ACROSS THE UNIVERSE

THE DC UNIVERSE STORIES OF

ALAN MOORE

D C   C O M I C S

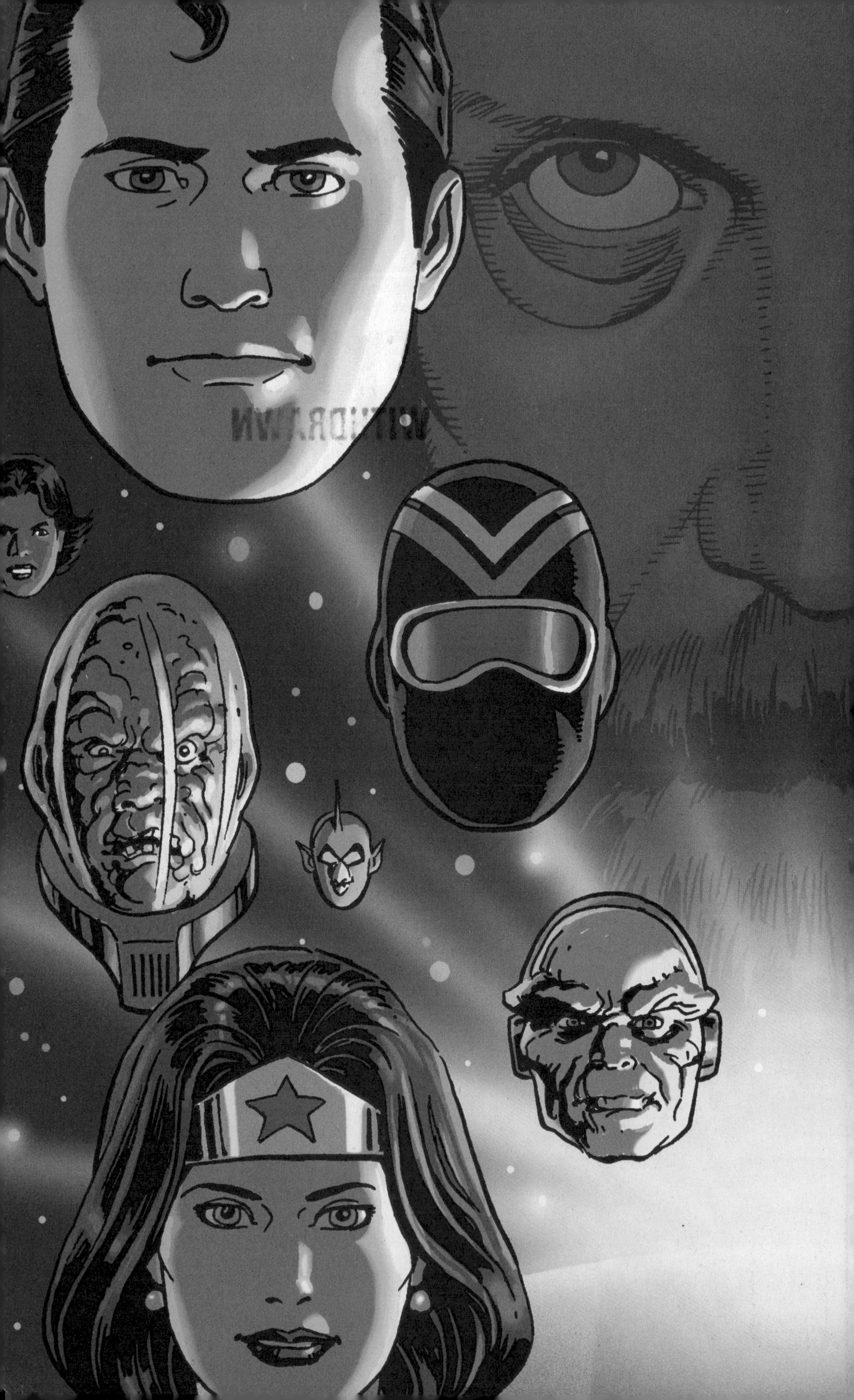

ACROSS THE UNIVERSE

THE DC UNIVERSE STORIES OF

ALAN MOORE

DC COMICS

Dan Didio
VP-Executive Editor

Dale Crain
Senior Editor-Collected Edition

Robbin Brosterman
Senior Art Director

Paul Levitz
President & Publisher

Georg Brewer
*VP-Design & Retail Product
Development*

Richard Bruning
VP-Creative Director

Patrick Caldon
Senior VP-Finance & Operations

Chris Caramalis
VP-Finance

Terri Cunningham
VP-Managing Editor

Alison Gill
VP-Manufacturing

Lillian Laserson
Senior VP & General Counsel

David McKillips
VP- Advertising

John Nee
VP-Business Development

Cheryl Rubin
VP-Licensing & Merchandising

Bob Wayne
VP-Sales & Marketing

Selected black-and-white reconstruction by Rick Keene.
Selected color reconstruction by Jamison.
Cover illustration by Dave Gibbons.
Publication design by Brainchild Studios/NYC.

Superman created by Jerry Siegel and Joe Shuster.
Batman created by Bob Kane.
Wonder Woman created by William Moulton Marston.
Swamp Thing created by Len Wein and Berni Wrightson.
Vigilante created by Marv Wolfman and George Pérez.
The Omega Men created by Keith Giffen and Roger Slifer.

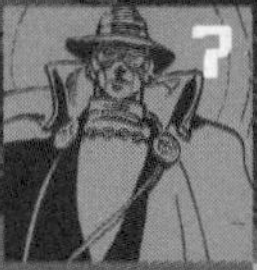

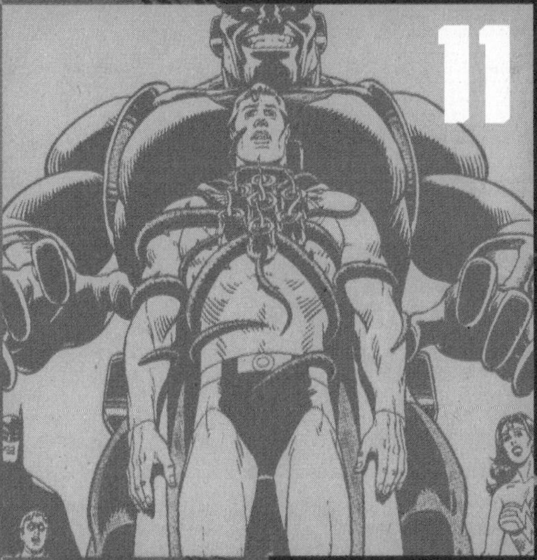

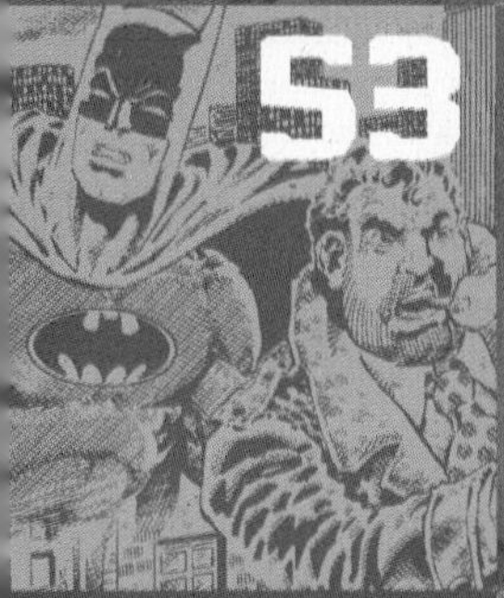

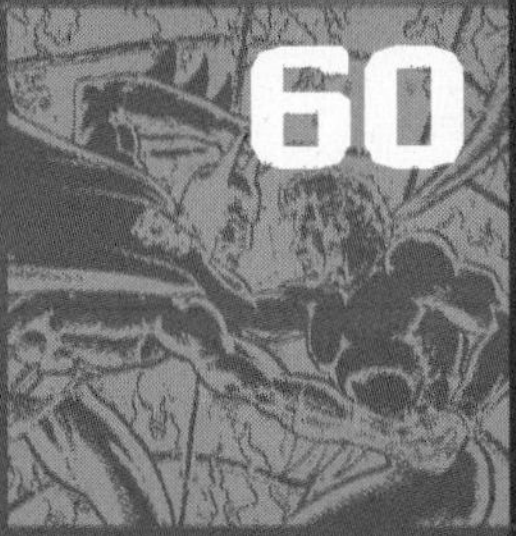

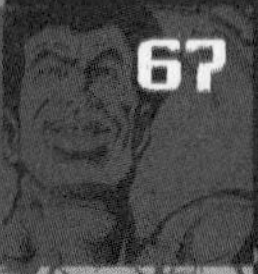

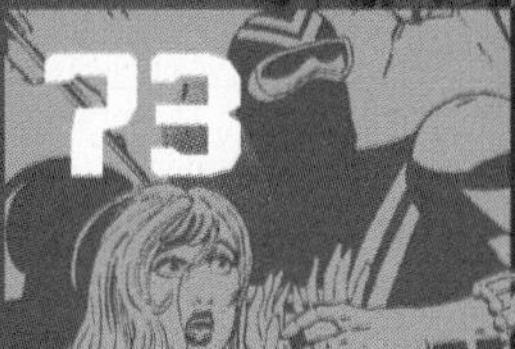

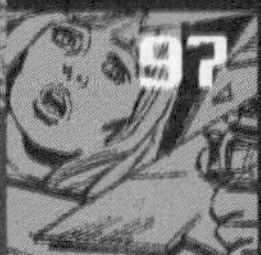

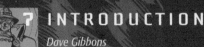

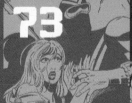

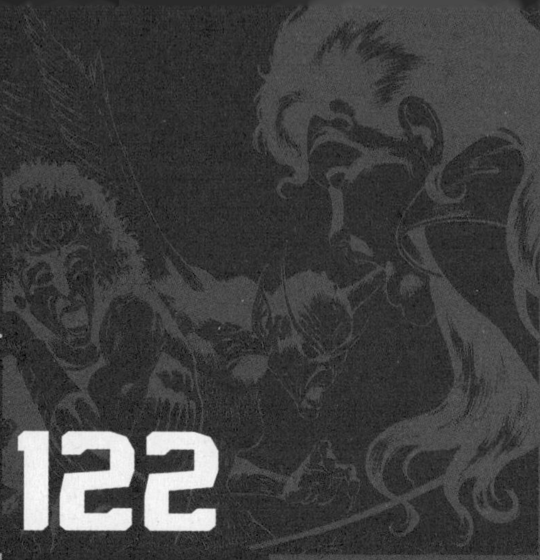

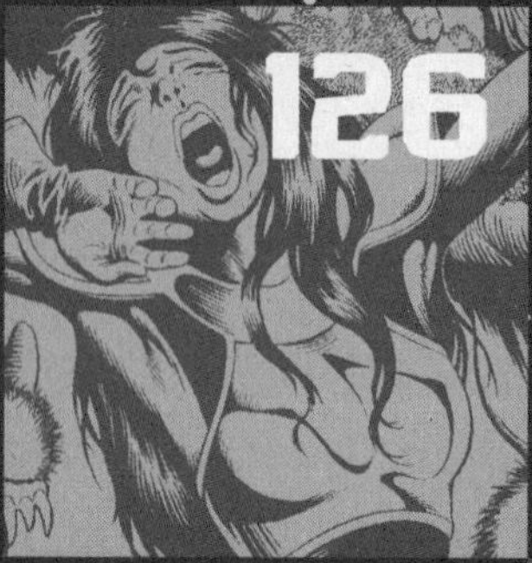

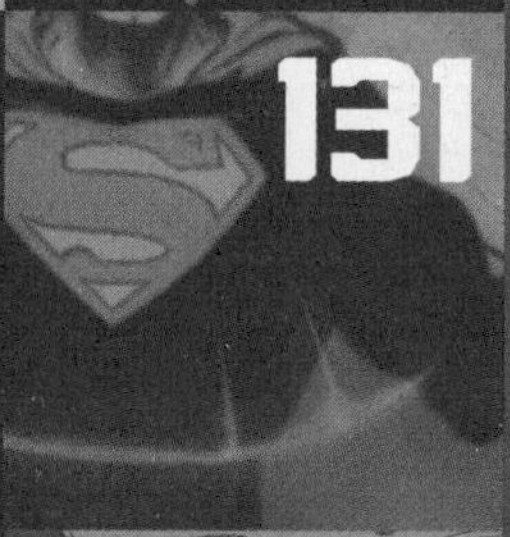

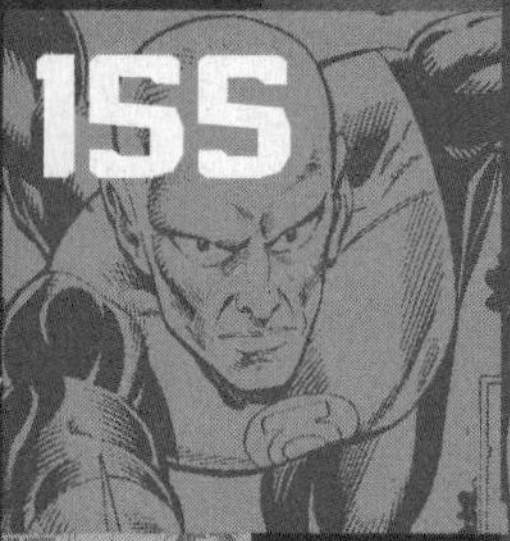

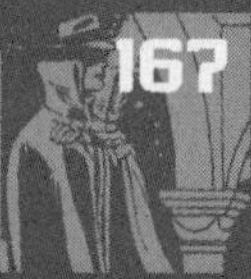

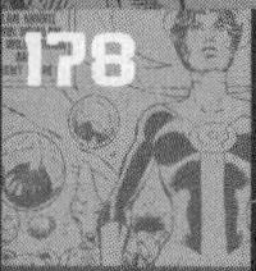

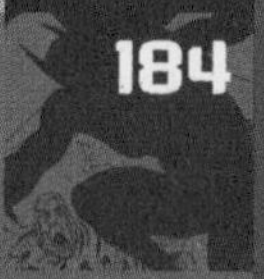

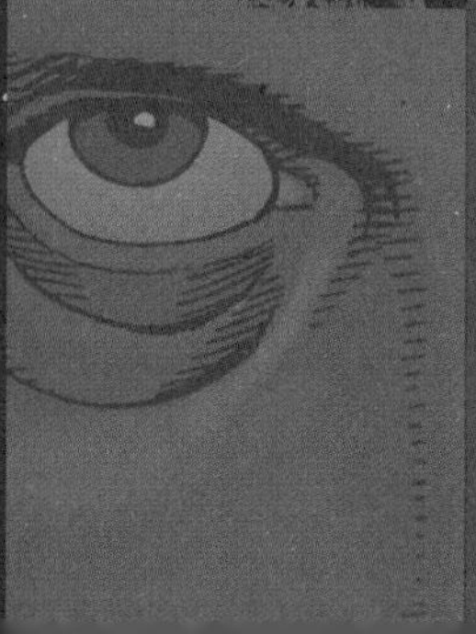

INTRODUCTION

THERE'S BEEN A LOT SAID ABOUT ALAN MOORE'S WRITING TALENT. IT'S CLEAR TO ANYONE WHO'S READ EVEN ONE OF HIS STORIES THAT HE POSSESSES A REMARKABLE COMMAND OF LANGUAGE AND IS A MASTER OF DESCRIPTION AND DIALOGUE.

His work connects on both an intellectual and emotional level, in a way that's unmatched in today's comics. I share in the admiration of his writing skills, both as a reader and a frequent collaborator. As the latter, I've experienced firsthand his ability to write amazingly well, amazingly fast, and have been privy to the parts of his writing that the reader never sees: namely, the extensive scene- and mood-setting descriptions that have enabled me and his other artistic partners to produce perhaps the best work of our careers.

I could easily fill this introduction with praise for his creative prowess but I'd rather talk about something else — the capacity without which his writing skills would be superfluous, the talent that is truly at the root of his genius. And that is his abilty to closely observe the universe around him.

Of course, the universe that surrounds Alan is the same universe that you and I also inhabit, but we just don't see the details that he sees. We don't hear the resonant chords he hears. We overlook the connections he makes us aware of. To one degree or another, we take things for granted, we go through the motions, we see what we expect to see.

But not Alan. Not in our "real" universe, and not in the fictional universes which he has given his attention to.

Now, it may be that "universe" is too grand a term for the interwoven comic-book narratives that, by their consensus, form the DC Universe. But, from the randomly conceived episodes of the nineteen forties to the deliberate constructions of later years, the stories of DC's heroic characters have, at least, aggregated into a wonderful, tantalizingly complex vista.

It was comic books' equivalent of the Big Bang. And Alan was there, watching, listening, absorbing...

Alan, from an early age, was observing that imaginary continuum, absorbing the detail, the connections, the magic. For a boy in the Britain of the late fifties and early sixties, DC Comics, even as mere objects, held an extraordinary appeal. They were vivid artifacts of a distant, more exciting civilization, a colorful land a million miles away from the grey uniformity of mundane reality.

And, once within their pages, there was a joyous escape into the gaudy, hard-focus, proto-universes of the characters themselves. In those days,

only the stories of the Superman and Batman "families" were widely available, with their B-list supporters, J'onn J'onzz, Green Arrow, Aquaman, and the like. Back then, their worlds had not merged, beyond the pairing of Superman and Batman or the briefest of caption foot-notes. But the potential was clearly there, although only dreamt-of by the readers, until the day that the first advertisement for the Justice League of America saw print:

"Just Imagine… The Mightiest Heroes of Our Time have banded TOGETHER as the JUSTICE LEAGUE OF AMERICA"

It was comic books' equivalent of the Big Bang. And Alan was there, watching, listening, absorbing, and, no doubt, just imagining…

As the DC Universe rapidly expanded to incorporate the earlier, more limited con-tinuities of its forties' "Golden Age" stars, the characters of former four-color rivals from Quality Comics and eventually even the world of archcompetitor Captain Marvel himself, Alan kept vigil.

He didn't miss a thing. He wandered those imaginary worlds, taking in everything that he was shown but clearly also wondering about what he wasn't shown. Wondering just what it was really like to have super-powers, a Fortress of Solitude, a Power Ring, a secret identity, a kid sidekick. What it really felt like to be the last survivor of a doomed world, to want to strike fear into the hearts of evildoers, to be the fastest man alive, or the tiniest.

Like a lot of early fans and would-be professionals, Alan concocted his own stories and grandiose plotlines featuring DC characters, dreaming that one day, he might get his chance to guide their destinies himself.

As a near contemporary of Alan's, I shared the same dream and, like him, was one of those fortunate enough to realize it. It was a dream made all the more improbable by the real-world existence of the North Atlantic Ocean but, somehow, by luck and circumstance, it came true.

I managed to get my toe in DC's door a little ahead of Alan, although, by then, I'd already worked with him professionally on short stories for Britain's *2000AD* weekly. I knew him and his work well enough to want to work with him more.

> ### He didn't miss a thing. He wandered those imaginary worlds, taking in everything that he was shown...

We'd talk often about doing something together for DC, and he even typed up a couple of outlines for proposed series that we could submit jointly. One, a complex, continuity-ranging saga prominently featuring the Challengers of the Unknown, made far-reaching changes to the entire DC Universe. I mentioned it to a contact at DC, prior to making a full proposal, but was told that the Challengers had been "promised" to another writer, and that there was no point in our continuing.

Another proposal, this time for the Martian Manhunter, was a much less ambitious notion, setting an alien being against a fifties backdrop of McCarthyism and small-town paranoia.

Unfortunately, we learned that someone else was already revamping the character and so that, too, went no further.

After such a lot of unpaid and frustrated work on Alan's part, his eventual arrival at DC Comics was quite easily achieved. My phone rang one evening and Len Wein, then an editor/writer at DC, asked me if I had the number of a writer called Alan Moore. He'd read some of the work Alan had done for Britain's *Warrior* magazine and thought he might be able to revitalize Swamp Thing…

The rest, as they say, is comic-book history.

The rest, as they say, is comic-book history.

Before he eventually parted company with DC Comics, to explore and create other universes, Alan wrote some of the most resonant tales about their characters, both major and minor, that have ever seen print. Most of those stories are presented here. They range from the whimsical to the poetic to the disturbingly real. They give some idea of the breadth of Alan's writing, his command of language, and mastery of description and dialogue. But, above all, they show what magic there can be in the universe, if you really pay attention.

— Dave Gibbons
March 20, 2003

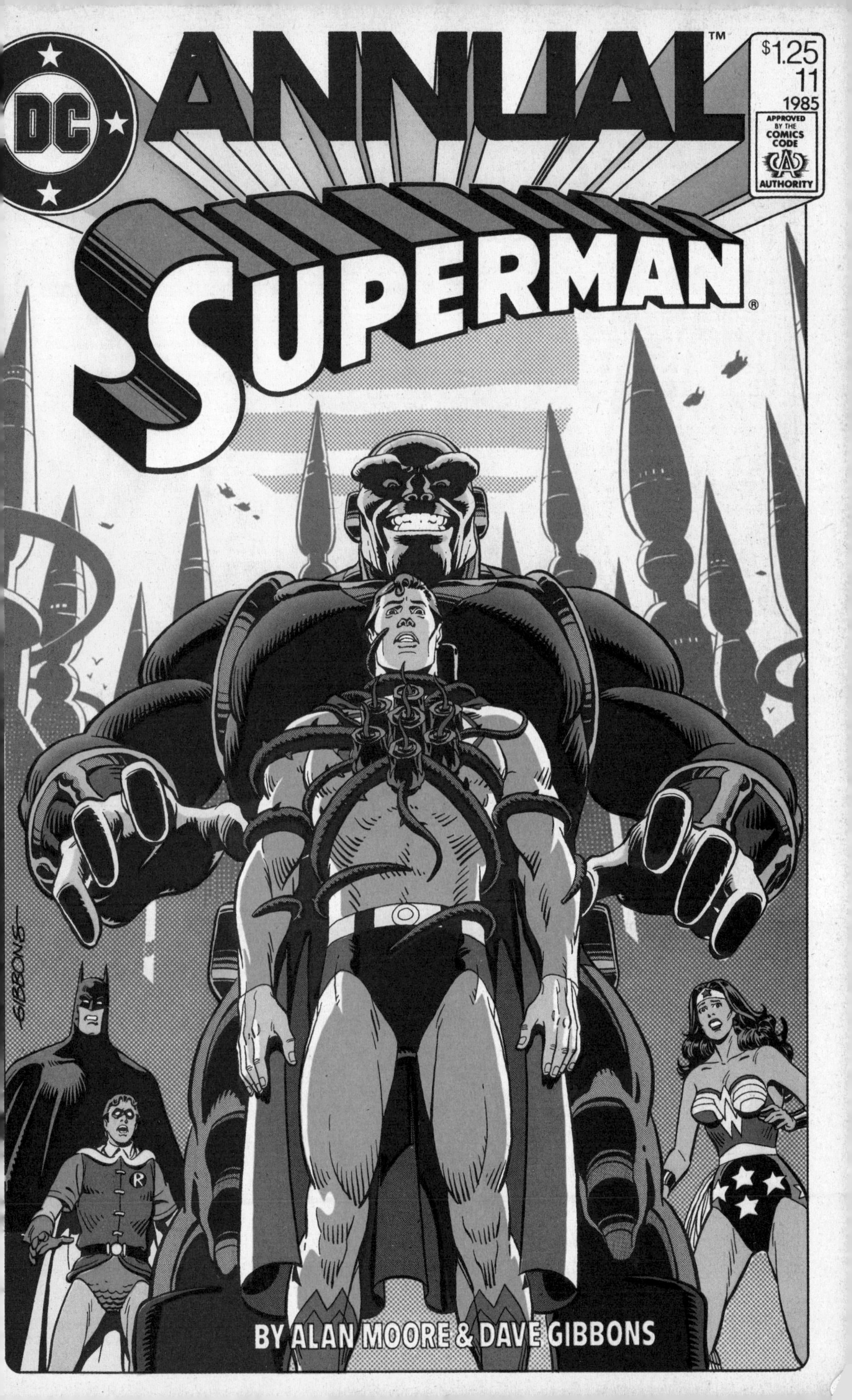
DC
ANNUAL™
$1.25
11
1985
APPROVED BY THE COMICS CODE AUTHORITY
SUPERMAN®
GIBBONS
BY ALAN MOORE & DAVE GIBBONS

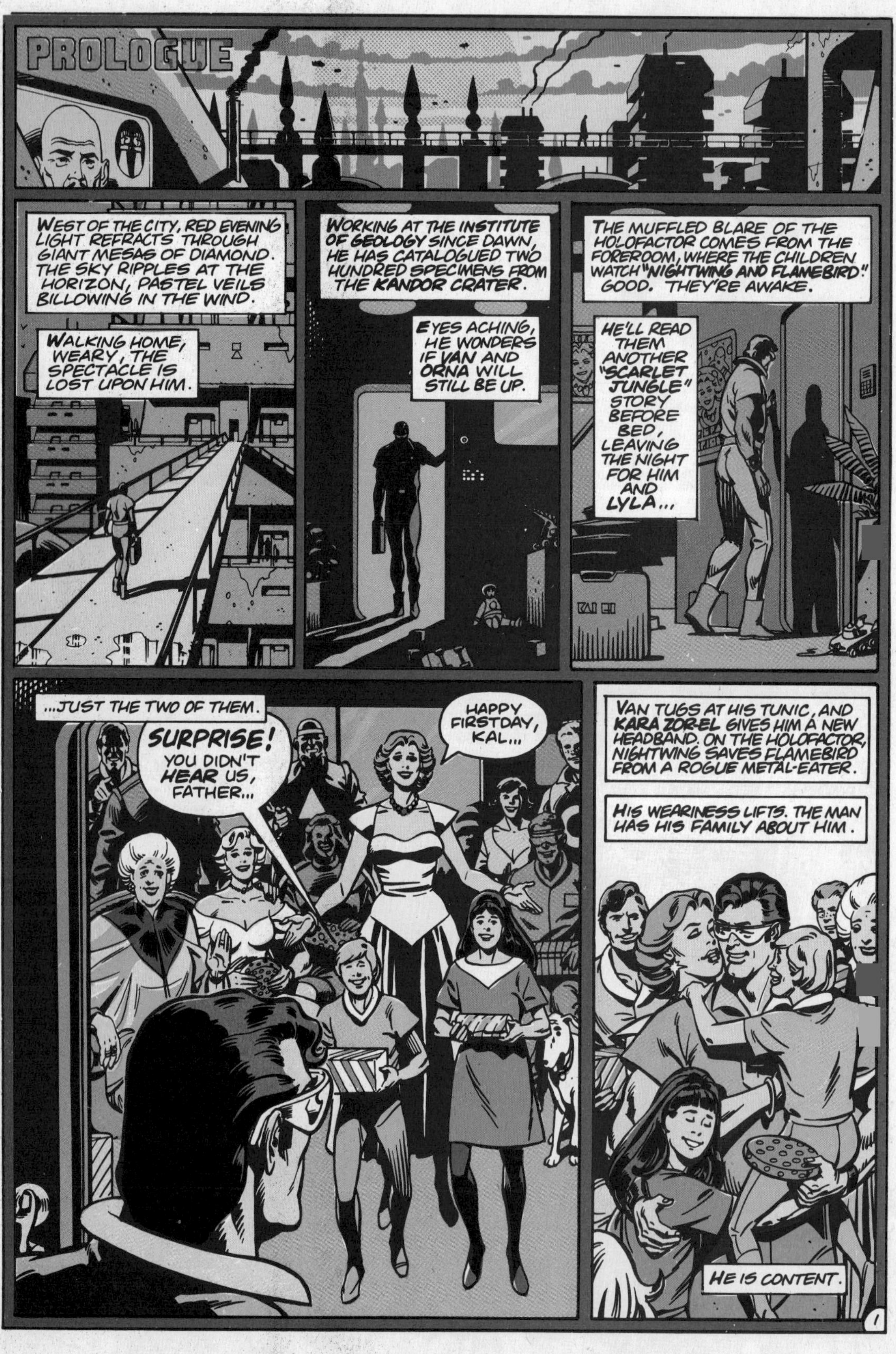
PROLOGUE
WEST OF THE CITY, RED EVENING LIGHT REFRACTS THROUGH GIANT MESAS OF DIAMOND. THE SKY RIPPLES AT THE HORIZON, PASTEL VEILS BILLOWING IN THE WIND.
WALKING HOME, WEARY, THE SPECTACLE IS LOST UPON HIM.
WORKING AT THE INSTITUTE OF GEOLOGY SINCE DAWN, HE HAS CATALOGUED TWO HUNDRED SPECIMENS FROM THE KANDOR CRATER.
EYES ACHING, HE WONDERS IF VAN AND ORNA WILL STILL BE UP.
THE MUFFLED BLARE OF THE HOLOFACTOR COMES FROM THE FOREROOM, WHERE THE CHILDREN WATCH "NIGHTWING AND FLAMEBIRD." GOOD. THEY'RE AWAKE.
HE'LL READ THEM ANOTHER "SCARLET JUNGLE" STORY BEFORE BED, LEAVING THE NIGHT FOR HIM AND LYLA...
...JUST THE TWO OF THEM.
SURPRISE! YOU DIDN'T HEAR US, FATHER...
HAPPY FIRSTDAY, KAL...
VAN TUGS AT HIS TUNIC, AND KARA ZOR-EL GIVES HIM A NEW HEADBAND. ON THE HOLOFACTOR, NIGHTWING SAVES FLAMEBIRD FROM A ROGUE METAL-EATER.
HIS WEARINESS LIFTS. THE MAN HAS HIS FAMILY ABOUT HIM.
HE IS CONTENT.
1

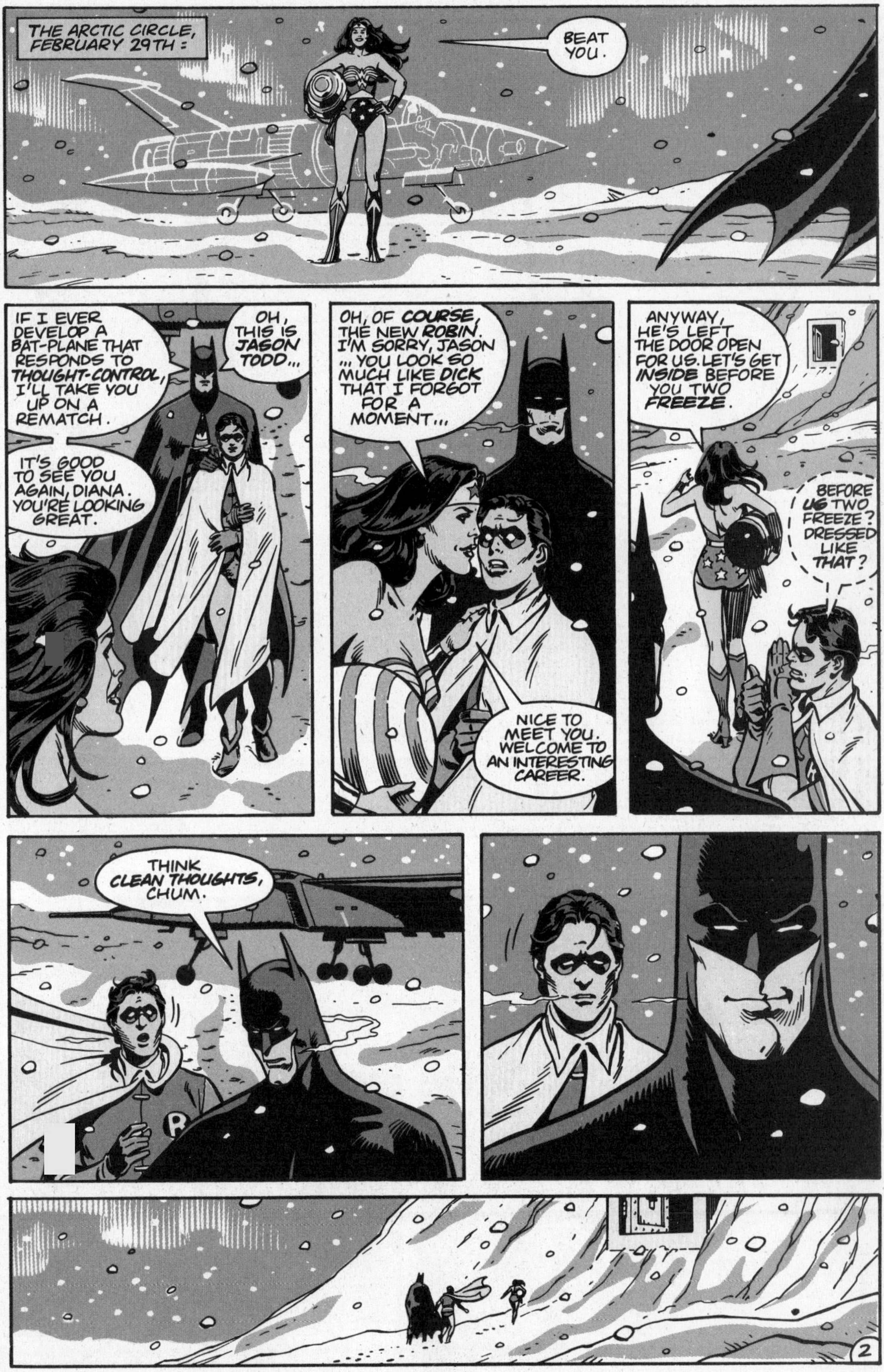
THE ARCTIC CIRCLE, FEBRUARY 29TH:
BEAT YOU.
IF I EVER DEVELOP A BAT-PLANE THAT RESPONDS TO THOUGHT-CONTROL, I'LL TAKE YOU UP ON A REMATCH.
IT'S GOOD TO SEE YOU AGAIN, DIANA. YOU'RE LOOKING GREAT.
OH, THIS IS JASON TODD...
OH, OF COURSE, THE NEW ROBIN. I'M SORRY, JASON ... YOU LOOK SO MUCH LIKE DICK THAT I FORGOT FOR A MOMENT...
NICE TO MEET YOU. WELCOME TO AN INTERESTING CAREER.
ANYWAY, HE'S LEFT THE DOOR OPEN FOR US. LET'S GET INSIDE BEFORE YOU TWO FREEZE.
BEFORE US TWO FREEZE? DRESSED LIKE THAT?
THINK CLEAN THOUGHTS, CHUM.
2

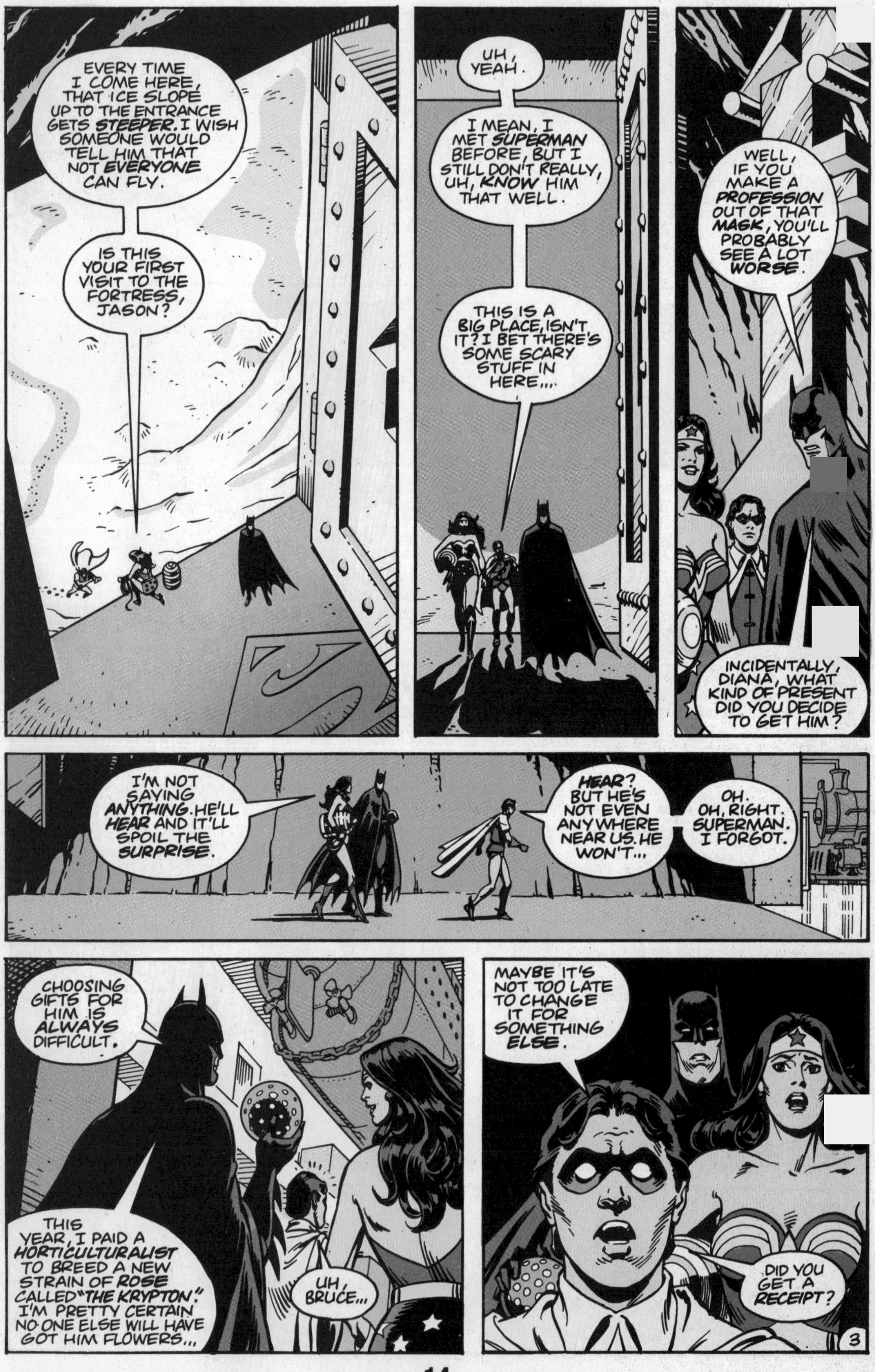
EVERY TIME I COME HERE, THAT ICE SLOPE UP TO THE ENTRANCE GETS STEEPER. I WISH SOMEONE WOULD TELL HIM THAT NOT EVERYONE CAN FLY.
IS THIS YOUR FIRST VISIT TO THE FORTRESS, JASON?
UH, YEAH.
I MEAN, I MET SUPERMAN BEFORE, BUT I STILL DON'T REALLY, UH, KNOW HIM THAT WELL.
THIS IS A BIG PLACE, ISN'T IT? I BET THERE'S SOME SCARY STUFF IN HERE....
WELL, IF YOU MAKE A PROFESSION OUT OF THAT MASK, YOU'LL PROBABLY SEE A LOT WORSE.
INCIDENTALLY, DIANA, WHAT KIND OF PRESENT DID YOU DECIDE TO GET HIM?
I'M NOT SAYING ANYTHING. HE'LL HEAR AND IT'LL SPOIL THE SURPRISE.
HEAR? BUT HE'S NOT EVEN ANYWHERE NEAR US. HE WON'T...
OH. OH, RIGHT. SUPERMAN. I FORGOT.
CHOOSING GIFTS FOR HIM IS ALWAYS DIFFICULT.
THIS YEAR, I PAID A HORTICULTURALIST TO BREED A NEW STRAIN OF ROSE CALLED "THE KRYPTON". I'M PRETTY CERTAIN NO ONE ELSE WILL HAVE GOT HIM FLOWERS...
UH, BRUCE...
MAYBE IT'S NOT TOO LATE TO CHANGE IT FOR SOMETHING ELSE.
DID YOU GET A RECEIPT?
3

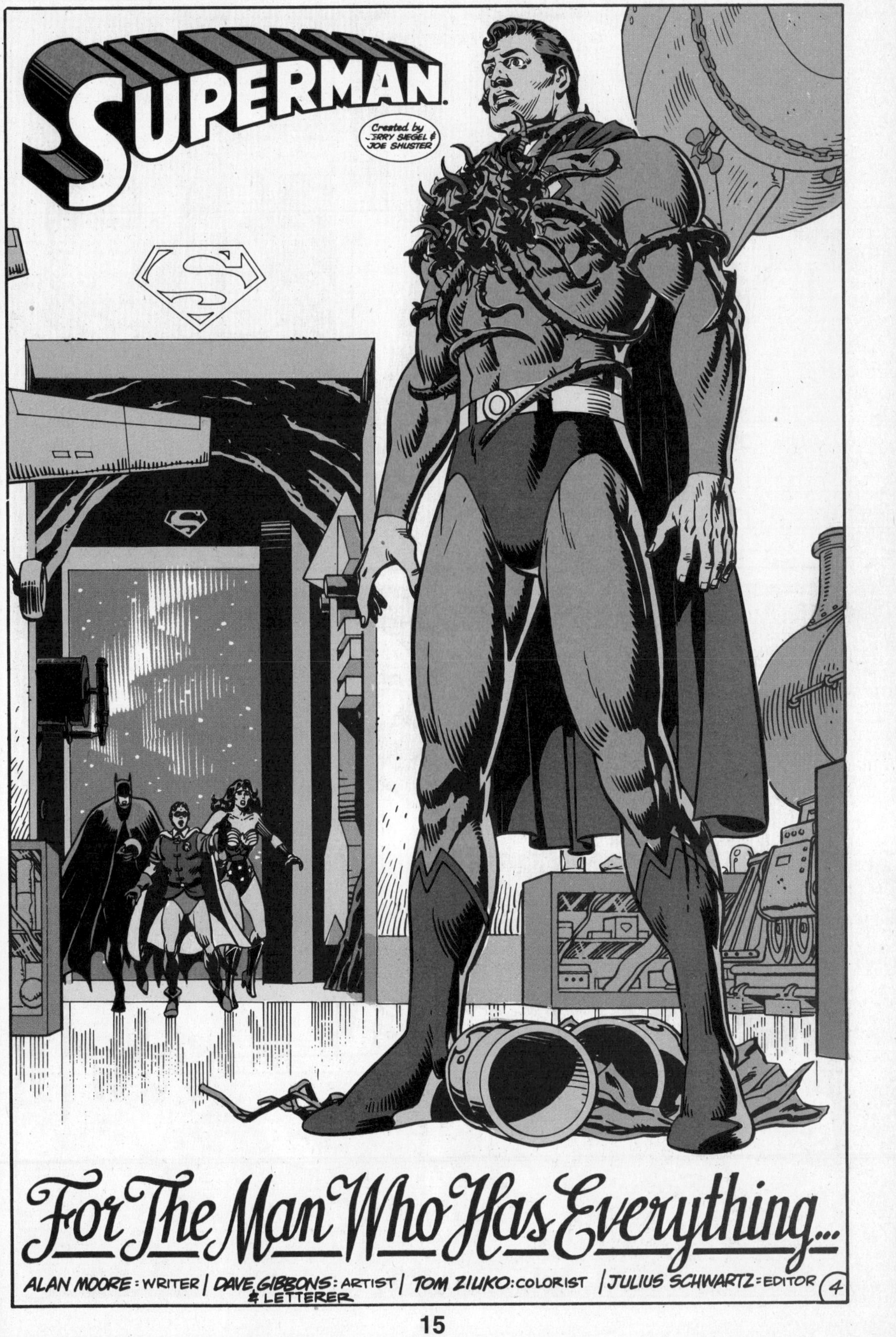
SUPERMAN
Created by JERRY SIEGEL & JOE SHUSTER
For The Man Who Has Everything...
ALAN MOORE: WRITER | DAVE GIBBONS: ARTIST & LETTERER | TOM ZIUKO: COLORIST | JULIUS SCHWARTZ: EDITOR
4

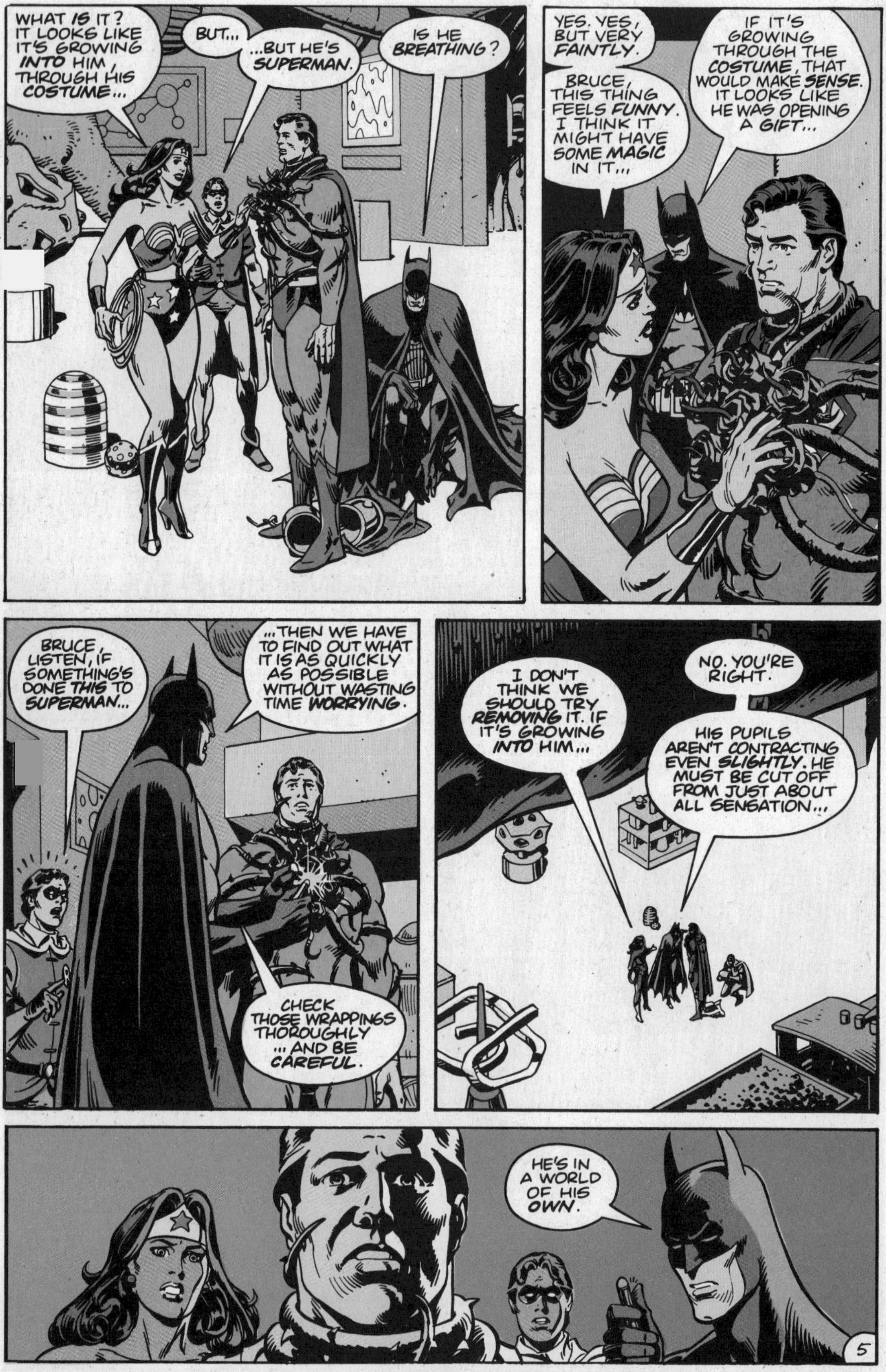
WHAT IS IT? IT LOOKS LIKE IT'S GROWING INTO HIM, THROUGH HIS COSTUME...
BUT...
...BUT HE'S SUPERMAN.
IS HE BREATHING?
YES. YES, BUT VERY FAINTLY.
BRUCE, THIS THING FEELS FUNNY. I THINK IT MIGHT HAVE SOME MAGIC IN IT...
IF IT'S GROWING THROUGH THE COSTUME, THAT WOULD MAKE SENSE. IT LOOKS LIKE HE WAS OPENING A GIFT...
BRUCE, LISTEN, IF SOMETHING'S DONE THIS TO SUPERMAN...
...THEN WE HAVE TO FIND OUT WHAT IT IS AS QUICKLY AS POSSIBLE WITHOUT WASTING TIME WORRYING.
CHECK THOSE WRAPPINGS THOROUGHLY ...AND BE CAREFUL.
I DON'T THINK WE SHOULD TRY REMOVING IT. IF IT'S GROWING INTO HIM...
NO. YOU'RE RIGHT.
HIS PUPILS AREN'T CONTRACTING EVEN SLIGHTLY. HE MUST BE CUT OFF FROM JUST ABOUT ALL SENSATION...
HE'S IN A WORLD OF HIS OWN.
5

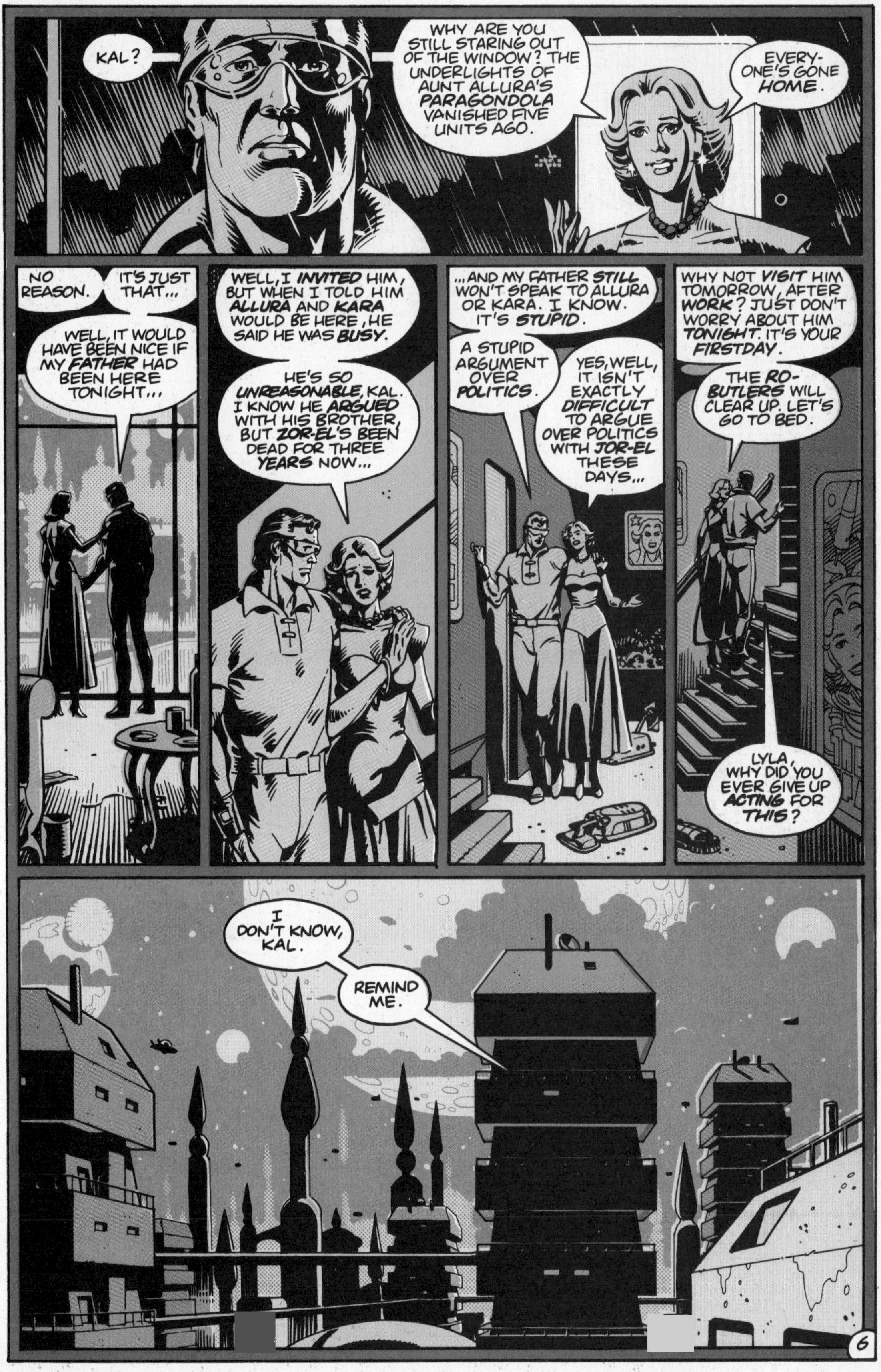
KAL?
WHY ARE YOU STILL STARING OUT OF THE WINDOW? THE UNDERLIGHTS OF AUNT ALLURA'S PARAGONDOLA VANISHED FIVE UNITS AGO.
EVERY-ONE'S GONE HOME.
NO REASON.
IT'S JUST THAT...
WELL, IT WOULD HAVE BEEN NICE IF MY FATHER HAD BEEN HERE TONIGHT...
WELL, I INVITED HIM, BUT WHEN I TOLD HIM ALLURA AND KARA WOULD BE HERE, HE SAID HE WAS BUSY.
HE'S SO UNREASONABLE, KAL. I KNOW HE ARGUED WITH HIS BROTHER, BUT ZOR-EL'S BEEN DEAD FOR THREE YEARS NOW...
...AND MY FATHER STILL WON'T SPEAK TO ALLURA OR KARA. I KNOW. IT'S STUPID.
A STUPID ARGUMENT OVER POLITICS.
YES, WELL, IT ISN'T EXACTLY DIFFICULT TO ARGUE OVER POLITICS WITH JOR-EL THESE DAYS...
WHY NOT VISIT HIM TOMORROW, AFTER WORK? JUST DON'T WORRY ABOUT HIM TONIGHT. IT'S YOUR FIRSTDAY.
THE RO-BUTLERS WILL CLEAR UP. LET'S GO TO BED.
LYLA, WHY DID YOU EVER GIVE UP ACTING FOR THIS?
I DON'T KNOW, KAL.
REMIND ME.
6

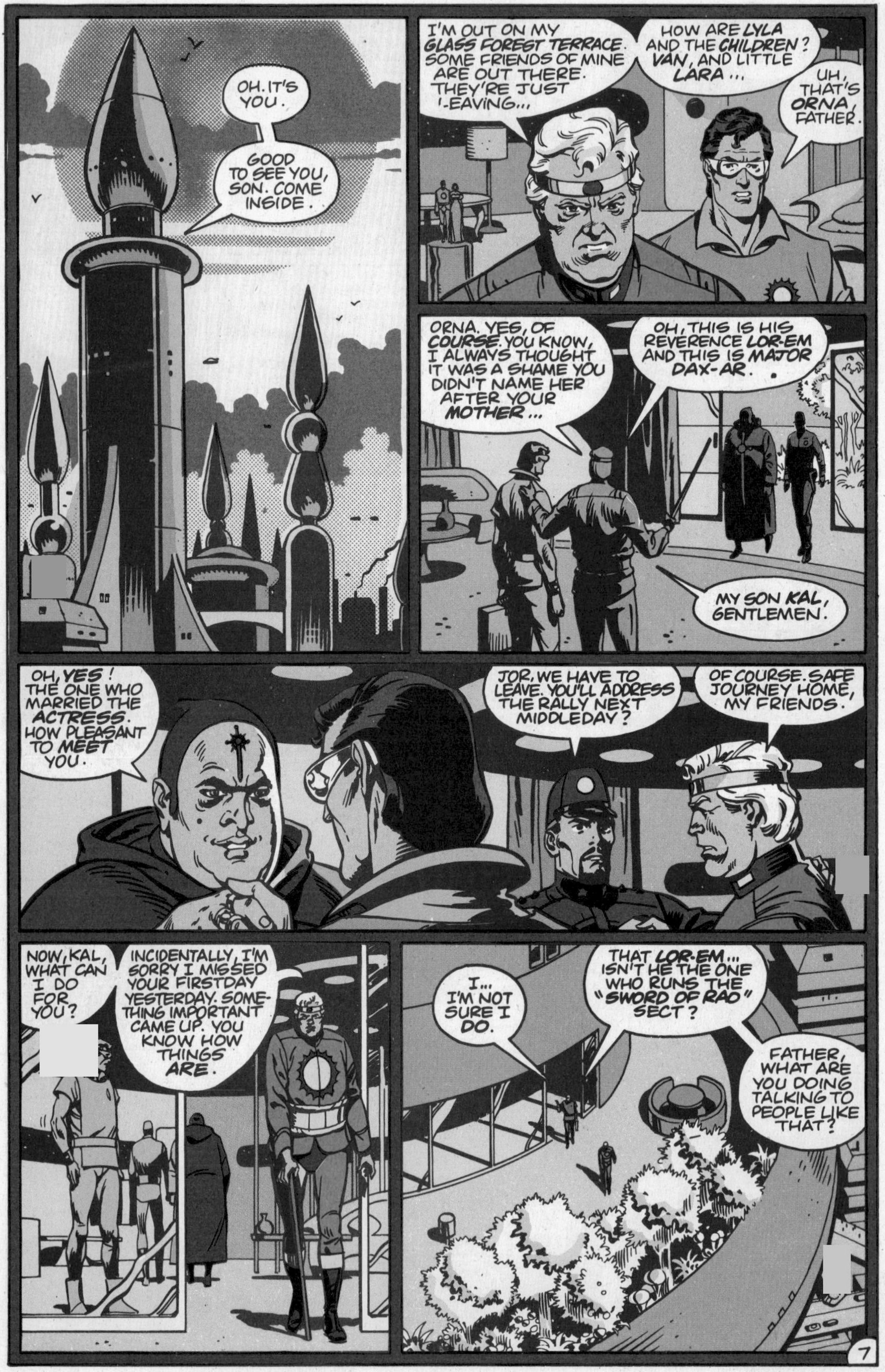
OH. IT'S YOU.
GOOD TO SEE YOU, SON. COME INSIDE.
I'M OUT ON MY GLASS FOREST TERRACE. SOME FRIENDS OF MINE ARE OUT THERE. THEY'RE JUST LEAVING...
HOW ARE LYLA AND THE CHILDREN? VAN, AND LITTLE LARA...
UH, THAT'S ORNA, FATHER.
ORNA. YES, OF COURSE. YOU KNOW, I ALWAYS THOUGHT IT WAS A SHAME YOU DIDN'T NAME HER AFTER YOUR MOTHER...
OH, THIS IS HIS REVERENCE LOR-EM AND THIS IS MAJOR DAX-AR.
MY SON KAL, GENTLEMEN.
OH, YES! THE ONE WHO MARRIED THE ACTRESS. HOW PLEASANT TO MEET YOU.
JOR, WE HAVE TO LEAVE. YOU'LL ADDRESS THE RALLY NEXT MIDDLEDAY?
OF COURSE. SAFE JOURNEY HOME, MY FRIENDS.
NOW, KAL, WHAT CAN I DO FOR YOU?
INCIDENTALLY, I'M SORRY I MISSED YOUR FIRSTDAY YESTERDAY. SOMETHING IMPORTANT CAME UP. YOU KNOW HOW THINGS ARE.
I... I'M NOT SURE I DO.
THAT LOR-EM... ISN'T HE THE ONE WHO RUNS THE "SWORD OF RAO" SECT?
FATHER, WHAT ARE YOU DOING TALKING TO PEOPLE LIKE THAT?
7

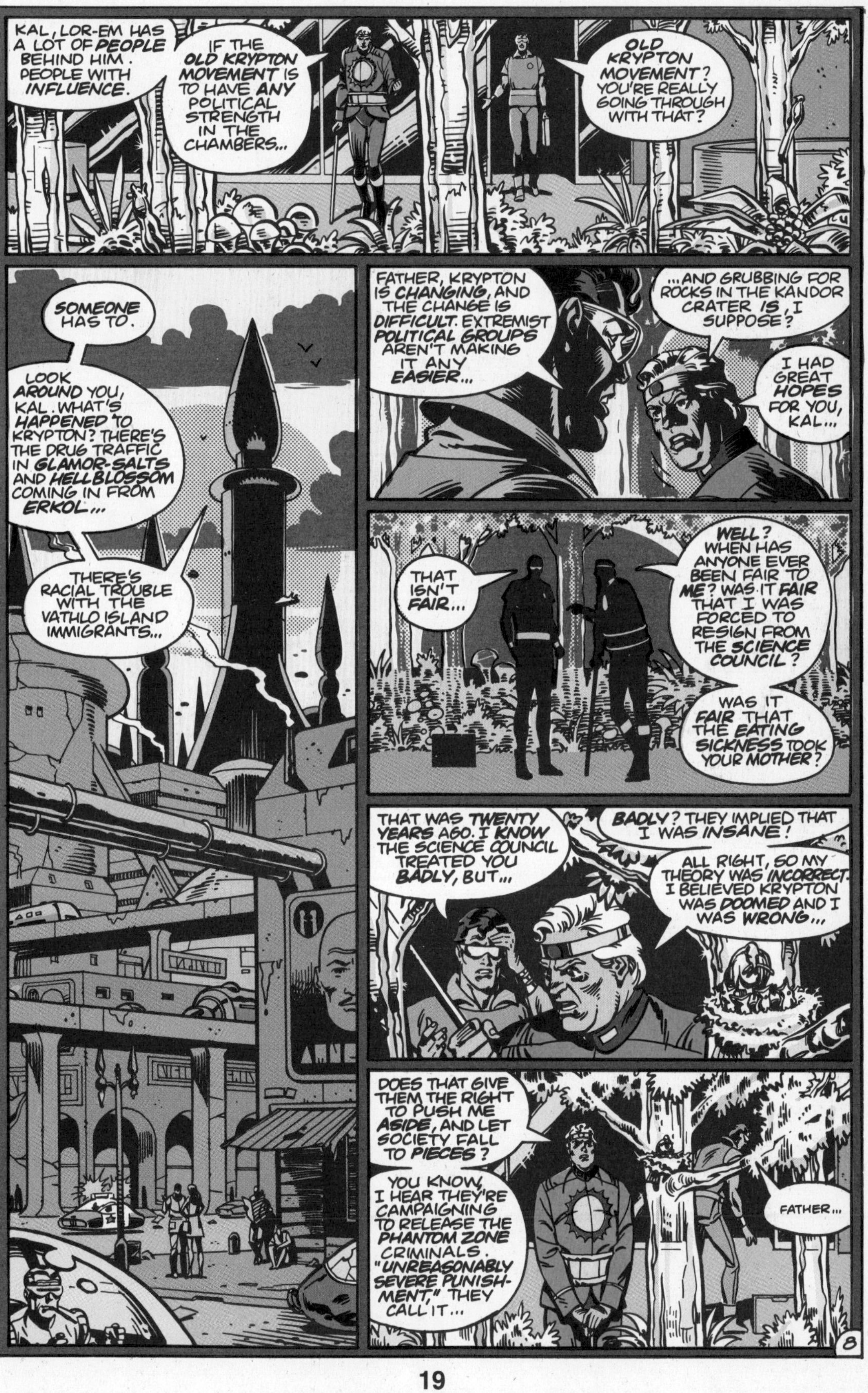
KAL, LOR-EM HAS A LOT OF PEOPLE BEHIND HIM. PEOPLE WITH INFLUENCE.
IF THE OLD KRYPTON MOVEMENT IS TO HAVE ANY POLITICAL STRENGTH IN THE CHAMBERS...
OLD KRYPTON MOVEMENT? YOU'RE REALLY GOING THROUGH WITH THAT?
SOMEONE HAS TO.
LOOK AROUND YOU, KAL. WHAT'S HAPPENED TO KRYPTON? THERE'S THE DRUG TRAFFIC IN GLAMOR-SALTS AND HELLBLOSSOM COMING IN FROM ERKOL...
THERE'S RACIAL TROUBLE WITH THE VATHLO ISLAND IMMIGRANTS...
FATHER, KRYPTON IS CHANGING, AND THE CHANGE IS DIFFICULT. EXTREMIST POLITICAL GROUPS AREN'T MAKING IT ANY EASIER...
...AND GRUBBING FOR ROCKS IN THE KANDOR CRATER IS, I SUPPOSE?
I HAD GREAT HOPES FOR YOU, KAL...
THAT ISN'T FAIR...
WELL? WHEN HAS ANYONE EVER BEEN FAIR TO ME? WAS IT FAIR THAT I WAS FORCED TO RESIGN FROM THE SCIENCE COUNCIL?
WAS IT FAIR THAT THE EATING SICKNESS TOOK YOUR MOTHER?
THAT WAS TWENTY YEARS AGO. I KNOW THE SCIENCE COUNCIL TREATED YOU BADLY, BUT...
BADLY? THEY IMPLIED THAT I WAS INSANE!
ALL RIGHT, SO MY THEORY WAS INCORRECT. I BELIEVED KRYPTON WAS DOOMED AND I WAS WRONG...
DOES THAT GIVE THEM THE RIGHT TO PUSH ME ASIDE, AND LET SOCIETY FALL TO PIECES?
YOU KNOW, I HEAR THEY'RE CAMPAIGNING TO RELEASE THE PHANTOM ZONE CRIMINALS. "UNREASONABLY SEVERE PUNISHMENT," THEY CALL IT...
FATHER...
8

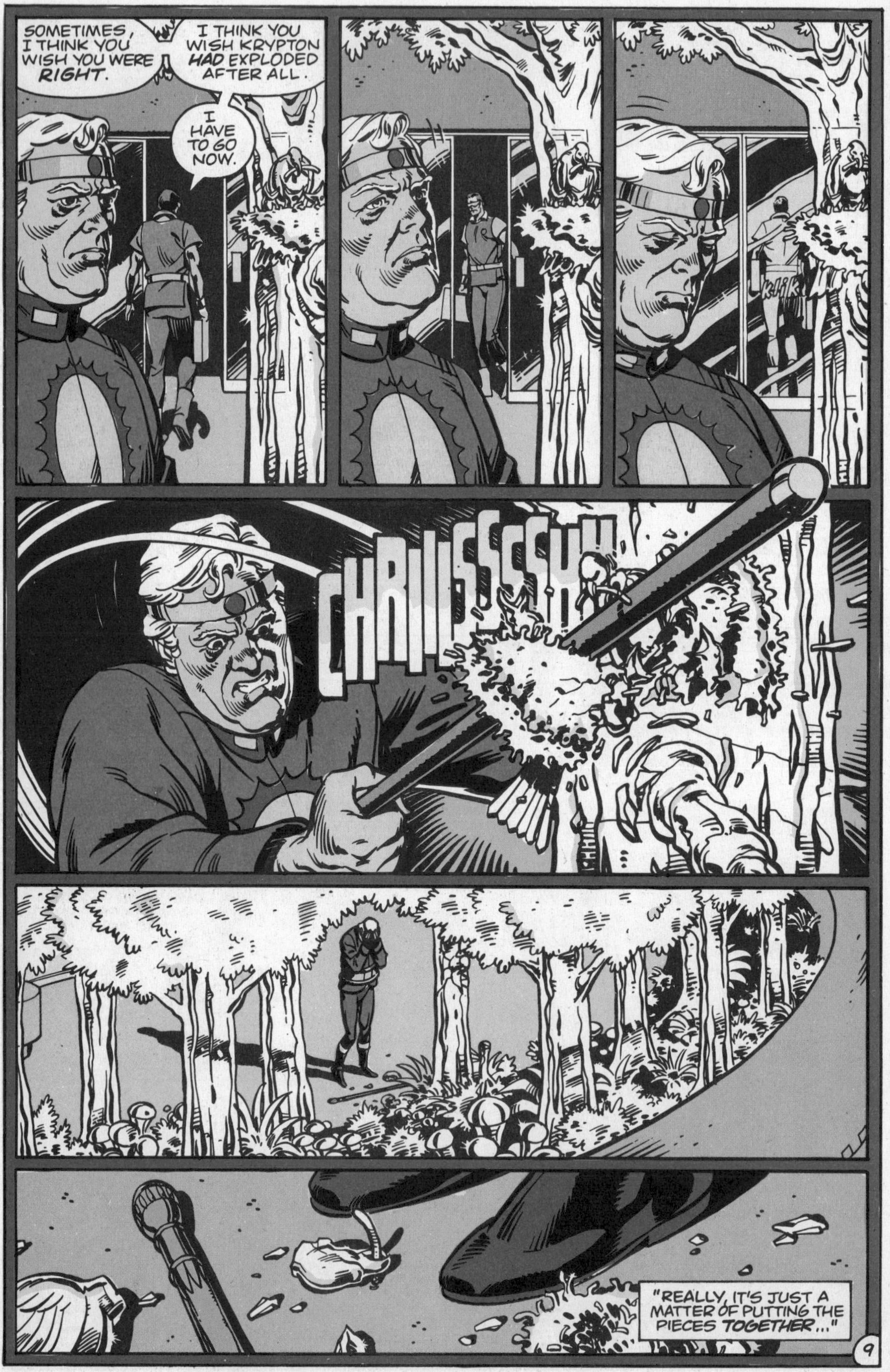
SOMETIMES, I THINK YOU WISH YOU WERE RIGHT.
I THINK YOU WISH KRYPTON HAD EXPLODED AFTER ALL.
I HAVE TO GO NOW.
"REALLY, IT'S JUST A MATTER OF PUTTING THE PIECES TOGETHER..."
9

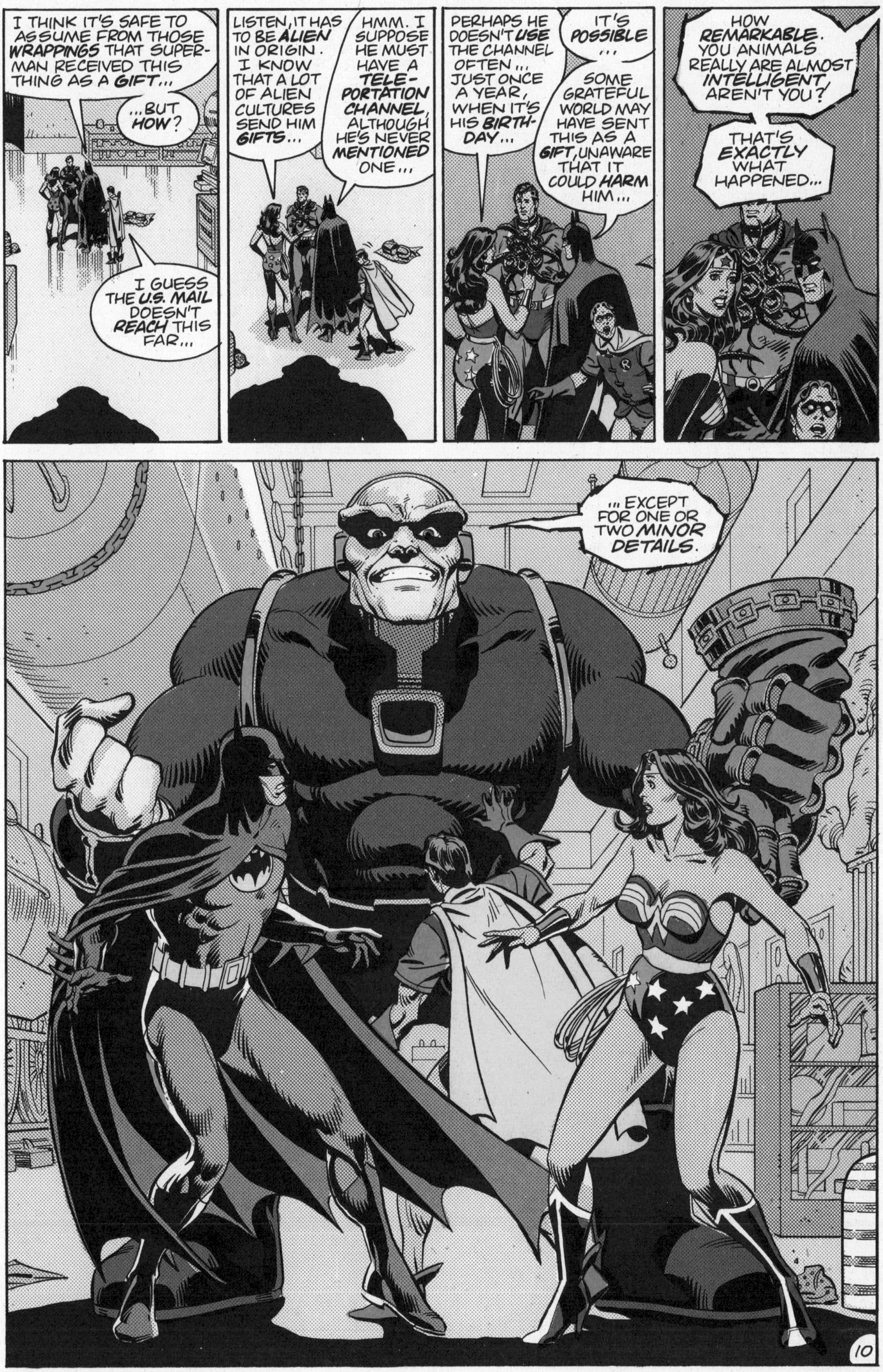

I THINK IT'S SAFE TO ASSUME FROM THOSE WRAPPINGS THAT SUPERMAN RECEIVED THIS THING AS A GIFT...
...BUT HOW?
I GUESS THE U.S. MAIL DOESN'T REACH THIS FAR...
LISTEN, IT HAS TO BE ALIEN IN ORIGIN. I KNOW THAT A LOT OF ALIEN CULTURES SEND HIM GIFTS...
HMM. I SUPPOSE HE MUST HAVE A TELEPORTATION CHANNEL, ALTHOUGH HE'S NEVER MENTIONED ONE...
PERHAPS HE DOESN'T USE THE CHANNEL OFTEN... JUST ONCE A YEAR, WHEN IT'S HIS BIRTHDAY...
IT'S POSSIBLE...
SOME GRATEFUL WORLD MAY HAVE SENT THIS AS A GIFT, UNAWARE THAT IT COULD HARM HIM...
HOW REMARKABLE. YOU ANIMALS REALLY ARE ALMOST INTELLIGENT, AREN'T YOU?
THAT'S EXACTLY WHAT HAPPENED...
...EXCEPT FOR ONE OR TWO MINOR DETAILS.
10

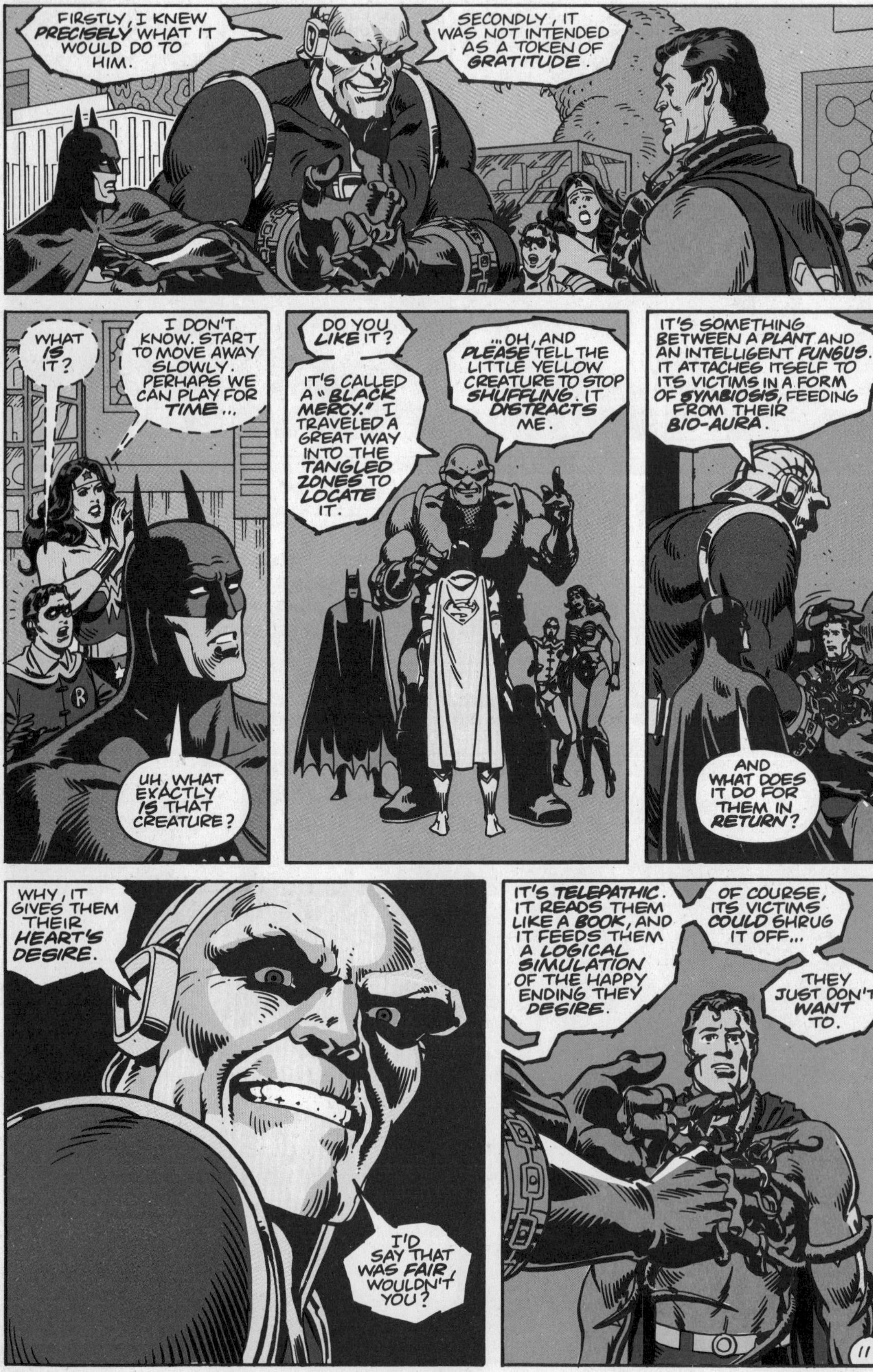
FIRSTLY, I KNEW PRECISELY WHAT IT WOULD DO TO HIM.
SECONDLY, IT WAS NOT INTENDED AS A TOKEN OF GRATITUDE.
WHAT IS IT?
I DON'T KNOW. START TO MOVE AWAY SLOWLY. PERHAPS WE CAN PLAY FOR TIME...
UH, WHAT EXACTLY IS THAT CREATURE?
DO YOU LIKE IT?
IT'S CALLED A "BLACK MERCY." I TRAVELED A GREAT WAY INTO THE TANGLED ZONES TO LOCATE IT.
...OH, AND PLEASE TELL THE LITTLE YELLOW CREATURE TO STOP SHUFFLING. IT DISTRACTS ME.
IT'S SOMETHING BETWEEN A PLANT AND AN INTELLIGENT FUNGUS. IT ATTACHES ITSELF TO ITS VICTIMS IN A FORM OF SYMBIOSIS, FEEDING FROM THEIR BIO-AURA.
AND WHAT DOES IT DO FOR THEM IN RETURN?
WHY, IT GIVES THEM THEIR HEART'S DESIRE.
I'D SAY THAT WAS FAIR, WOULDN'T YOU?
IT'S TELEPATHIC. IT READS THEM LIKE A BOOK, AND IT FEEDS THEM A LOGICAL SIMULATION OF THE HAPPY ENDING THEY DESIRE.
OF COURSE, ITS VICTIMS COULD SHRUG IT OFF...
THEY JUST DON'T WANT TO.
11

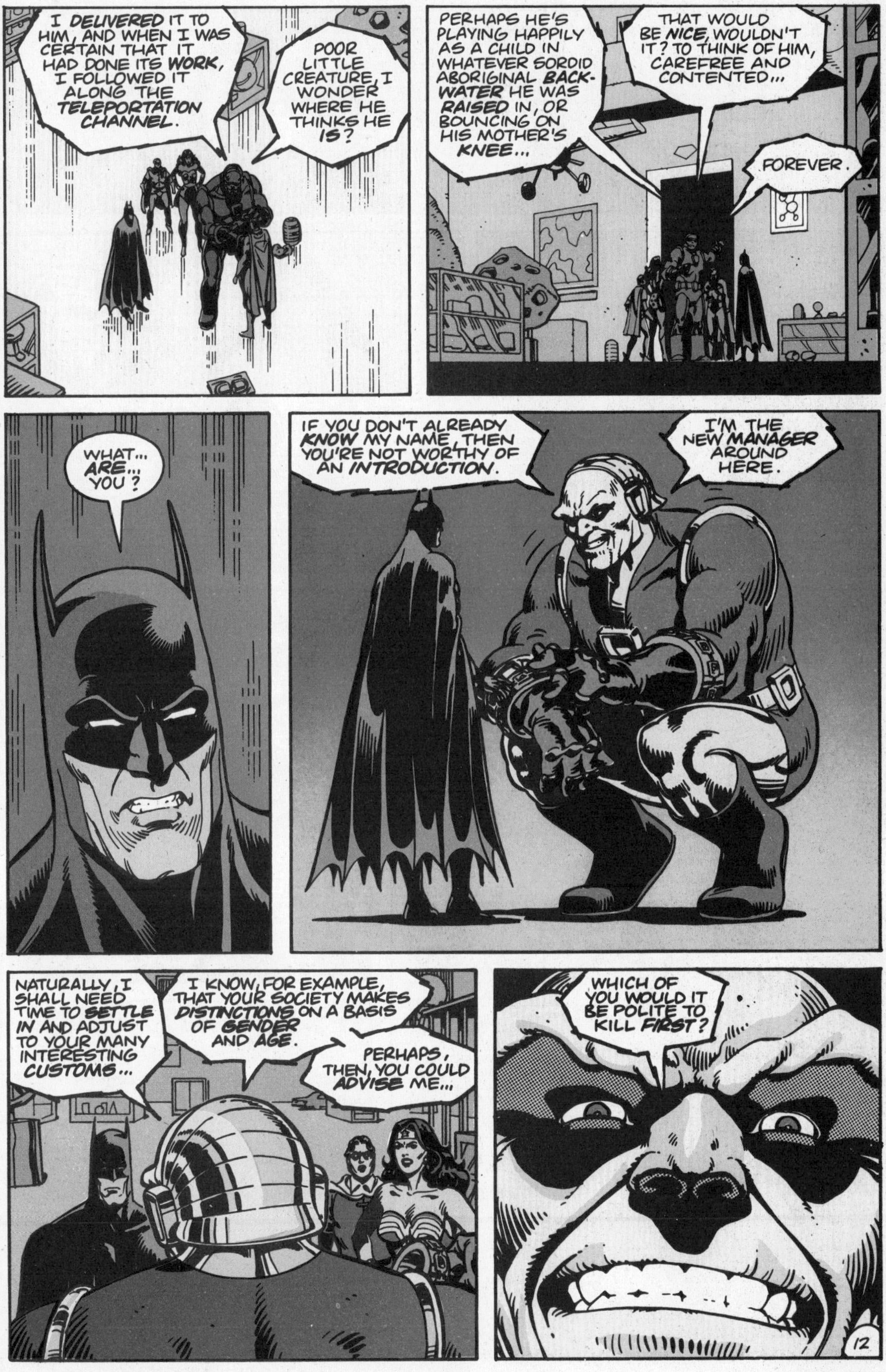
I DELIVERED IT TO HIM, AND WHEN I WAS CERTAIN THAT IT HAD DONE ITS WORK, I FOLLOWED IT ALONG THE TELEPORTATION CHANNEL.
POOR LITTLE CREATURE, I WONDER WHERE HE THINKS HE IS?
PERHAPS HE'S PLAYING HAPPILY AS A CHILD IN WHATEVER SORDID ABORIGINAL BACK-WATER HE WAS RAISED IN, OR BOUNCING ON HIS MOTHER'S KNEE...
THAT WOULD BE NICE, WOULDN'T IT? TO THINK OF HIM, CAREFREE AND CONTENTED...
FOREVER.
WHAT... ARE... YOU?
IF YOU DON'T ALREADY KNOW MY NAME, THEN YOU'RE NOT WORTHY OF AN INTRODUCTION.
I'M THE NEW MANAGER AROUND HERE.
NATURALLY, I SHALL NEED TIME TO SETTLE IN AND ADJUST TO YOUR MANY INTERESTING CUSTOMS...
I KNOW, FOR EXAMPLE, THAT YOUR SOCIETY MAKES DISTINCTIONS ON A BASIS OF GENDER AND AGE.
PERHAPS, THEN, YOU COULD ADVISE ME...
WHICH OF YOU WOULD IT BE POLITE TO KILL FIRST?
12

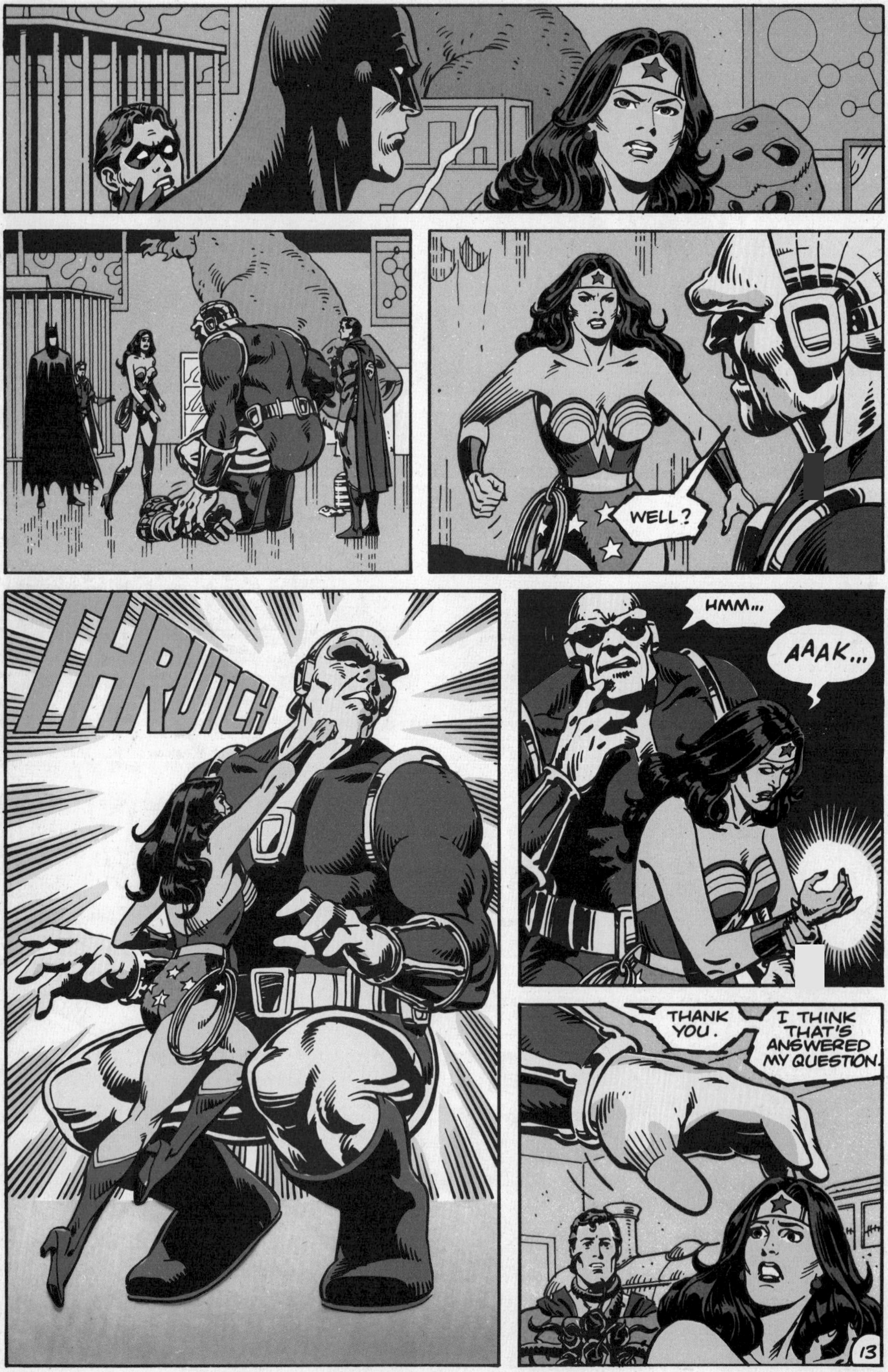
WELL?
THRUTCH
HMM...
AAAK...
THANK YOU.
I THINK THAT'S ANSWERED MY QUESTION!
13

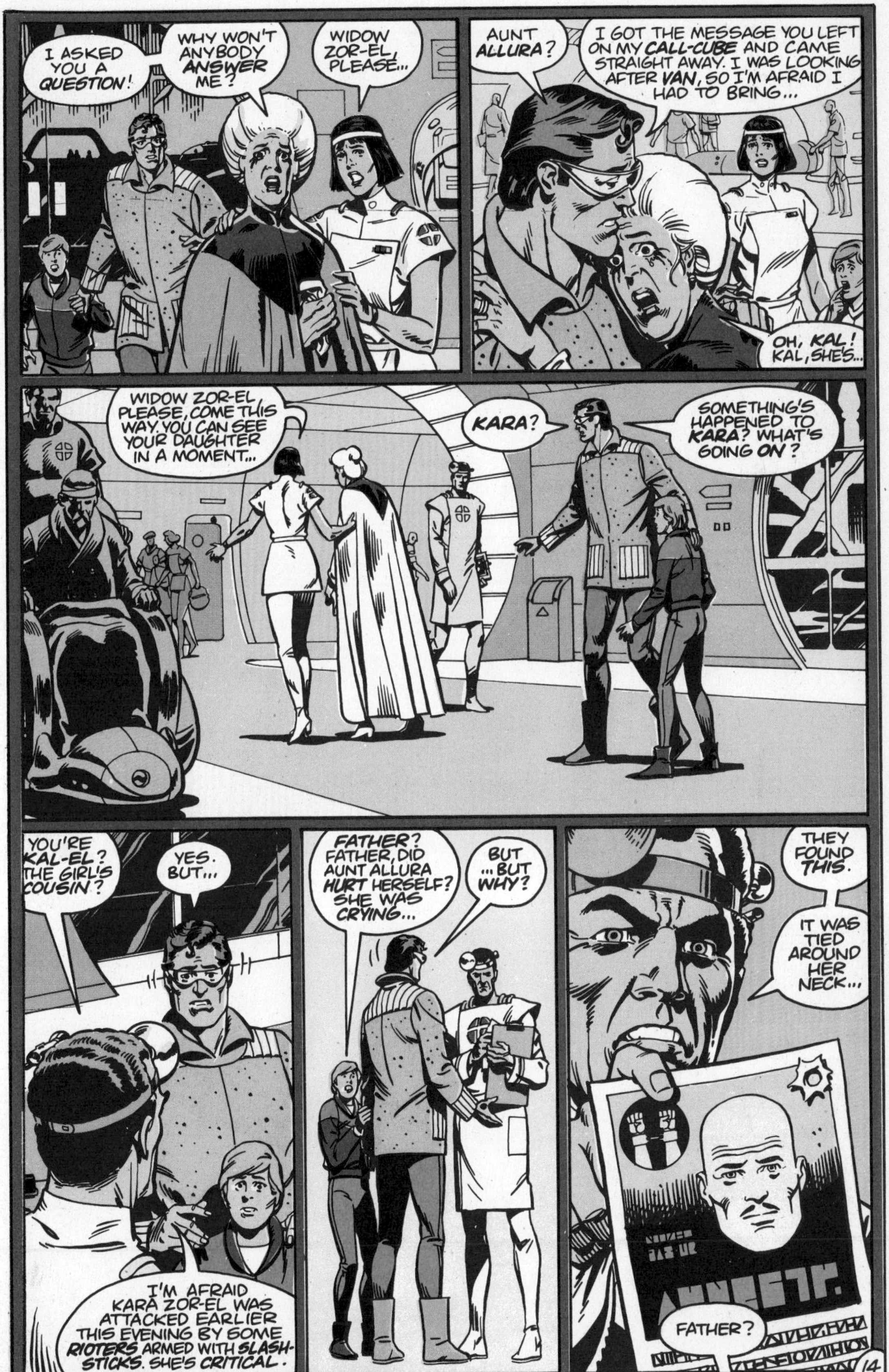
I ASKED YOU A QUESTION!
WHY WON'T ANYBODY ANSWER ME?
WIDOW ZOR-EL, PLEASE...
AUNT ALLURA?
I GOT THE MESSAGE YOU LEFT ON MY CALL-CUBE AND CAME STRAIGHT AWAY. I WAS LOOKING AFTER VAN, SO I'M AFRAID I HAD TO BRING...
OH, KAL! KAL, SHE'S...
WIDOW ZOR-EL PLEASE, COME THIS WAY. YOU CAN SEE YOUR DAUGHTER IN A MOMENT...
KARA?
SOMETHING'S HAPPENED TO KARA? WHAT'S GOING ON?
YOU'RE KAL-EL? THE GIRL'S COUSIN?
YES. BUT...
I'M AFRAID KARA ZOR-EL WAS ATTACKED EARLIER THIS EVENING BY SOME RIOTERS ARMED WITH SLASH-STICKS. SHE'S CRITICAL.
FATHER? FATHER, DID AUNT ALLURA HURT HERSELF? SHE WAS CRYING...
BUT ...BUT WHY?
THEY FOUND THIS.
IT WAS TIED AROUND HER NECK...
FATHER?
14

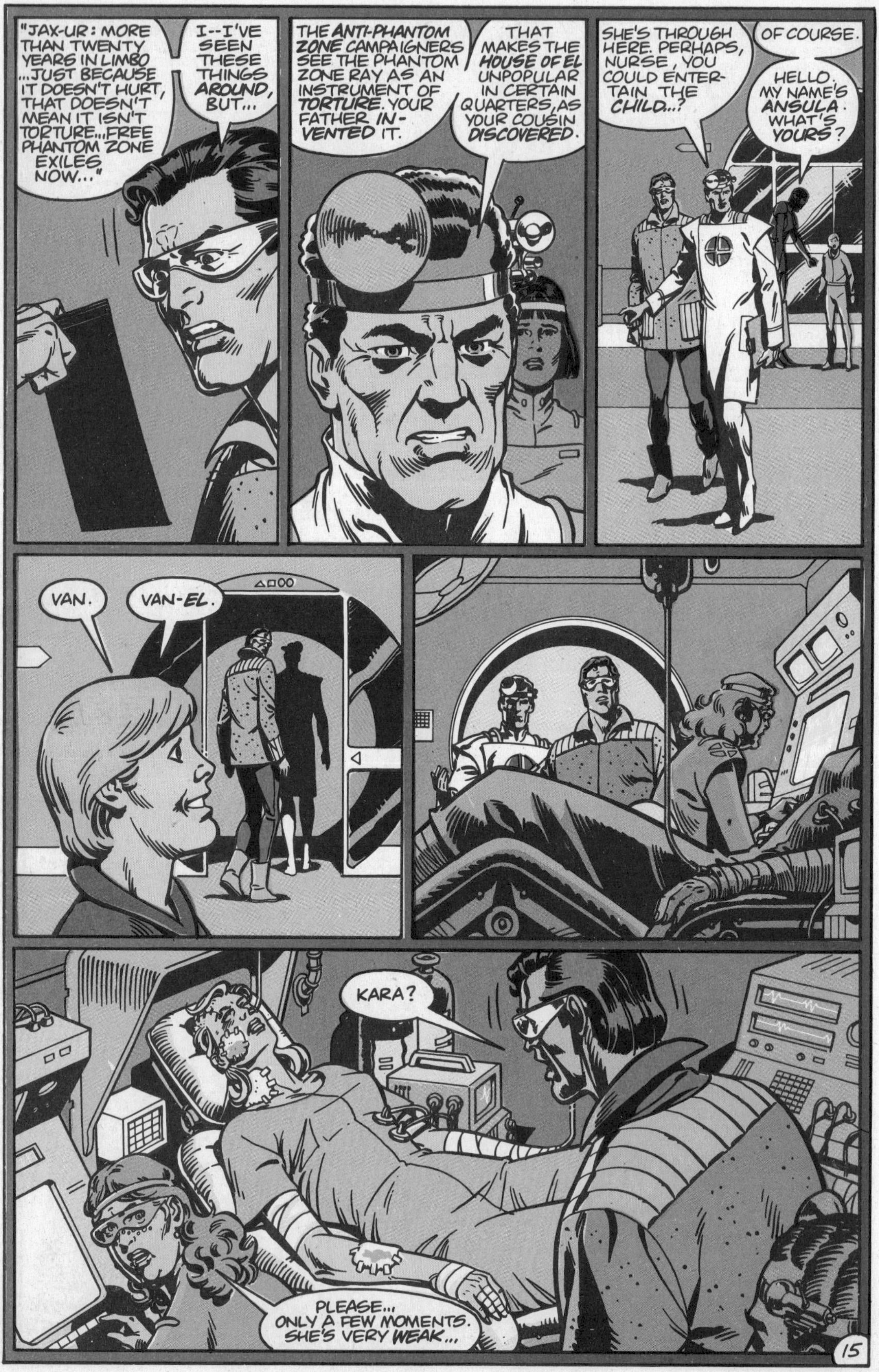

"JAX-UR: MORE THAN TWENTY YEARS IN LIMBO ...JUST BECAUSE IT DOESN'T HURT, THAT DOESN'T MEAN IT ISN'T TORTURE...FREE PHANTOM ZONE EXILES NOW..."
I--I'VE SEEN THESE THINGS AROUND, BUT...
THE ANTI-PHANTOM ZONE CAMPAIGNERS SEE THE PHANTOM ZONE RAY AS AN INSTRUMENT OF TORTURE. YOUR FATHER INVENTED IT.
THAT MAKES THE HOUSE OF EL UNPOPULAR IN CERTAIN QUARTERS, AS YOUR COUSIN DISCOVERED.
SHE'S THROUGH HERE. PERHAPS, NURSE, YOU COULD ENTERTAIN THE CHILD...?
OF COURSE.
HELLO. MY NAME'S ANSULA. WHAT'S YOURS?
VAN.
VAN-EL.
KARA?
PLEASE... ONLY A FEW MOMENTS. SHE'S VERY WEAK...
15

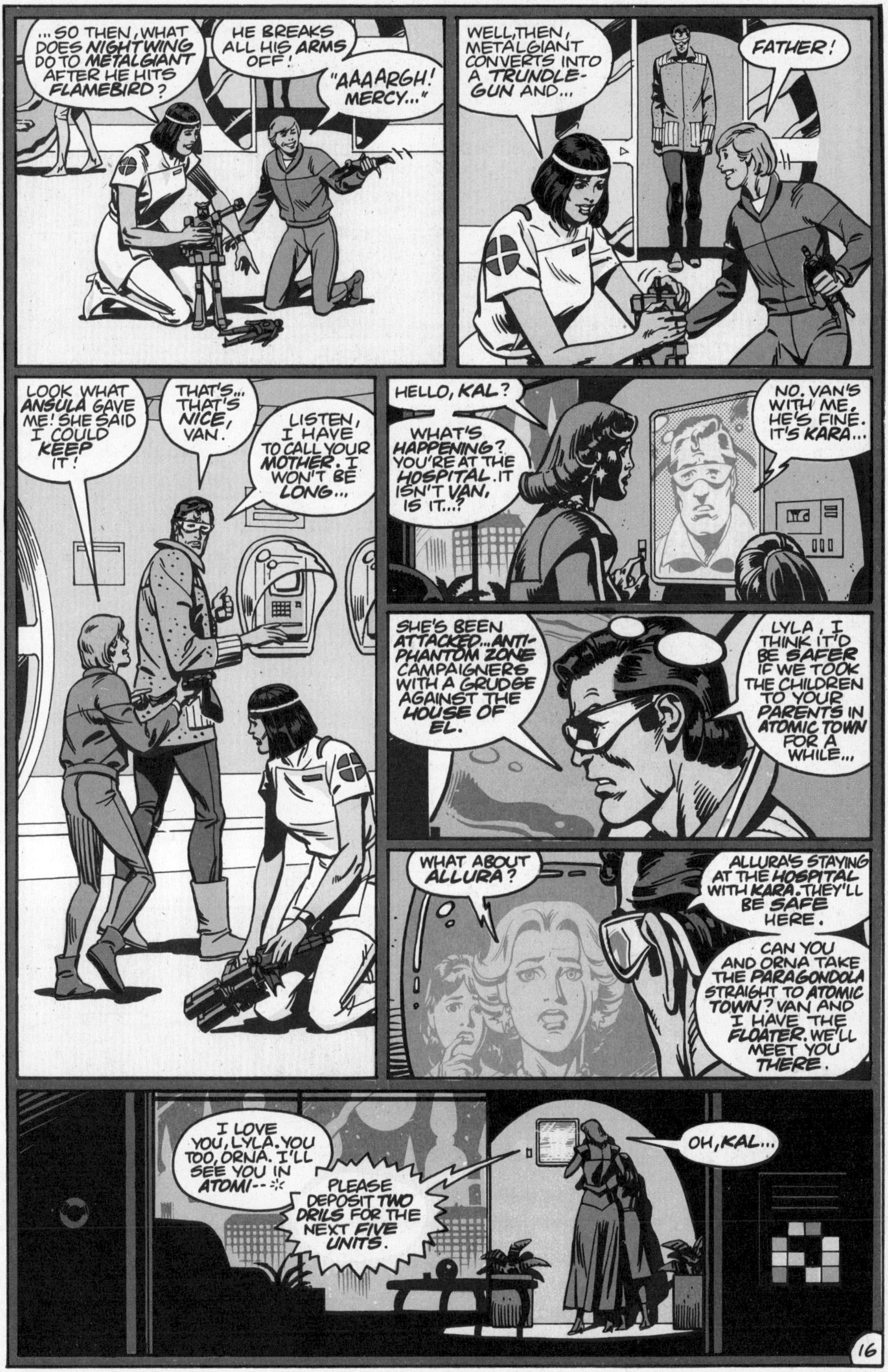
...SO THEN, WHAT DOES NIGHTWING DO TO METALGIANT AFTER HE HITS FLAMEBIRD?
HE BREAKS ALL HIS ARMS OFF!
"AAAARGH! MERCY..."
WELL, THEN, METALGIANT CONVERTS INTO A TRUNDLE-GUN AND...
FATHER!
LOOK WHAT ANSULA GAVE ME! SHE SAID I COULD KEEP IT!
THAT'S... THAT'S NICE, VAN.
LISTEN, I HAVE TO CALL YOUR MOTHER. I WON'T BE LONG...
HELLO, KAL?
WHAT'S HAPPENING? YOU'RE AT THE HOSPITAL. IT ISN'T VAN, IS IT...?
NO. VAN'S WITH ME. HE'S FINE. IT'S KARA...
SHE'S BEEN ATTACKED...ANTI-PHANTOM ZONE CAMPAIGNERS WITH A GRUDGE AGAINST THE HOUSE OF EL.
LYLA, I THINK IT'D BE SAFER IF WE TOOK THE CHILDREN TO YOUR PARENTS IN ATOMIC TOWN FOR A WHILE...
WHAT ABOUT ALLURA?
ALLURA'S STAYING AT THE HOSPITAL WITH KARA. THEY'LL BE SAFE HERE.
CAN YOU AND ORNA TAKE THE PARAGONDOLA STRAIGHT TO ATOMIC TOWN? VAN AND I HAVE THE FLOATER. WE'LL MEET YOU THERE.
I LOVE YOU, LYLA. YOU TOO, ORNA. I'LL SEE YOU IN ATOMI--
PLEASE DEPOSIT TWO DRILS FOR THE NEXT FIVE UNITS.
OH, KAL...
16

28

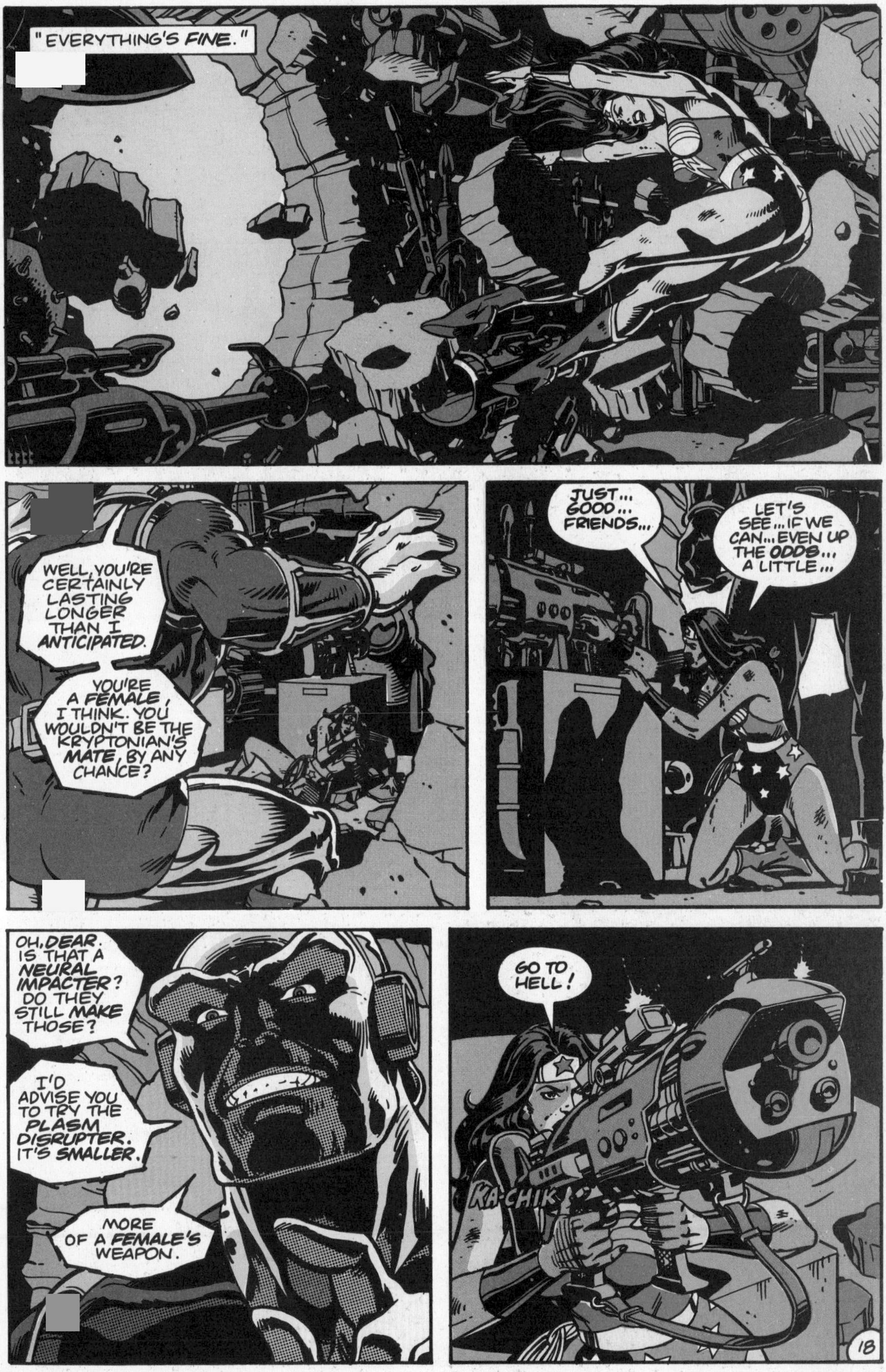
"EVERYTHING'S FINE."
WELL, YOU'RE CERTAINLY LASTING LONGER THAN I ANTICIPATED.
YOU'RE A FEMALE, I THINK. YOU WOULDN'T BE THE KRYPTONIAN'S MATE, BY ANY CHANCE?
JUST... GOOD... FRIENDS...
LET'S SEE... IF WE CAN... EVEN UP THE ODDS... A LITTLE...
OH, DEAR. IS THAT A NEURAL IMPACTER? DO THEY STILL MAKE THOSE?
I'D ADVISE YOU TO TRY THE PLASM DISRUPTER. IT'S SMALLER.
MORE OF A FEMALE'S WEAPON.
GO TO HELL!
KA-CHIK
18

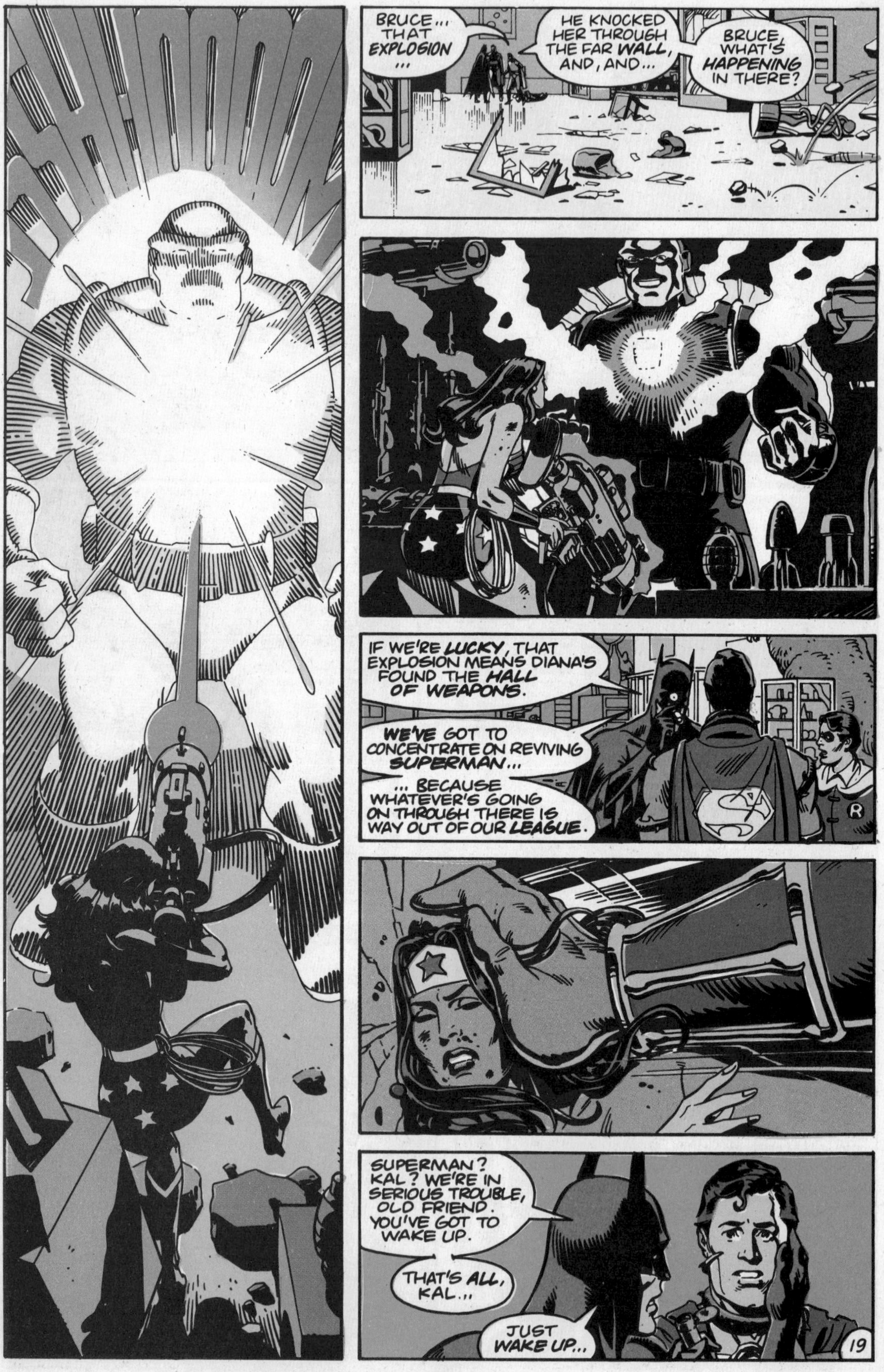
BRUCE... THAT EXPLOSION ...
HE KNOCKED HER THROUGH THE FAR WALL, AND, AND...
BRUCE, WHAT'S HAPPENING IN THERE?
IF WE'RE LUCKY, THAT EXPLOSION MEANS DIANA'S FOUND THE HALL OF WEAPONS.
WE'VE GOT TO CONCENTRATE ON REVIVING SUPERMAN...
... BECAUSE WHATEVER'S GOING ON THROUGH THERE IS WAY OUT OF OUR LEAGUE.
SUPERMAN? KAL? WE'RE IN SERIOUS TROUBLE, OLD FRIEND. YOU'VE GOT TO WAKE UP.
THAT'S ALL, KAL...
JUST WAKE UP...
19

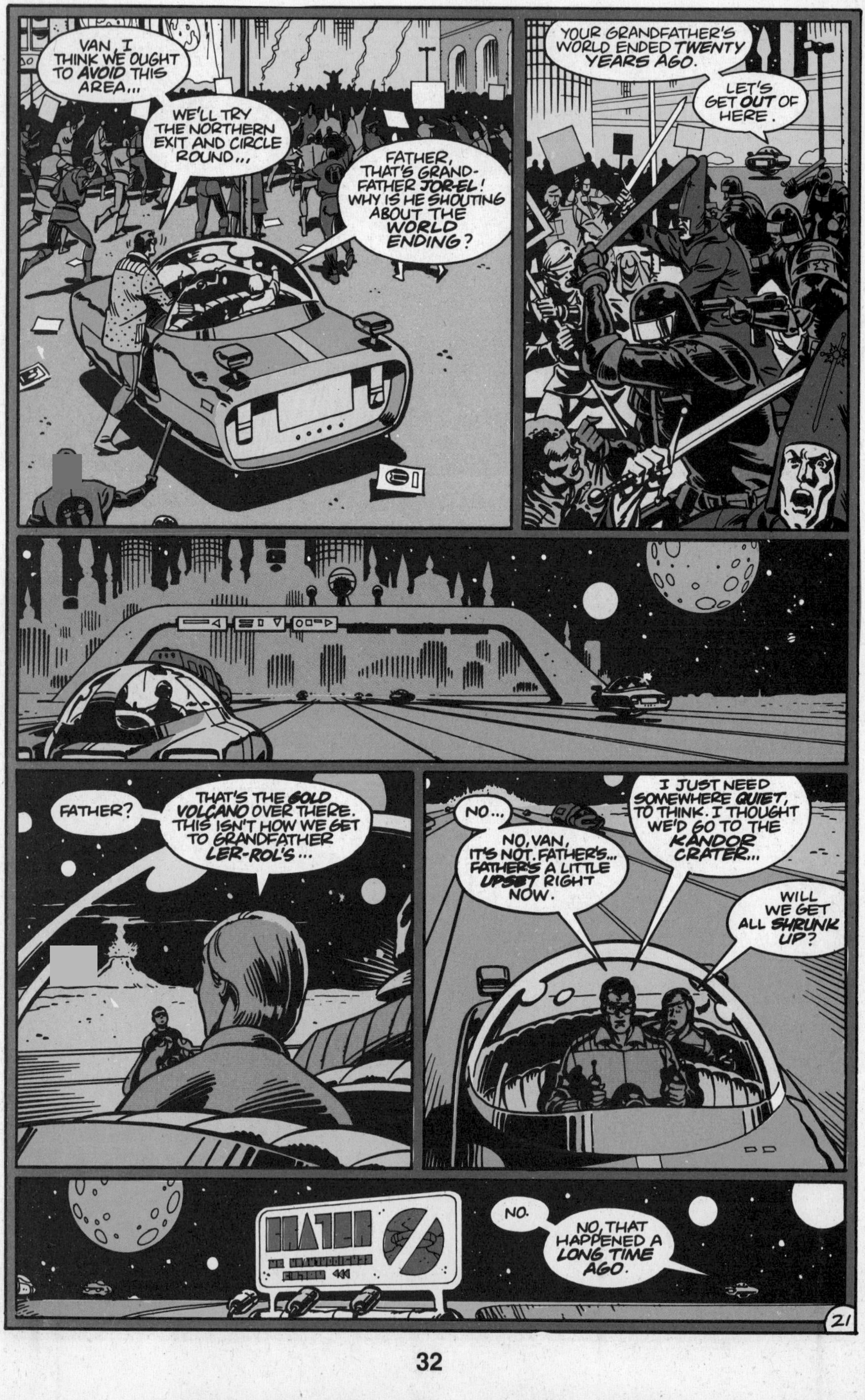
VAN, I THINK WE OUGHT TO AVOID THIS AREA...
WE'LL TRY THE NORTHERN EXIT AND CIRCLE ROUND...
FATHER, THAT'S GRAND-FATHER JOR-EL! WHY IS HE SHOUTING ABOUT THE WORLD ENDING?
YOUR GRANDFATHER'S WORLD ENDED TWENTY YEARS AGO.
LET'S GET OUT OF HERE.
FATHER?
THAT'S THE GOLD VOLCANO OVER THERE. THIS ISN'T HOW WE GET TO GRANDFATHER LER-ROL'S...
NO...
NO, VAN, IT'S NOT. FATHER'S... FATHER'S A LITTLE UPSET RIGHT NOW.
I JUST NEED SOMEWHERE QUIET, TO THINK. I THOUGHT WE'D GO TO THE KANDOR CRATER...
WILL WE GET ALL SHRUNK UP?
NO.
NO, THAT HAPPENED A LONG TIME AGO.
21

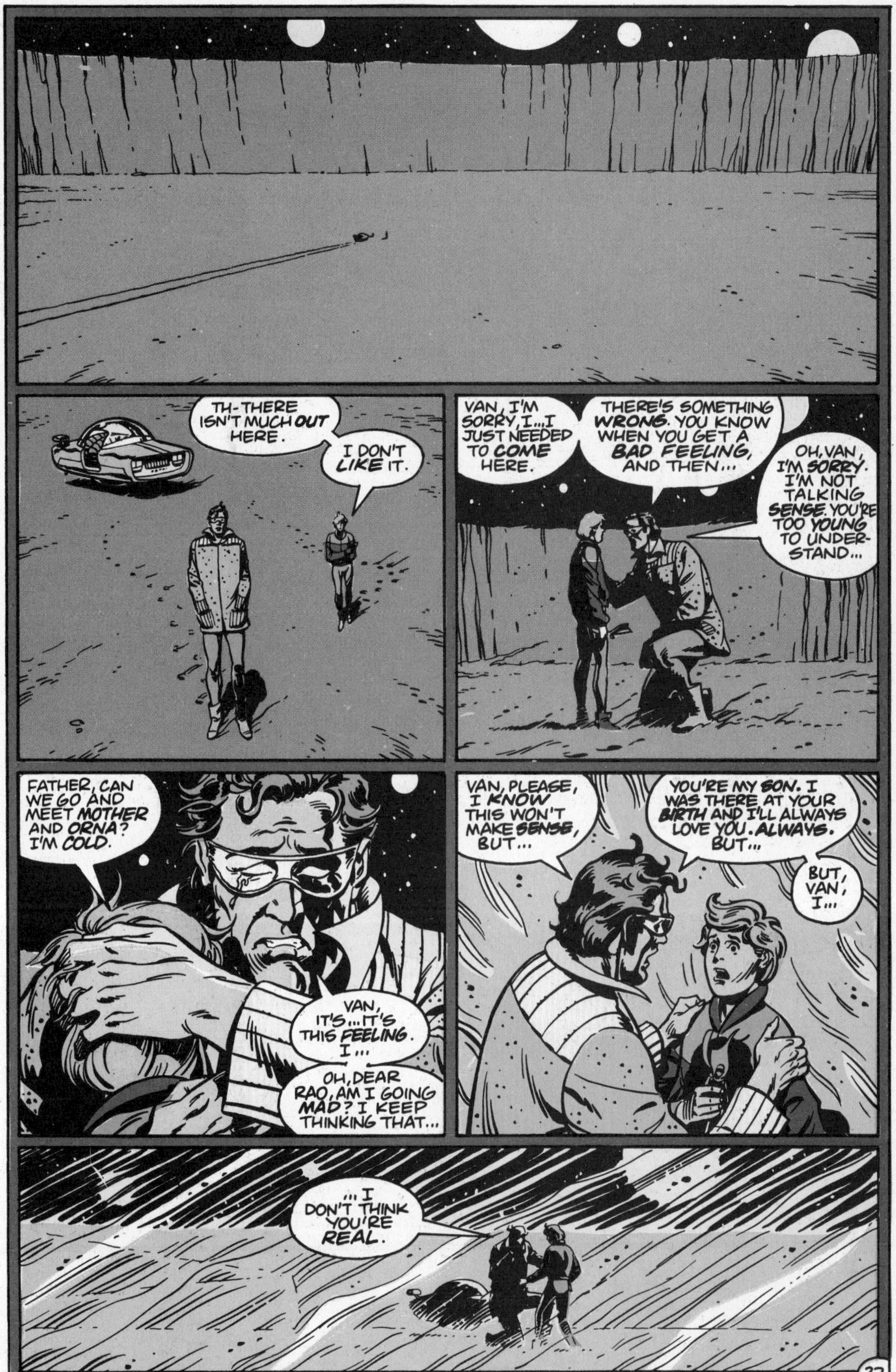
TH-THERE ISN'T MUCH OUT HERE.
I DON'T LIKE IT.
VAN, I'M SORRY, I...I JUST NEEDED TO COME HERE.
THERE'S SOMETHING WRONG. YOU KNOW WHEN YOU GET A BAD FEELING, AND THEN...
OH, VAN, I'M SORRY. I'M NOT TALKING SENSE. YOU'RE TOO YOUNG TO UNDER-STAND...
FATHER, CAN WE GO AND MEET MOTHER AND ORNA? I'M COLD.
VAN, IT'S...IT'S THIS FEELING. I...
OH, DEAR RAO, AM I GOING MAD? I KEEP THINKING THAT...
VAN, PLEASE, I KNOW THIS WON'T MAKE SENSE, BUT...
YOU'RE MY SON. I WAS THERE AT YOUR BIRTH AND I'LL ALWAYS LOVE YOU. ALWAYS. BUT...
BUT, VAN, I...
...I DON'T THINK YOU'RE REAL.
22

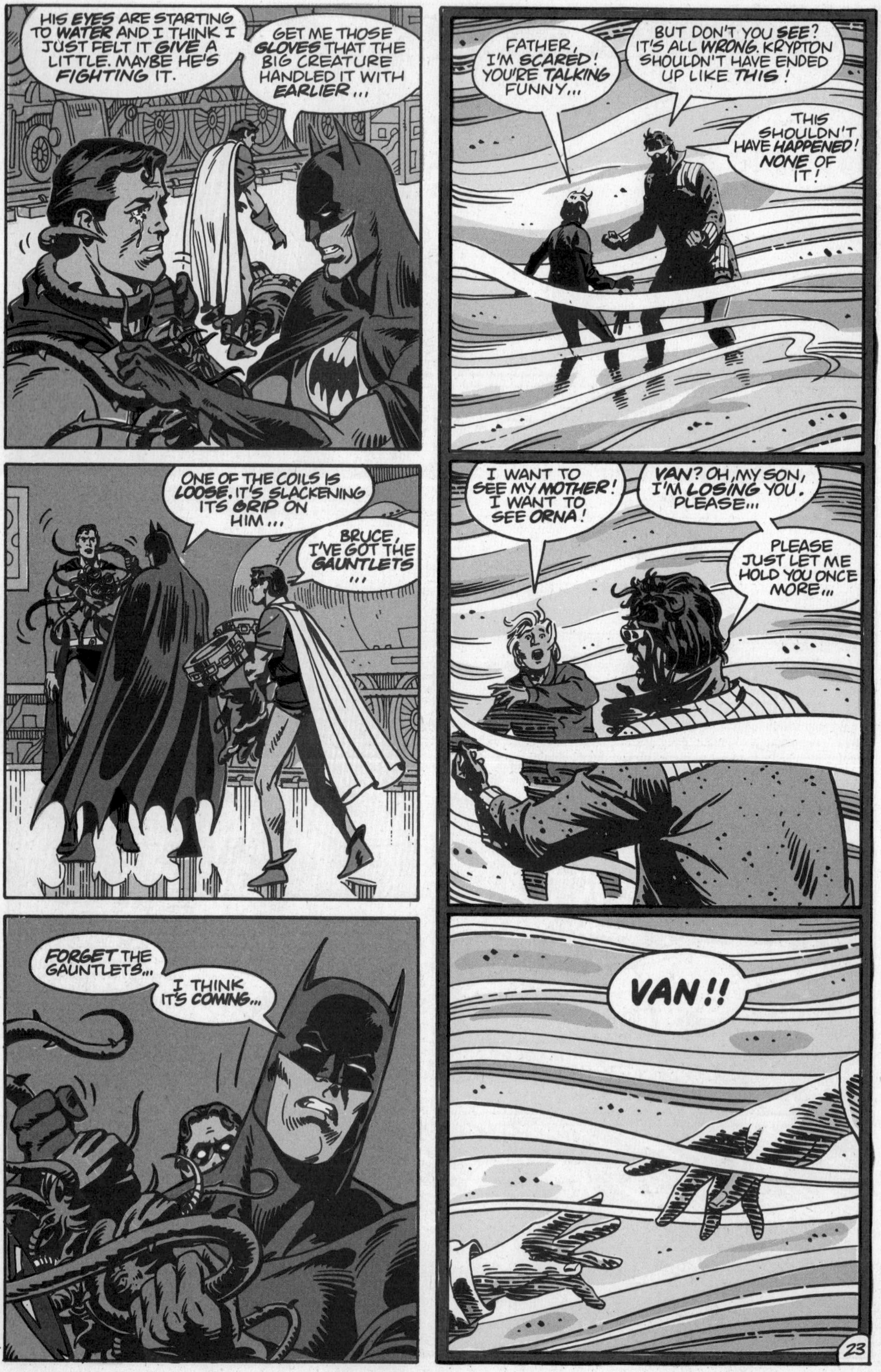
HIS EYES ARE STARTING TO WATER AND I THINK I JUST FELT IT GIVE A LITTLE. MAYBE HE'S FIGHTING IT.
GET ME THOSE GLOVES THAT THE BIG CREATURE HANDLED IT WITH EARLIER...
FATHER, I'M SCARED! YOU'RE TALKING FUNNY...
BUT DON'T YOU SEE? IT'S ALL WRONG. KRYPTON SHOULDN'T HAVE ENDED UP LIKE THIS!
THIS SHOULDN'T HAVE HAPPENED! NONE OF IT!
ONE OF THE COILS IS LOOSE. IT'S SLACKENING ITS GRIP ON HIM...
BRUCE, I'VE GOT THE GAUNTLETS...
I WANT TO SEE MY MOTHER! I WANT TO SEE ORNA!
VAN? OH, MY SON, I'M LOSING YOU. PLEASE...
PLEASE JUST LET ME HOLD YOU ONCE MORE...
FORGET THE GAUNTLETS...
I THINK IT'S COMING...
VAN!!
23

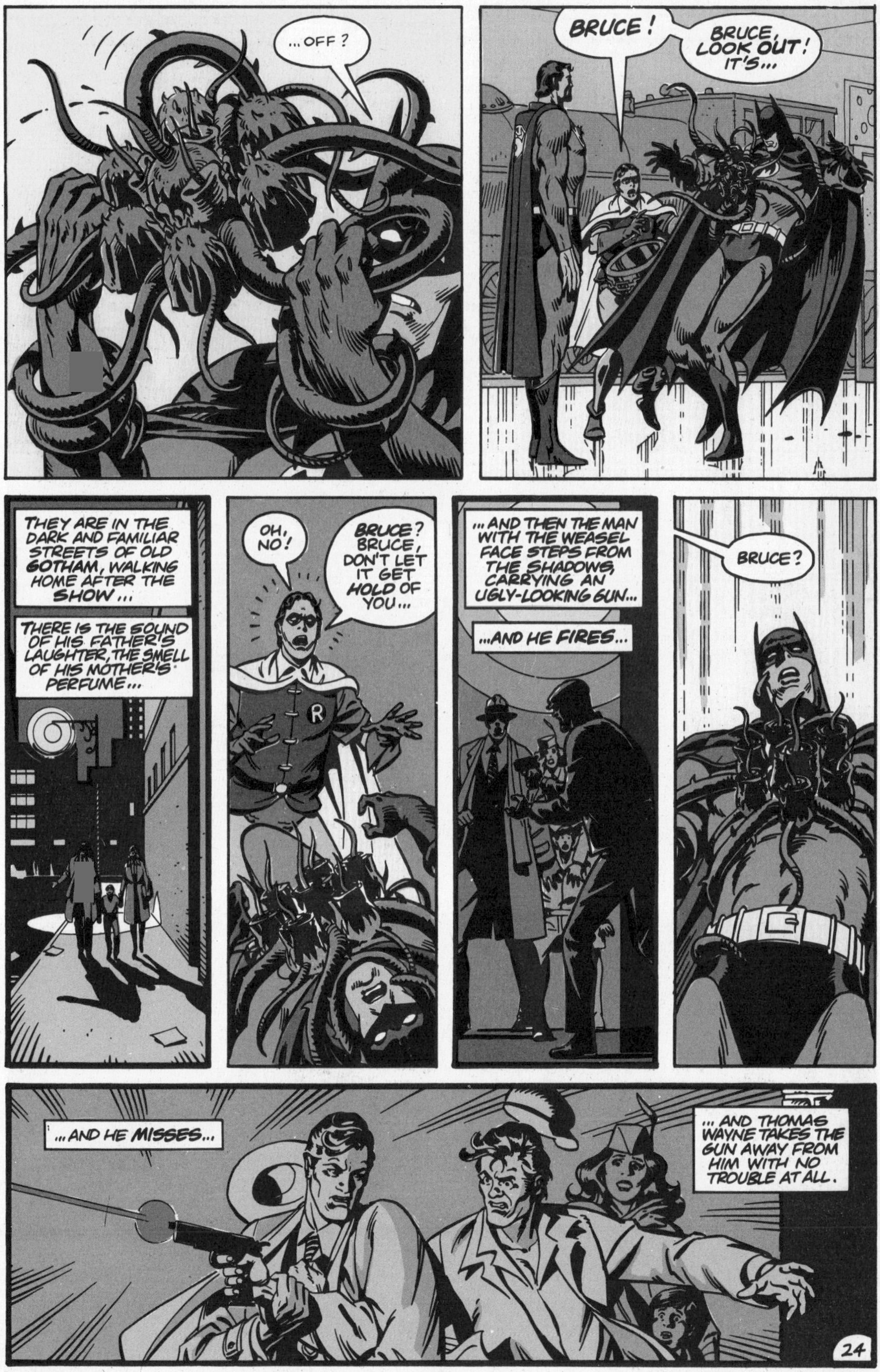
...OFF?
BRUCE!
BRUCE, LOOK OUT! IT'S...
THEY ARE IN THE DARK AND FAMILIAR STREETS OF OLD GOTHAM, WALKING HOME AFTER THE SHOW...
THERE IS THE SOUND OF HIS FATHER'S LAUGHTER, THE SMELL OF HIS MOTHER'S PERFUME...
OH, NO!
BRUCE? BRUCE, DON'T LET IT GET HOLD OF YOU...
...AND THEN THE MAN WITH THE WEASEL FACE STEPS FROM THE SHADOWS, CARRYING AN UGLY-LOOKING GUN...
...AND HE FIRES...
BRUCE?
...AND HE MISSES...
...AND THOMAS WAYNE TAKES THE GUN AWAY FROM HIM WITH NO TROUBLE AT ALL.
24

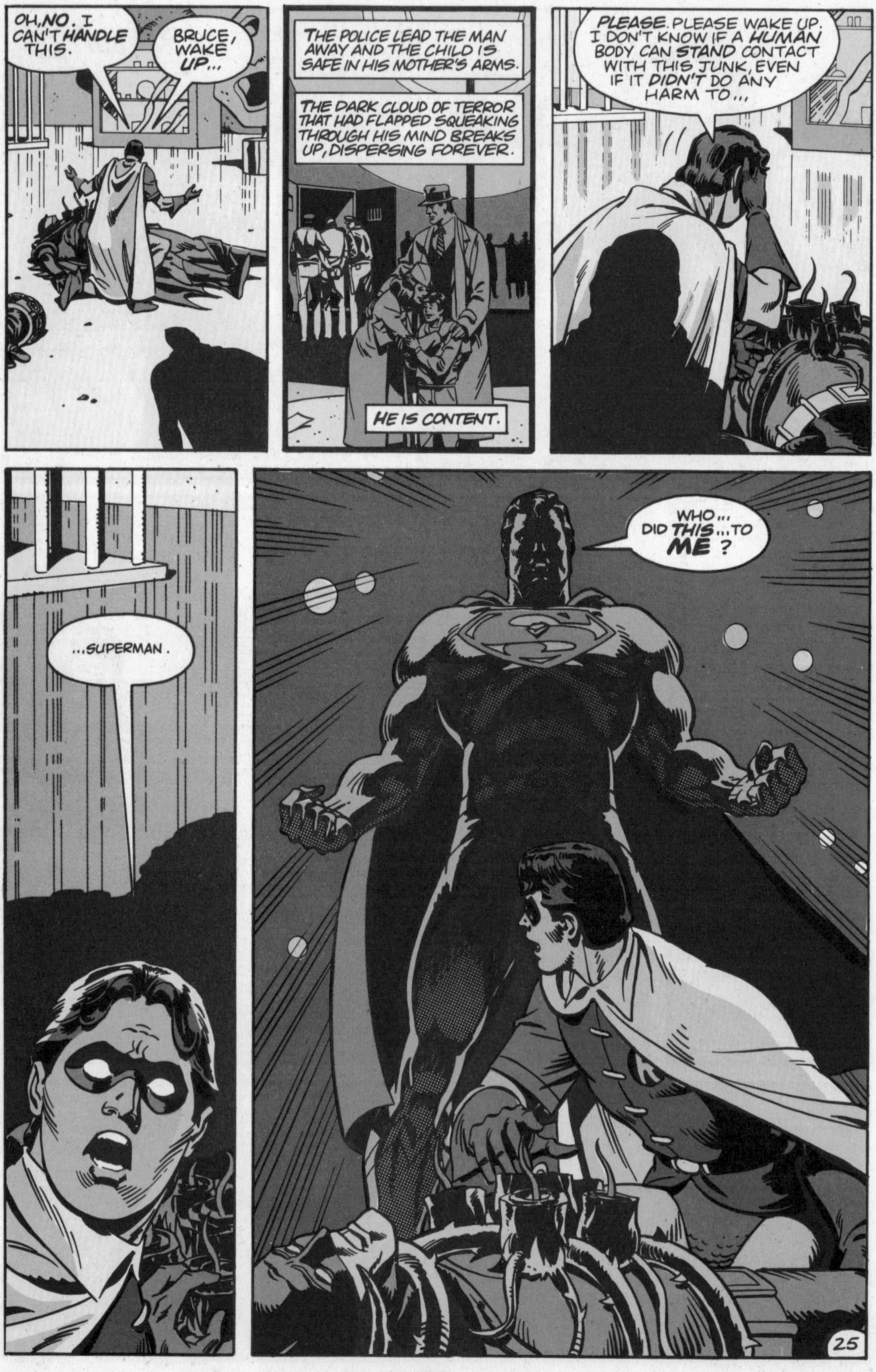
OH, NO. I CAN'T HANDLE THIS.
BRUCE, WAKE UP...
THE POLICE LEAD THE MAN AWAY AND THE CHILD IS SAFE IN HIS MOTHER'S ARMS.
THE DARK CLOUD OF TERROR THAT HAD FLAPPED SQUEAKING THROUGH HIS MIND BREAKS UP, DISPERSING FOREVER.
HE IS CONTENT.
PLEASE. PLEASE WAKE UP. I DON'T KNOW IF A HUMAN BODY CAN STAND CONTACT WITH THIS JUNK, EVEN IF IT DIDN'T DO ANY HARM TO...
...SUPERMAN.
WHO... DID THIS... TO ME?
25

I ...I DON'T KNOW.

A BIG YELLOW GUY. HE'S THROUGH THERE HURTING *WONDER WOMAN* NOW ...

SUPERMAN? ARE YOU OKAY? YOU LOOK SORTA, UH...

MONGUL ...

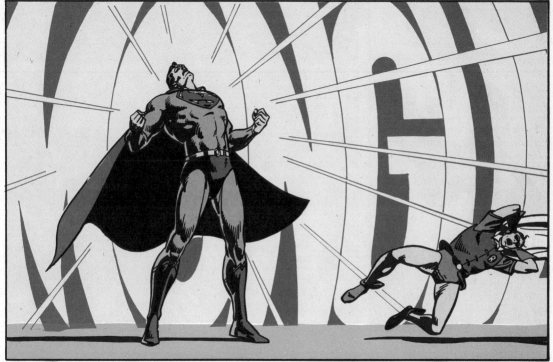

SUPERMAN! WAIT...

FFWOOSH

HE HEARS A VOICE LIKE ARMAGEDDON SHOUTING HIS NAME, AND HE STARTS TO TURN...

HE KNOWS HE HAS PERHAPS LESS THAN HALF A SECOND IN WHICH TO DEFEND HIMSELF...

26

WHAT AM I GOING TO DO ABOUT *BRUCE?* I CAN'T...

UH...

HE STARTS TO REACH TOWARDS HIS ARMOR'S WEAPON SYSTEMS, LETTING THE UNCONSCIOUS WOMAN CRUMPLE TO THE FLOOR...

...BUT THE ROCK OF THE FAR WALL SEEMS TO RIPPLE OUTWARDS IN A SUDDEN CASCADE OF POWDER...

...AND A FOUR-HUNDRED-MILE-AN-HOUR WIND SLAMS INTO HIM LIKE A STEAM HAMMER AS BIG AS THE WORLD...

...AND HE KNOWS THAT HE IS FAR TOO LATE.

27

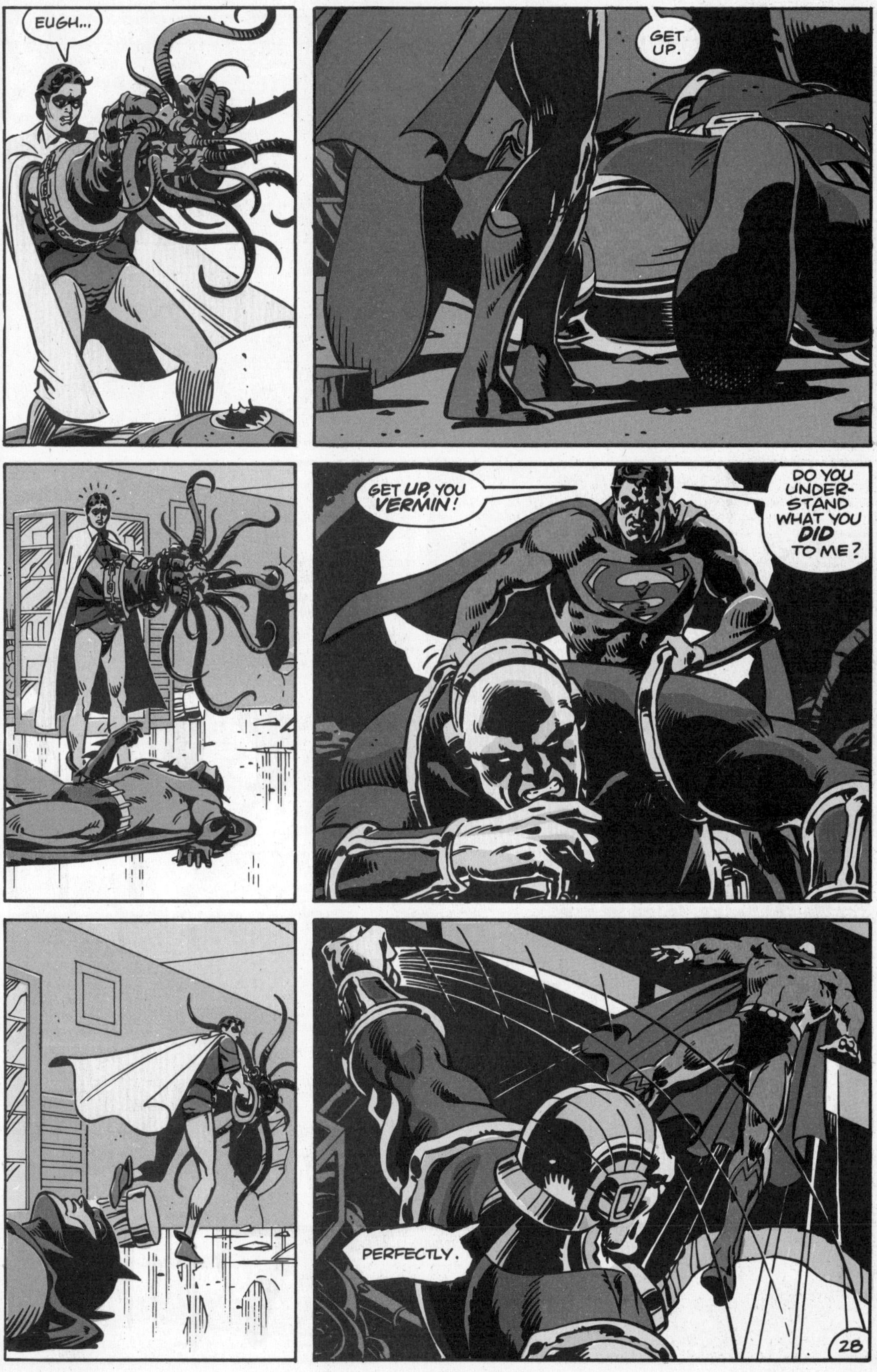
EUGH...
GET UP.
GET UP, YOU VERMIN!
DO YOU UNDERSTAND WHAT YOU DID TO ME?
PERFECTLY.
28

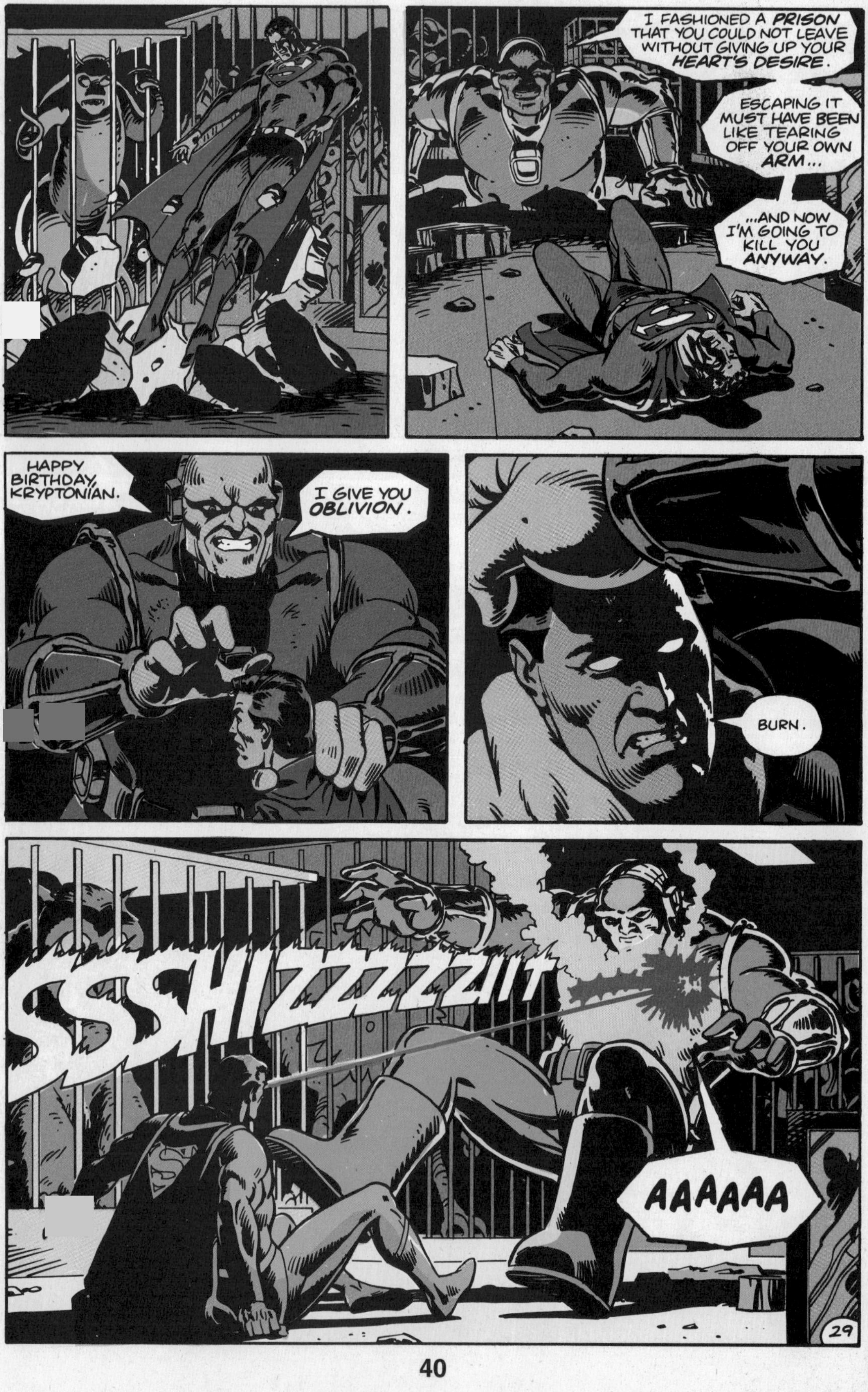

I FASHIONED A PRISON THAT YOU COULD NOT LEAVE WITHOUT GIVING UP YOUR HEART'S DESIRE.
ESCAPING IT MUST HAVE BEEN LIKE TEARING OFF YOUR OWN ARM...
...AND NOW I'M GOING TO KILL YOU ANYWAY.
HAPPY BIRTHDAY, KRYPTONIAN.
I GIVE YOU OBLIVION.
BURN.
SSHIZZZZZIIT
AAAAAA
29

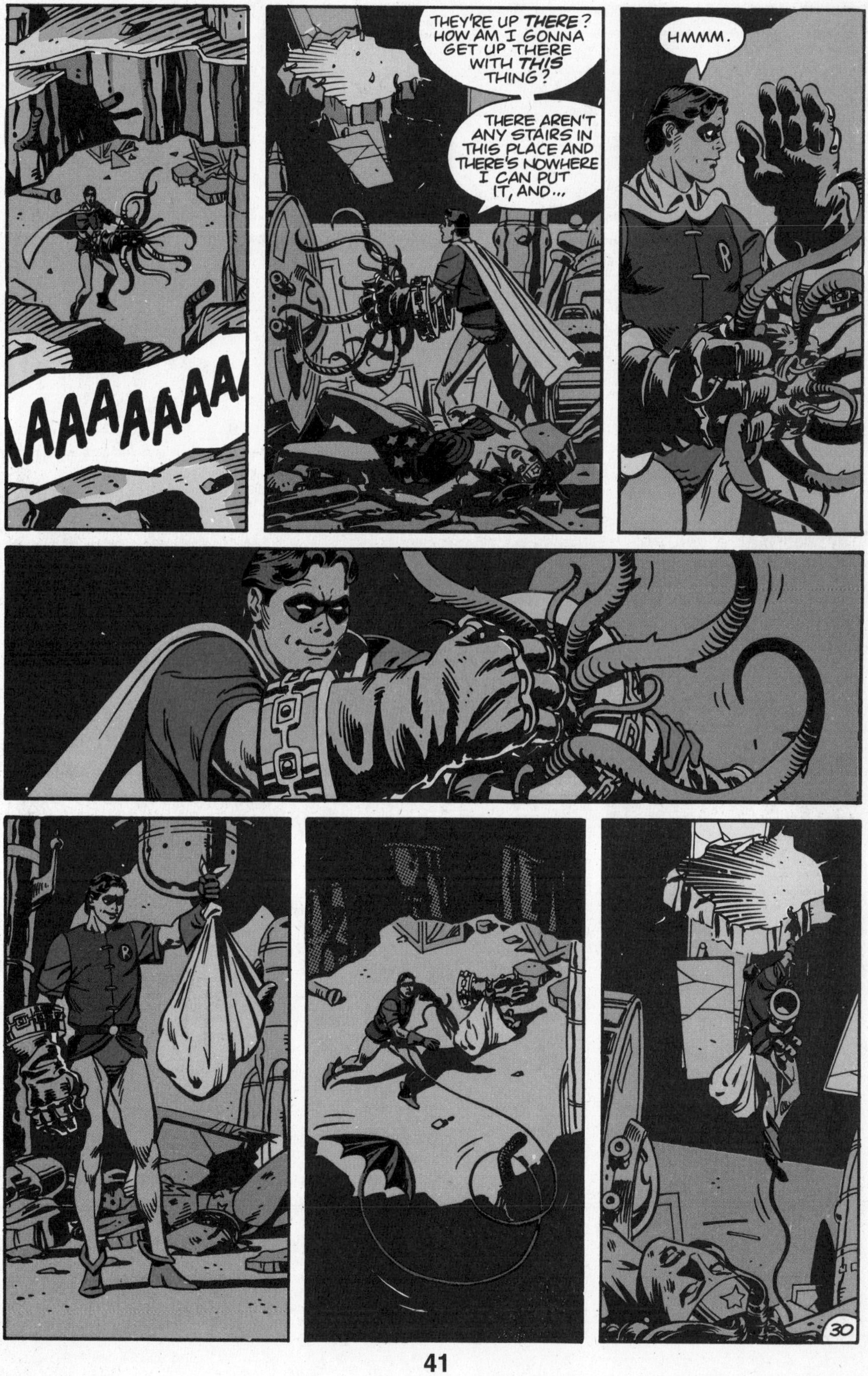
AAAAAAAAA
THEY'RE UP THERE? HOW AM I GONNA GET UP THERE WITH THIS THING?
THERE AREN'T ANY STAIRS IN THIS PLACE AND THERE'S NOWHERE I CAN PUT IT, AND...
HMMM.
30

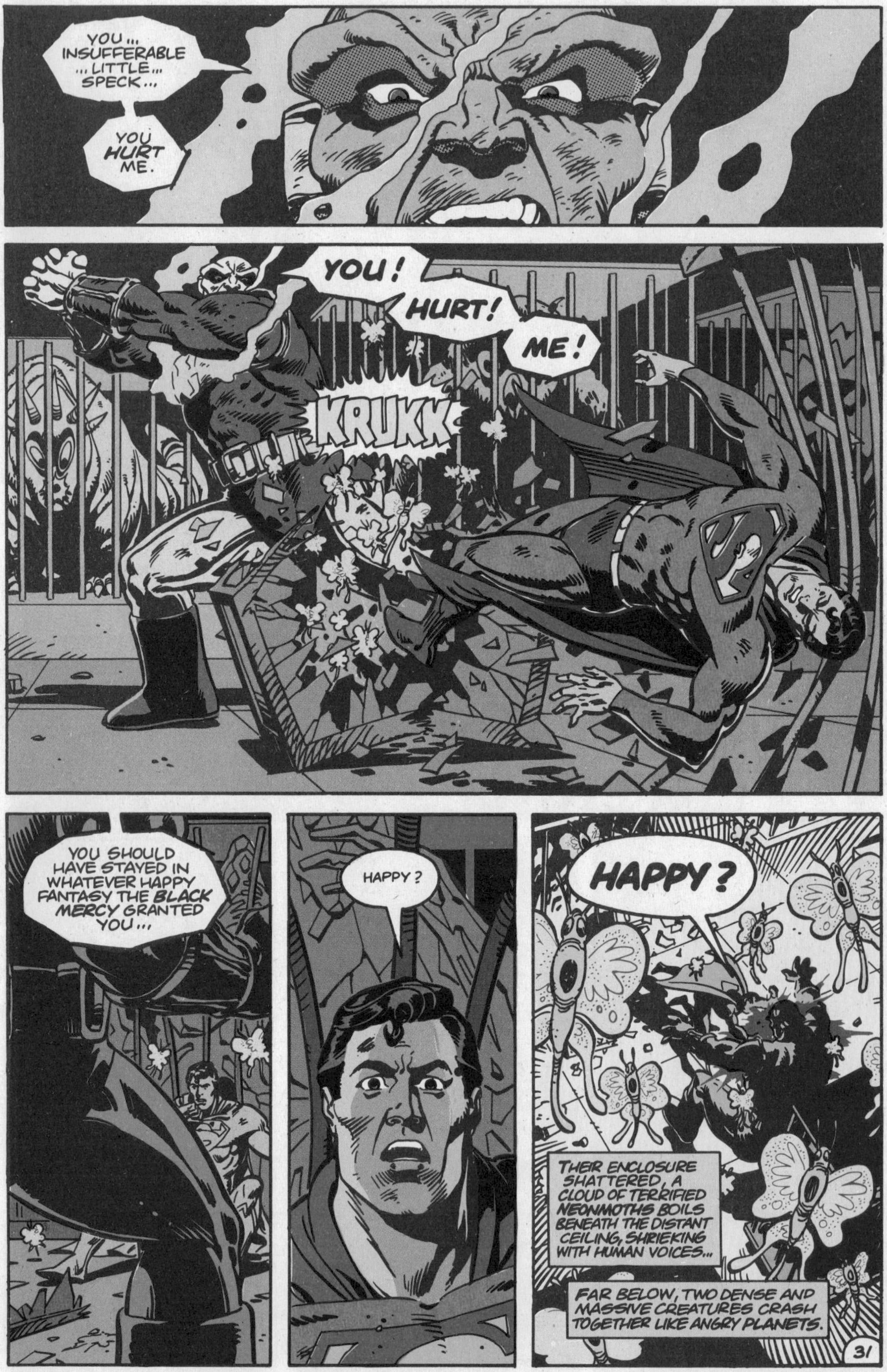

YOU... INSUFFERABLE ...LITTLE... SPECK...
YOU HURT ME.
YOU!
HURT!
ME!
KRUKK
YOU SHOULD HAVE STAYED IN WHATEVER HAPPY FANTASY THE BLACK MERCY GRANTED YOU...
HAPPY?
HAPPY?
THEIR ENCLOSURE SHATTERED, A CLOUD OF TERRIFIED NEONMOTHS BOILS BENEATH THE DISTANT CEILING, SHRIEKING WITH HUMAN VOICES...
FAR BELOW, TWO DENSE AND MASSIVE CREATURES CRASH TOGETHER LIKE ANGRY PLANETS.
31

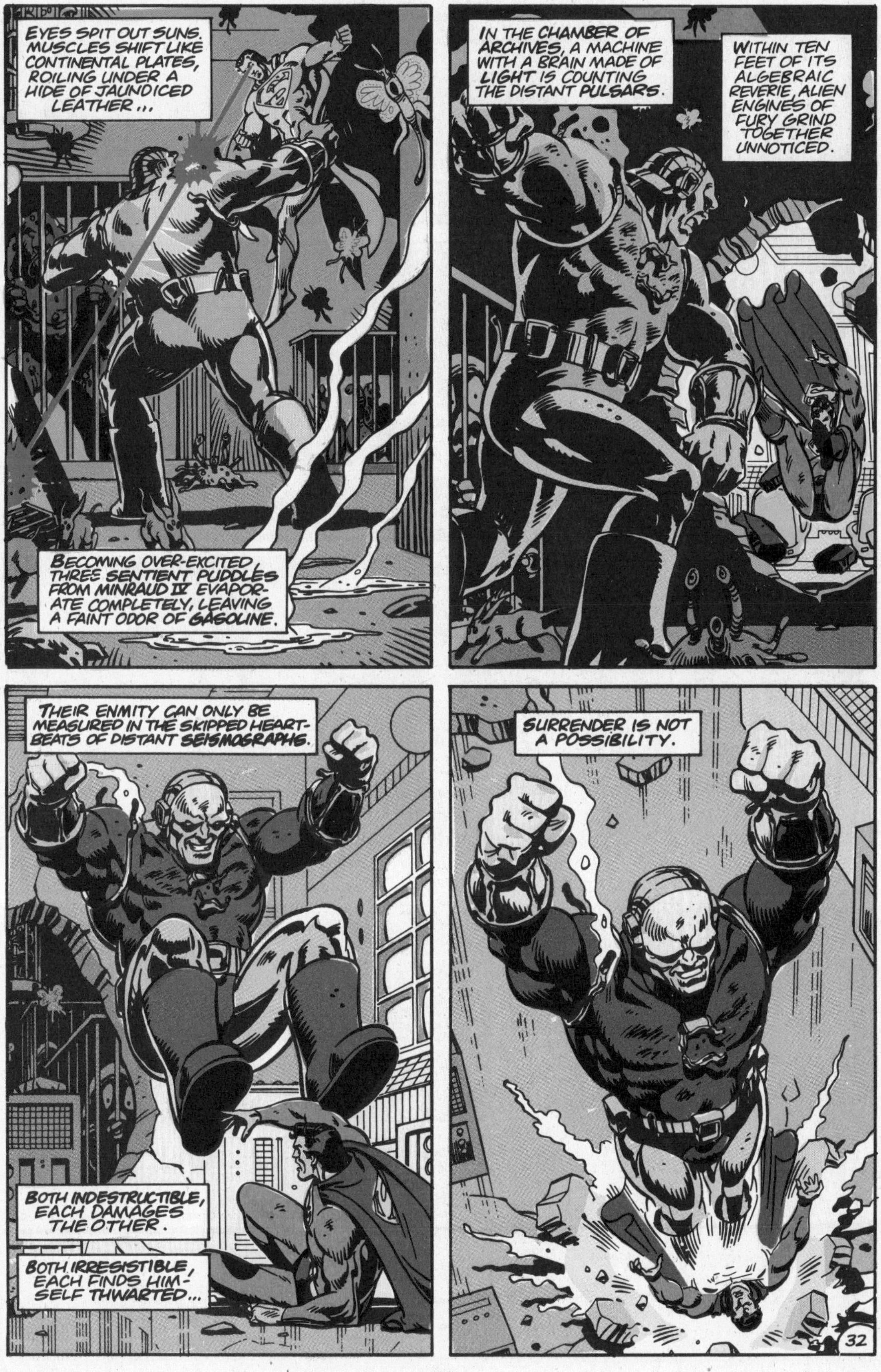
EYES SPIT OUT SUNS. MUSCLES SHIFT LIKE CONTINENTAL PLATES, ROILING UNDER A HIDE OF JAUNDICED LEATHER...
BECOMING OVER-EXCITED, THREE SENTIENT PUDDLES FROM MINRAUD IV EVAPORATE COMPLETELY, LEAVING A FAINT ODOR OF GASOLINE.
IN THE CHAMBER OF ARCHIVES, A MACHINE WITH A BRAIN MADE OF LIGHT IS COUNTING THE DISTANT PULSARS.
WITHIN TEN FEET OF ITS ALGEBRAIC REVERIE, ALIEN ENGINES OF FURY GRIND TOGETHER UNNOTICED.
THEIR ENMITY CAN ONLY BE MEASURED IN THE SKIPPED HEARTBEATS OF DISTANT SEISMOGRAPHS.
BOTH INDESTRUCTIBLE, EACH DAMAGES THE OTHER.
BOTH IRRESISTIBLE, EACH FINDS HIMSELF THWARTED...
SURRENDER IS NOT A POSSIBILITY.
32

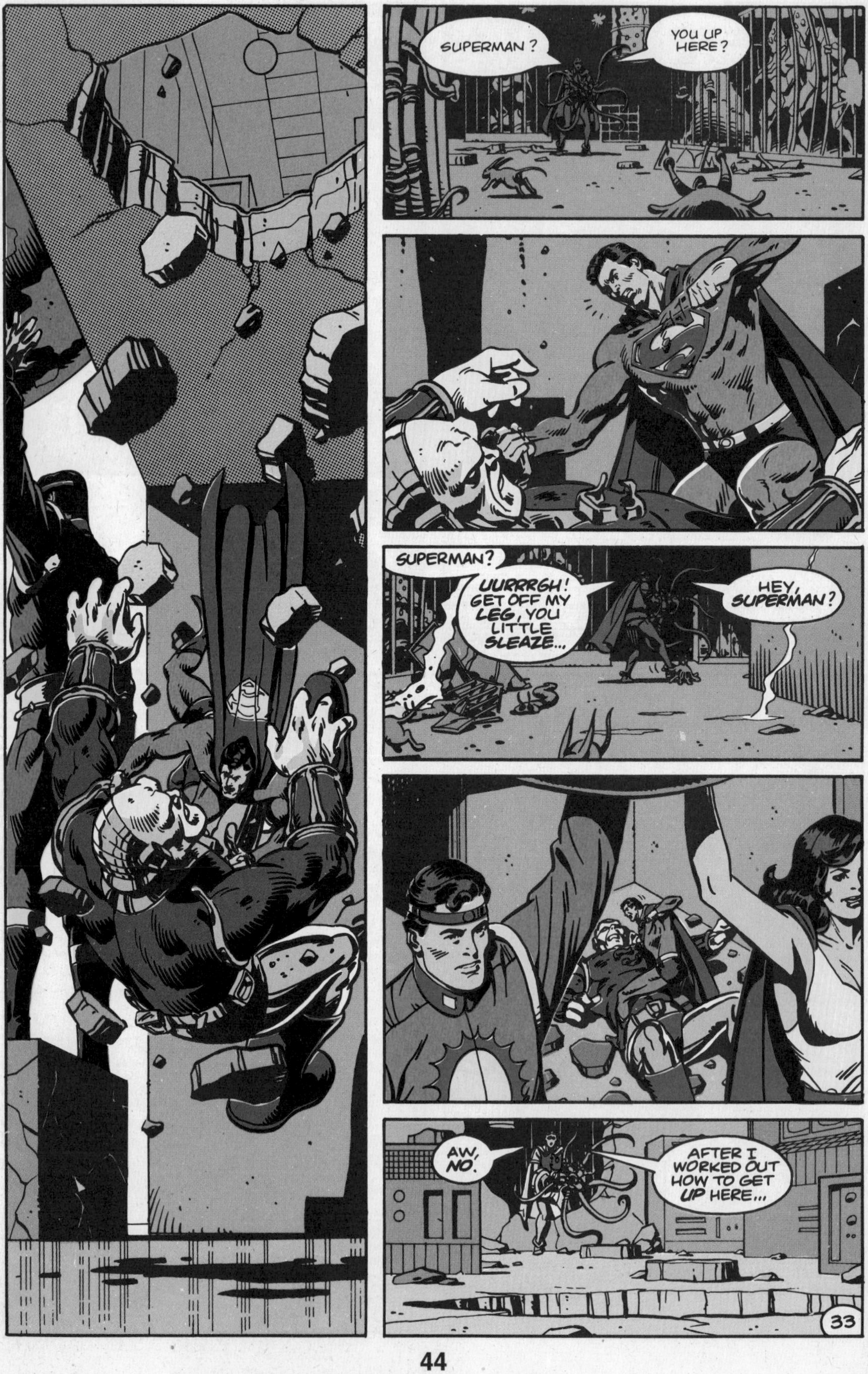
SUPERMAN?
YOU UP HERE?
SUPERMAN?
UURRRGH! GET OFF MY LEG, YOU LITTLE SLEAZE...
HEY, SUPERMAN?
AW, NO.
AFTER I WORKED OUT HOW TO GET UP HERE...
33

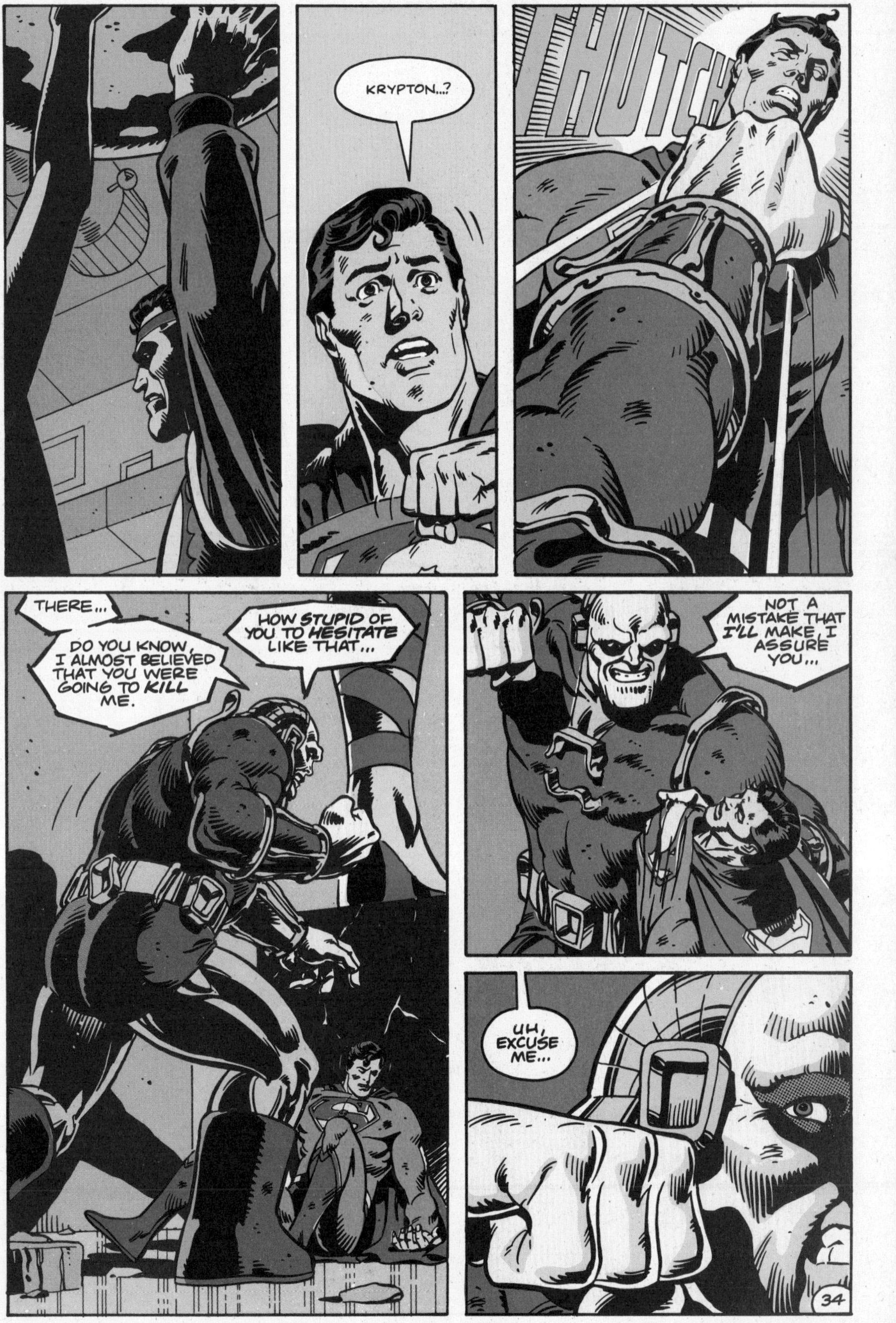
KRYPTON...?
THUTCH
THERE...
DO YOU KNOW, I ALMOST BELIEVED THAT YOU WERE GOING TO KILL ME.
HOW STUPID OF YOU TO HESITATE LIKE THAT...
NOT A MISTAKE THAT I'LL MAKE, I ASSURE YOU...
UH, EXCUSE ME...
34

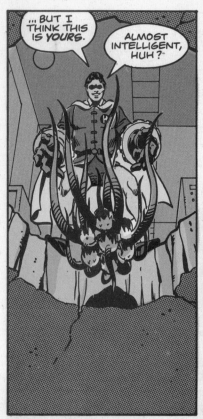

...BUT I THINK THIS IS YOURS.

ALMOST INTELLIGENT, HUH?~

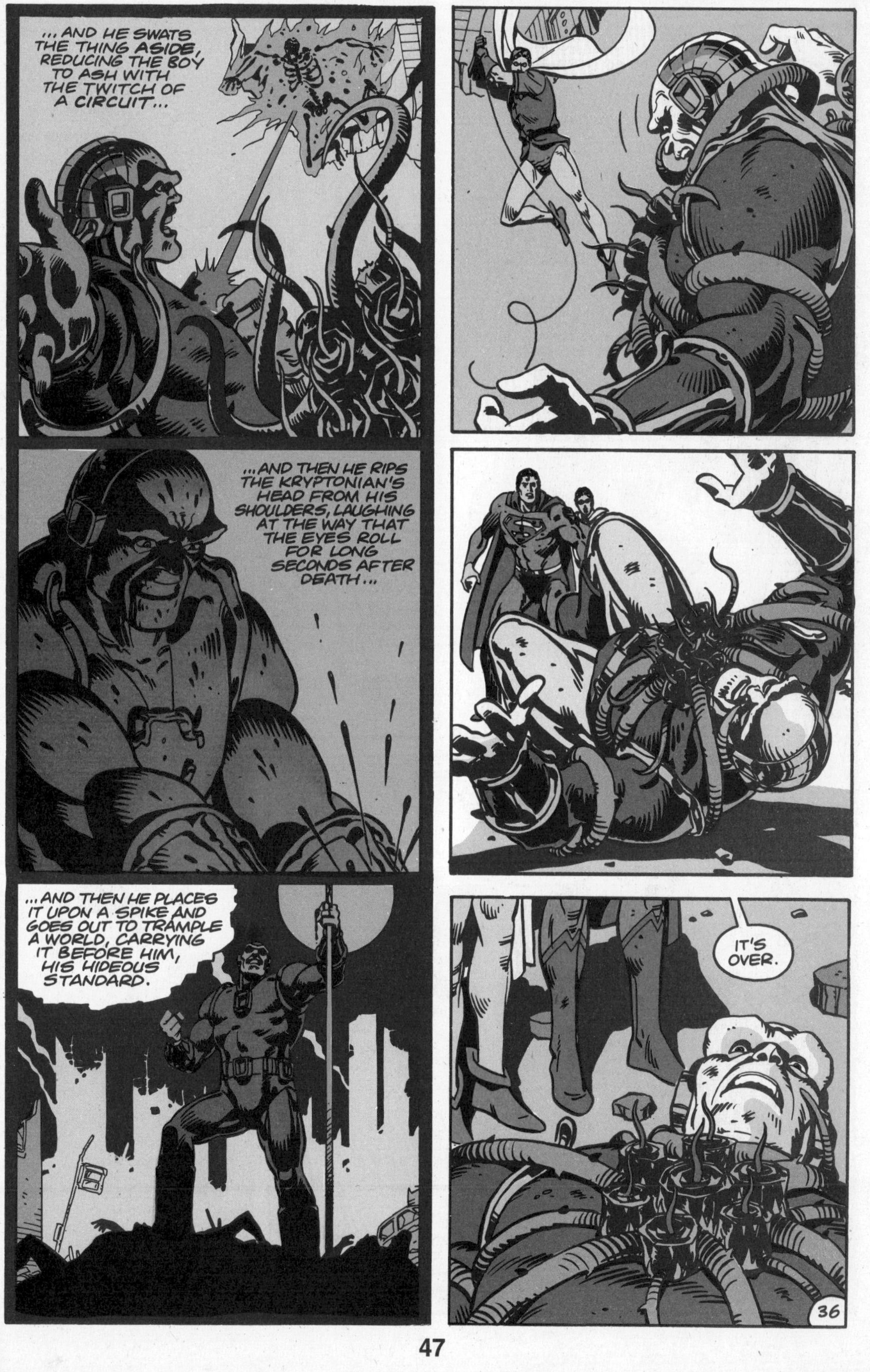
...AND HE SWATS THE THING ASIDE, REDUCING THE BOY TO ASH WITH THE TWITCH OF A CIRCUIT...
...AND THEN HE RIPS THE KRYPTONIAN'S HEAD FROM HIS SHOULDERS, LAUGHING AT THE WAY THAT THE EYES ROLL FOR LONG SECONDS AFTER DEATH...
...AND THEN HE PLACES IT UPON A SPIKE AND GOES OUT TO TRAMPLE A WORLD, CARRYING IT BEFORE HIM, HIS HIDEOUS STANDARD.
IT'S OVER.
36

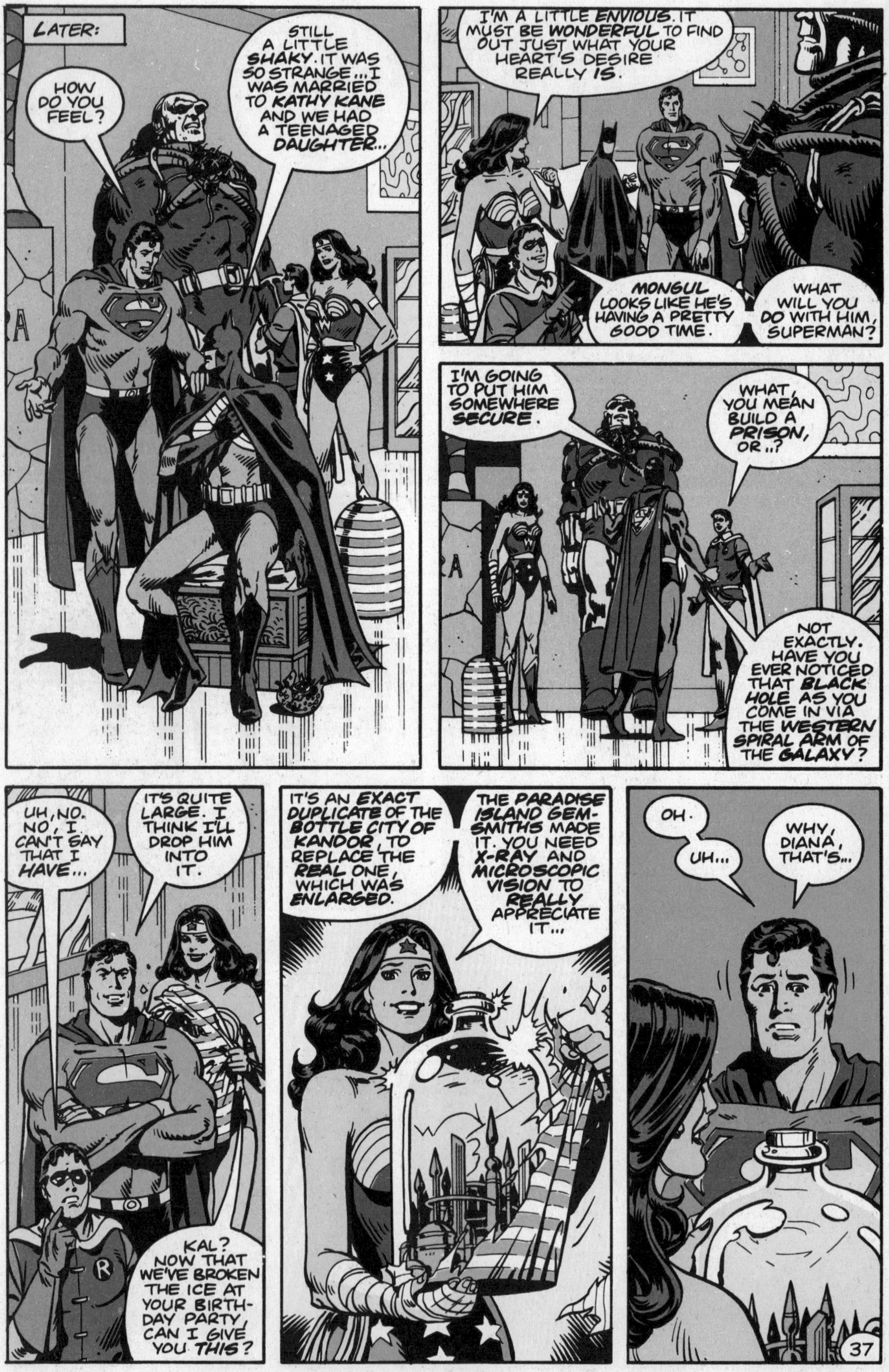
LATER:
HOW DO YOU FEEL?
STILL A LITTLE SHAKY. IT WAS SO STRANGE... I WAS MARRIED TO KATHY KANE AND WE HAD A TEENAGED DAUGHTER...
I'M A LITTLE ENVIOUS. IT MUST BE WONDERFUL TO FIND OUT JUST WHAT YOUR HEART'S DESIRE REALLY IS.
MONGUL LOOKS LIKE HE'S HAVING A PRETTY GOOD TIME.
WHAT WILL YOU DO WITH HIM, SUPERMAN?
I'M GOING TO PUT HIM SOMEWHERE SECURE.
WHAT, YOU MEAN BUILD A PRISON, OR..?
NOT EXACTLY. HAVE YOU EVER NOTICED THAT BLACK HOLE AS YOU COME IN VIA THE WESTERN SPIRAL ARM OF THE GALAXY?
UH, NO. NO, I CAN'T SAY THAT I HAVE...
IT'S QUITE LARGE. I THINK I'LL DROP HIM INTO IT.
KAL? NOW THAT WE'VE BROKEN THE ICE AT YOUR BIRTHDAY PARTY, CAN I GIVE YOU THIS?
IT'S AN EXACT DUPLICATE OF THE BOTTLE CITY OF KANDOR, TO REPLACE THE REAL ONE, WHICH WAS ENLARGED.
THE PARADISE ISLAND GEM-SMITHS MADE IT. YOU NEED X-RAY AND MICROSCOPIC VISION TO REALLY APPRECIATE IT...
OH.
UH...
WHY, DIANA, THAT'S...
37

...JUST...

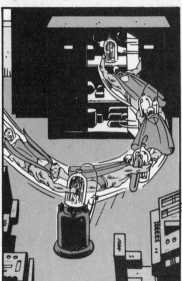

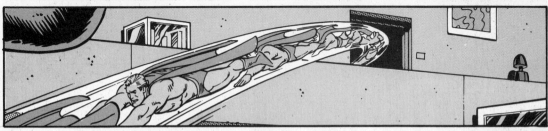

...JUST...

38

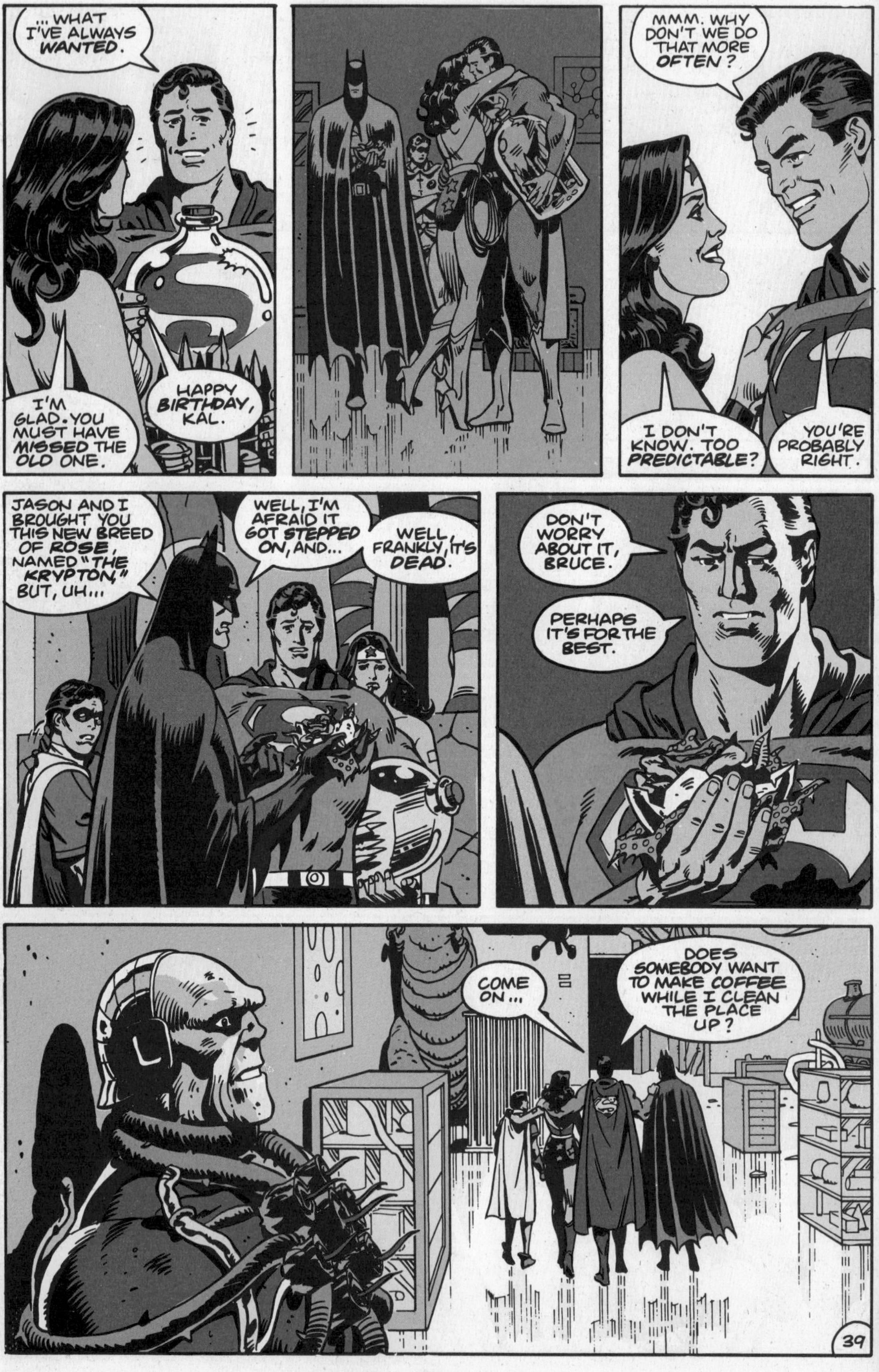

... WHAT I'VE ALWAYS WANTED.
I'M GLAD. YOU MUST HAVE MISSED THE OLD ONE.
HAPPY BIRTHDAY, KAL.
MMM. WHY DON'T WE DO THAT MORE OFTEN?
I DON'T KNOW. TOO PREDICTABLE?
YOU'RE PROBABLY RIGHT.
JASON AND I BROUGHT YOU THIS NEW BREED OF ROSE, NAMED "THE KRYPTON," BUT, UH...
WELL, I'M AFRAID IT GOT STEPPED ON, AND...
WELL, FRANKLY, IT'S DEAD.
DON'T WORRY ABOUT IT, BRUCE.
PERHAPS IT'S FOR THE BEST.
COME ON...
DOES SOMEBODY WANT TO MAKE COFFEE WHILE I CLEAN THE PLACE UP?
39

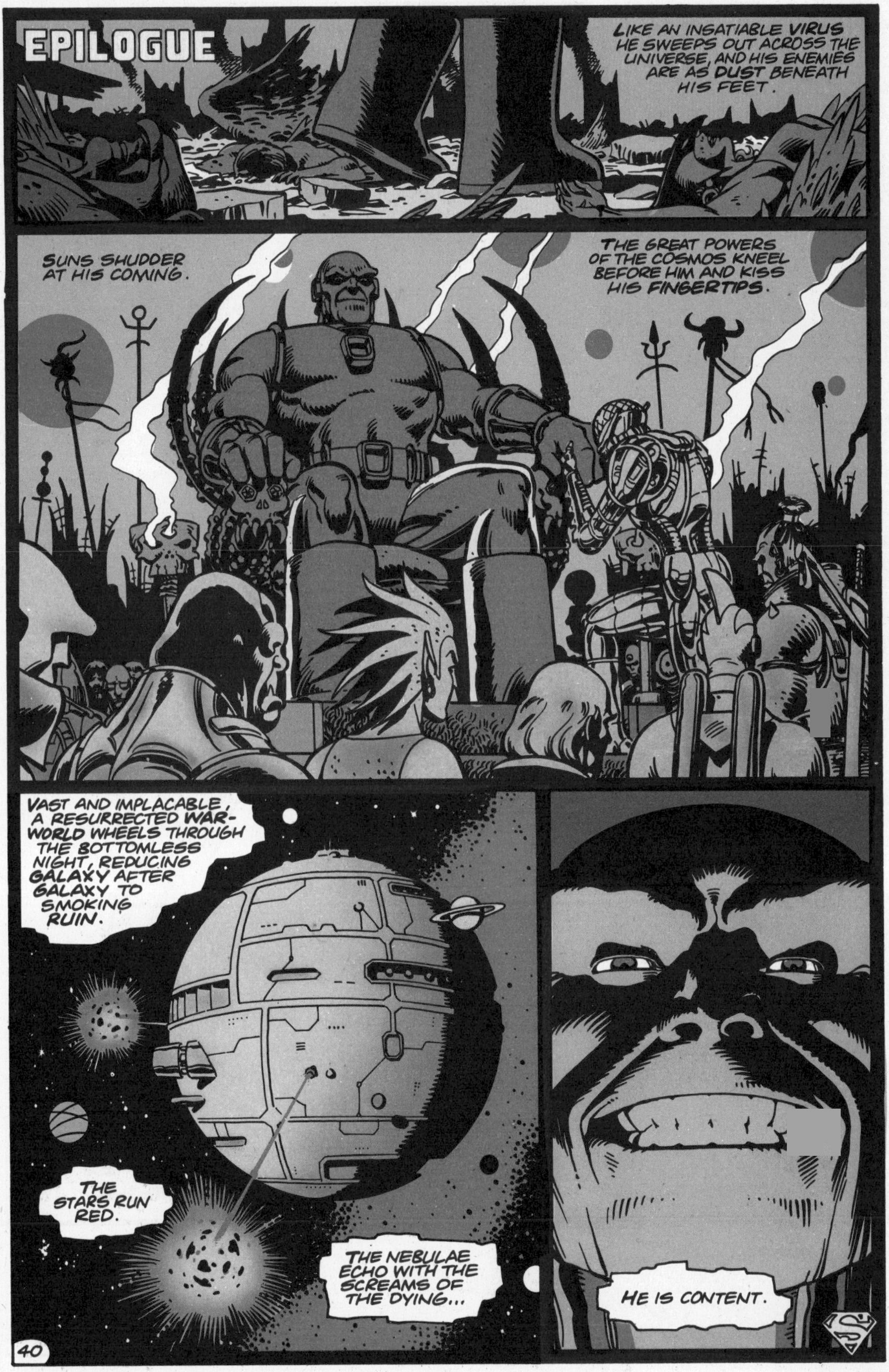
EPILOGUE
LIKE AN INSATIABLE VIRUS HE SWEEPS OUT ACROSS THE UNIVERSE, AND HIS ENEMIES ARE AS DUST BENEATH HIS FEET.
SUNS SHUDDER AT HIS COMING.
THE GREAT POWERS OF THE COSMOS KNEEL BEFORE HIM AND KISS HIS FINGERTIPS.
VAST AND IMPLACABLE, A RESURRECTED WAR-WORLD WHEELS THROUGH THE BOTTOMLESS NIGHT, REDUCING GALAXY AFTER GALAXY TO SMOKING RUIN.
THE STARS RUN RED.
THE NEBULAE ECHO WITH THE SCREAMS OF THE DYING...
HE IS CONTENT.
40

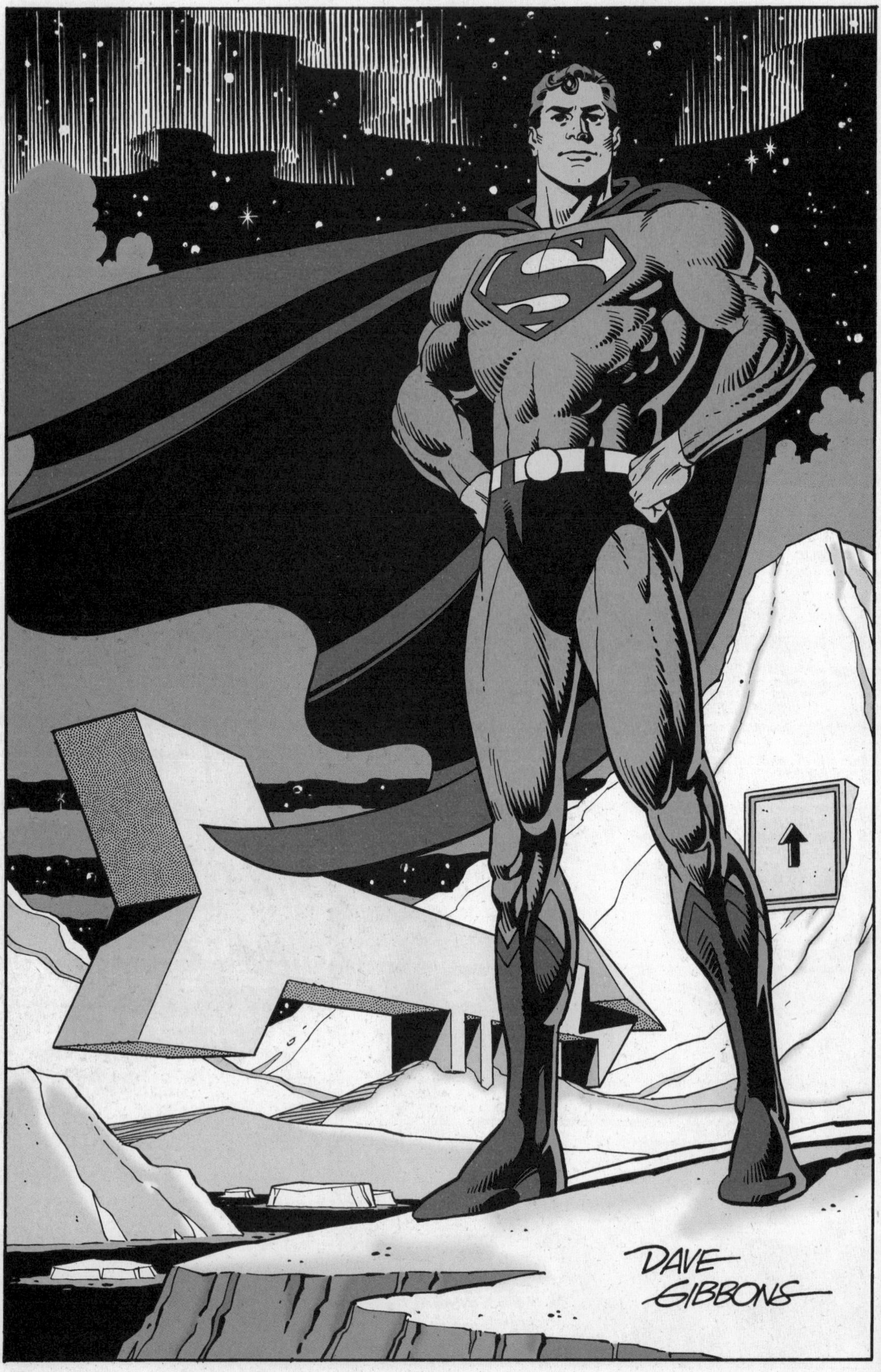
DAVE GIBBONS

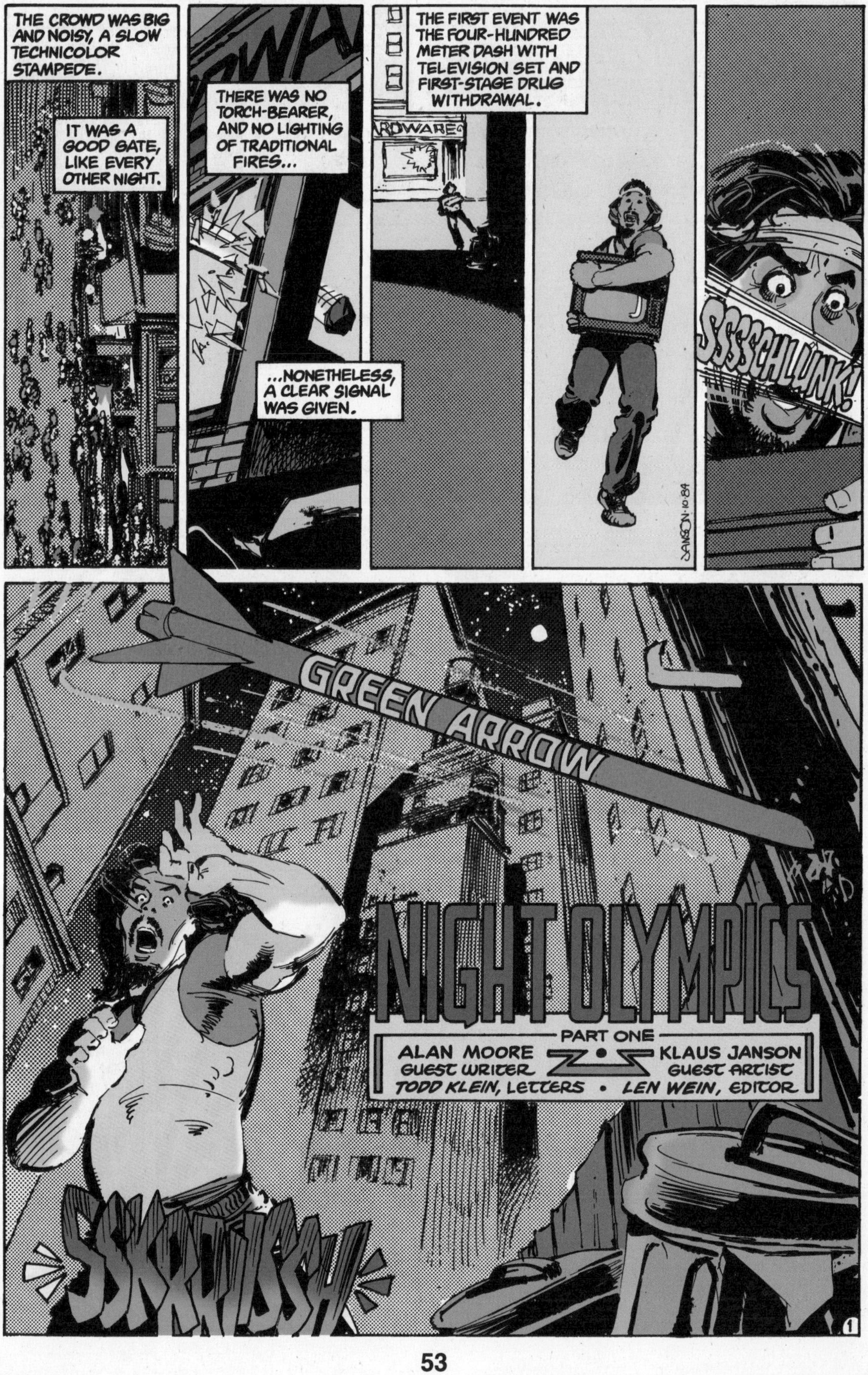
THE CROWD WAS BIG AND NOISY, A SLOW TECHNICOLOR STAMPEDE.
IT WAS A GOOD GATE, LIKE EVERY OTHER NIGHT.
THERE WAS NO TORCH-BEARER, AND NO LIGHTING OF TRADITIONAL FIRES...
...NONETHELESS, A CLEAR SIGNAL WAS GIVEN.
THE FIRST EVENT WAS THE FOUR-HUNDRED METER DASH WITH TELEVISION SET AND FIRST-STAGE DRUG WITHDRAWAL.
ARDWARE
JANSON 10-84
SSSCHLUNK!
GREEN ARROW
NIGHT OLYMPICS
PART ONE
ALAN MOORE GUEST WRITER
KLAUS JANSON GUEST ARTIST
TODD KLEIN, LETTERS • LEN WEIN, EDITOR
SSKKHUSSH
1

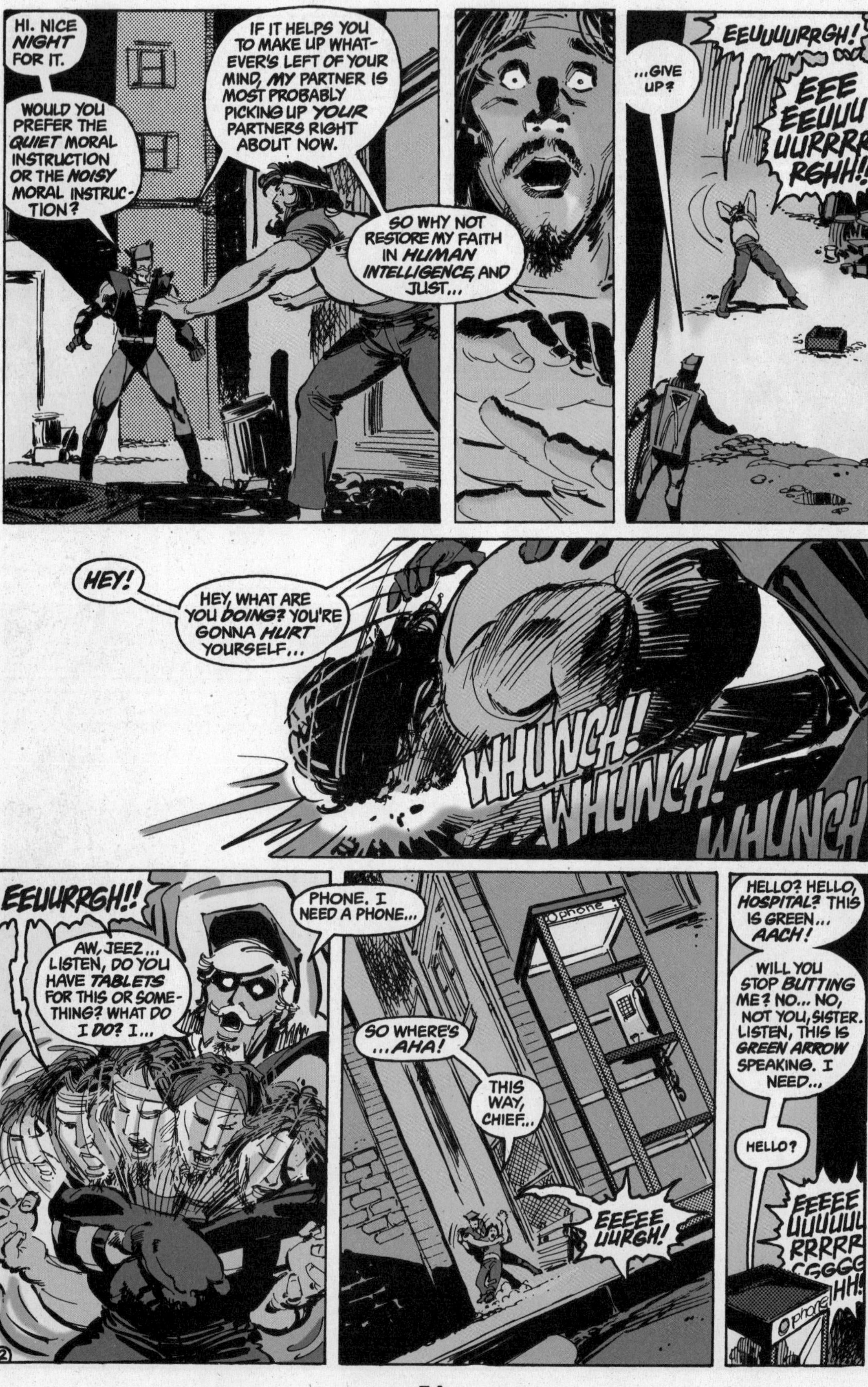
HI. NICE NIGHT FOR IT.
WOULD YOU PREFER THE QUIET MORAL INSTRUCTION OR THE NOISY MORAL INSTRUCTION?
IF IT HELPS YOU TO MAKE UP WHATEVER'S LEFT OF YOUR MIND, MY PARTNER IS MOST PROBABLY PICKING UP YOUR PARTNERS RIGHT ABOUT NOW.
SO WHY NOT RESTORE MY FAITH IN HUMAN INTELLIGENCE, AND JUST...
...GIVE UP?
EEUUUUURRGH!
EEE EEUUU UURRRR RGHH!!
HEY!
HEY, WHAT ARE YOU DOING? YOU'RE GONNA HURT YOURSELF...
WHUNCH! WHUNCH! WHUNCH
EEUURRGH!!
AW, JEEZ... LISTEN, DO YOU HAVE TABLETS FOR THIS OR SOMETHING? WHAT DO I DO? I...
PHONE. I NEED A PHONE...
SO WHERE'S ...AHA!
THIS WAY, CHIEF...
EEEEE UURGH!
HELLO? HELLO, HOSPITAL? THIS IS GREEN... AACH!
WILL YOU STOP BUTTING ME? NO... NO, NOT YOU, SISTER. LISTEN, THIS IS GREEN ARROW SPEAKING. I NEED...
HELLO?
EEEEE UUUUUU RRRRR GGGG HH!!

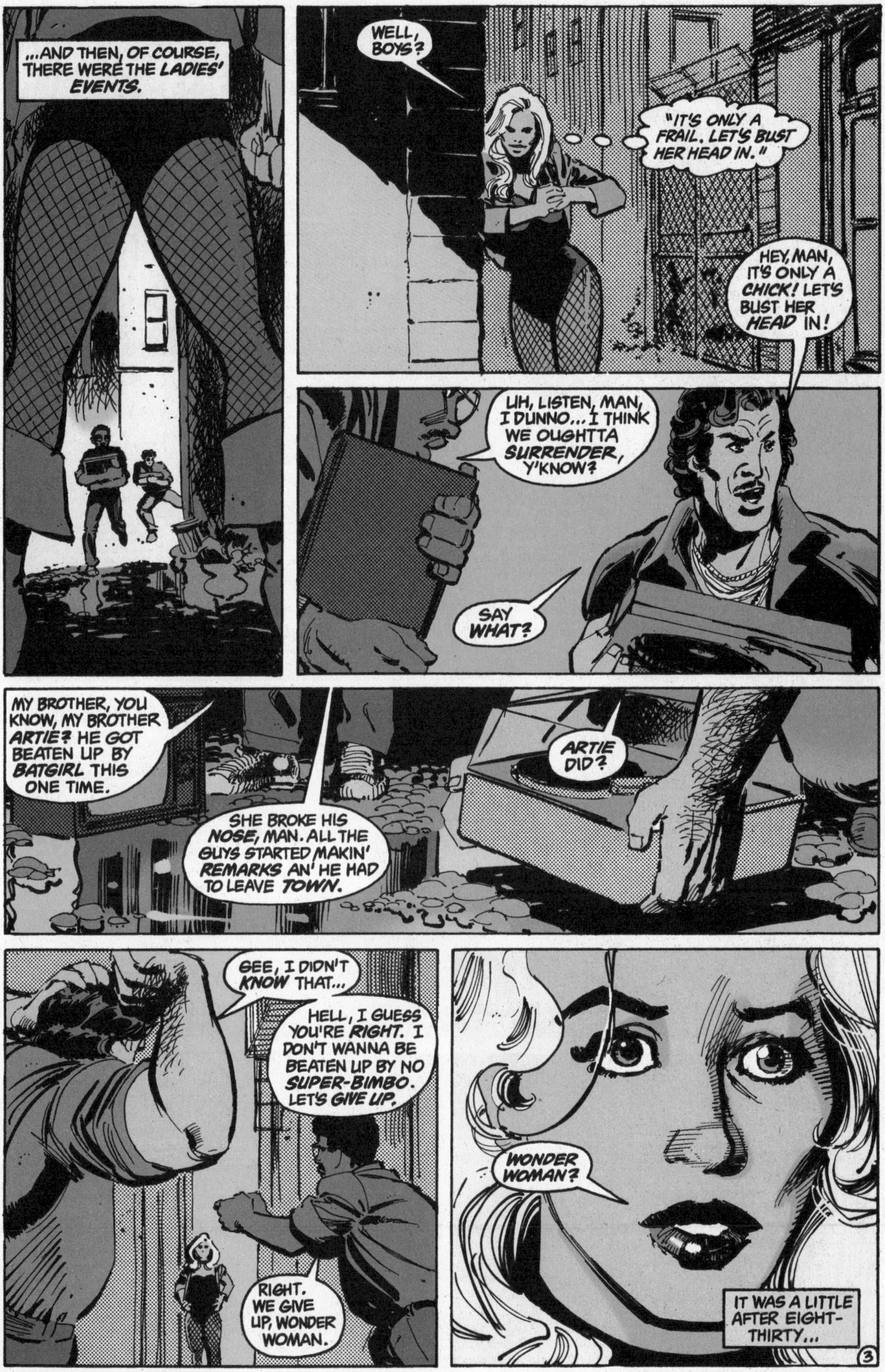
...AND THEN, OF COURSE, THERE WERE THE LADIES' EVENTS.
WELL, BOYS?
"IT'S ONLY A FRAIL. LET'S BUST HER HEAD IN."
HEY, MAN, IT'S ONLY A CHICK! LET'S BUST HER HEAD IN!
UH, LISTEN, MAN, I DUNNO... I THINK WE OUGHTTA SURRENDER, Y'KNOW?
SAY WHAT?
MY BROTHER, YOU KNOW, MY BROTHER ARTIE? HE GOT BEATEN UP BY BATGIRL THIS ONE TIME.
ARTIE DID?
SHE BROKE HIS NOSE, MAN. ALL THE GUYS STARTED MAKIN' REMARKS AN' HE HAD TO LEAVE TOWN.
GEE, I DIDN'T KNOW THAT...
HELL, I GUESS YOU'RE RIGHT. I DON'T WANNA BE BEATEN UP BY NO SUPER-BIMBO. LET'S GIVE UP.
RIGHT. WE GIVE UP, WONDER WOMAN.
WONDER WOMAN?
IT WAS A LITTLE AFTER EIGHT-THIRTY...
3

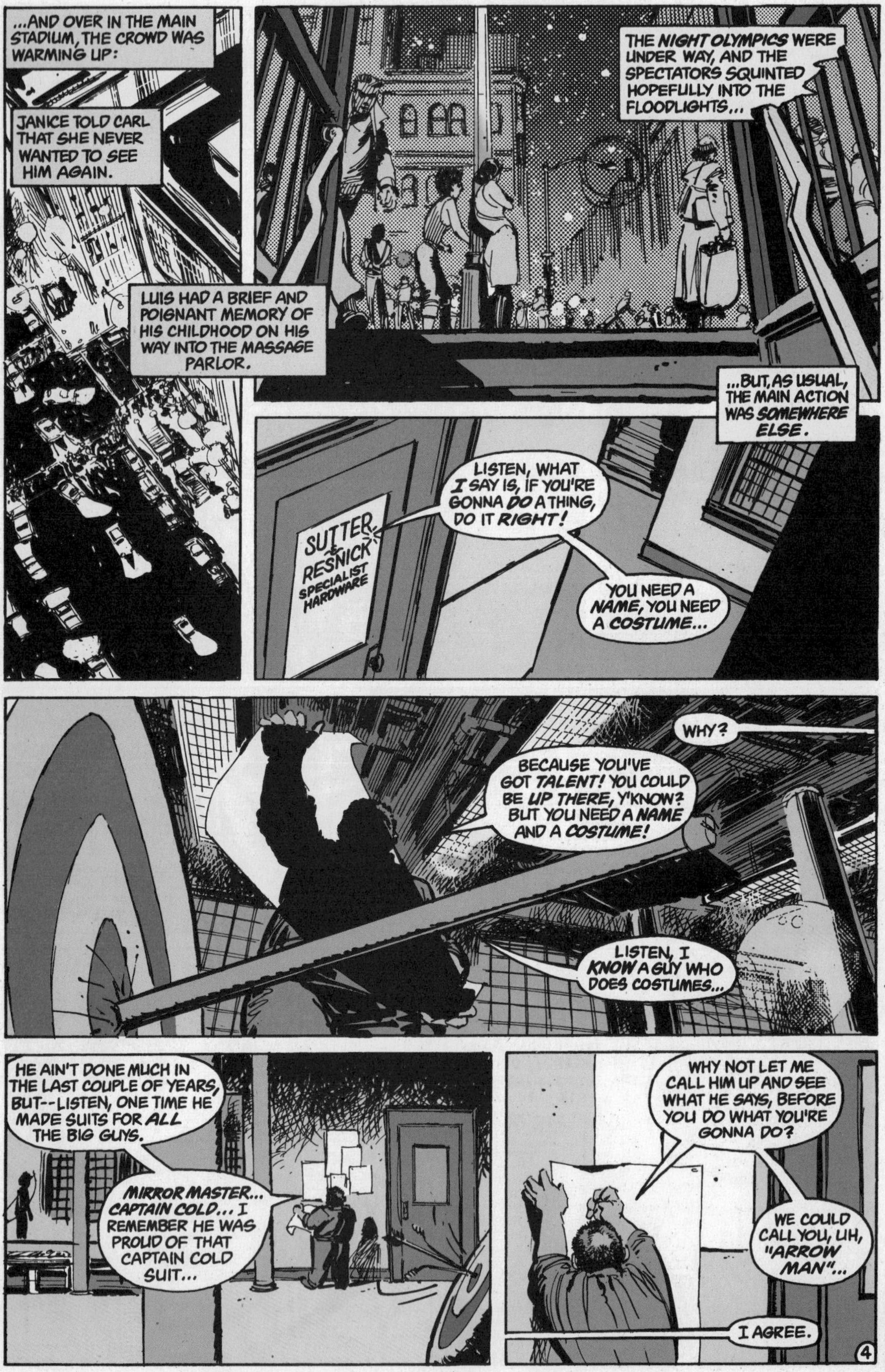
...AND OVER IN THE MAIN STADIUM, THE CROWD WAS WARMING UP:
JANICE TOLD CARL THAT SHE NEVER WANTED TO SEE HIM AGAIN.
LUIS HAD A BRIEF AND POIGNANT MEMORY OF HIS CHILDHOOD ON HIS WAY INTO THE MASSAGE PARLOR.
THE NIGHT OLYMPICS WERE UNDER WAY, AND THE SPECTATORS SQUINTED HOPEFULLY INTO THE FLOODLIGHTS...
...BUT, AS USUAL, THE MAIN ACTION WAS SOMEWHERE ELSE.
SUTTER & RESNICK SPECIALIST HARDWARE
LISTEN, WHAT I SAY IS, IF YOU'RE GONNA DO A THING, DO IT RIGHT!
YOU NEED A NAME, YOU NEED A COSTUME...
WHY?
BECAUSE YOU'VE GOT TALENT! YOU COULD BE UP THERE, Y'KNOW? BUT YOU NEED A NAME AND A COSTUME!
LISTEN, I KNOW A GUY WHO DOES COSTUMES...
HE AIN'T DONE MUCH IN THE LAST COUPLE OF YEARS, BUT--LISTEN, ONE TIME HE MADE SUITS FOR ALL THE BIG GUYS.
MIRROR MASTER... CAPTAIN COLD... I REMEMBER HE WAS PROUD OF THAT CAPTAIN COLD SUIT...
WHY NOT LET ME CALL HIM UP AND SEE WHAT HE SAYS, BEFORE YOU DO WHAT YOU'RE GONNA DO?
WE COULD CALL YOU, UH, "ARROW MAN"...
I AGREE.
4

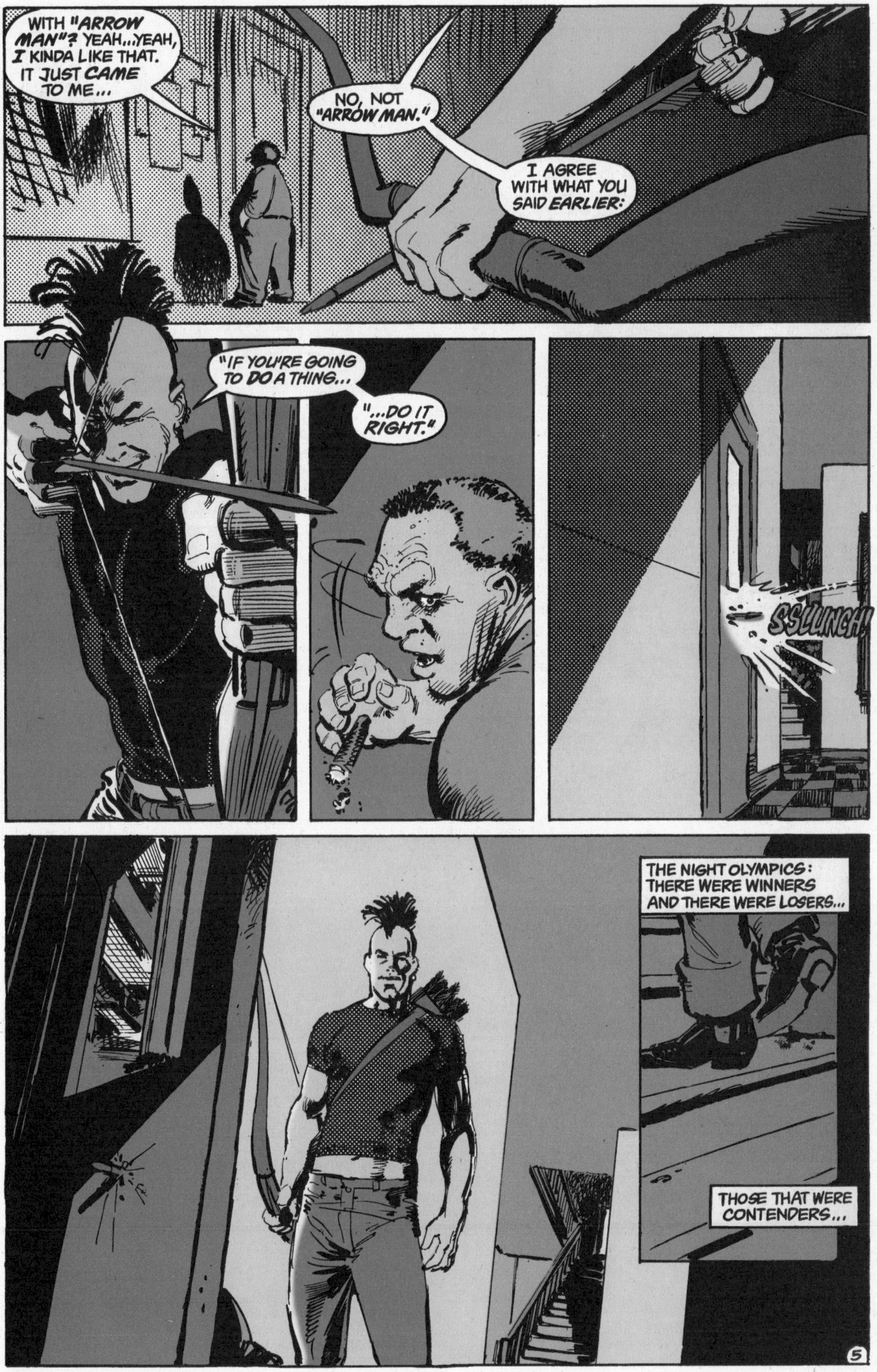

WITH "ARROW MAN"? YEAH...YEAH, I KINDA LIKE THAT. IT JUST CAME TO ME...
NO, NOT "ARROW MAN."
I AGREE WITH WHAT YOU SAID EARLIER:
"IF YOU'RE GOING TO DO A THING...
"...DO IT RIGHT."
SSLUNCH!
THE NIGHT OLYMPICS: THERE WERE WINNERS AND THERE WERE LOSERS...
THOSE THAT WERE CONTENDERS...
5

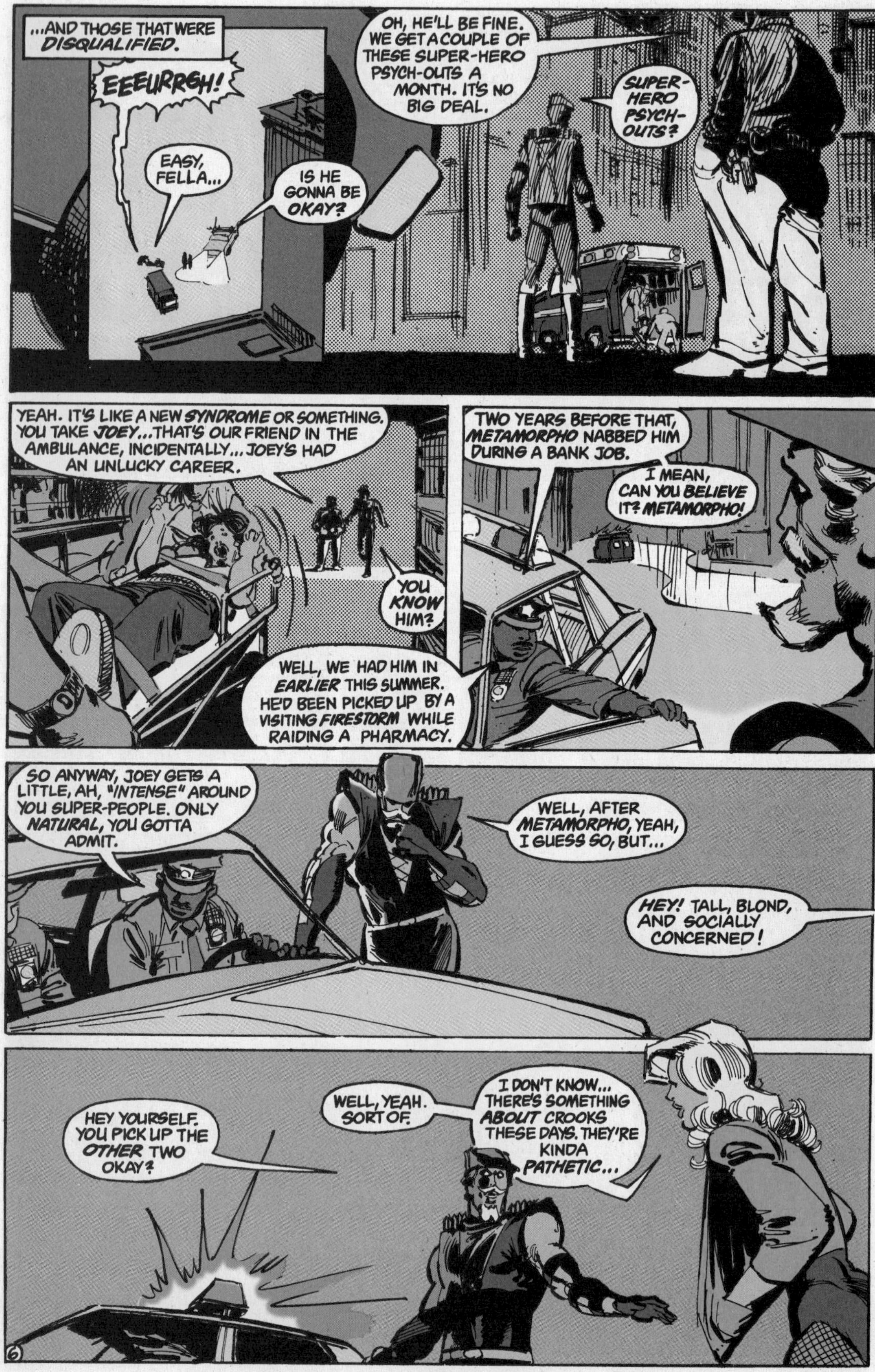

...AND THOSE THAT WERE DISQUALIFIED.
EEEURRGH!
EASY, FELLA...
IS HE GONNA BE OKAY?
OH, HE'LL BE FINE. WE GET A COUPLE OF THESE SUPER-HERO PSYCH-OUTS A MONTH. IT'S NO BIG DEAL.
SUPER-HERO PSYCH-OUTS?
YEAH. IT'S LIKE A NEW SYNDROME OR SOMETHING. YOU TAKE JOEY...THAT'S OUR FRIEND IN THE AMBULANCE, INCIDENTALLY... JOEY'S HAD AN UNLUCKY CAREER.
YOU KNOW HIM?
WELL, WE HAD HIM IN EARLIER THIS SUMMER. HE'D BEEN PICKED UP BY A VISITING FIRESTORM WHILE RAIDING A PHARMACY.
TWO YEARS BEFORE THAT, METAMORPHO NABBED HIM DURING A BANK JOB.
I MEAN, CAN YOU BELIEVE IT? METAMORPHO!
SO ANYWAY, JOEY GETS A LITTLE, AH, "INTENSE" AROUND YOU SUPER-PEOPLE. ONLY NATURAL, YOU GOTTA ADMIT.
WELL, AFTER METAMORPHO, YEAH, I GUESS SO, BUT...
HEY! TALL, BLOND, AND SOCIALLY CONCERNED!
HEY YOURSELF. YOU PICK UP THE OTHER TWO OKAY?
WELL, YEAH. SORT OF.
I DON'T KNOW... THERE'S SOMETHING ABOUT CROOKS THESE DAYS. THEY'RE KINDA PATHETIC...
6

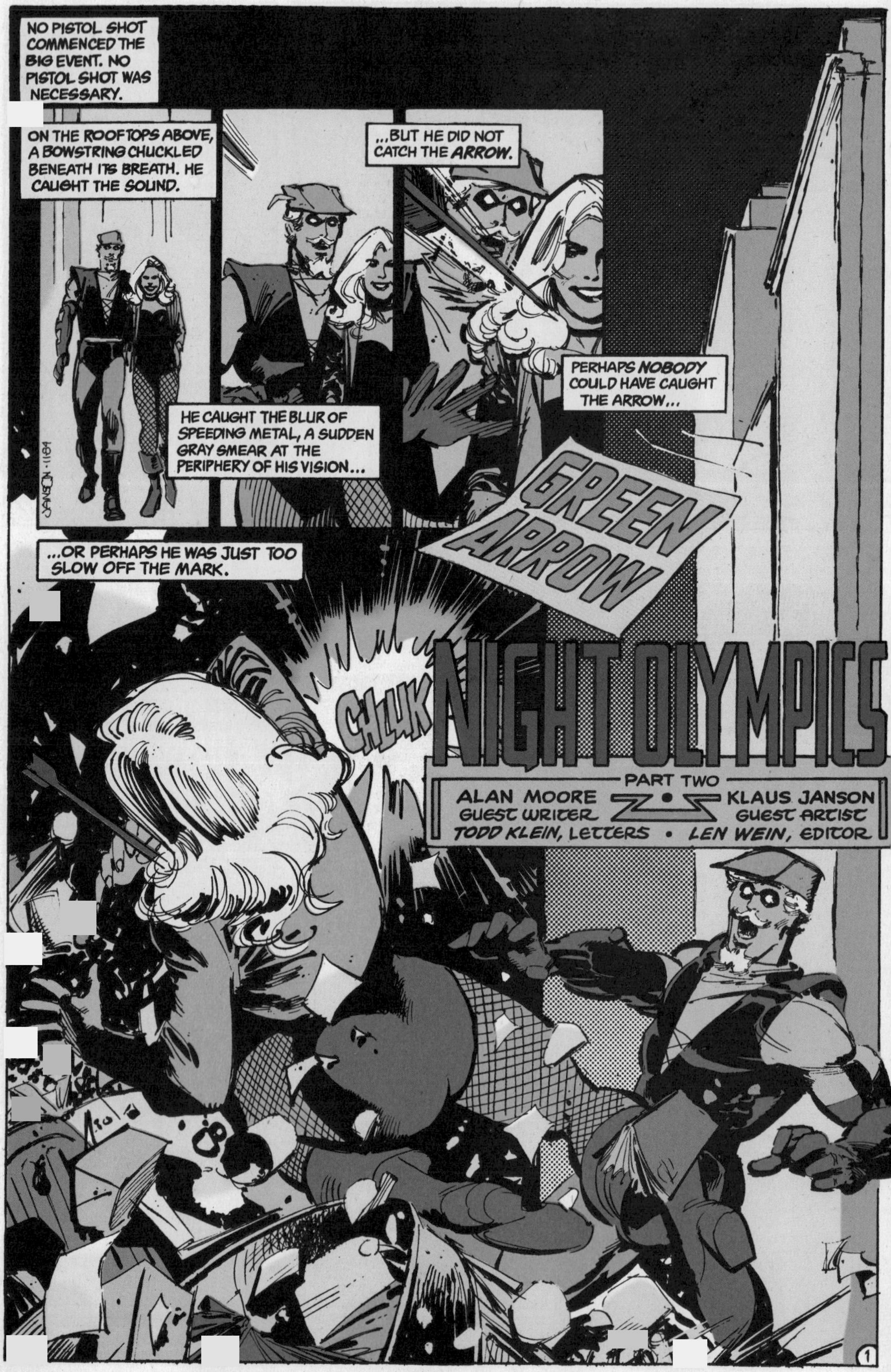
NO PISTOL SHOT COMMENCED THE BIG EVENT. NO PISTOL SHOT WAS NECESSARY.
ON THE ROOFTOPS ABOVE, A BOWSTRING CHUCKLED BENEATH ITS BREATH. HE CAUGHT THE SOUND.
HE CAUGHT THE BLUR OF SPEEDING METAL, A SUDDEN GRAY SMEAR AT THE PERIPHERY OF HIS VISION...
...BUT HE DID NOT CATCH THE ARROW.
PERHAPS NOBODY COULD HAVE CAUGHT THE ARROW...
...OR PERHAPS HE WAS JUST TOO SLOW OFF THE MARK.
GREEN ARROW
CHLUK
NIGHT OLYMPICS
PART TWO
ALAN MOORE GUEST WRITER
KLAUS JANSON GUEST ARTIST
TODD KLEIN, LETTERS • LEN WEIN, EDITOR
1

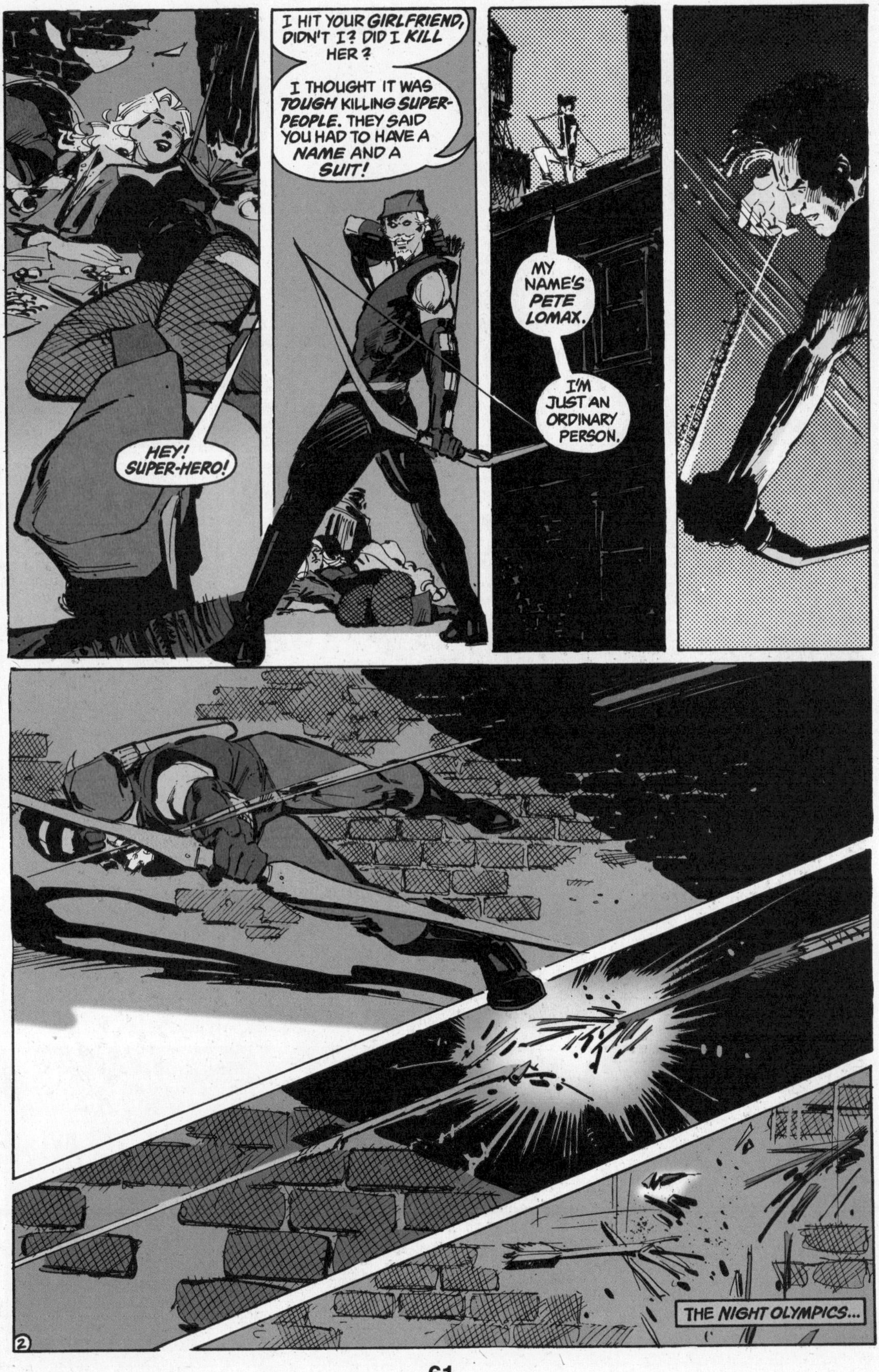
HEY! SUPER-HERO!
I HIT YOUR GIRLFRIEND, DIDN'T I? DID I KILL HER?
I THOUGHT IT WAS TOUGH KILLING SUPER-PEOPLE. THEY SAID YOU HAD TO HAVE A NAME AND A SUIT!
MY NAME'S PETE LOMAX.
I'M JUST AN ORDINARY PERSON.
THE NIGHT OLYMPICS...
2

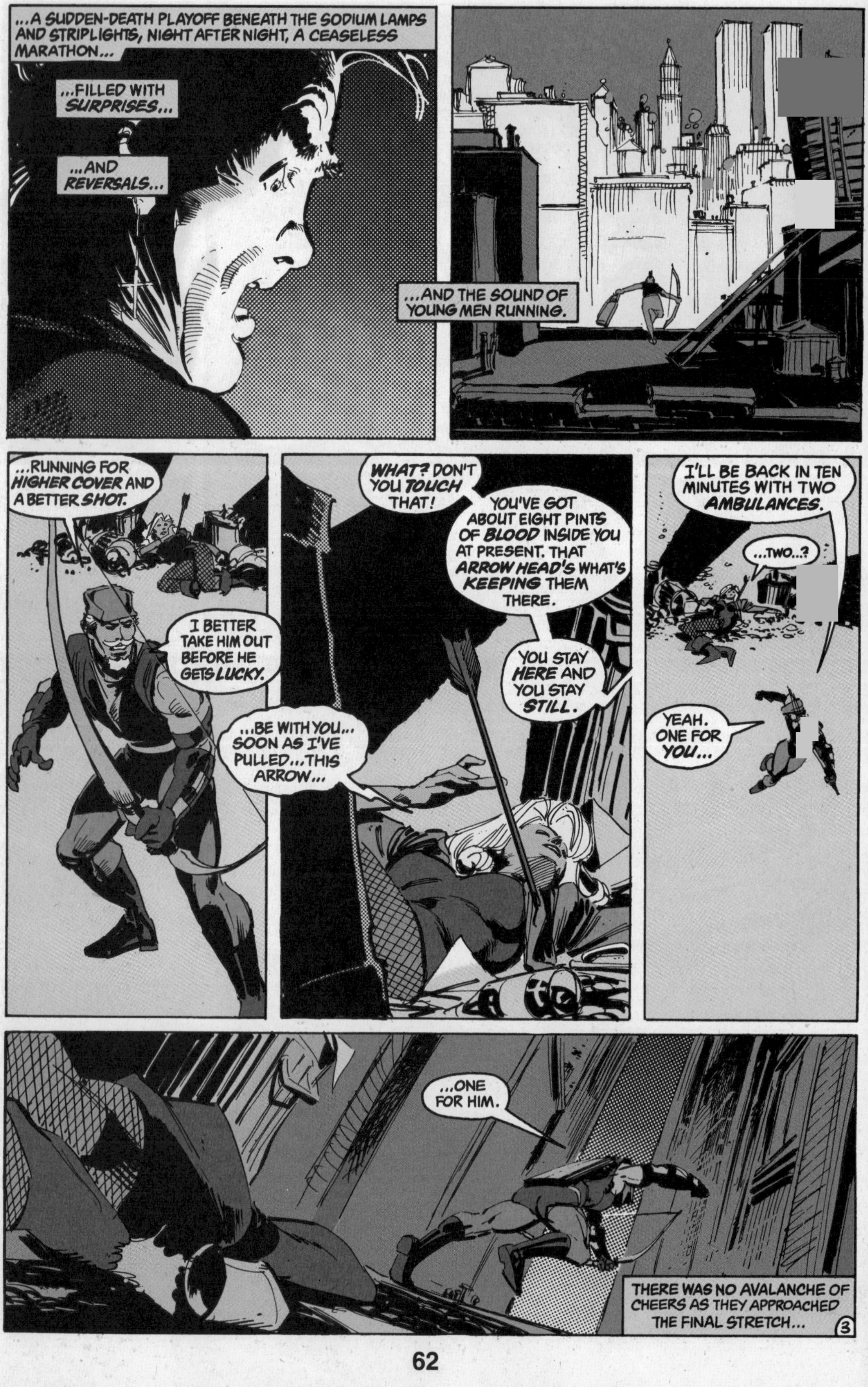

...A SUDDEN-DEATH PLAYOFF BENEATH THE SODIUM LAMPS AND STRIPLIGHTS, NIGHT AFTER NIGHT, A CEASELESS MARATHON...
...FILLED WITH SURPRISES...
...AND REVERSALS...
...AND THE SOUND OF YOUNG MEN RUNNING.
...RUNNING FOR HIGHER COVER AND A BETTER SHOT.
I BETTER TAKE HIM OUT BEFORE HE GETS LUCKY.
...BE WITH YOU... SOON AS I'VE PULLED...THIS ARROW...
WHAT? DON'T YOU TOUCH THAT!
YOU'VE GOT ABOUT EIGHT PINTS OF BLOOD INSIDE YOU AT PRESENT. THAT ARROW HEAD'S WHAT'S KEEPING THEM THERE.
YOU STAY HERE AND YOU STAY STILL.
I'LL BE BACK IN TEN MINUTES WITH TWO AMBULANCES.
...TWO...?
YEAH. ONE FOR YOU...
...ONE FOR HIM.
THERE WAS NO AVALANCHE OF CHEERS AS THEY APPROACHED THE FINAL STRETCH...
3

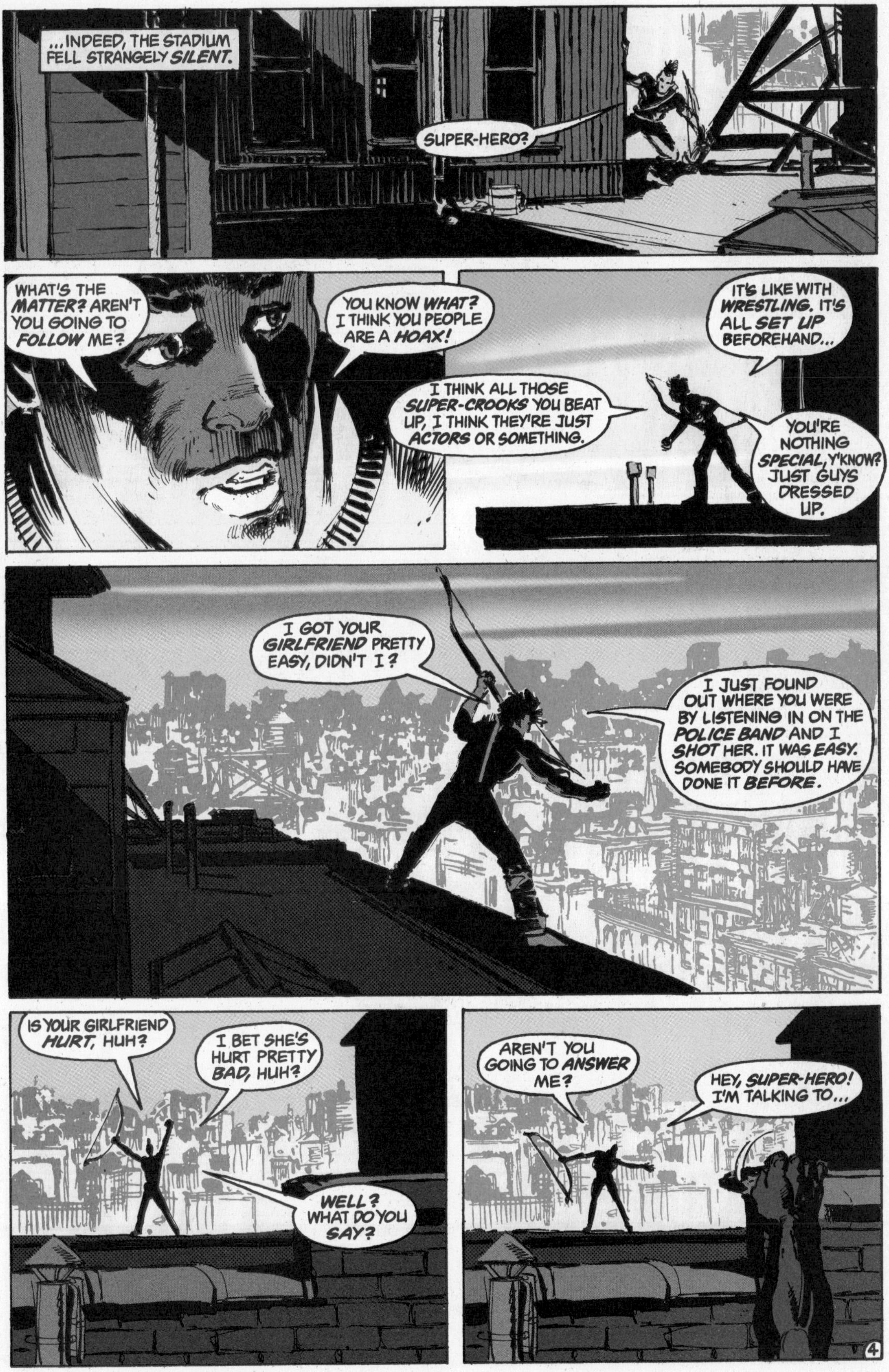
...INDEED, THE STADIUM FELL STRANGELY SILENT.
SUPER-HERO?
WHAT'S THE MATTER? AREN'T YOU GOING TO FOLLOW ME?
YOU KNOW WHAT? I THINK YOU PEOPLE ARE A HOAX!
IT'S LIKE WITH WRESTLING. IT'S ALL SET UP BEFOREHAND...
I THINK ALL THOSE SUPER-CROOKS YOU BEAT UP, I THINK THEY'RE JUST ACTORS OR SOMETHING.
YOU'RE NOTHING SPECIAL, Y'KNOW? JUST GUYS DRESSED UP.
I GOT YOUR GIRLFRIEND PRETTY EASY, DIDN'T I?
I JUST FOUND OUT WHERE YOU WERE BY LISTENING IN ON THE POLICE BAND AND I SHOT HER. IT WAS EASY. SOMEBODY SHOULD HAVE DONE IT BEFORE.
IS YOUR GIRLFRIEND HURT, HUH?
I BET SHE'S HURT PRETTY BAD, HUH?
WELL? WHAT DO YOU SAY?
AREN'T YOU GOING TO ANSWER ME?
HEY, SUPER-HERO! I'M TALKING TO...
4

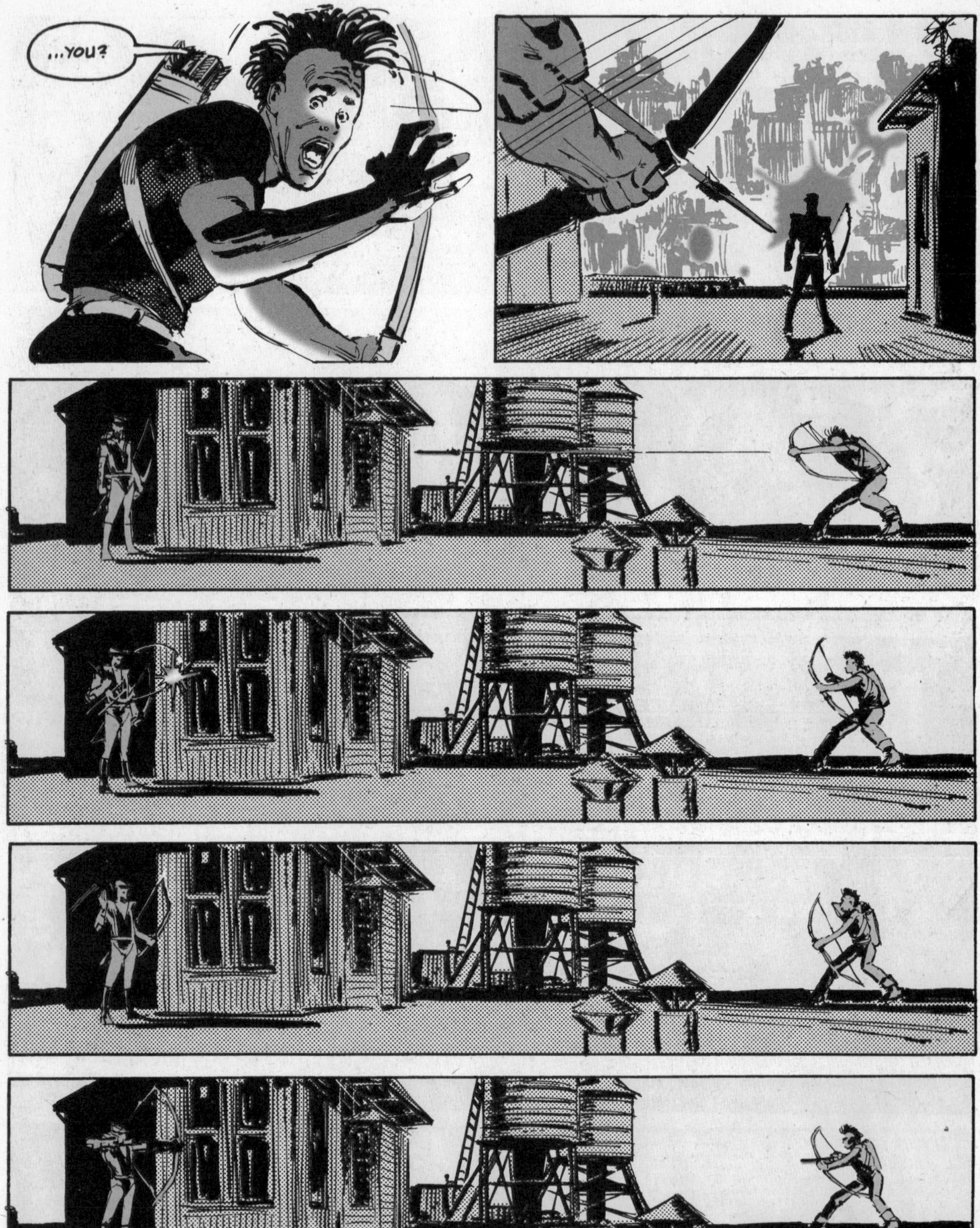
...YOU?
5

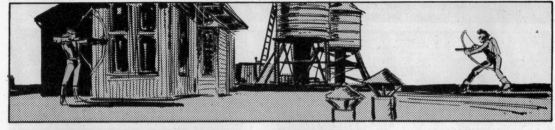

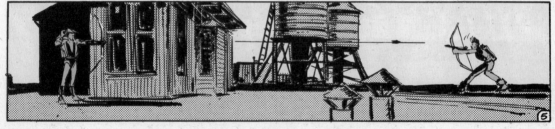

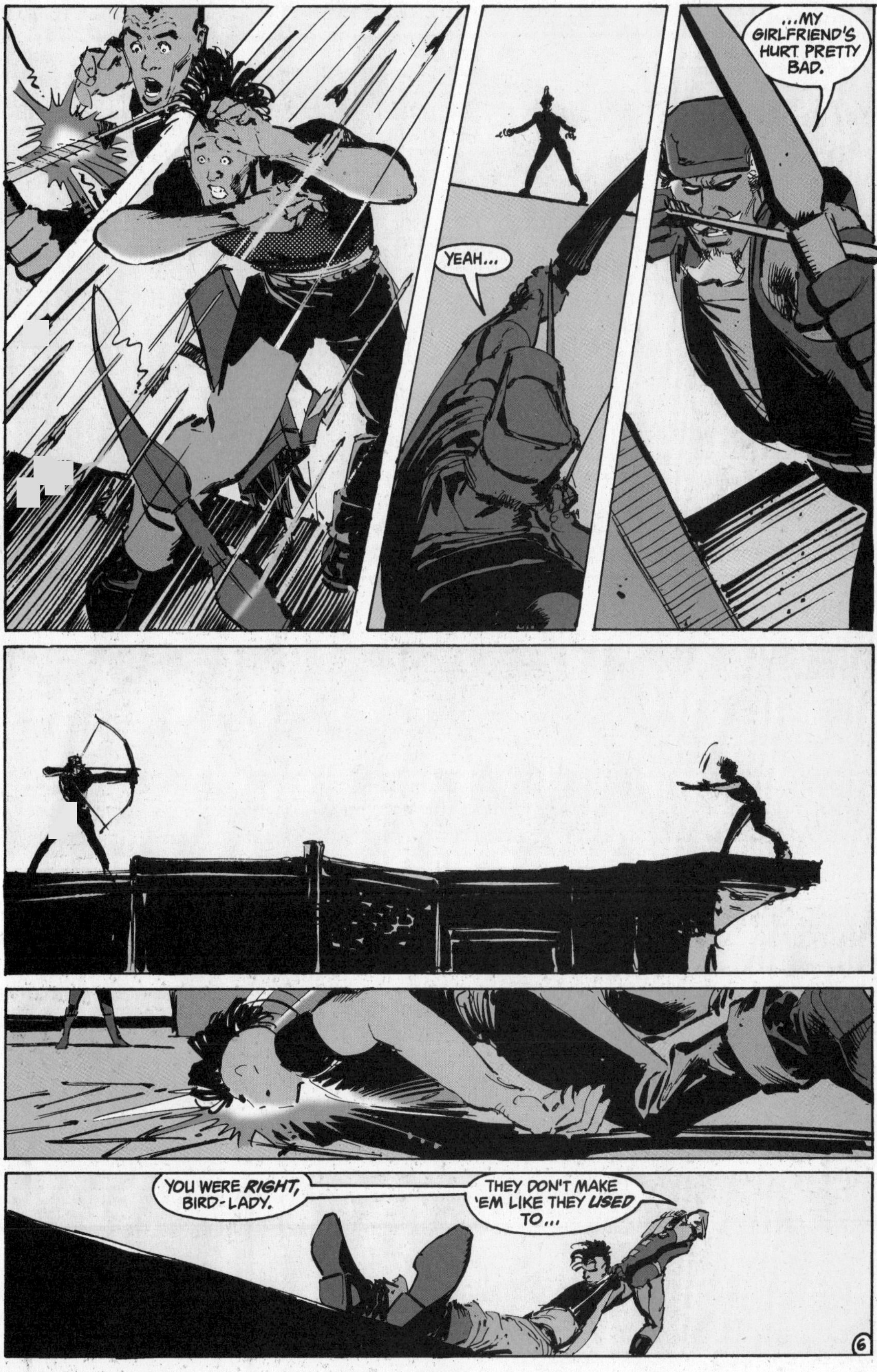
YEAH...
...MY GIRLFRIEND'S HURT PRETTY BAD.
YOU WERE RIGHT, BIRD-LADY.
THEY DON'T MAKE 'EM LIKE THEY USED TO...
6

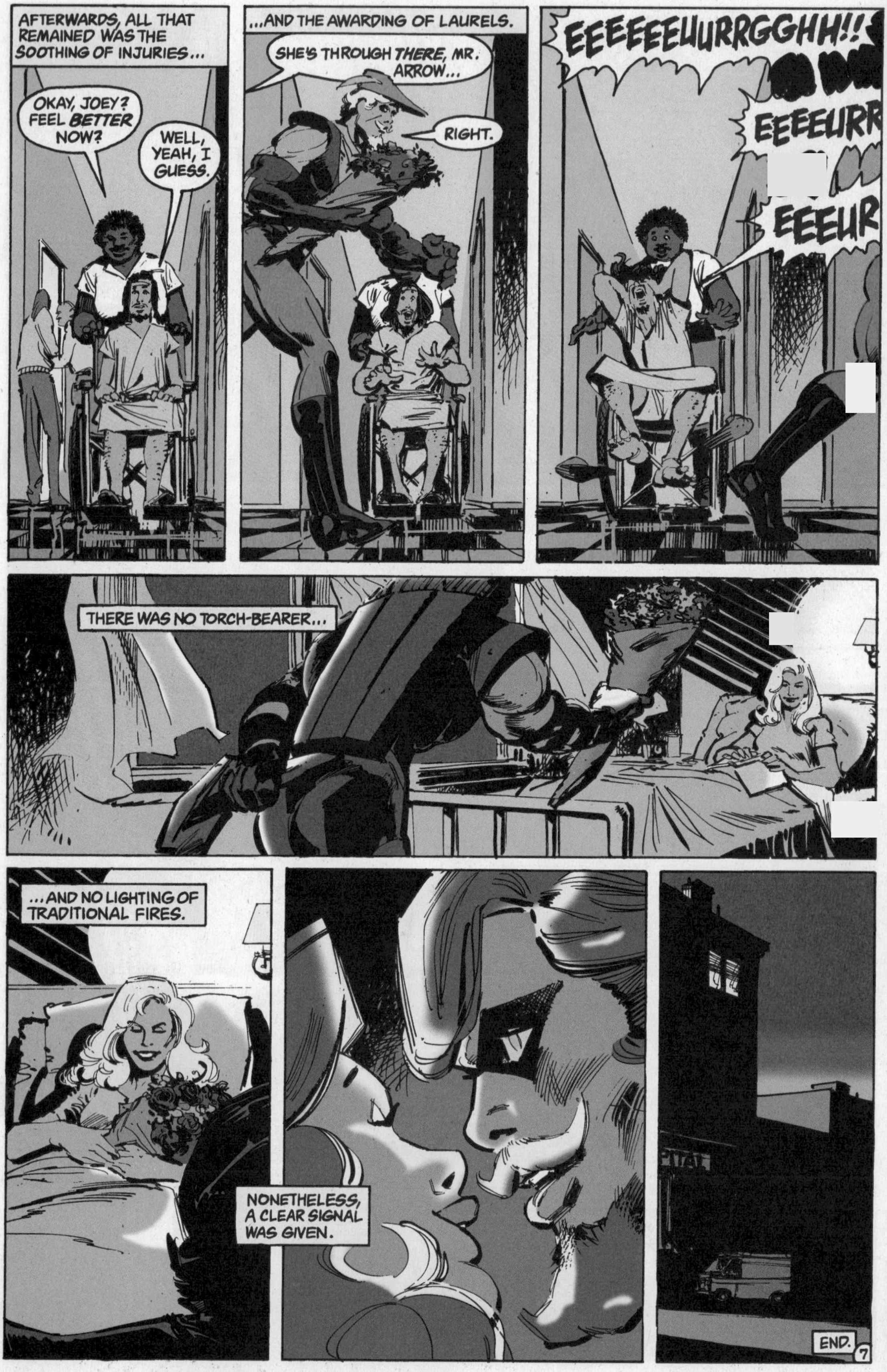

AFTERWARDS, ALL THAT REMAINED WAS THE SOOTHING OF INJURIES...
OKAY, JOEY? FEEL BETTER NOW?
WELL, YEAH, I GUESS.
...AND THE AWARDING OF LAURELS.
SHE'S THROUGH THERE, MR. ARROW...
RIGHT.
EEEEEEUURRGGHH!!
EEEEURR
EEEUR
THERE WAS NO TORCH-BEARER...
...AND NO LIGHTING OF TRADITIONAL FIRES.
NONETHELESS, A CLEAR SIGNAL WAS GIVEN.
END.
7

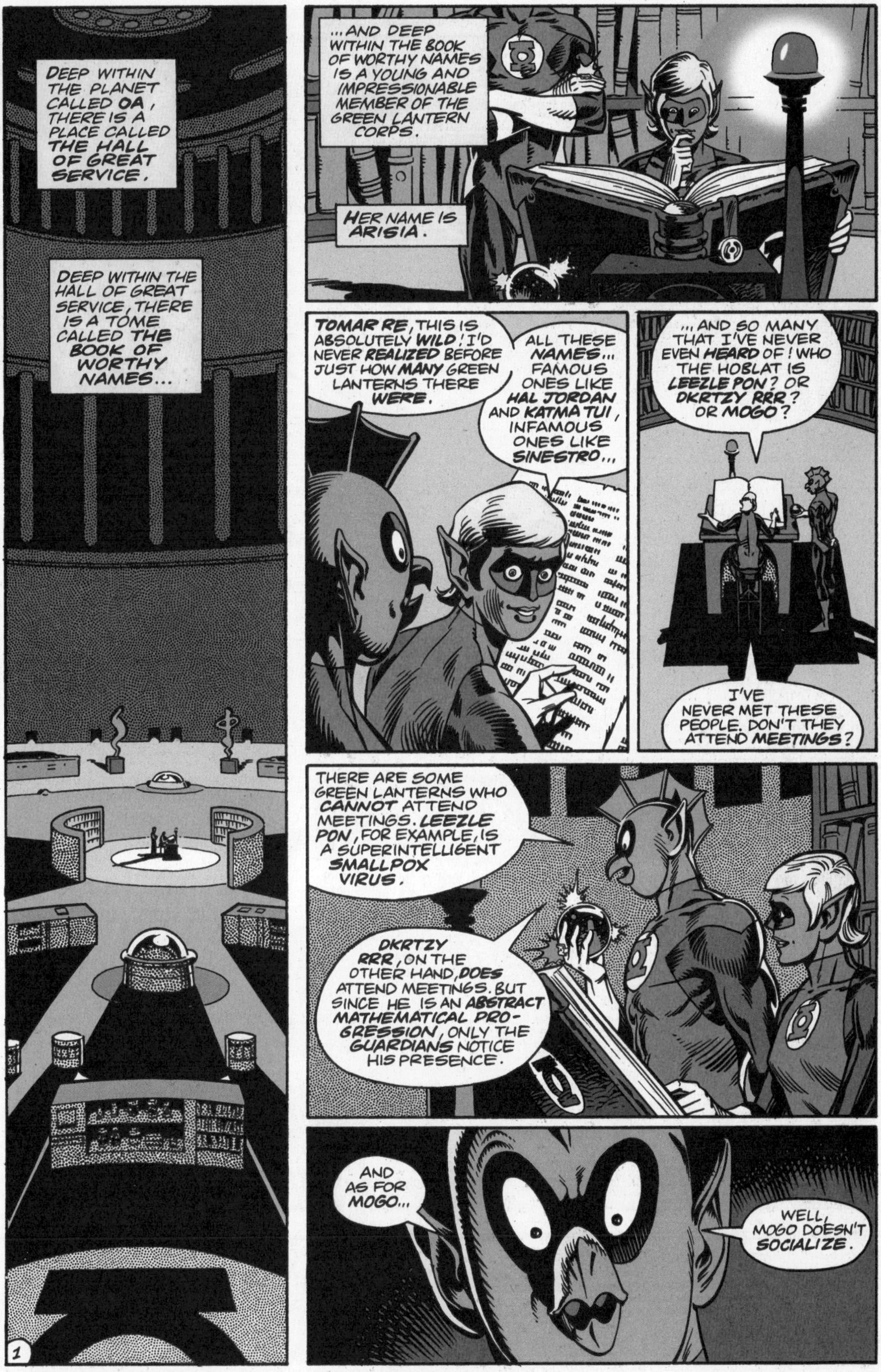
DEEP WITHIN THE PLANET CALLED OA, THERE IS A PLACE CALLED THE HALL OF GREAT SERVICE.
DEEP WITHIN THE HALL OF GREAT SERVICE, THERE IS A TOME CALLED THE BOOK OF WORTHY NAMES...
1
...AND DEEP WITHIN THE BOOK OF WORTHY NAMES IS A YOUNG AND IMPRESSIONABLE MEMBER OF THE GREEN LANTERN CORPS.
HER NAME IS ARISIA.
TOMAR RE, THIS IS ABSOLUTELY WILD! I'D NEVER REALIZED BEFORE JUST HOW MANY GREEN LANTERNS THERE WERE.
ALL THESE NAMES... FAMOUS ONES LIKE HAL JORDAN AND KATMA TUI, INFAMOUS ONES LIKE SINESTRO...
...AND SO MANY THAT I'VE NEVER EVEN HEARD OF! WHO THE HOBLAT IS LEEZLE PON? OR DKRTZY RRR? OR MOGO?
I'VE NEVER MET THESE PEOPLE. DON'T THEY ATTEND MEETINGS?
THERE ARE SOME GREEN LANTERNS WHO CANNOT ATTEND MEETINGS. LEEZLE PON, FOR EXAMPLE, IS A SUPERINTELLIGENT SMALLPOX VIRUS.
DKRTZY RRR, ON THE OTHER HAND, DOES ATTEND MEETINGS. BUT SINCE HE IS AN ABSTRACT MATHEMATICAL PRO-GRESSION, ONLY THE GUARDIANS NOTICE HIS PRESENCE.
AND AS FOR MOGO...
WELL, MOGO DOESN'T SOCIALIZE.

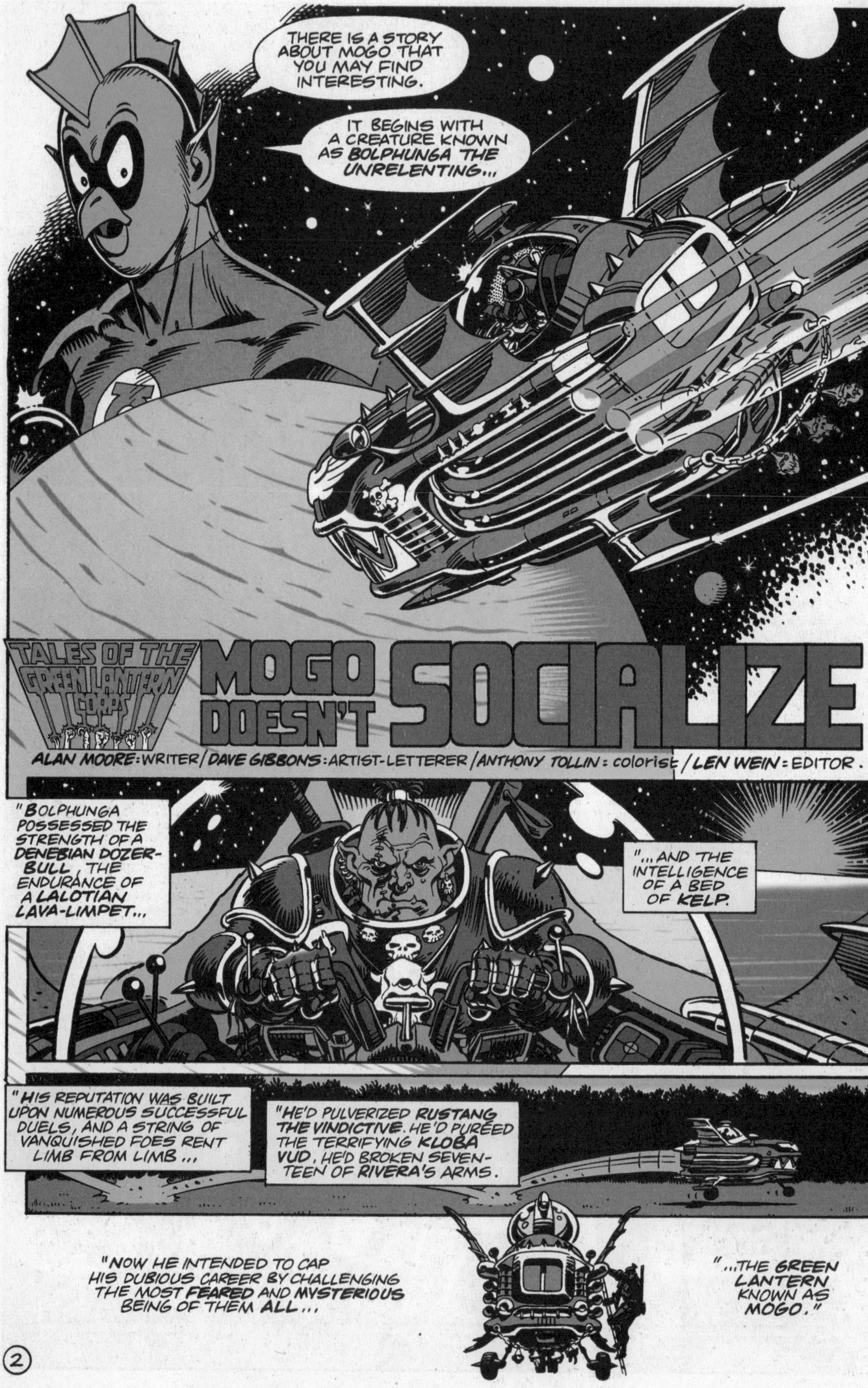
THERE IS A STORY ABOUT MOGO THAT YOU MAY FIND INTERESTING.
IT BEGINS WITH A CREATURE KNOWN AS BOLPHUNGA THE UNRELENTING...
TALES OF THE GREEN LANTERN CORPS
MOGO DOESN'T SOCIALIZE
ALAN MOORE: WRITER / DAVE GIBBONS: ARTIST-LETTERER / ANTHONY TOLLIN: colorist / LEN WEIN: EDITOR.
"BOLPHUNGA POSSESSED THE STRENGTH OF A DENEBIAN DOZER-BULL, THE ENDURANCE OF A LALOTIAN LAVA-LIMPET...
"...AND THE INTELLIGENCE OF A BED OF KELP.
"HIS REPUTATION WAS BUILT UPON NUMEROUS SUCCESSFUL DUELS, AND A STRING OF VANQUISHED FOES RENT LIMB FROM LIMB...
"HE'D PULVERIZED RUSTANG THE VINDICTIVE. HE'D PUREED THE TERRIFYING KLOBA VUD, HE'D BROKEN SEVENTEEN OF RIVERA'S ARMS.
"NOW HE INTENDED TO CAP HIS DUBIOUS CAREER BY CHALLENGING THE MOST FEARED AND MYSTERIOUS BEING OF THEM ALL...
"...THE GREEN LANTERN KNOWN AS MOGO."
2

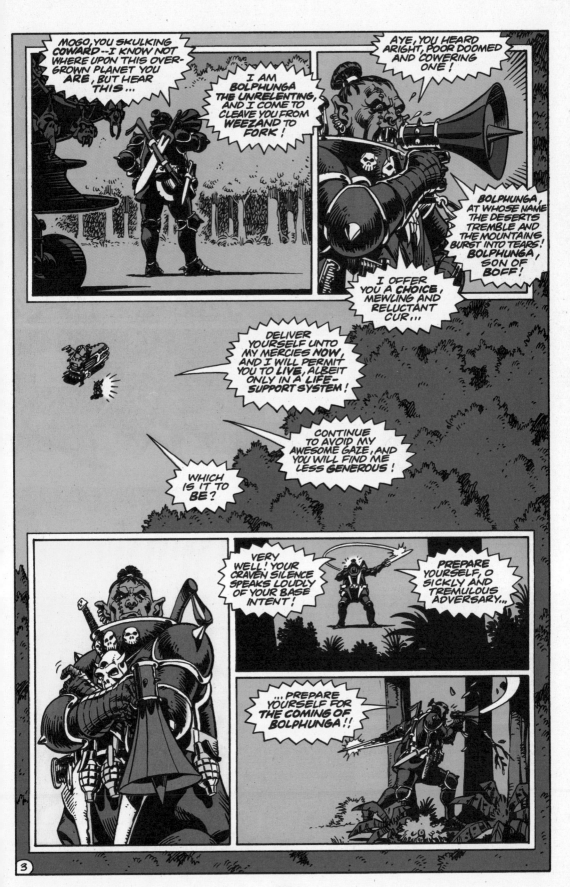

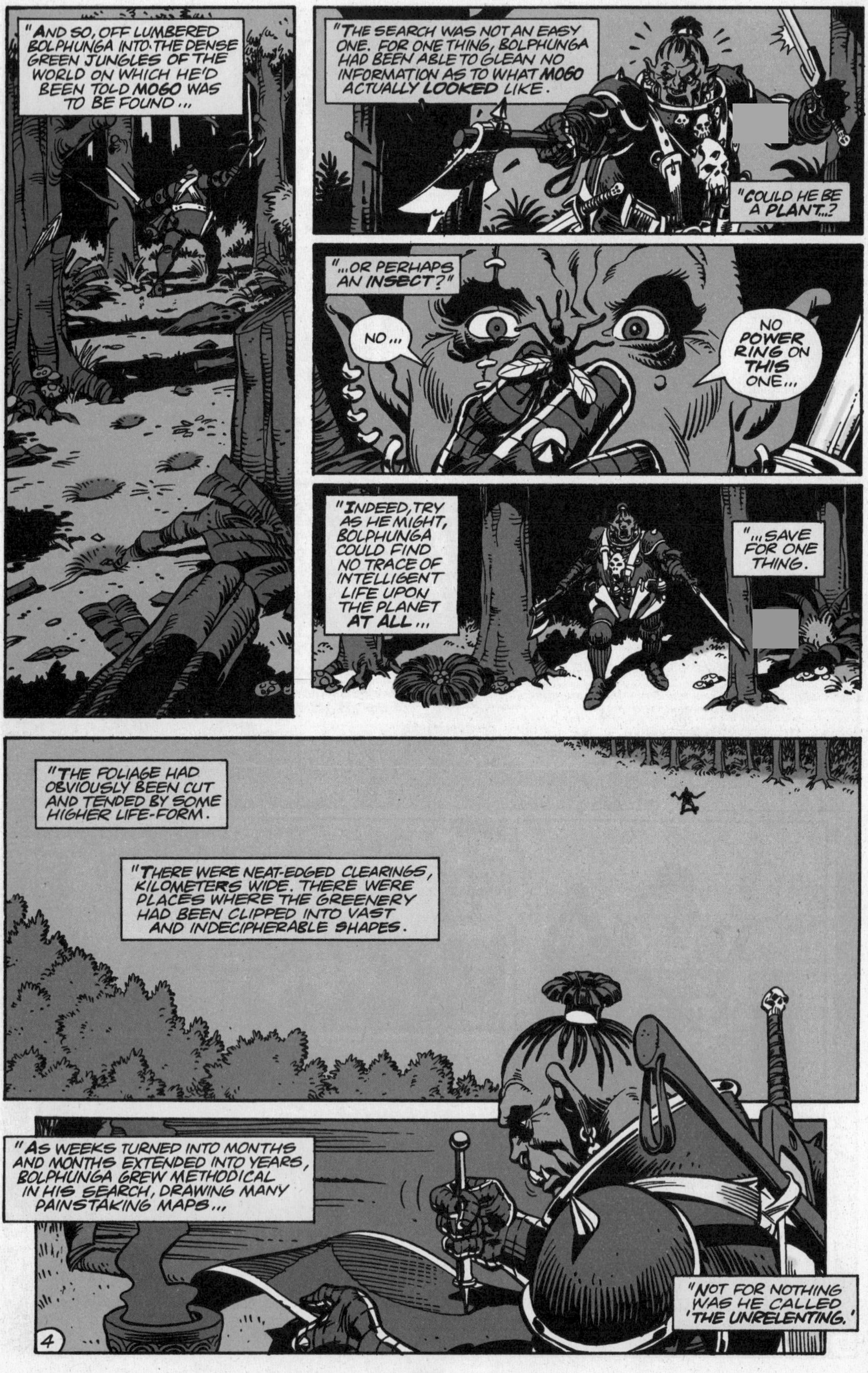
"AND SO, OFF LUMBERED BOLPHUNGA INTO THE DENSE GREEN JUNGLES OF THE WORLD ON WHICH HE'D BEEN TOLD MOGO WAS TO BE FOUND...
"THE SEARCH WAS NOT AN EASY ONE. FOR ONE THING, BOLPHUNGA HAD BEEN ABLE TO GLEAN NO INFORMATION AS TO WHAT MOGO ACTUALLY LOOKED LIKE.
"COULD HE BE A PLANT...?
"...OR PERHAPS AN INSECT?"
NO...
NO POWER RING ON THIS ONE...
"INDEED, TRY AS HE MIGHT, BOLPHUNGA COULD FIND NO TRACE OF INTELLIGENT LIFE UPON THE PLANET AT ALL...
"...SAVE FOR ONE THING.
"THE FOLIAGE HAD OBVIOUSLY BEEN CUT AND TENDED BY SOME HIGHER LIFE-FORM.
"THERE WERE NEAT-EDGED CLEARINGS, KILOMETERS WIDE. THERE WERE PLACES WHERE THE GREENERY HAD BEEN CLIPPED INTO VAST AND INDECIPHERABLE SHAPES.
"AS WEEKS TURNED INTO MONTHS AND MONTHS EXTENDED INTO YEARS, BOLPHUNGA GREW METHODICAL IN HIS SEARCH, DRAWING MANY PAINSTAKING MAPS...
"NOT FOR NOTHING WAS HE CALLED 'THE UNRELENTING.'
4

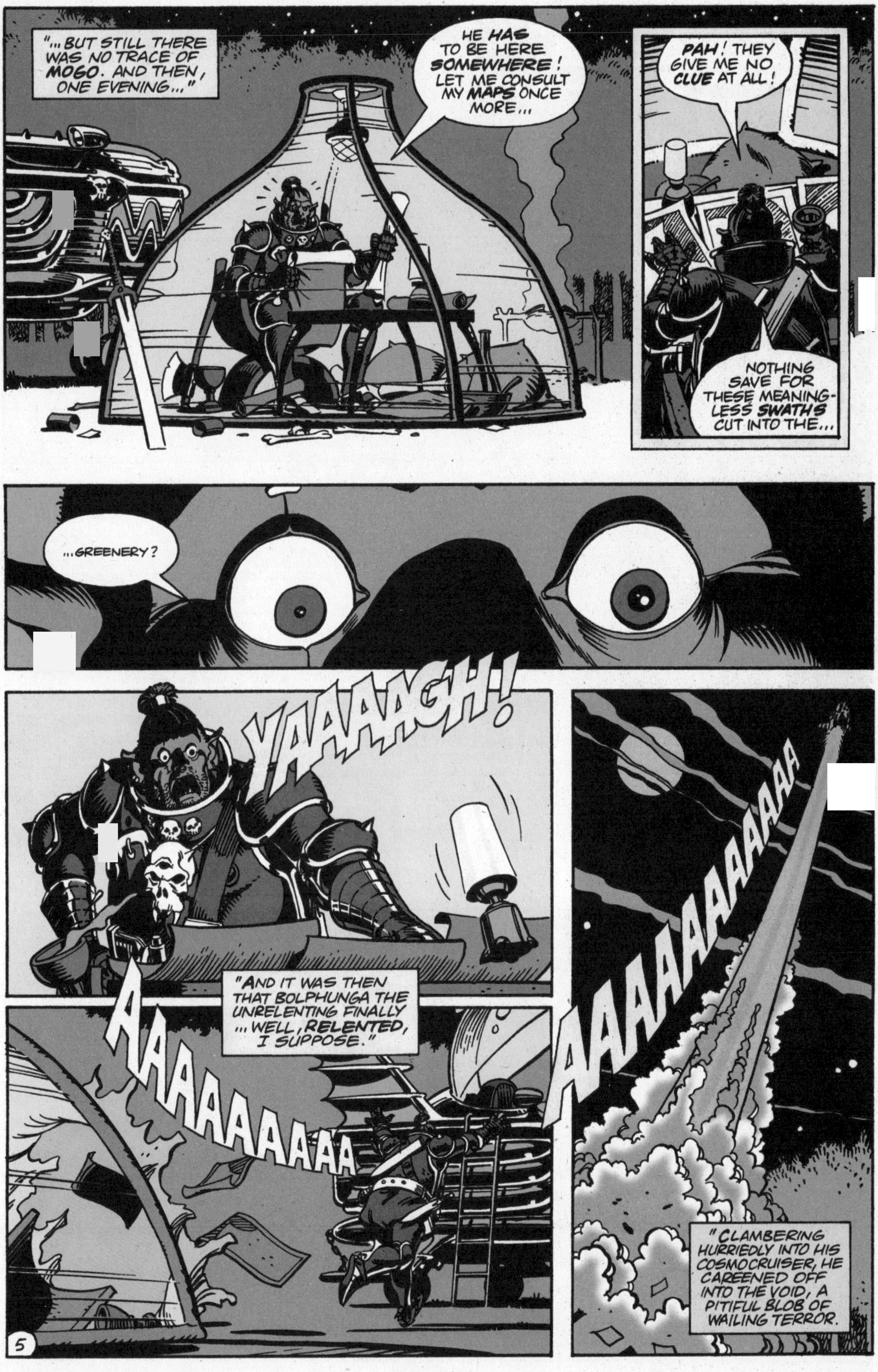
"...BUT STILL THERE WAS NO TRACE OF MOGO. AND THEN, ONE EVENING..."
HE HAS TO BE HERE SOMEWHERE! LET ME CONSULT MY MAPS ONCE MORE...
PAH! THEY GIVE ME NO CLUE AT ALL!
NOTHING SAVE FOR THESE MEANING-LESS SWATHS CUT INTO THE...
...GREENERY?
YAAAAGH!
AAAAAAAAAAA
"AND IT WAS THEN THAT BOLPHUNGA THE UNRELENTING FINALLY ...WELL, RELENTED, I SUPPOSE."
AAAAAAAAAAAAAAAAAA
"CLAMBERING HURRIEDLY INTO HIS COSMOCRUISER, HE CAREENED OFF INTO THE VOID, A PITIFUL BLOB OF WAILING TERROR.
5

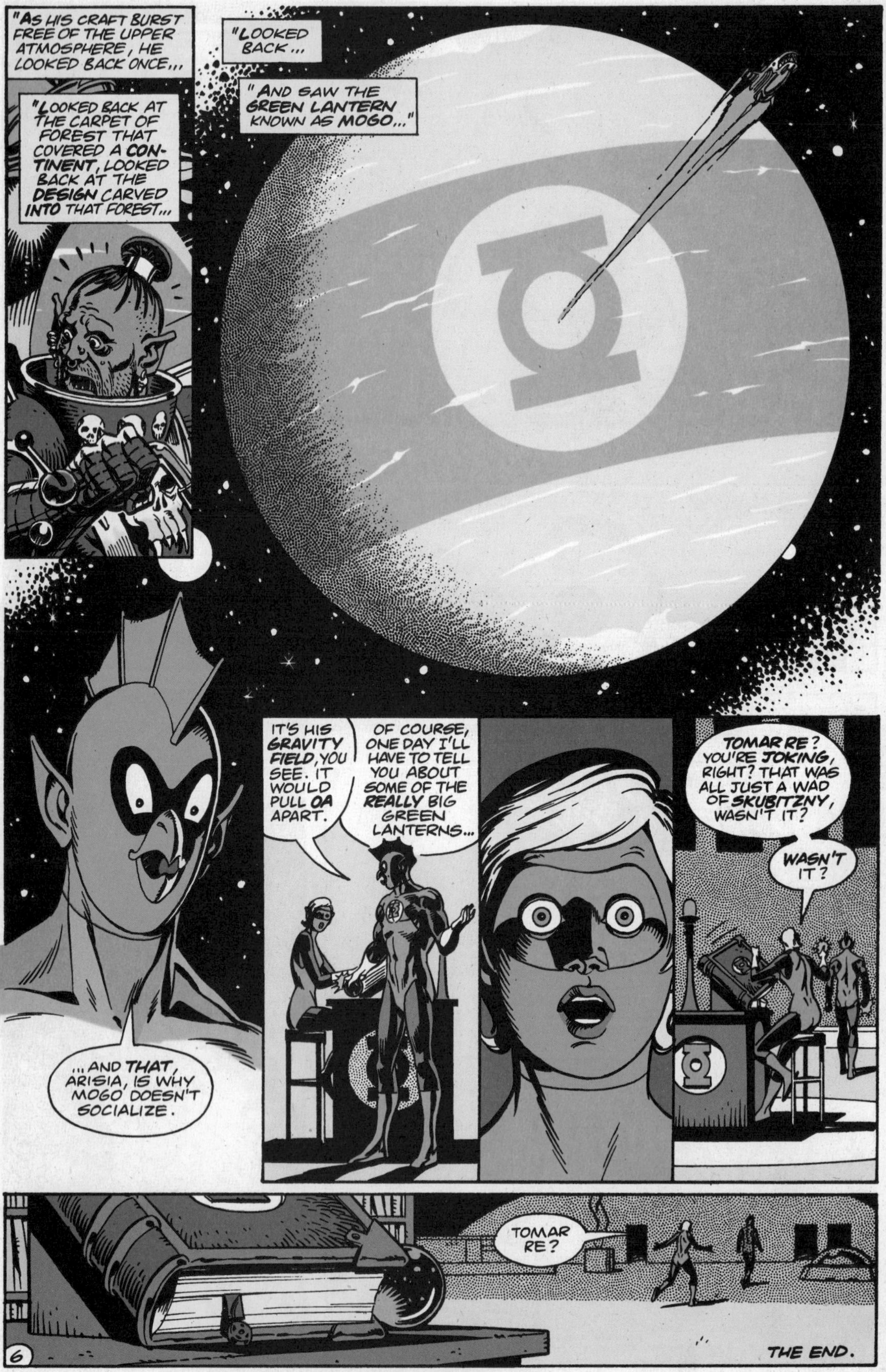
"AS HIS CRAFT BURST FREE OF THE UPPER ATMOSPHERE, HE LOOKED BACK ONCE...
"LOOKED BACK AT THE CARPET OF FOREST THAT COVERED A CONTINENT, LOOKED BACK AT THE DESIGN CARVED INTO THAT FOREST...
"LOOKED BACK...
"AND SAW THE GREEN LANTERN KNOWN AS MOGO..."
...AND THAT, ARISIA, IS WHY MOGO DOESN'T SOCIALIZE.
IT'S HIS GRAVITY FIELD, YOU SEE. IT WOULD PULL OA APART.
OF COURSE, ONE DAY I'LL HAVE TO TELL YOU ABOUT SOME OF THE REALLY BIG GREEN LANTERNS...
TOMAR RE? YOU'RE JOKING, RIGHT? THAT WAS ALL JUST A WAD OF SKUBITZNY, WASN'T IT?
WASN'T IT?
6
TOMAR RE?
THE END.

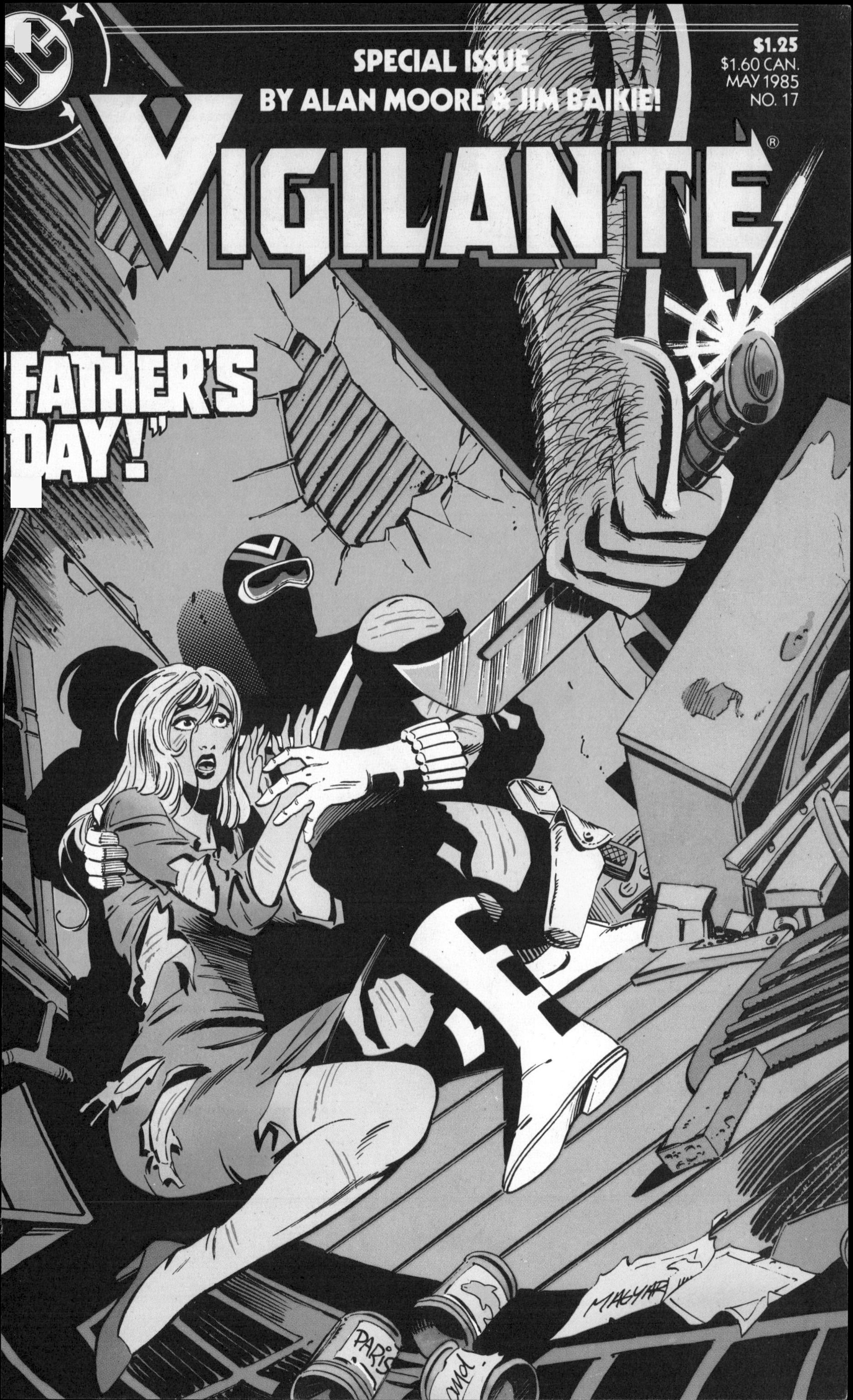

SPECIAL ISSUE
BY ALAN MOORE & JIM BAIKIE!
$1.25
$1.60 CAN.
MAY 1985
NO. 17
VIGILANTE®
"FATHER'S DAY!"
MAGYAR
PARIS

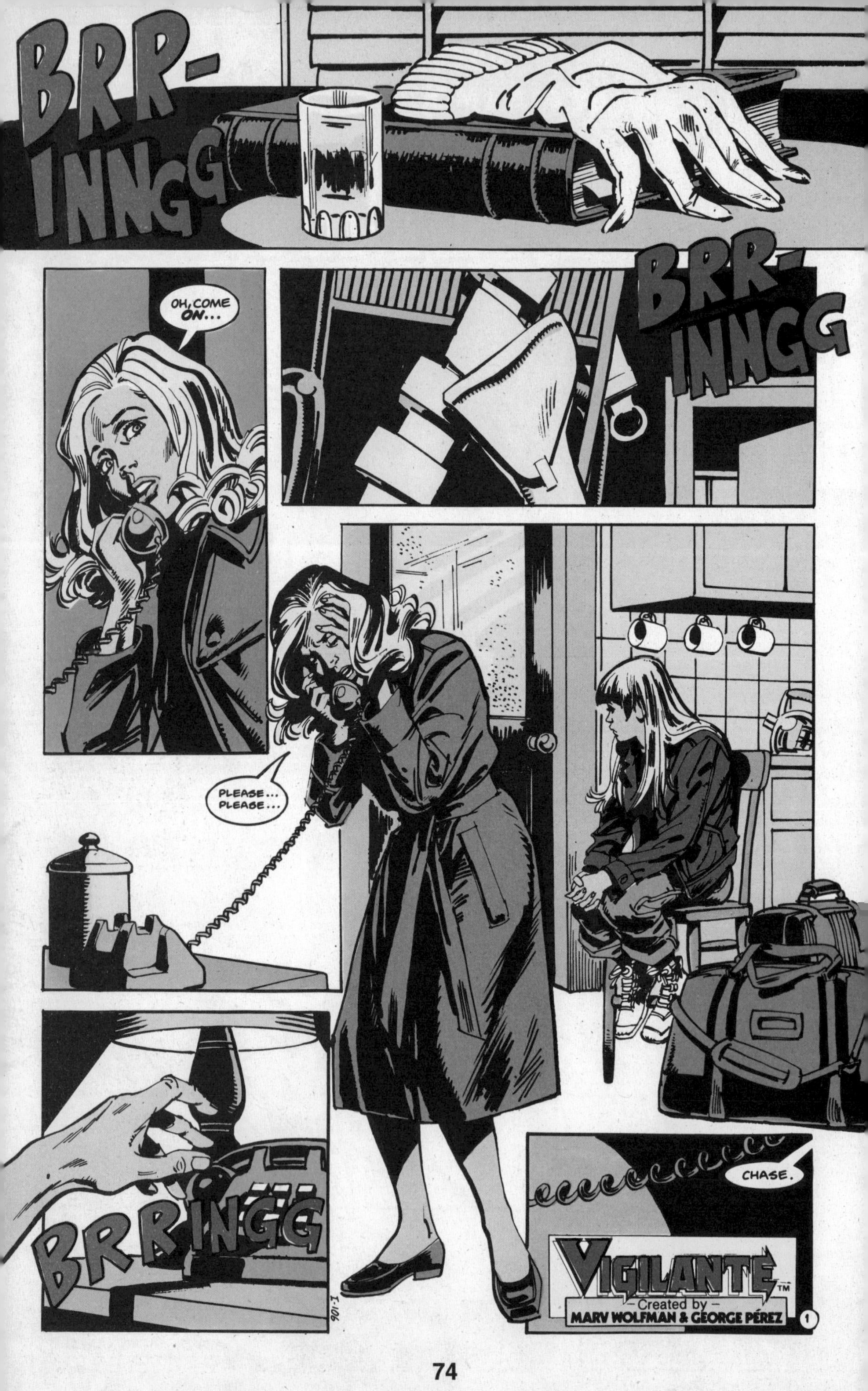

BRR-INNGG
OH, COME ON...
BRR-INNGG
PLEASE... PLEASE...
BRRINGG
CHASE.
VIGILANTE™
– Created by –
MARV WOLFMAN & GEORGE PÉREZ
1

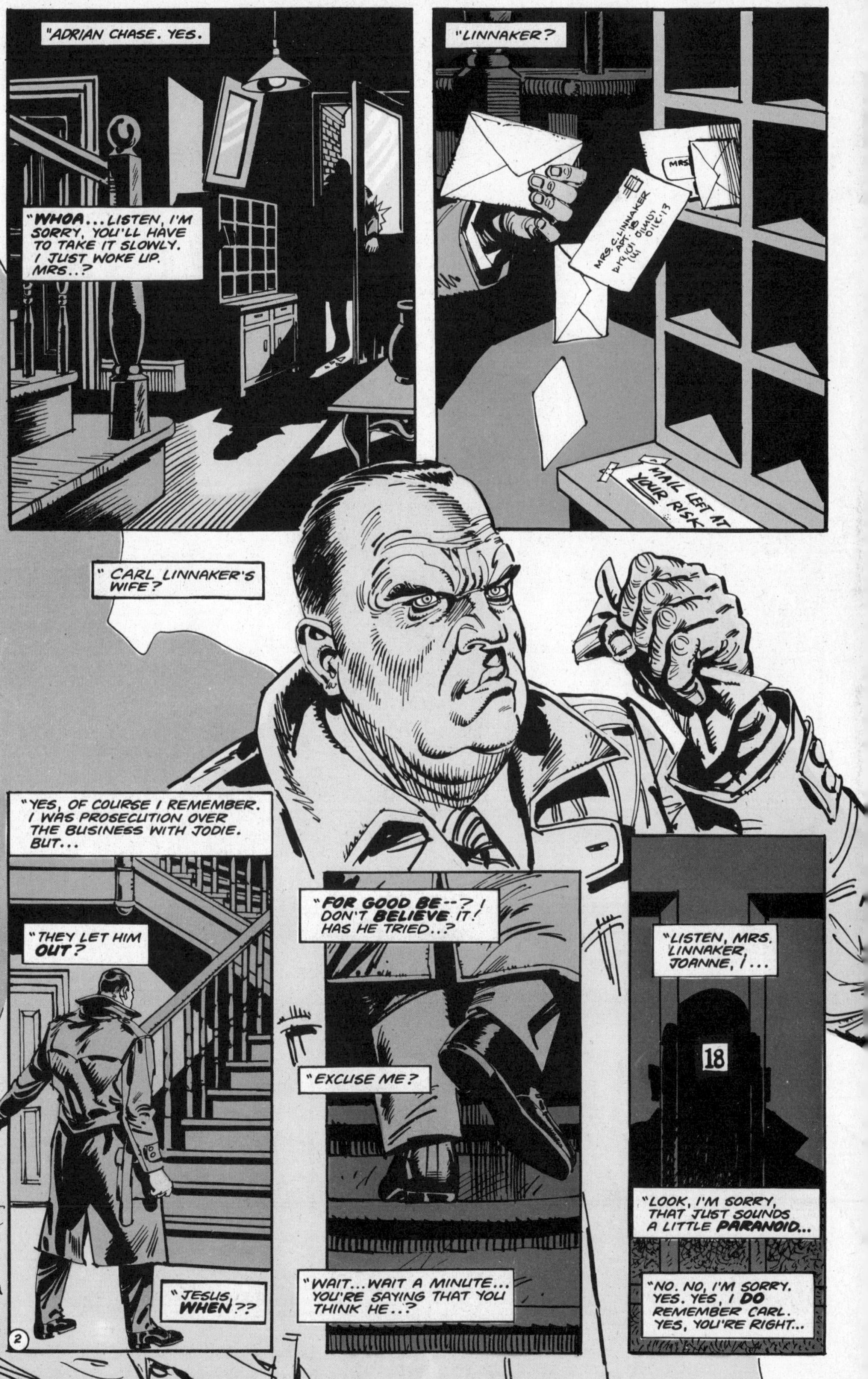
"ADRIAN CHASE. YES.
"WHOA... LISTEN, I'M SORRY, YOU'LL HAVE TO TAKE IT SLOWLY. I JUST WOKE UP. MRS..?
"LINNAKER?
MRS. C. LINNAKER APT. 18
MAIL LEFT AT YOUR RISK
" CARL LINNAKER'S WIFE?
"YES, OF COURSE I REMEMBER. I WAS PROSECUTION OVER THE BUSINESS WITH JODIE. BUT...
"THEY LET HIM OUT?
"JESUS, WHEN??
"FOR GOOD BE--? I DON'T BELIEVE IT! HAS HE TRIED..?
"EXCUSE ME?
"WAIT... WAIT A MINUTE... YOU'RE SAYING THAT YOU THINK HE..?
"LISTEN, MRS. LINNAKER, JOANNE, I...
18
"LOOK, I'M SORRY, THAT JUST SOUNDS A LITTLE PARANOID...
"NO. NO, I'M SORRY. YES. YES, I DO REMEMBER CARL. YES, YOU'RE RIGHT...
2

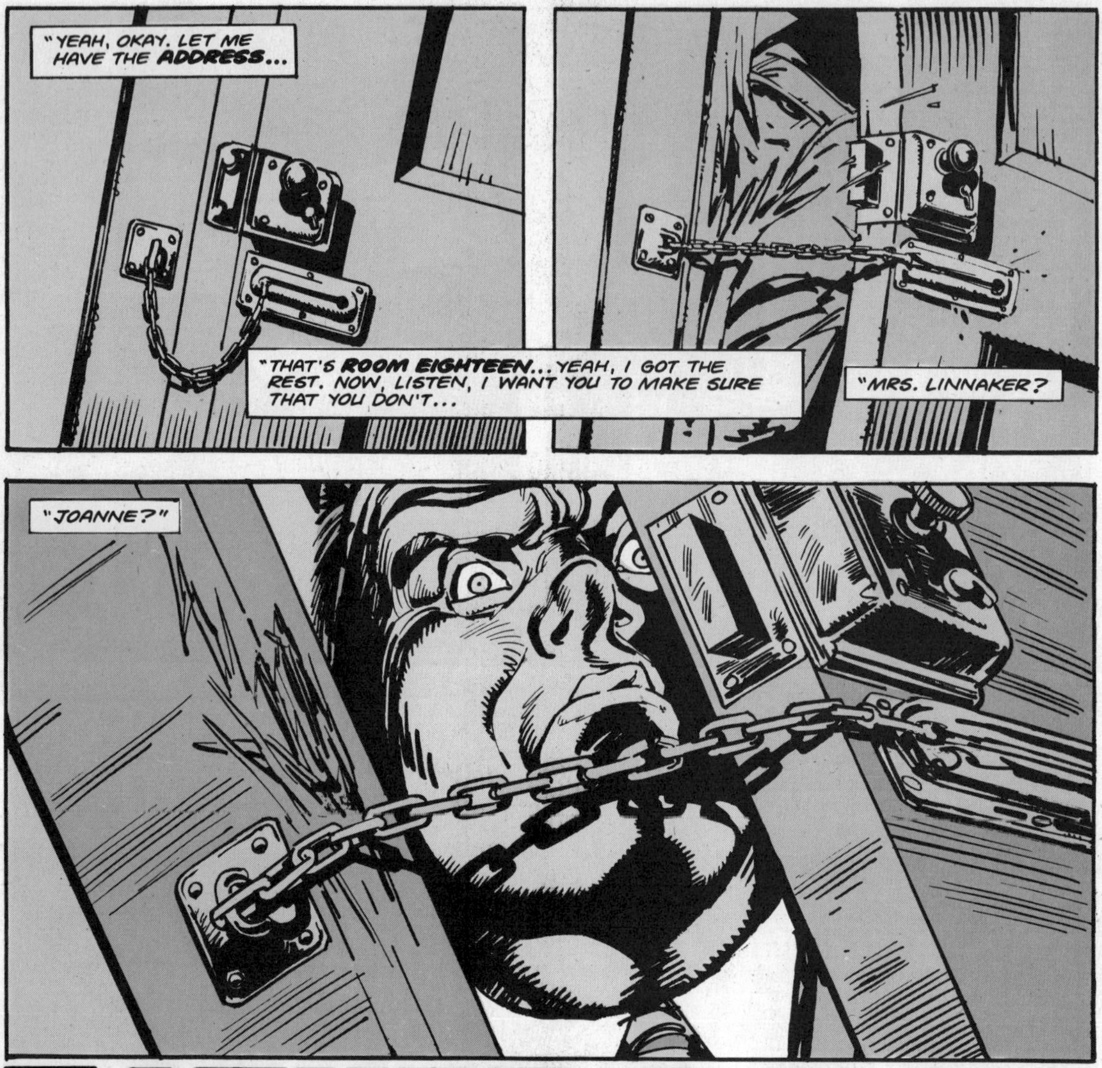
"YEAH, OKAY. LET ME HAVE THE ADDRESS...
"THAT'S ROOM EIGHTEEN... YEAH, I GOT THE REST. NOW, LISTEN, I WANT YOU TO MAKE SURE THAT YOU DON'T...
"MRS. LINNAKER?
"JOANNE?"

FATHER'S DAY

MARV WOLFMAN EDITOR | ALAN MOORE WRITER | JIM BAIKIE ARTIST | ANNIE HALFACREE LETTERER | TATJANA WOOD COLORIST

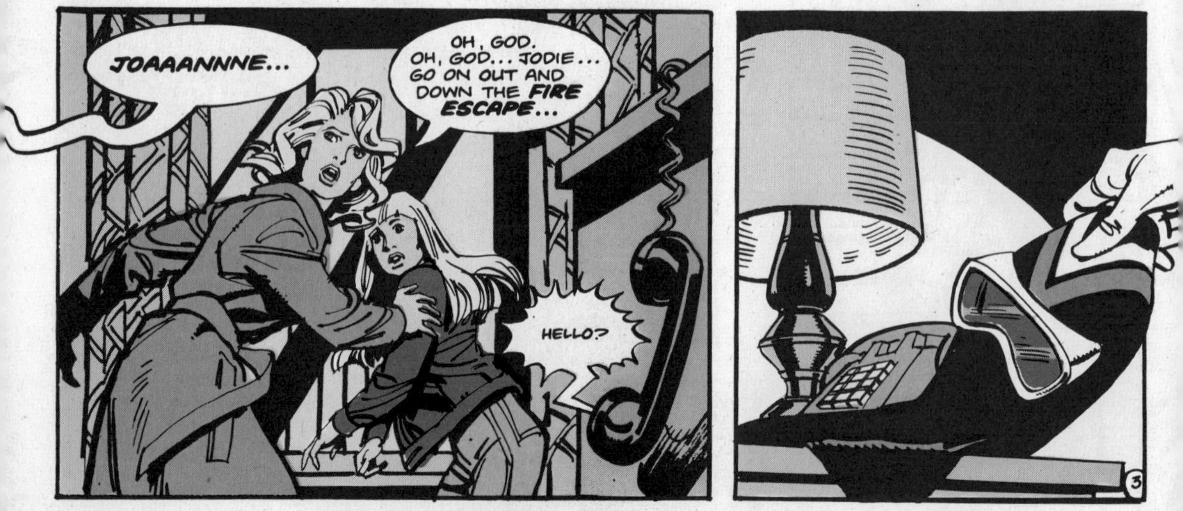
JOAAAANNNE...
OH, GOD. OH, GOD... JODIE... GO ON OUT AND DOWN THE FIRE ESCAPE...
HELLO?

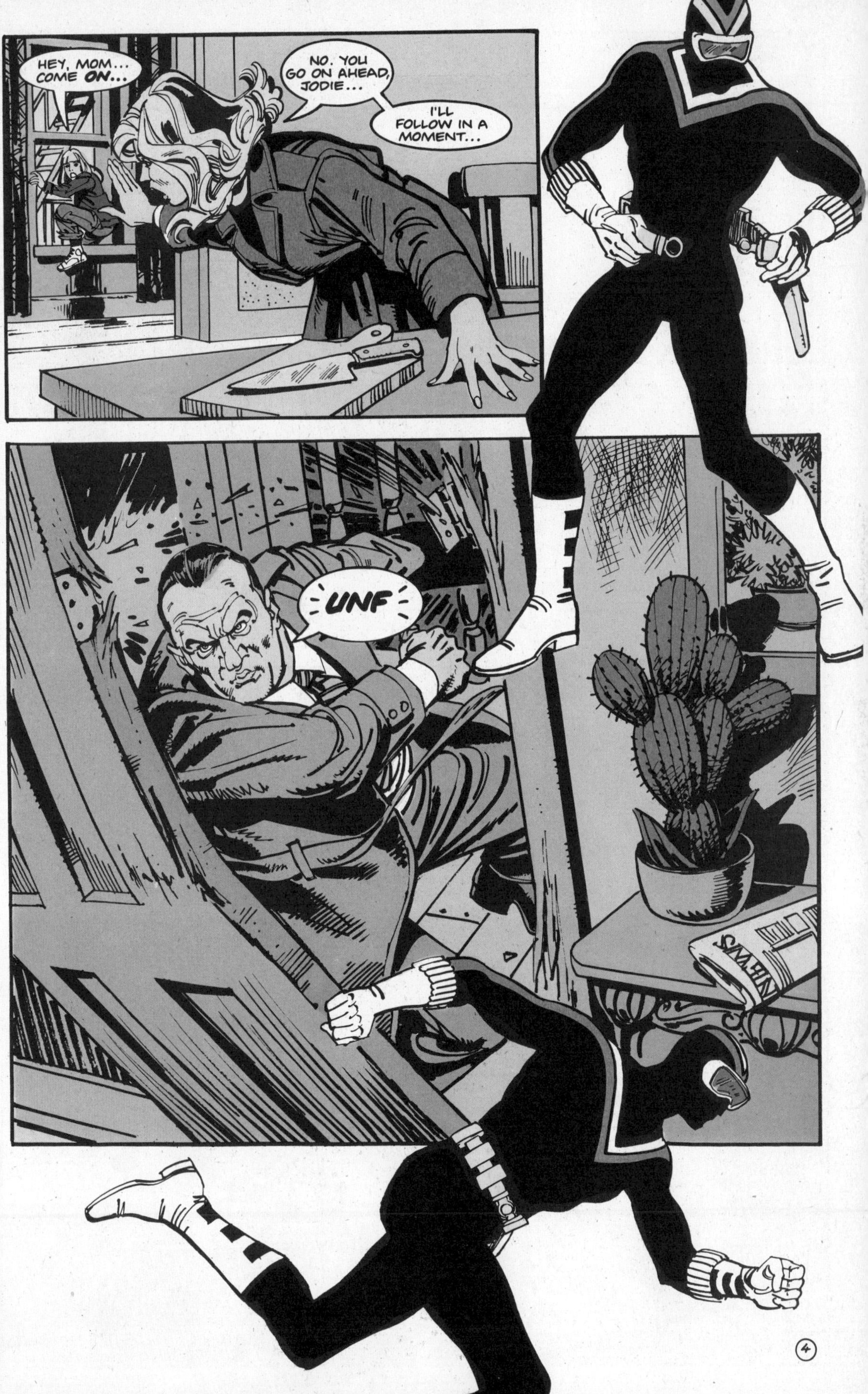
HEY, MOM... COME ON...
NO. YOU GO ON AHEAD, JODIE...
I'LL FOLLOW IN A MOMENT...
UNF
NEWS

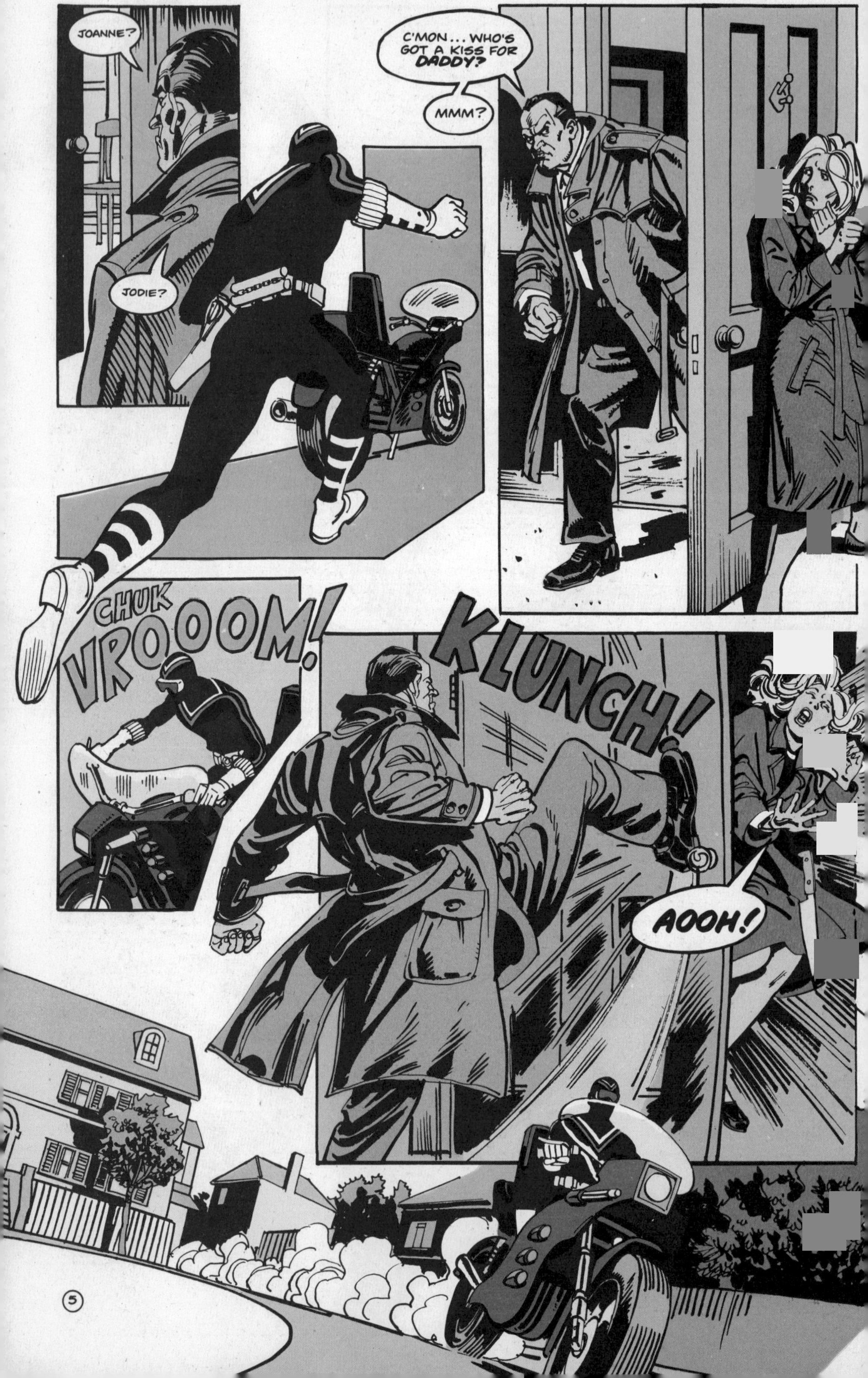
JOANNE?
JODIE?
C'MON... WHO'S GOT A KISS FOR DADDY?
MMM?
CHUK
VROOOM!
KLUNCH!
AOOH!

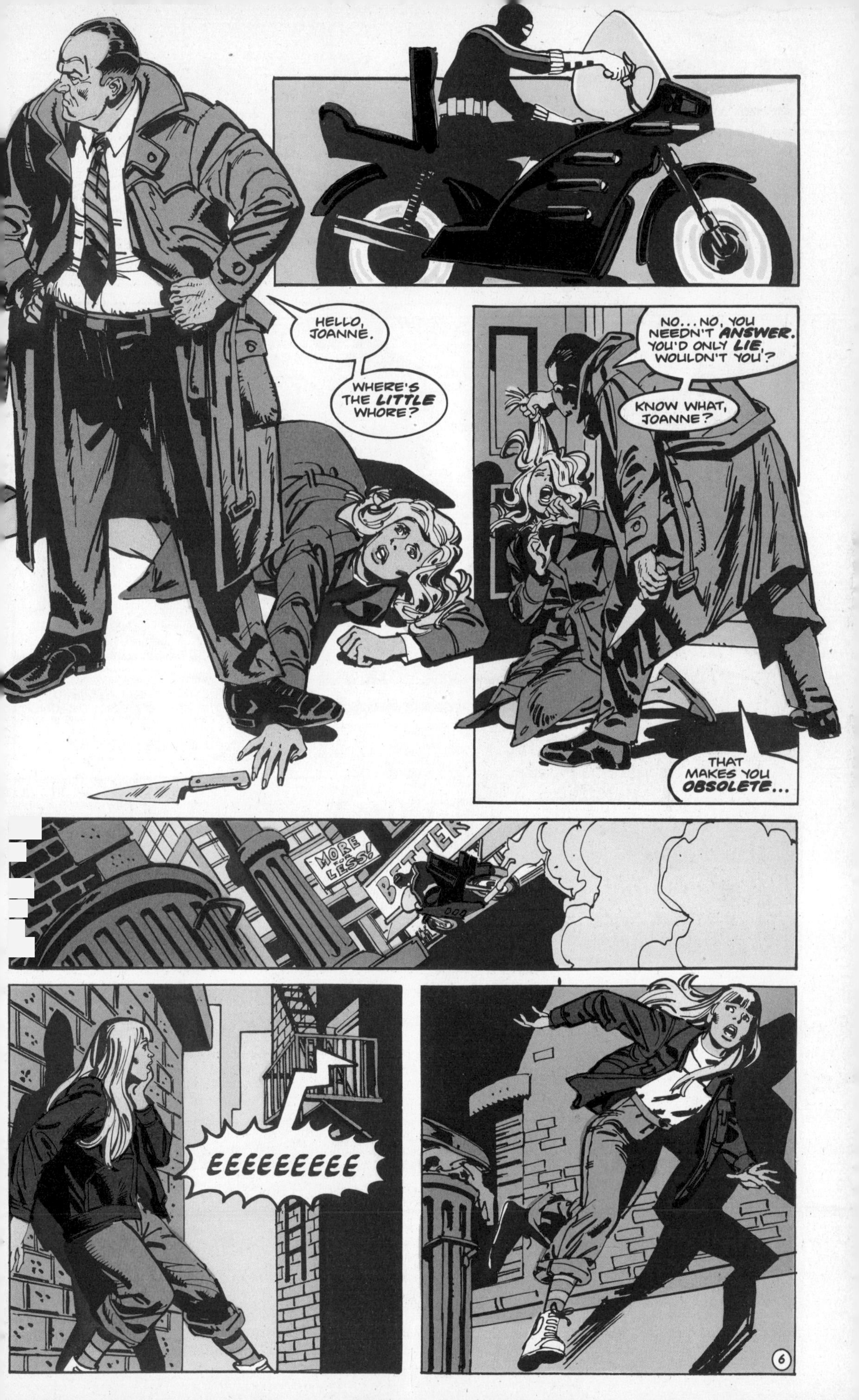
HELLO, JOANNE.
WHERE'S THE LITTLE WHORE?
NO... NO, YOU NEEDN'T ANSWER. YOU'D ONLY LIE, WOULDN'T YOU?
KNOW WHAT, JOANNE?
THAT MAKES YOU OBSOLETE...
MORE FOR LESS!
EEEEEEEEE

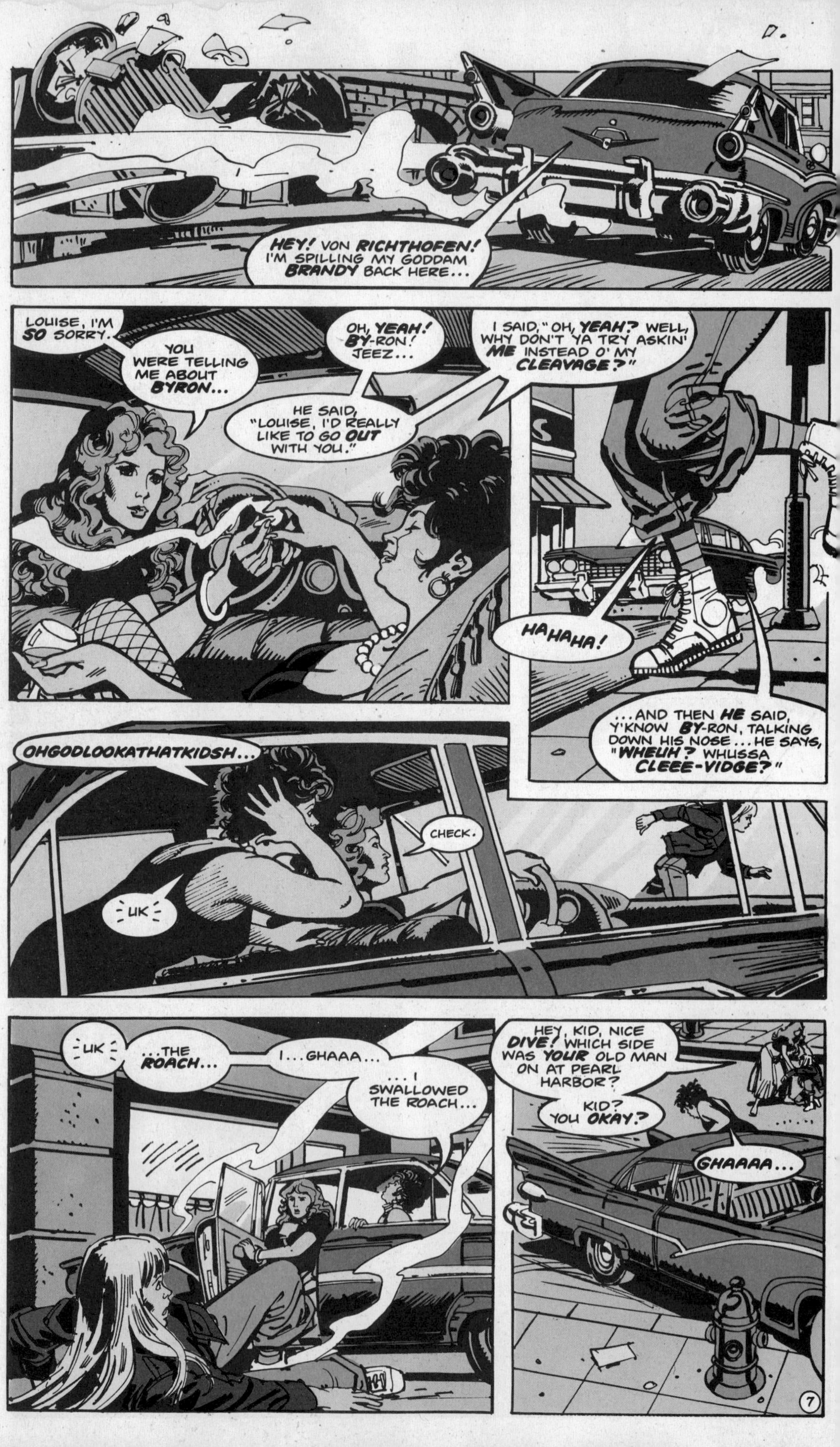

HEY! VON RICHTHOFEN! I'M SPILLING MY GODDAM BRANDY BACK HERE...
LOUISE, I'M SO SORRY.
YOU WERE TELLING ME ABOUT BYRON...
OH, YEAH! BY-RON! JEEZ...
HE SAID, "LOUISE, I'D REALLY LIKE TO GO OUT WITH YOU."
I SAID, "OH, YEAH? WELL, WHY DON'T YA TRY ASKIN' ME INSTEAD O' MY CLEAVAGE?"
HAHAHA!
...AND THEN HE SAID, Y'KNOW BY-RON, TALKING DOWN HIS NOSE... HE SAYS, "WHEUH? WHUSSA CLEEE-VIDGE?"
OHGODLOOKATHATKIDSH...
CHECK.
UK
UK
...THE ROACH...
I...GHAAA...
...I SWALLOWED THE ROACH...
HEY, KID, NICE DIVE! WHICH SIDE WAS YOUR OLD MAN ON AT PEARL HARBOR?
KID? YOU OKAY?
GHAAAA...

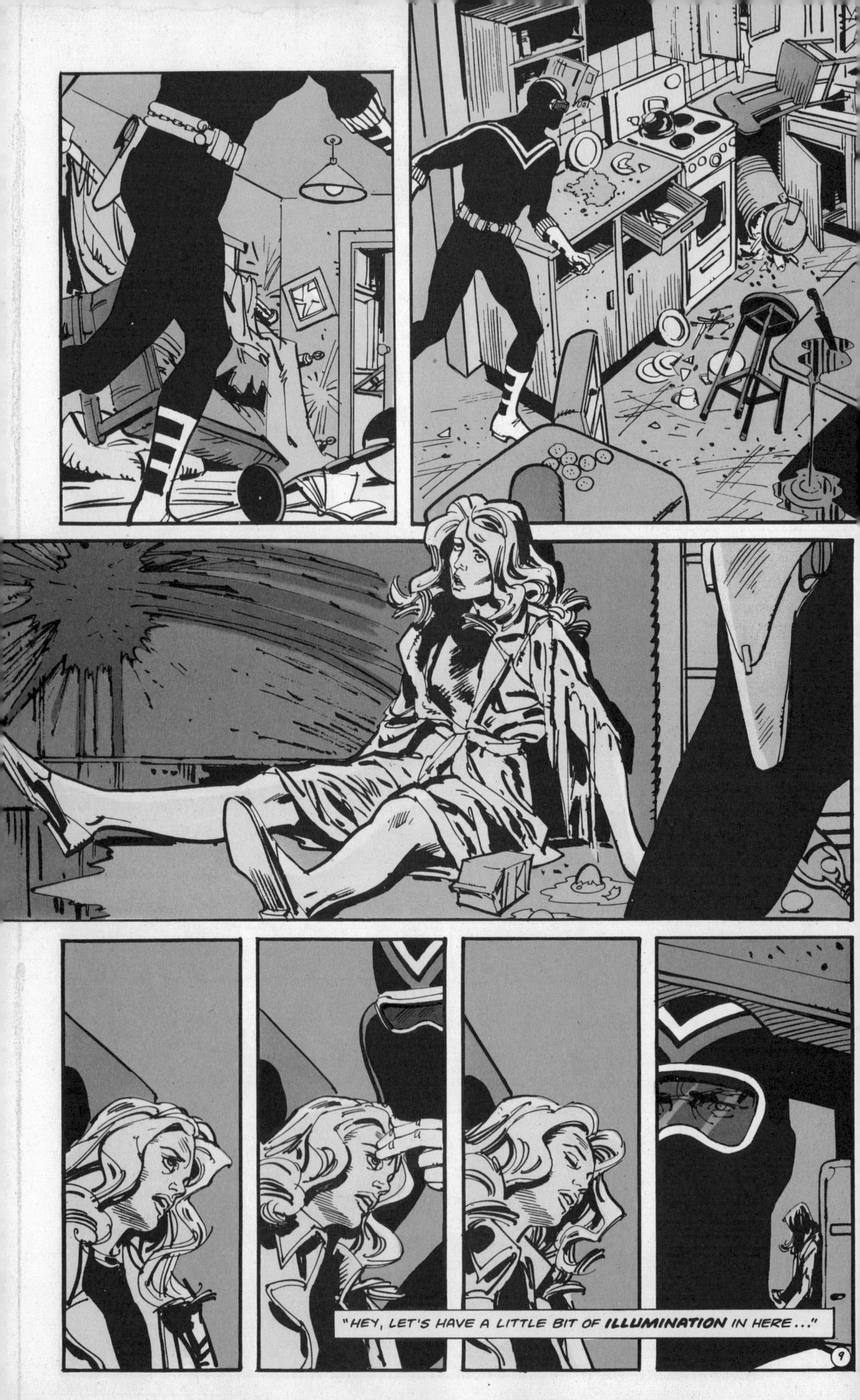
"HEY, LET'S HAVE A LITTLE BIT OF ILLUMINATION IN HERE..."
9

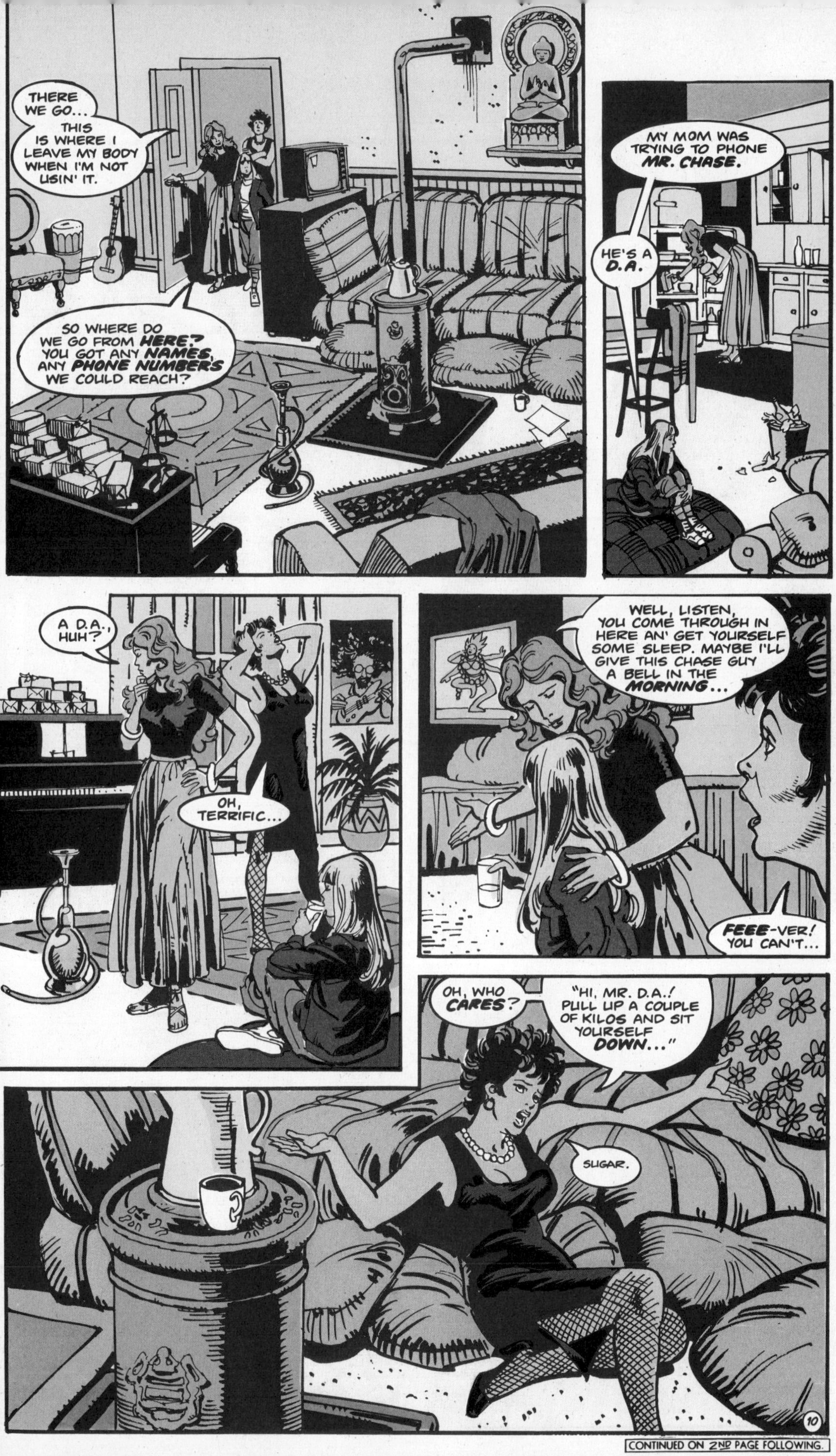
THERE WE GO... THIS IS WHERE I LEAVE MY BODY WHEN I'M NOT USIN' IT.
SO WHERE DO WE GO FROM HERE? YOU GOT ANY NAMES, ANY PHONE NUMBERS WE COULD REACH?
MY MOM WAS TRYING TO PHONE MR. CHASE.
HE'S A D.A.
A D.A., HUH?
OH, TERRIFIC...
WELL, LISTEN, YOU COME THROUGH IN HERE AN' GET YOURSELF SOME SLEEP. MAYBE I'LL GIVE THIS CHASE GUY A BELL IN THE MORNING...
FEEE-VER! YOU CAN'T...
OH, WHO CARES?
"HI, MR. D.A.! PULL UP A COUPLE OF KILOS AND SIT YOURSELF DOWN..."
SUGAR.
10

CONTINUED ON 2ND PAGE FOLLOWING.

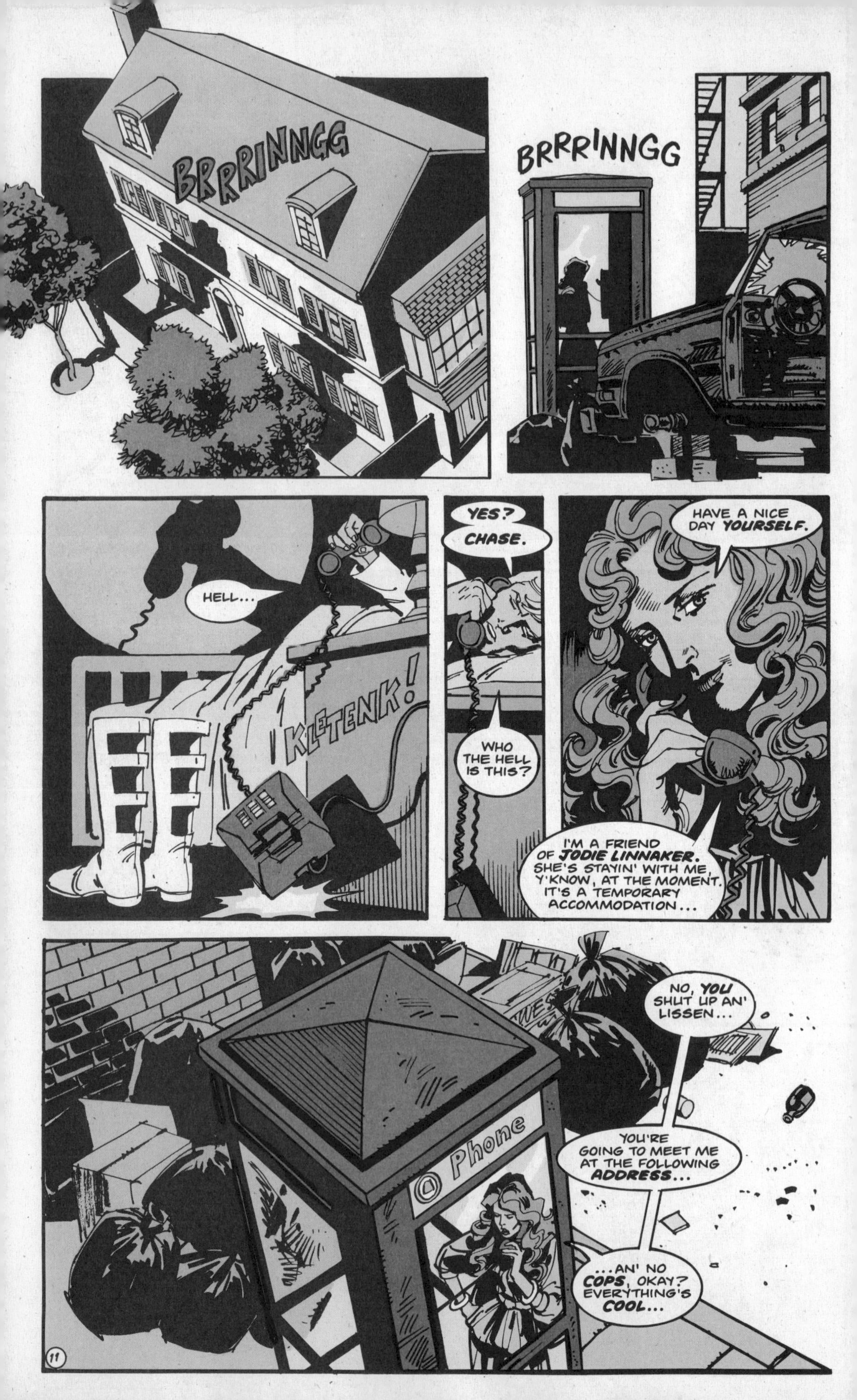
BRRRINNGG
BRRRINNGG
HELL...
KLETENK!
YES?
CHASE.
WHO THE HELL IS THIS?
HAVE A NICE DAY YOURSELF.
I'M A FRIEND OF JODIE LINNAKER. SHE'S STAYIN' WITH ME, Y'KNOW, AT THE MOMENT. IT'S A TEMPORARY ACCOMMODATION...
NO, YOU SHUT UP AN' LISSEN...
YOU'RE GOING TO MEET ME AT THE FOLLOWING ADDRESS...
...AN' NO COPS, OKAY? EVERYTHING'S COOL...
Phone
11

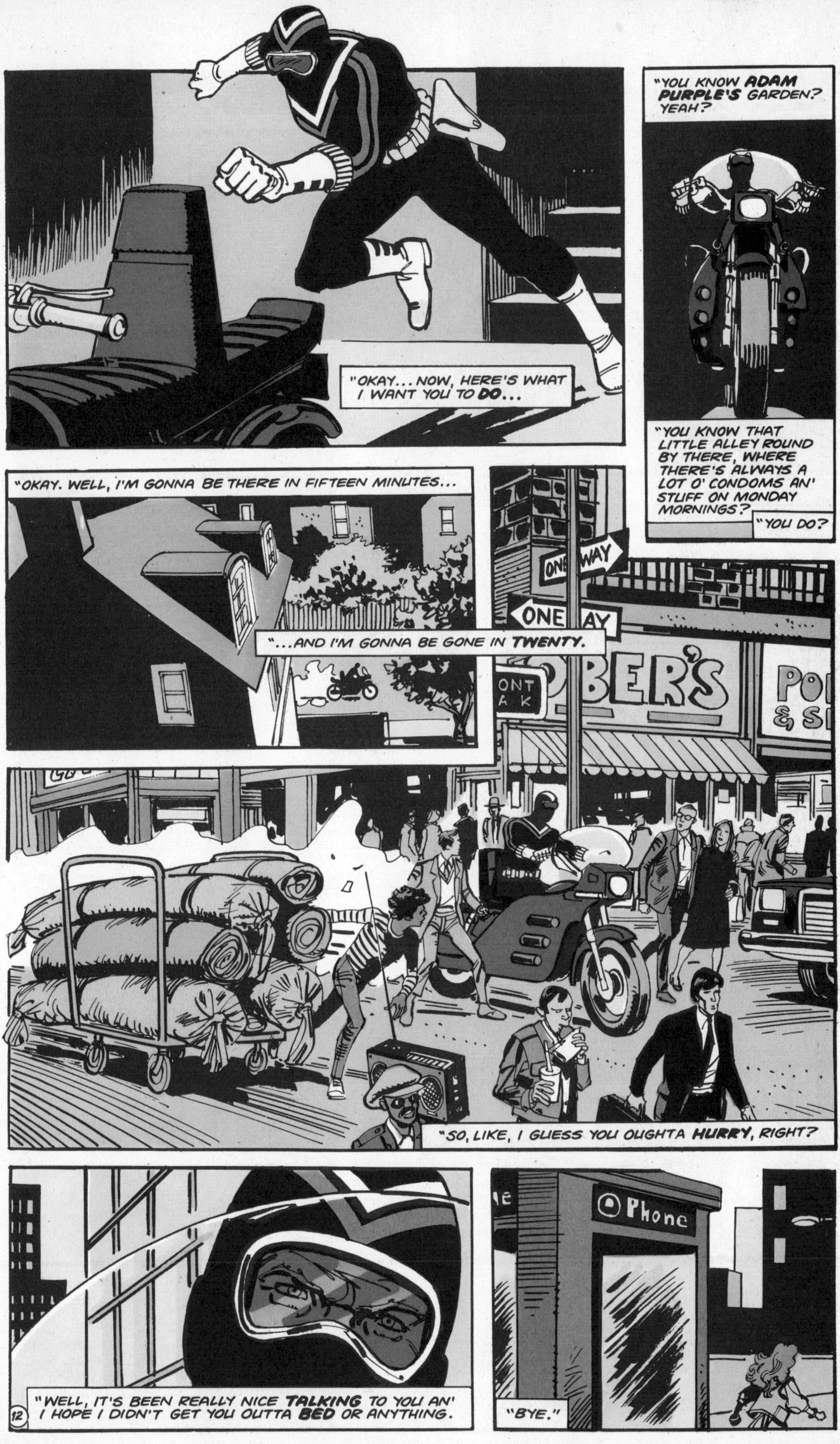
"OKAY... NOW, HERE'S WHAT I WANT YOU TO DO...
"YOU KNOW ADAM PURPLE'S GARDEN? YEAH?
"YOU KNOW THAT LITTLE ALLEY ROUND BY THERE, WHERE THERE'S ALWAYS A LOT O' CONDOMS AN' STUFF ON MONDAY MORNINGS?
"YOU DO?
"OKAY. WELL, I'M GONNA BE THERE IN FIFTEEN MINUTES...
"...AND I'M GONNA BE GONE IN TWENTY.
ONE WAY
ONE WAY
"SO, LIKE, I GUESS YOU OUGHTA HURRY, RIGHT?
"WELL, IT'S BEEN REALLY NICE TALKING TO YOU AN' I HOPE I DIDN'T GET YOU OUTTA BED OR ANYTHING.
Phone
"BYE."

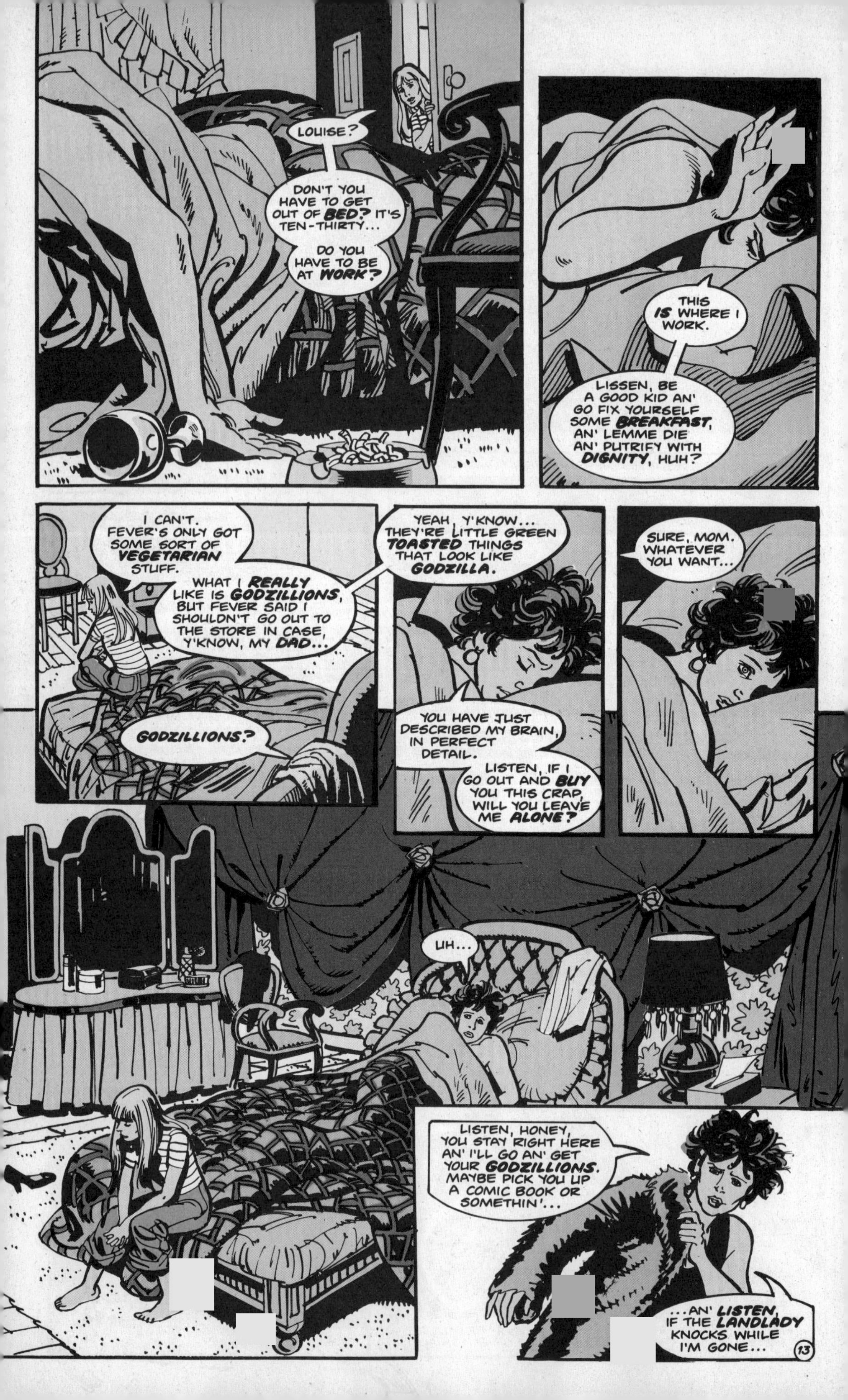
LOUISE?
DON'T YOU HAVE TO GET OUT OF BED? IT'S TEN-THIRTY...
DO YOU HAVE TO BE AT WORK?
THIS IS WHERE I WORK.
LISSEN, BE A GOOD KID AN' GO FIX YOURSELF SOME BREAKFAST, AN' LEMME DIE AN' PUTRIFY WITH DIGNITY, HUH?
I CAN'T. FEVER'S ONLY GOT SOME SORT OF VEGETARIAN STUFF.
WHAT I REALLY LIKE IS GODZILLIONS, BUT FEVER SAID I SHOULDN'T GO OUT TO THE STORE IN CASE, Y'KNOW, MY DAD...
GODZILLIONS?
YEAH, Y'KNOW... THEY'RE LITTLE GREEN TOASTED THINGS THAT LOOK LIKE GODZILLA.
YOU HAVE JUST DESCRIBED MY BRAIN, IN PERFECT DETAIL.
LISTEN, IF I GO OUT AND BUY YOU THIS CRAP, WILL YOU LEAVE ME ALONE?
SURE, MOM. WHATEVER YOU WANT...
UH...
LISTEN, HONEY, YOU STAY RIGHT HERE AN' I'LL GO AN' GET YOUR GODZILLIONS. MAYBE PICK YOU UP A COMIC BOOK OR SOMETHIN'...
...AN' LISTEN, IF THE LANDLADY KNOCKS WHILE I'M GONE...
13

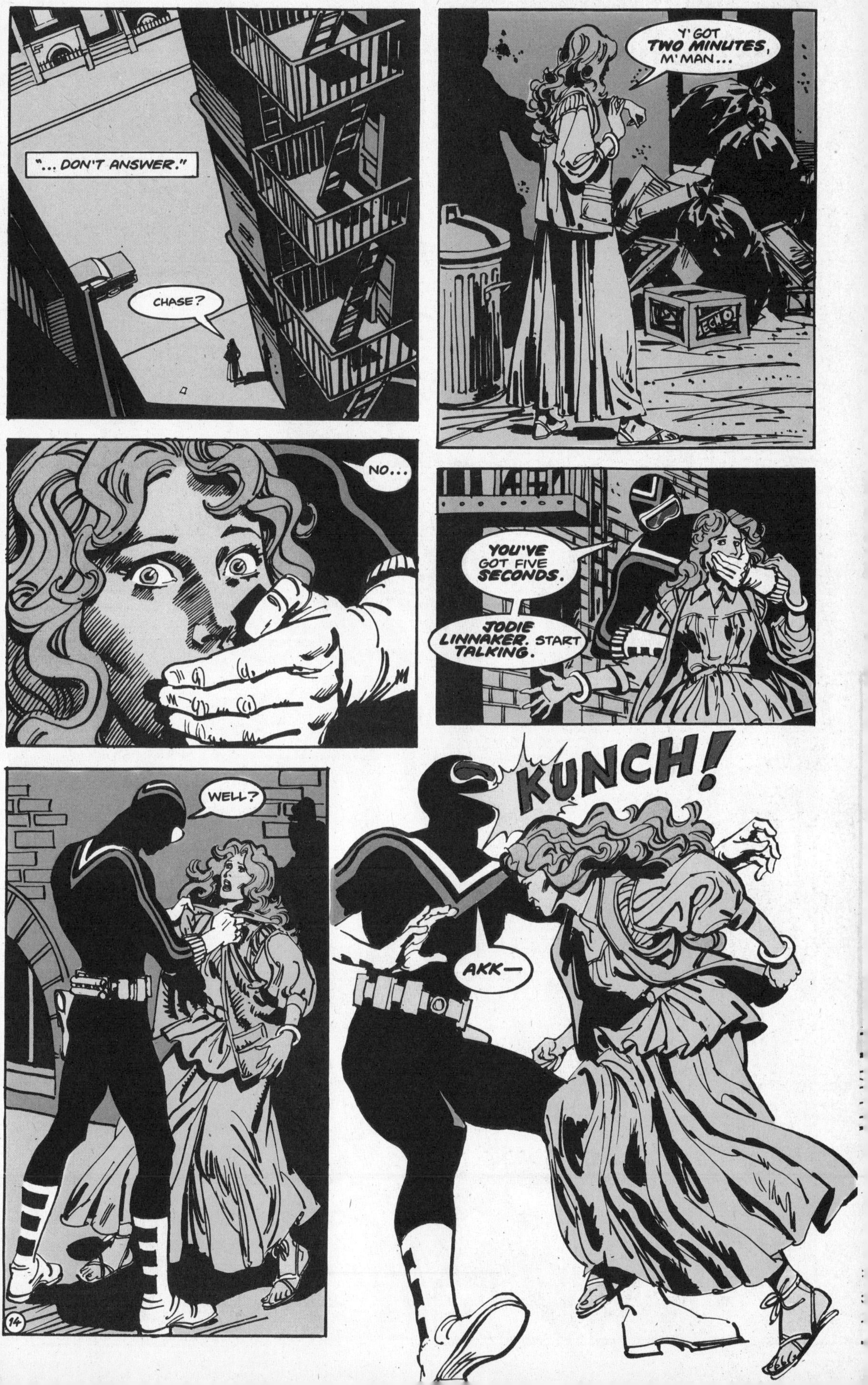

"... DON'T ANSWER."
CHASE?
Y' GOT TWO MINUTES, M' MAN...
NO...
YOU'VE GOT FIVE SECONDS.
JODIE LINNAKER. START TALKING.
WELL?
KUNCH!
AKK—
14

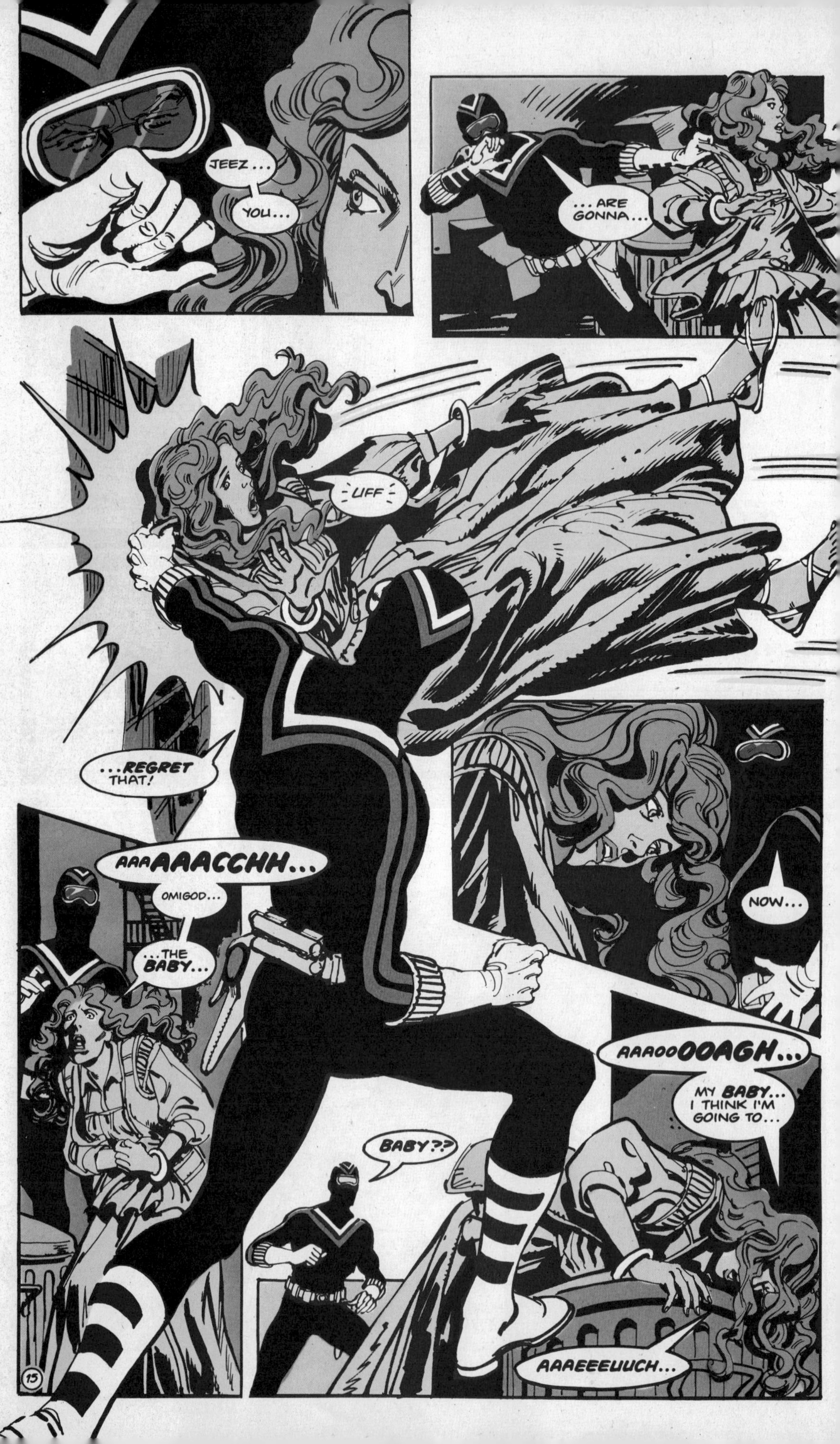
JEEZ...
YOU...
...ARE GONNA...
UFF
...REGRET THAT!
AAAAAACCHH...
OMIGOD...
...THE BABY...
NOW...
AAAOOOOAGH...
MY BABY... I THINK I'M GOING TO...
BABY??
AAAEEEUUCH...

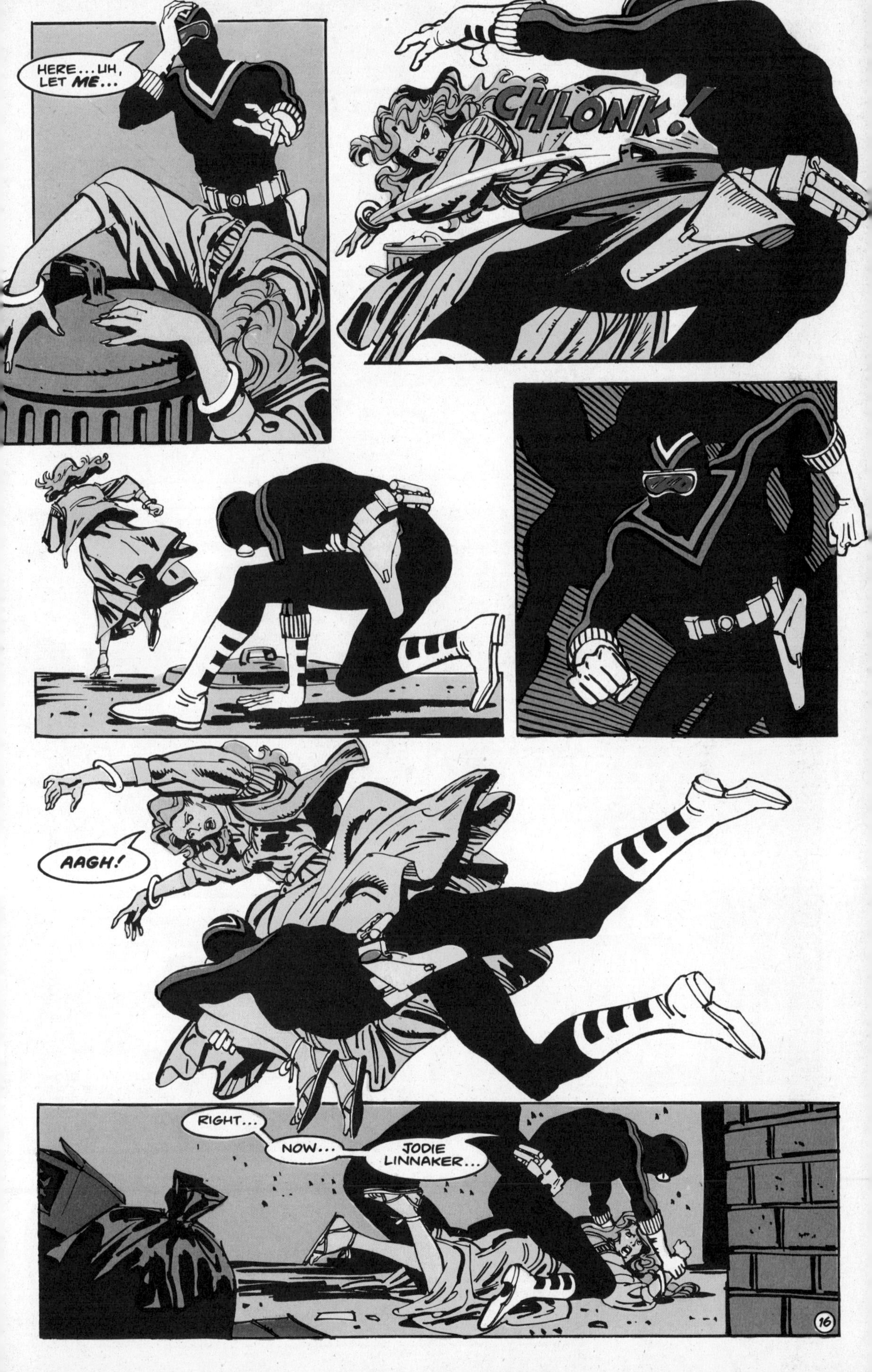
HERE... UH, LET ME...
CHLONK!
AAGH!
RIGHT...
NOW...
JODIE LINNAKER...
16

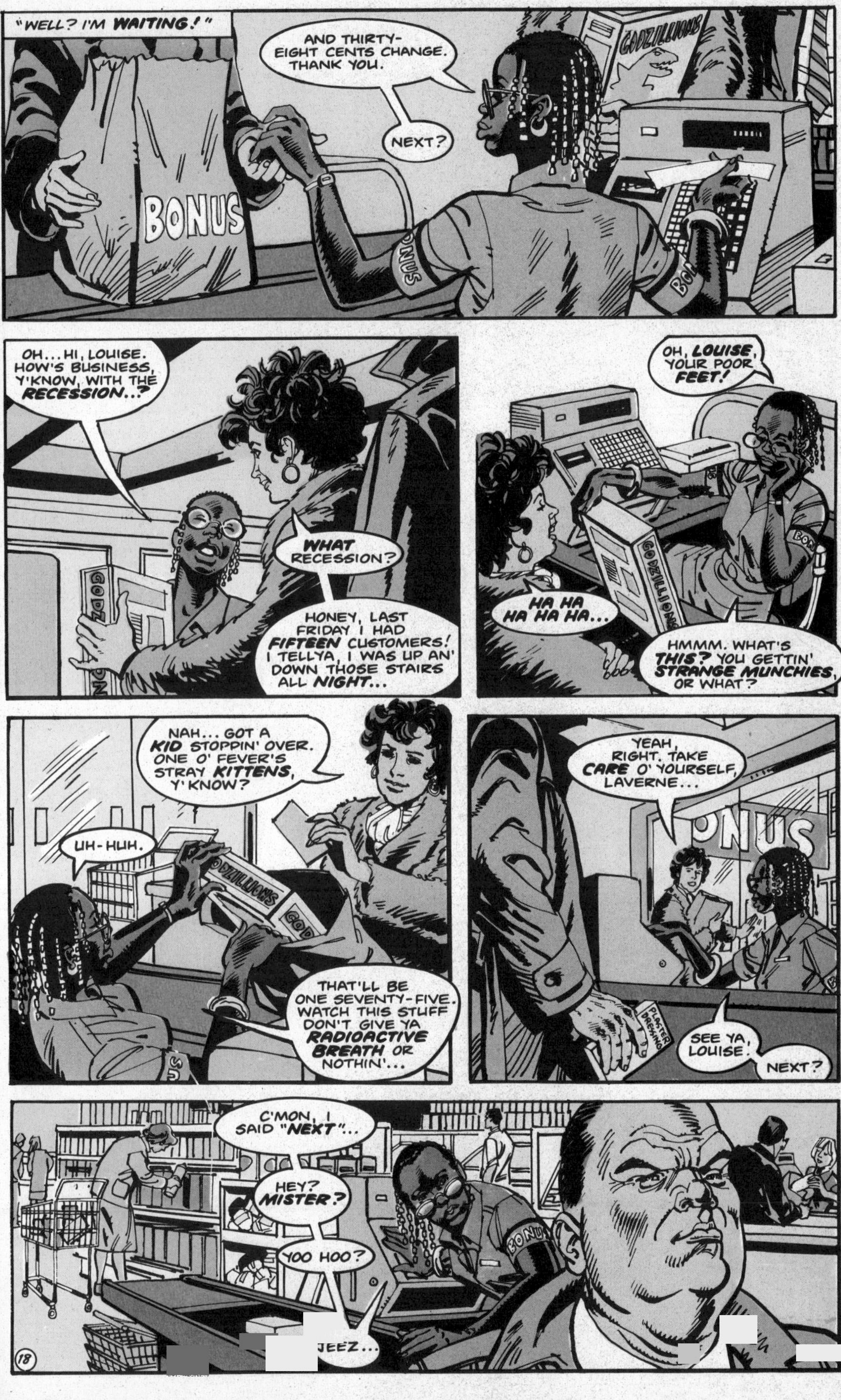
"WELL? I'M WAITING!"
AND THIRTY-EIGHT CENTS CHANGE. THANK YOU.
NEXT?
GODZILLIONS
BONUS
OH... HI, LOUISE. HOW'S BUSINESS, Y'KNOW, WITH THE RECESSION...?
WHAT RECESSION?
HONEY, LAST FRIDAY I HAD FIFTEEN CUSTOMERS! I TELLYA, I WAS UP AN' DOWN THOSE STAIRS ALL NIGHT...
OH, LOUISE, YOUR POOR FEET!
HA HA HA HA HA...
HMMM. WHAT'S THIS? YOU GETTIN' STRANGE MUNCHIES, OR WHAT?
NAH... GOT A KID STOPPIN' OVER. ONE O' FEVER'S STRAY KITTENS, Y'KNOW?
UH-HUH.
THAT'LL BE ONE SEVENTY-FIVE. WATCH THIS STUFF DON'T GIVE YA RADIOACTIVE BREATH OR NOTHIN'...
YEAH, RIGHT. TAKE CARE O' YOURSELF, LAVERNE...
PLASTER DRESSING
SEE YA, LOUISE.
NEXT?
C'MON, I SAID "NEXT"...
HEY? MISTER?
YOO HOO?
JEEZ...

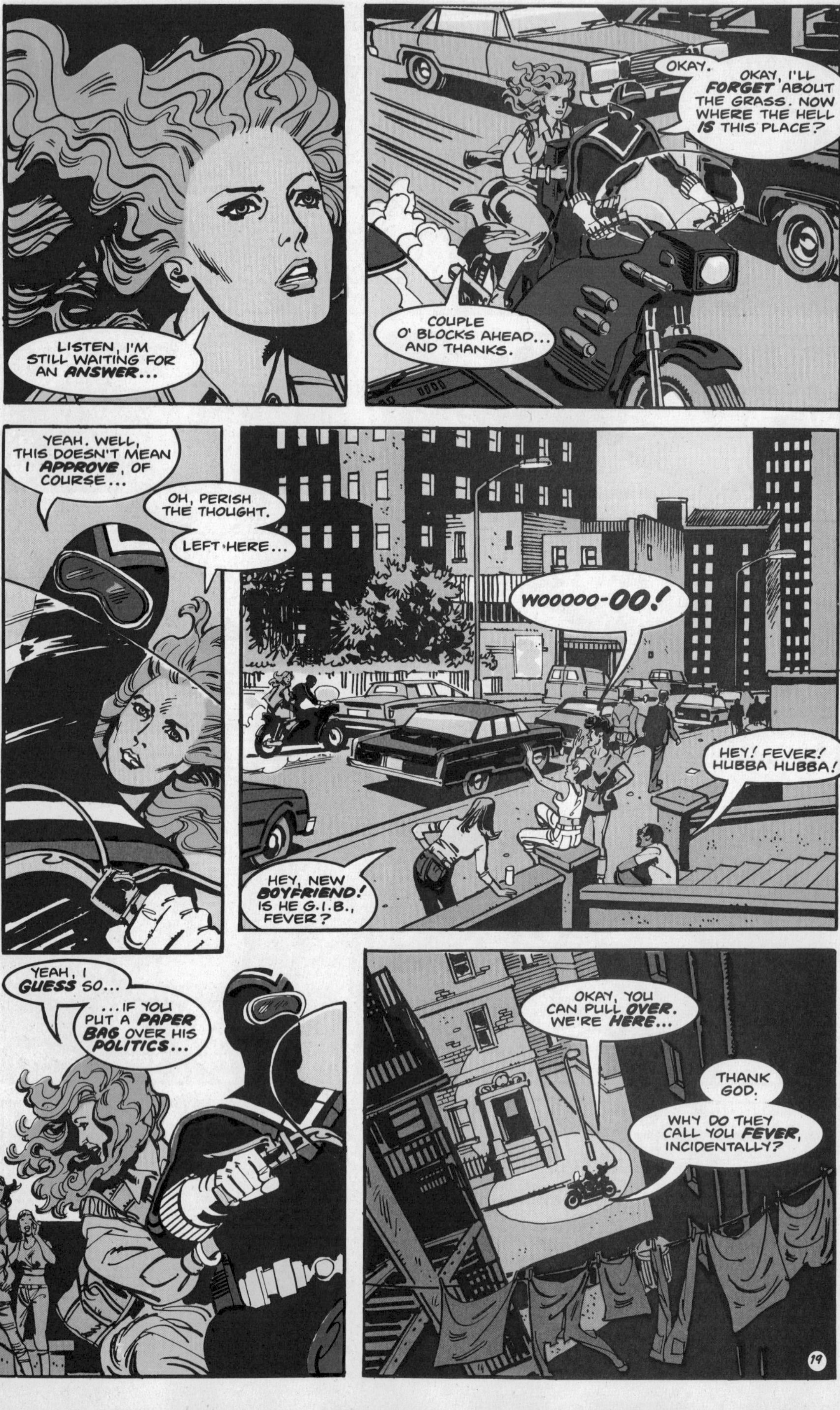

LISTEN, I'M STILL WAITING FOR AN ANSWER...
OKAY.
OKAY, I'LL FORGET ABOUT THE GRASS. NOW WHERE THE HELL IS THIS PLACE?
COUPLE O' BLOCKS AHEAD... AND THANKS.
YEAH. WELL, THIS DOESN'T MEAN I APPROVE, OF COURSE...
OH, PERISH THE THOUGHT.
LEFT HERE...
WOOOOO-OO!
HEY! FEVER! HUBBA HUBBA!
HEY, NEW BOYFRIEND! IS HE G.I.B., FEVER?
YEAH, I GUESS SO...
...IF YOU PUT A PAPER BAG OVER HIS POLITICS...
OKAY, YOU CAN PULL OVER. WE'RE HERE...
THANK GOD.
WHY DO THEY CALL YOU FEVER, INCIDENTALLY?

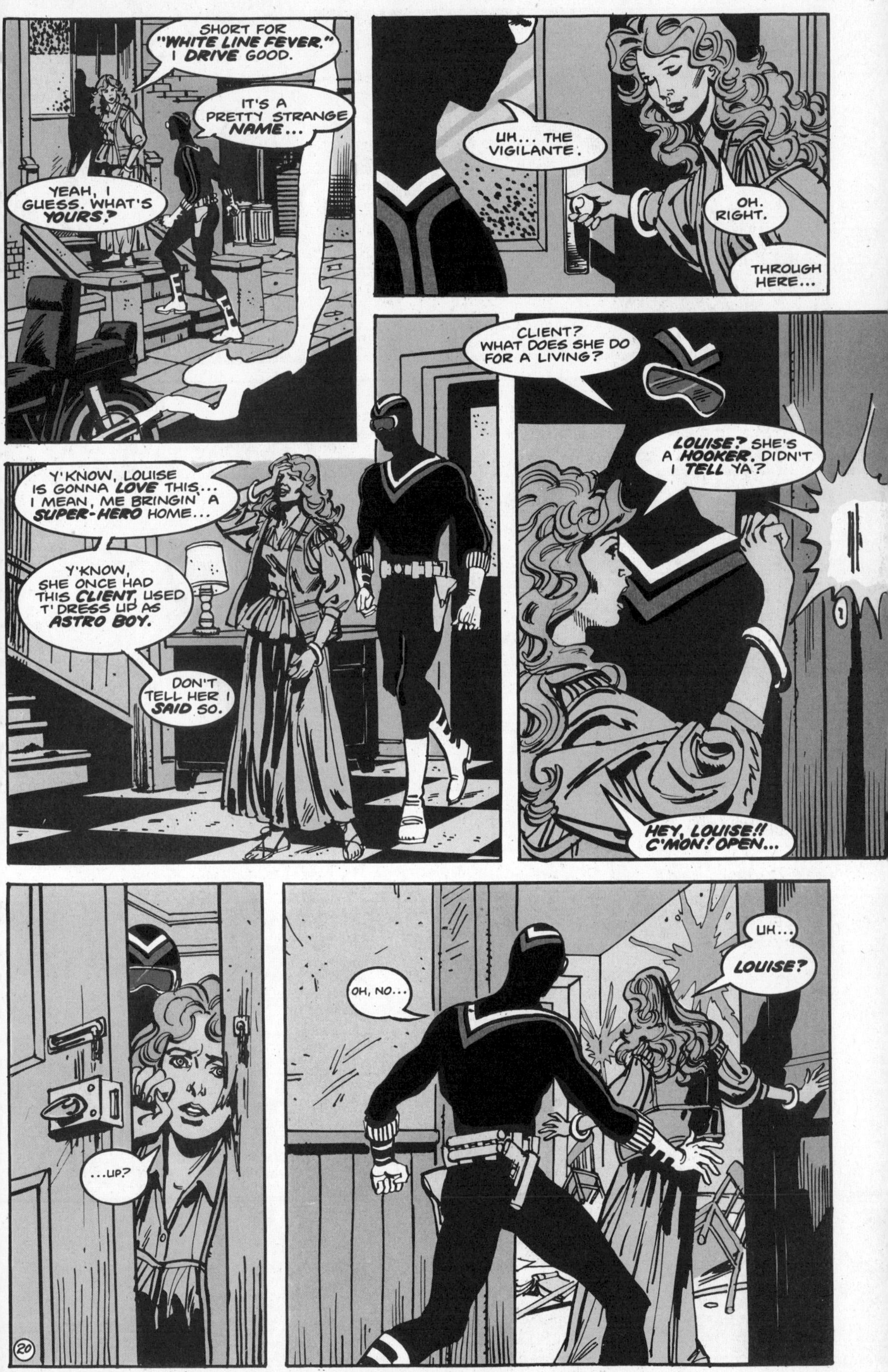
SHORT FOR "WHITE LINE FEVER." I DRIVE GOOD.
IT'S A PRETTY STRANGE NAME...
YEAH, I GUESS. WHAT'S YOURS?
UH... THE VIGILANTE.
OH. RIGHT.
THROUGH HERE...
Y'KNOW, LOUISE IS GONNA LOVE THIS... I MEAN, ME BRINGIN' A SUPER-HERO HOME...
Y'KNOW, SHE ONCE HAD THIS CLIENT, USED T' DRESS UP AS ASTRO BOY.
DON'T TELL HER I SAID SO.
CLIENT? WHAT DOES SHE DO FOR A LIVING?
LOUISE? SHE'S A HOOKER. DIDN'T I TELL YA?
HEY, LOUISE!! C'MON! OPEN...
...UP?
OH, NO...
UH...
LOUISE?
20

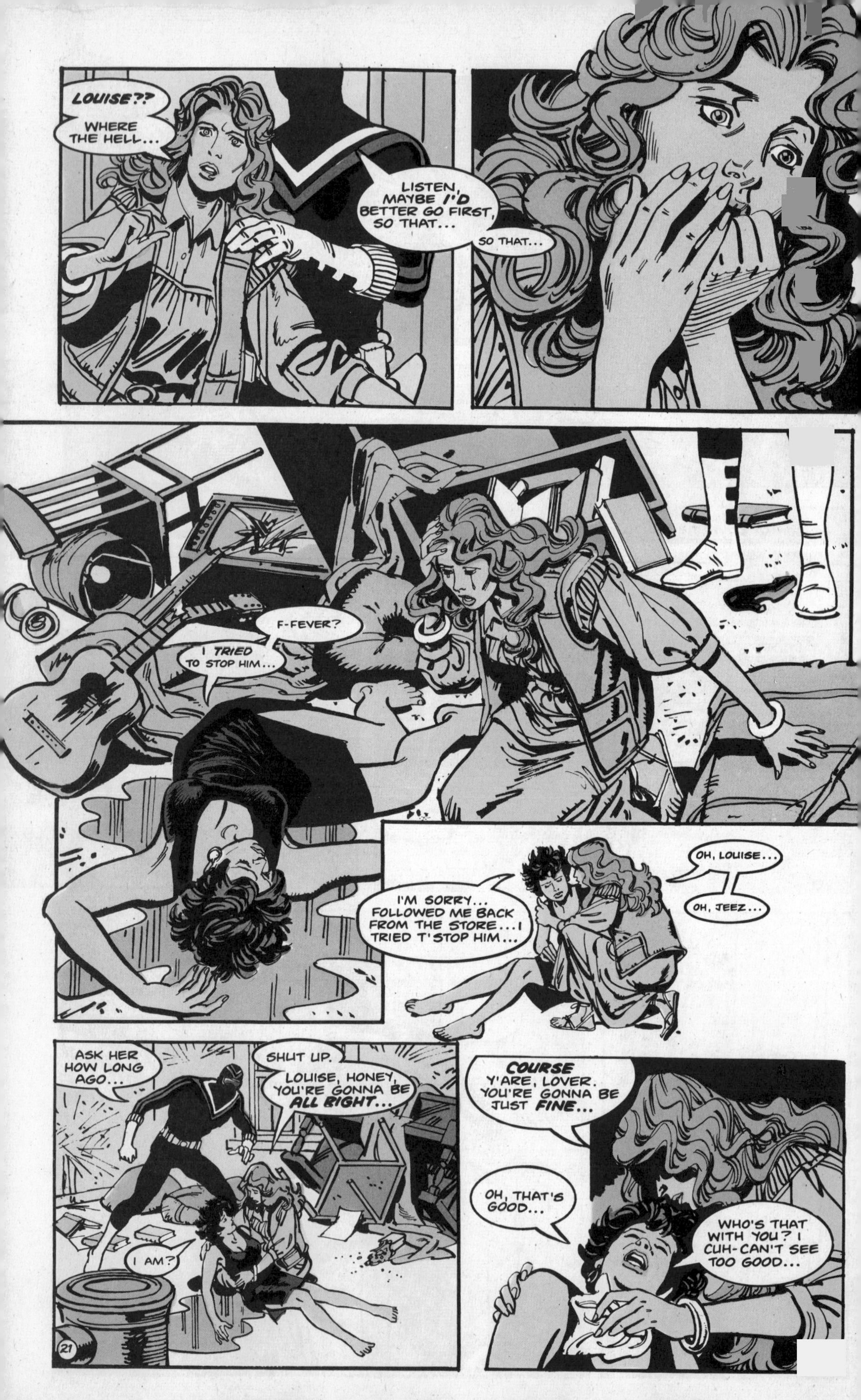
LOUISE??
WHERE THE HELL...
LISTEN, MAYBE I'D BETTER GO FIRST, SO THAT...
SO THAT...
F-FEVER?
I TRIED TO STOP HIM...
I'M SORRY... FOLLOWED ME BACK FROM THE STORE... I TRIED T' STOP HIM...
OH, LOUISE...
OH, JEEZ...
ASK HER HOW LONG AGO...
SHUT UP.
LOUISE, HONEY, YOU'RE GONNA BE ALL RIGHT...
I AM?
COURSE Y'ARE, LOVER. YOU'RE GONNA BE JUST FINE...
OH, THAT'S GOOD...
WHO'S THAT WITH YOU? I CUH-CAN'T SEE TOO GOOD...

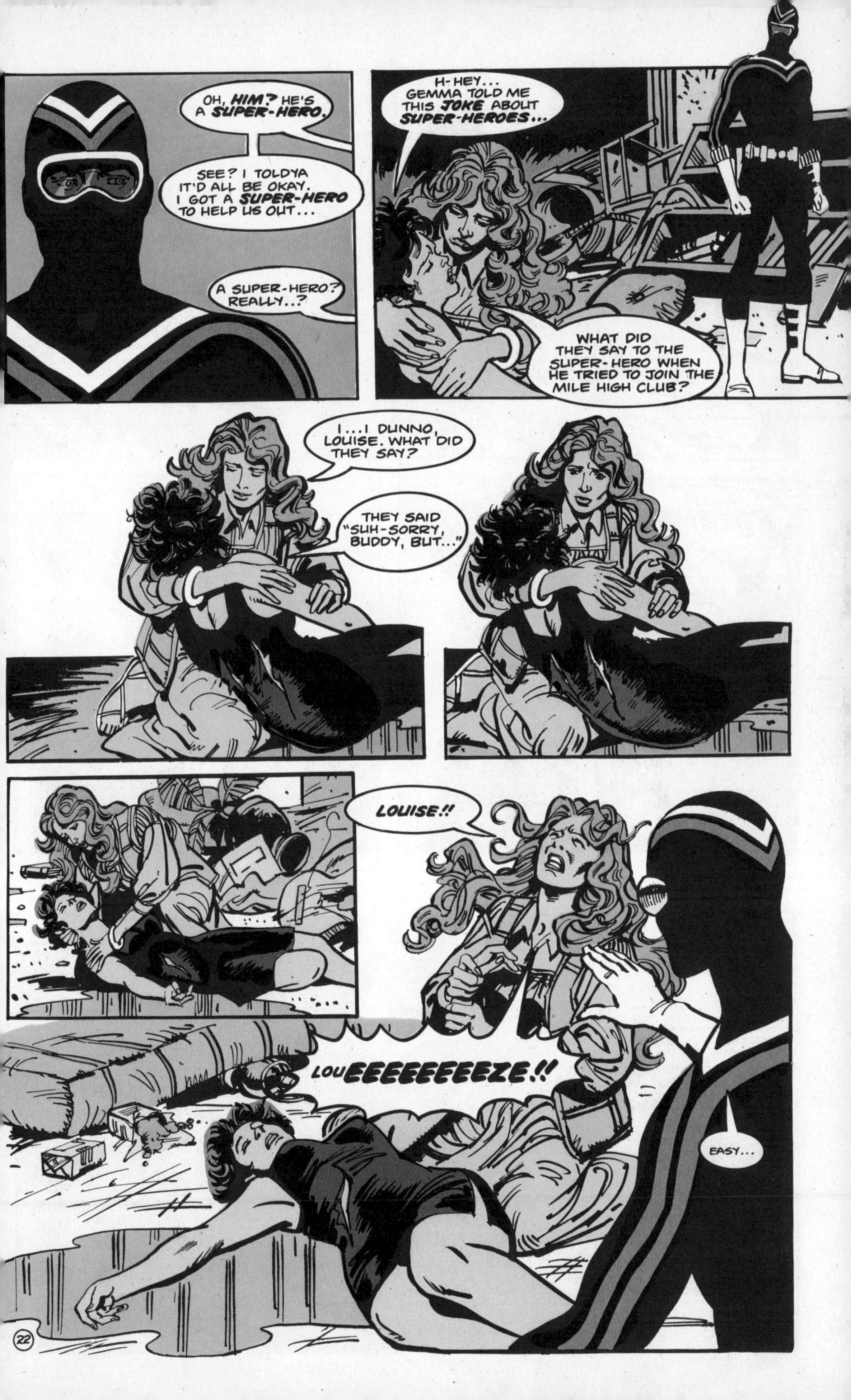
OH, HIM? HE'S A SUPER-HERO.
SEE? I TOLDYA IT'D ALL BE OKAY. I GOT A SUPER-HERO TO HELP US OUT...
A SUPER-HERO? REALLY...?
H-HEY... GEMMA TOLD ME THIS JOKE ABOUT SUPER-HEROES...
WHAT DID THEY SAY TO THE SUPER-HERO WHEN HE TRIED TO JOIN THE MILE HIGH CLUB?
I...I DUNNO, LOUISE. WHAT DID THEY SAY?
THEY SAID "SUH-SORRY, BUDDY, BUT..."
LOUISE!!
LOUEEEEEEEEEZE!!
EASY...

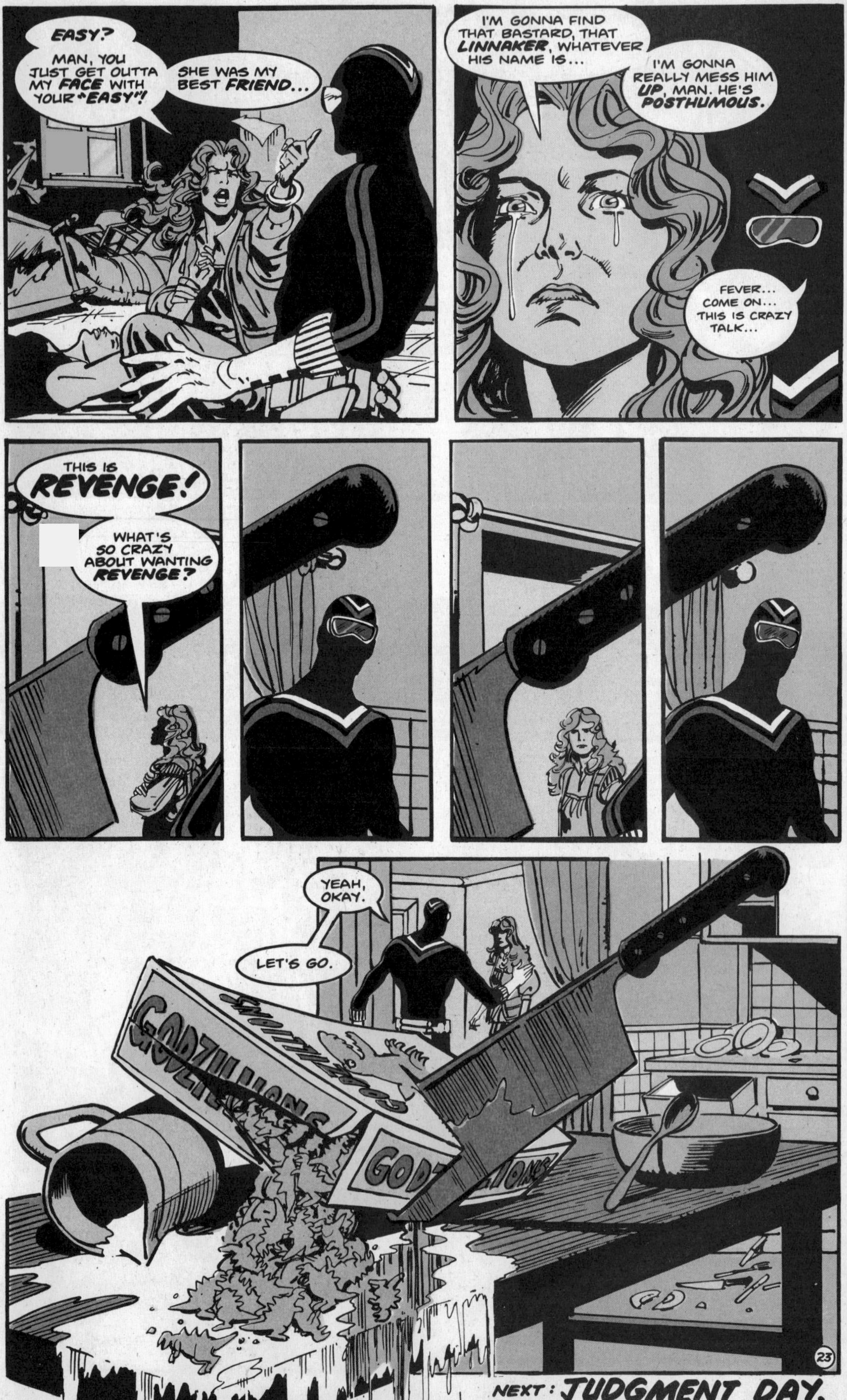
EASY?
MAN, YOU JUST GET OUTTA MY FACE WITH YOUR "EASY"!
SHE WAS MY BEST FRIEND...
I'M GONNA FIND THAT BASTARD, THAT LINNAKER, WHATEVER HIS NAME IS...
I'M GONNA REALLY MESS HIM UP, MAN. HE'S POSTHUMOUS.
FEVER... COME ON... THIS IS CRAZY TALK...
THIS IS REVENGE!
WHAT'S SO CRAZY ABOUT WANTING REVENGE?
YEAH, OKAY.
LET'S GO.
GODZILLIONS
GODZILLIONS
GOD...IONS
23
NEXT: JUDGMENT DAY.

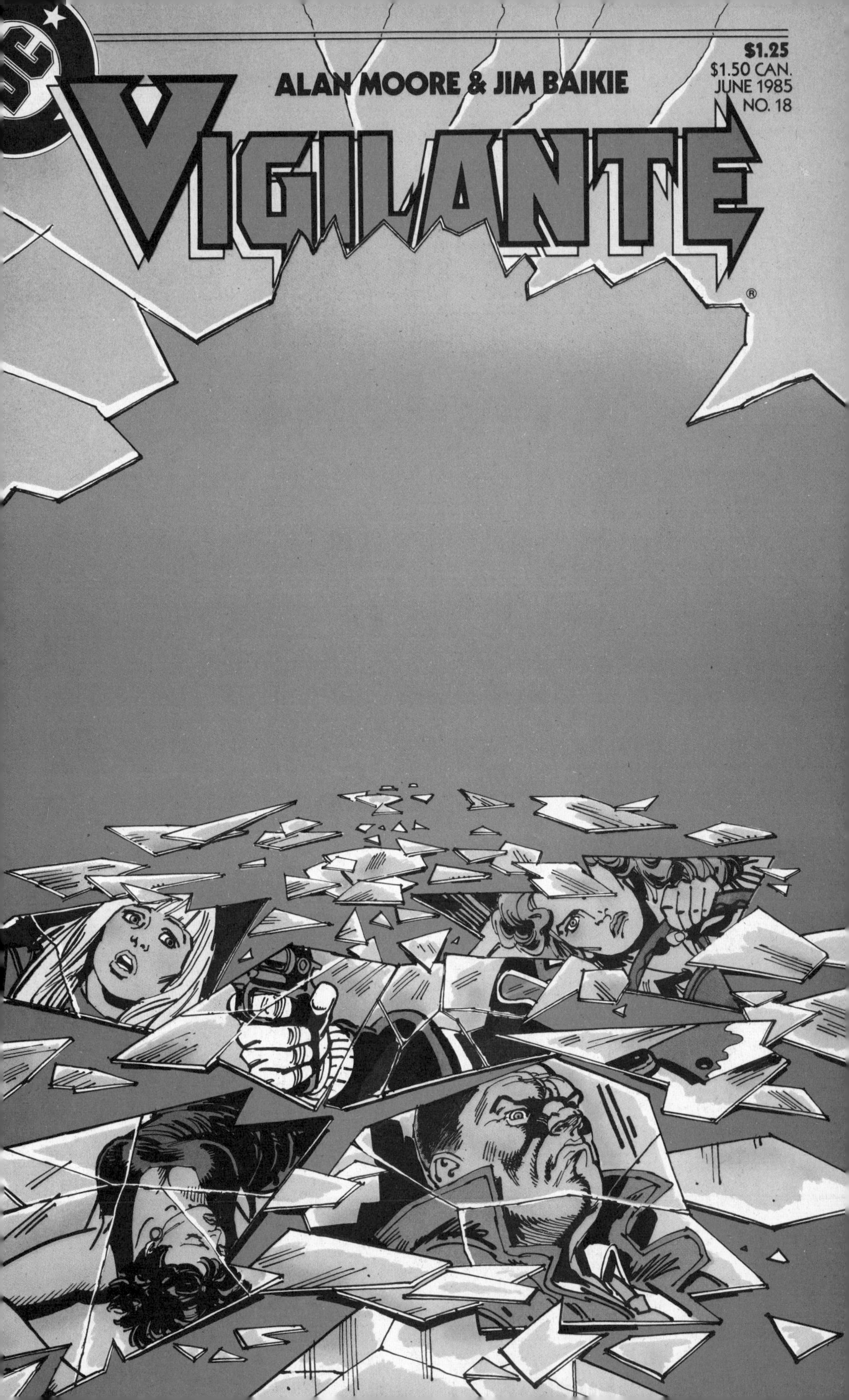
ALAN MOORE & JIM BAIKIE
VIGILANTE
$1.25
$1.50 CAN.
JUNE 1985
NO. 18

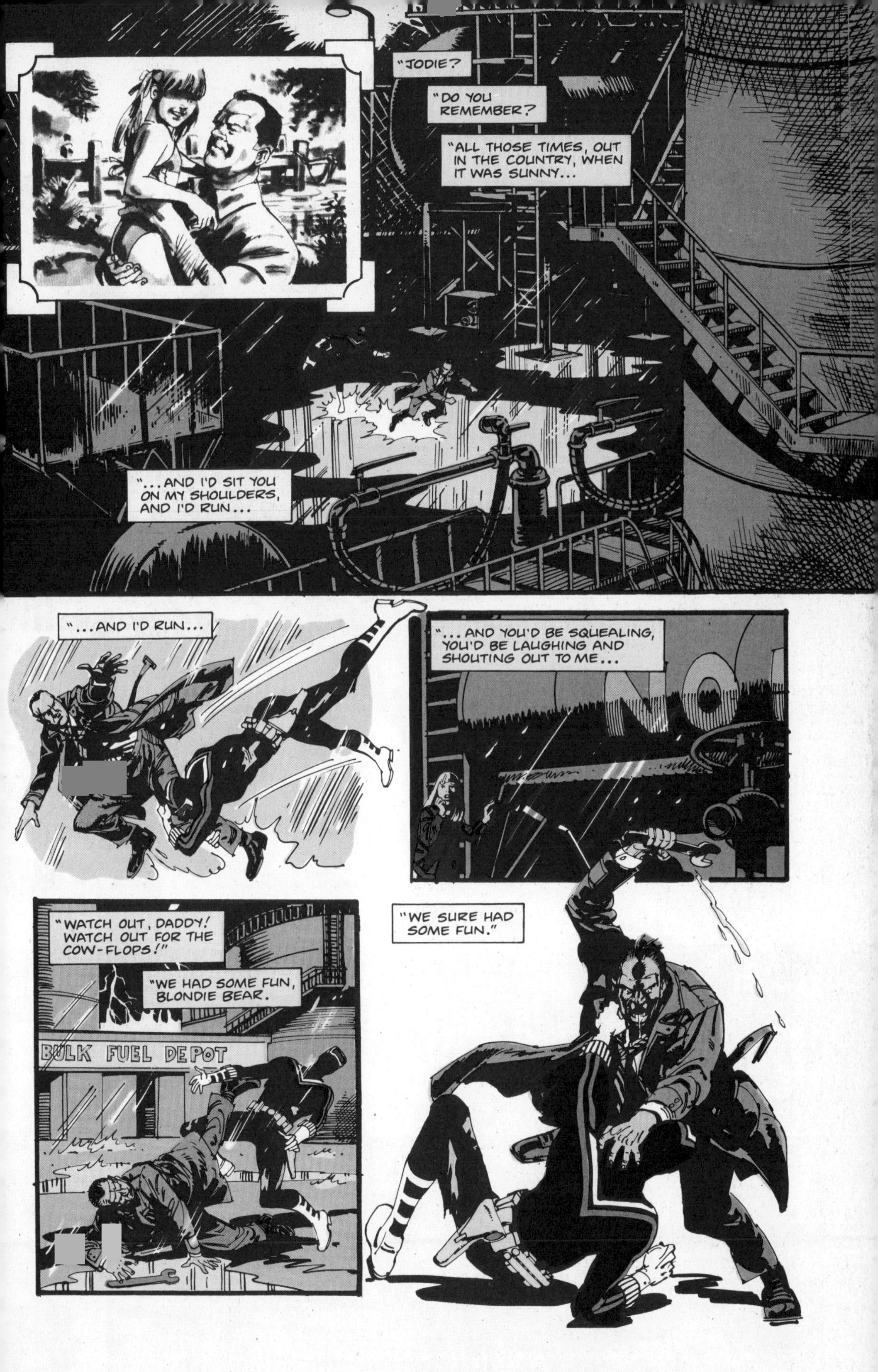
"JODIE?
"DO YOU REMEMBER?
"ALL THOSE TIMES, OUT IN THE COUNTRY, WHEN IT WAS SUNNY...
"...AND I'D SIT YOU ON MY SHOULDERS, AND I'D RUN...
"...AND I'D RUN...
"...AND YOU'D BE SQUEALING, YOU'D BE LAUGHING AND SHOUTING OUT TO ME...
"WATCH OUT, DADDY! WATCH OUT FOR THE COW-FLOPS!"
"WE HAD SOME FUN, BLONDIE BEAR.
BULK FUEL DEPOT
"WE SURE HAD SOME FUN."

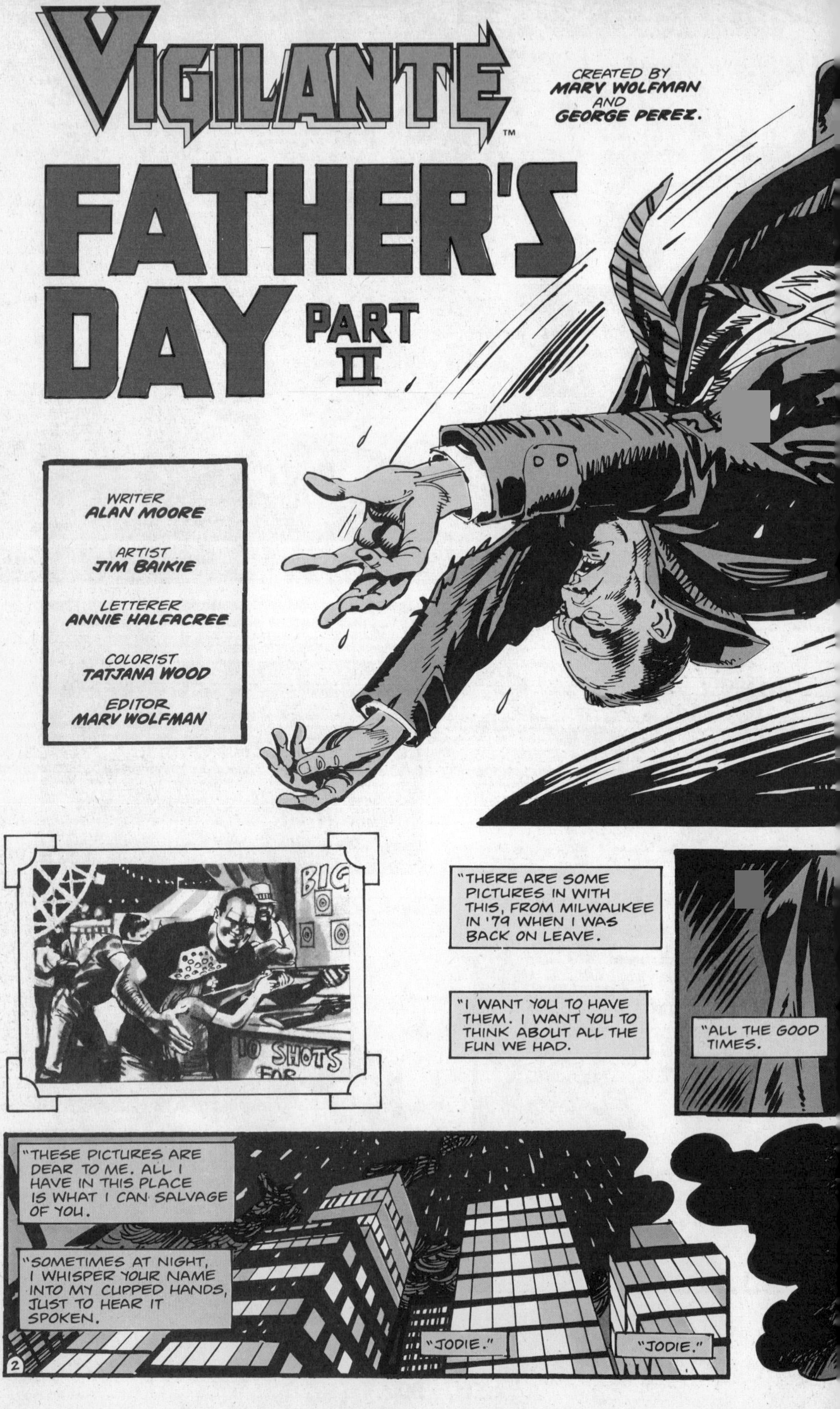

VIGILANTE™
CREATED BY MARV WOLFMAN AND GEORGE PEREZ.
FATHER'S DAY PART II
WRITER ALAN MOORE
ARTIST JIM BAIKIE
LETTERER ANNIE HALFACREE
COLORIST TATJANA WOOD
EDITOR MARV WOLFMAN
BIG
10 SHOTS FOR
"THERE ARE SOME PICTURES IN WITH THIS, FROM MILWAUKEE IN '79 WHEN I WAS BACK ON LEAVE.
"I WANT YOU TO HAVE THEM. I WANT YOU TO THINK ABOUT ALL THE FUN WE HAD.
"ALL THE GOOD TIMES.
"THESE PICTURES ARE DEAR TO ME. ALL I HAVE IN THIS PLACE IS WHAT I CAN SALVAGE OF YOU.
"SOMETIMES AT NIGHT, I WHISPER YOUR NAME INTO MY CUPPED HANDS, JUST TO HEAR IT SPOKEN.
"JODIE."
"JODIE."
2

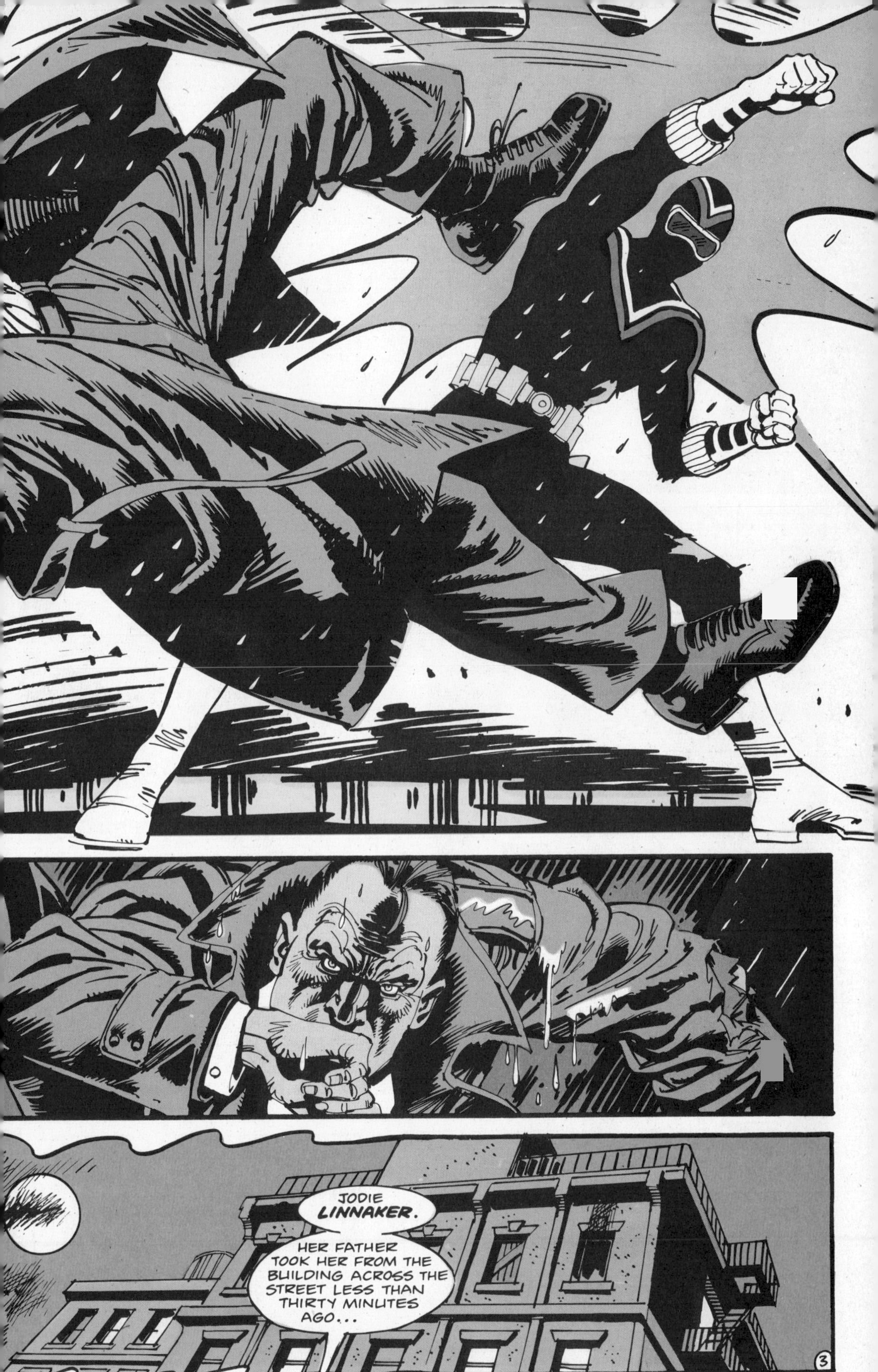
JODIE LINNAKER.
HER FATHER TOOK HER FROM THE BUILDING ACROSS THE STREET LESS THAN THIRTY MINUTES AGO...
3

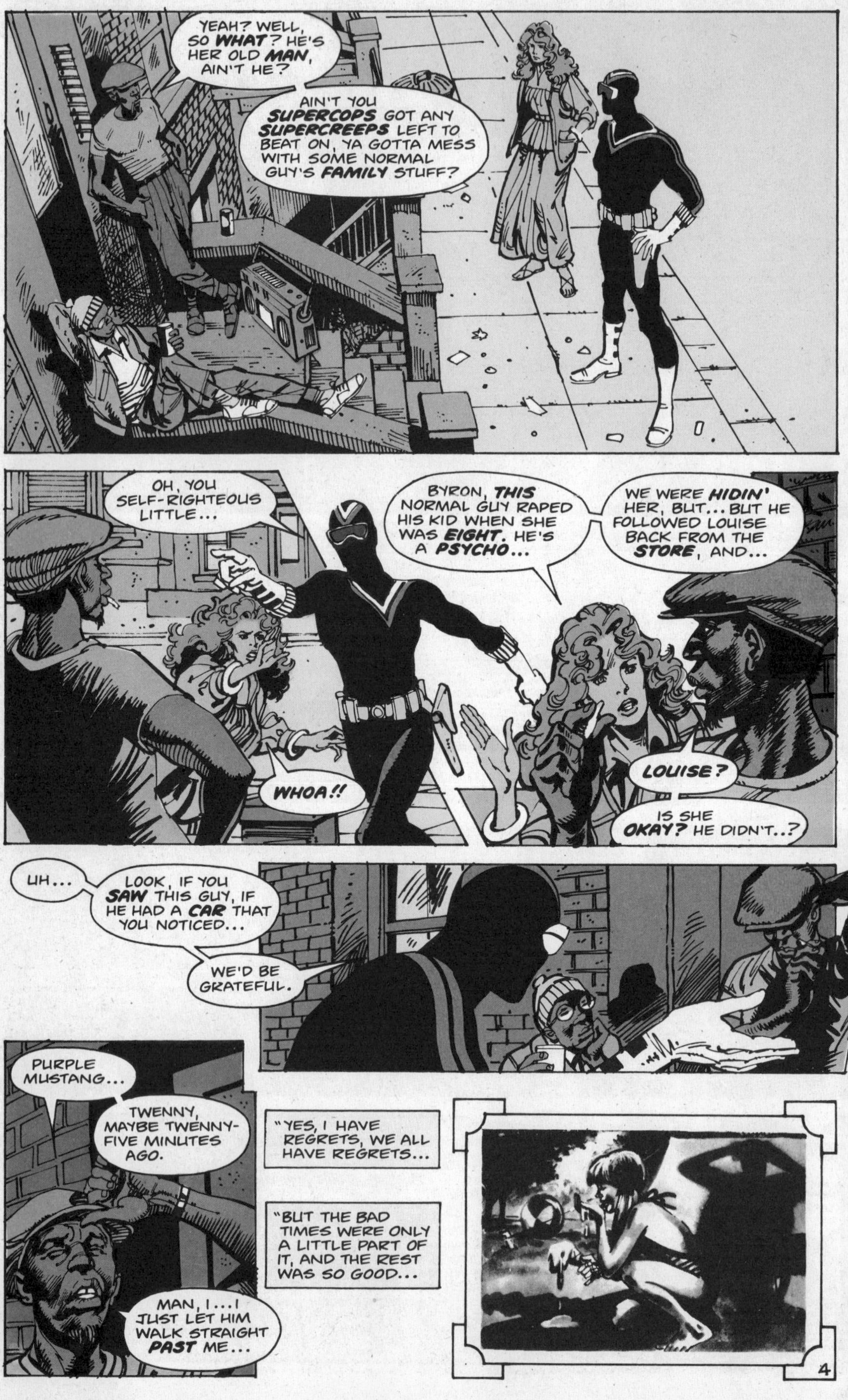

YEAH? WELL, SO WHAT? HE'S HER OLD MAN, AIN'T HE?
AIN'T YOU SUPERCOPS GOT ANY SUPERCREEPS LEFT TO BEAT ON, YA GOTTA MESS WITH SOME NORMAL GUY'S FAMILY STUFF?
OH, YOU SELF-RIGHTEOUS LITTLE...
BYRON, THIS NORMAL GUY RAPED HIS KID WHEN SHE WAS EIGHT. HE'S A PSYCHO...
WE WERE HIDIN' HER, BUT... BUT HE FOLLOWED LOUISE BACK FROM THE STORE, AND...
WHOA!!
LOUISE?
IS SHE OKAY? HE DIDN'T..?
UH...
LOOK, IF YOU SAW THIS GUY, IF HE HAD A CAR THAT YOU NOTICED...
WE'D BE GRATEFUL.
PURPLE MUSTANG...
TWENNY, MAYBE TWENNY-FIVE MINUTES AGO.
MAN, I...I JUST LET HIM WALK STRAIGHT PAST ME...
"YES, I HAVE REGRETS, WE ALL HAVE REGRETS...
"BUT THE BAD TIMES WERE ONLY A LITTLE PART OF IT, AND THE REST WAS SO GOOD...

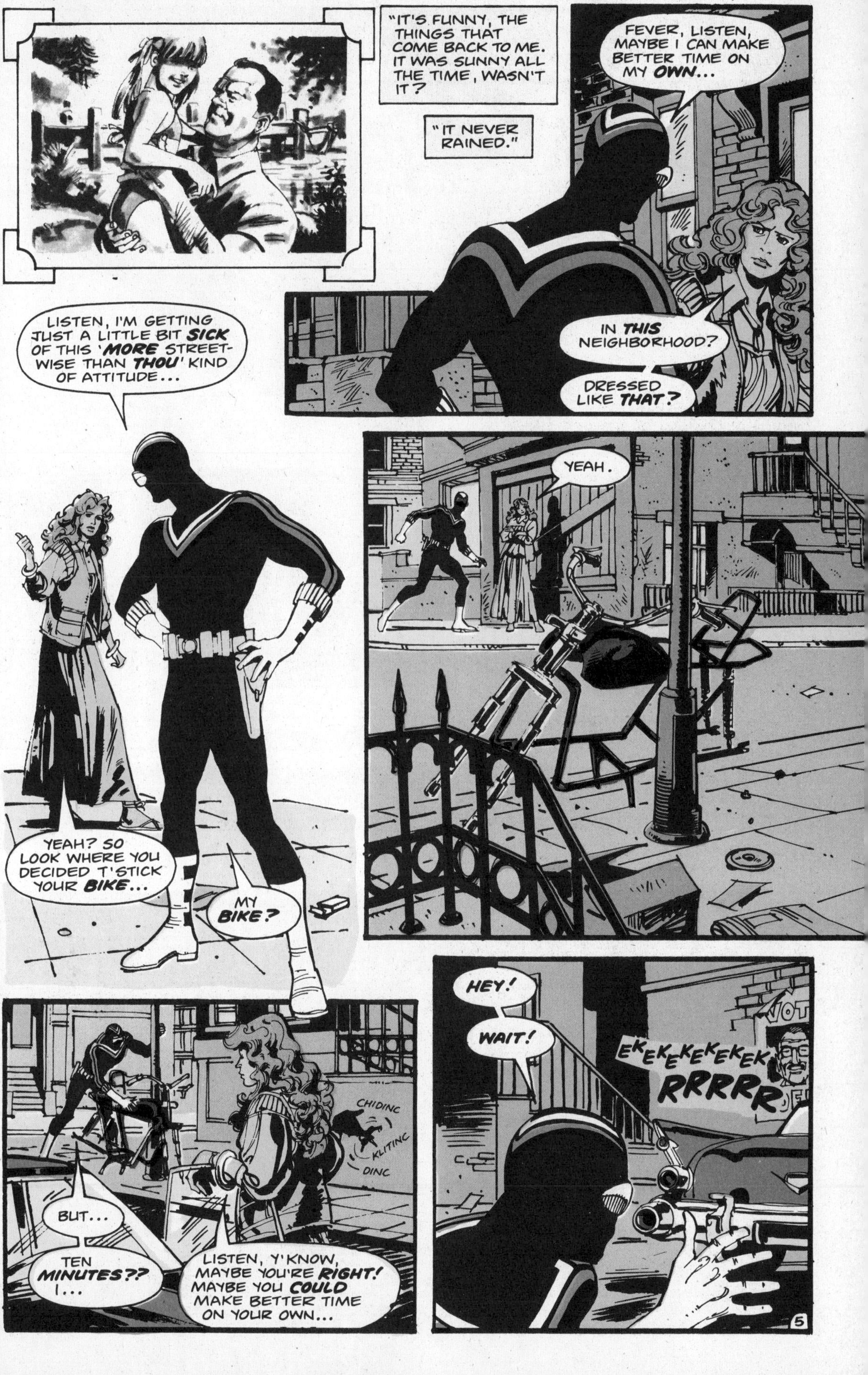

"IT'S FUNNY, THE THINGS THAT COME BACK TO ME. IT WAS SUNNY ALL THE TIME, WASN'T IT?
"IT NEVER RAINED."
FEVER, LISTEN, MAYBE I CAN MAKE BETTER TIME ON MY OWN...
IN THIS NEIGHBORHOOD?
DRESSED LIKE THAT?
LISTEN, I'M GETTING JUST A LITTLE BIT SICK OF THIS 'MORE STREET-WISE THAN THOU' KIND OF ATTITUDE...
YEAH? SO LOOK WHERE YOU DECIDED T'STICK YOUR BIKE...
MY BIKE?
YEAH.
CHIDINC
KLITINC
DINC
BUT...
TEN MINUTES?? I...
LISTEN, Y'KNOW, MAYBE YOU'RE RIGHT! MAYBE YOU COULD MAKE BETTER TIME ON YOUR OWN...
HEY!
WAIT!
EKEKEKEKEKEKEK
RRRRR

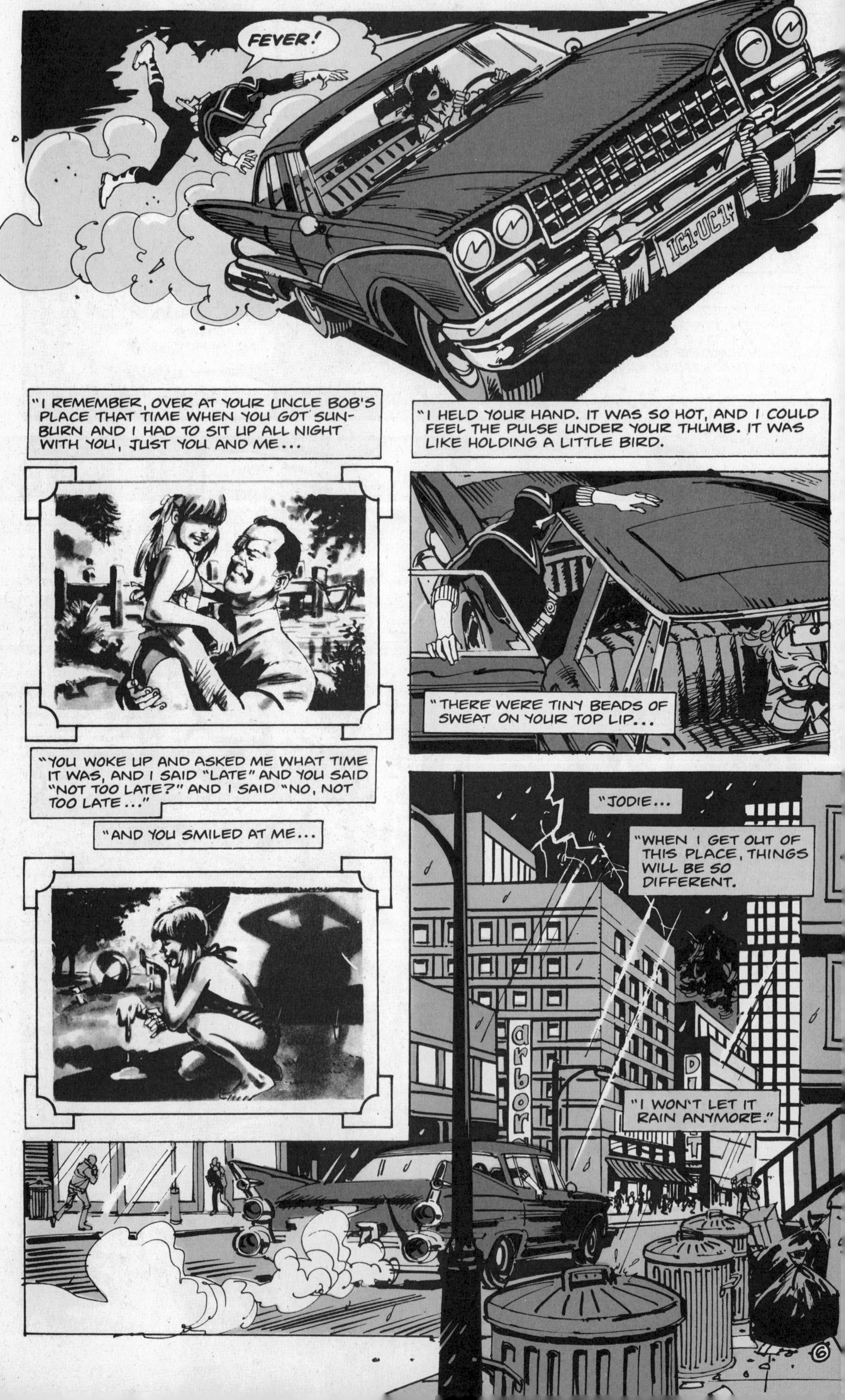

FEVER!
IC1·UC1
"I REMEMBER, OVER AT YOUR UNCLE BOB'S PLACE THAT TIME WHEN YOU GOT SUN-BURN AND I HAD TO SIT UP ALL NIGHT WITH YOU, JUST YOU AND ME...
"I HELD YOUR HAND. IT WAS SO HOT, AND I COULD FEEL THE PULSE UNDER YOUR THUMB. IT WAS LIKE HOLDING A LITTLE BIRD.
"THERE WERE TINY BEADS OF SWEAT ON YOUR TOP LIP...
"YOU WOKE UP AND ASKED ME WHAT TIME IT WAS, AND I SAID "LATE" AND YOU SAID "NOT TOO LATE?" AND I SAID "NO, NOT TOO LATE..."
"AND YOU SMILED AT ME...
"JODIE...
"WHEN I GET OUT OF THIS PLACE, THINGS WILL BE SO DIFFERENT.
arbor
"I WON'T LET IT RAIN ANYMORE."
6

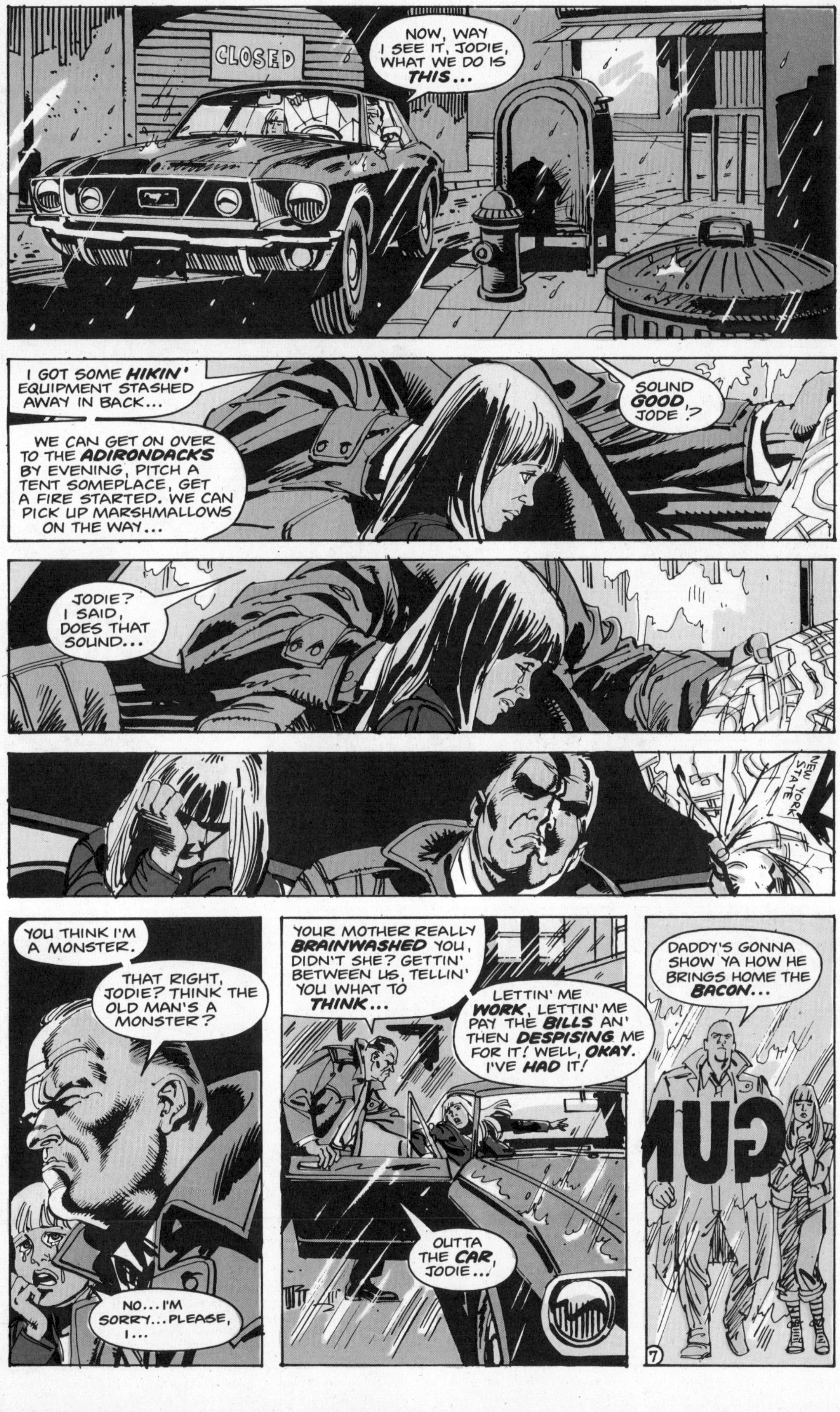

CLOSED
NOW, WAY I SEE IT, JODIE, WHAT WE DO IS THIS...
I GOT SOME HIKIN' EQUIPMENT STASHED AWAY IN BACK...
WE CAN GET ON OVER TO THE ADIRONDACKS BY EVENING, PITCH A TENT SOMEPLACE, GET A FIRE STARTED. WE CAN PICK UP MARSHMALLOWS ON THE WAY...
SOUND GOOD JODE !?
JODIE? I SAID, DOES THAT SOUND...
NEW YORK STATE
YOU THINK I'M A MONSTER.
THAT RIGHT, JODIE? THINK THE OLD MAN'S A MONSTER?
NO... I'M SORRY... PLEASE, I...
YOUR MOTHER REALLY BRAINWASHED YOU, DIDN'T SHE? GETTIN' BETWEEN US, TELLIN' YOU WHAT TO THINK...
LETTIN' ME WORK, LETTIN' ME PAY THE BILLS AN' THEN DESPISING ME FOR IT! WELL, OKAY. I'VE HAD IT!
OUTTA THE CAR, JODIE...!
DADDY'S GONNA SHOW YA HOW HE BRINGS HOME THE BACON...
GUN

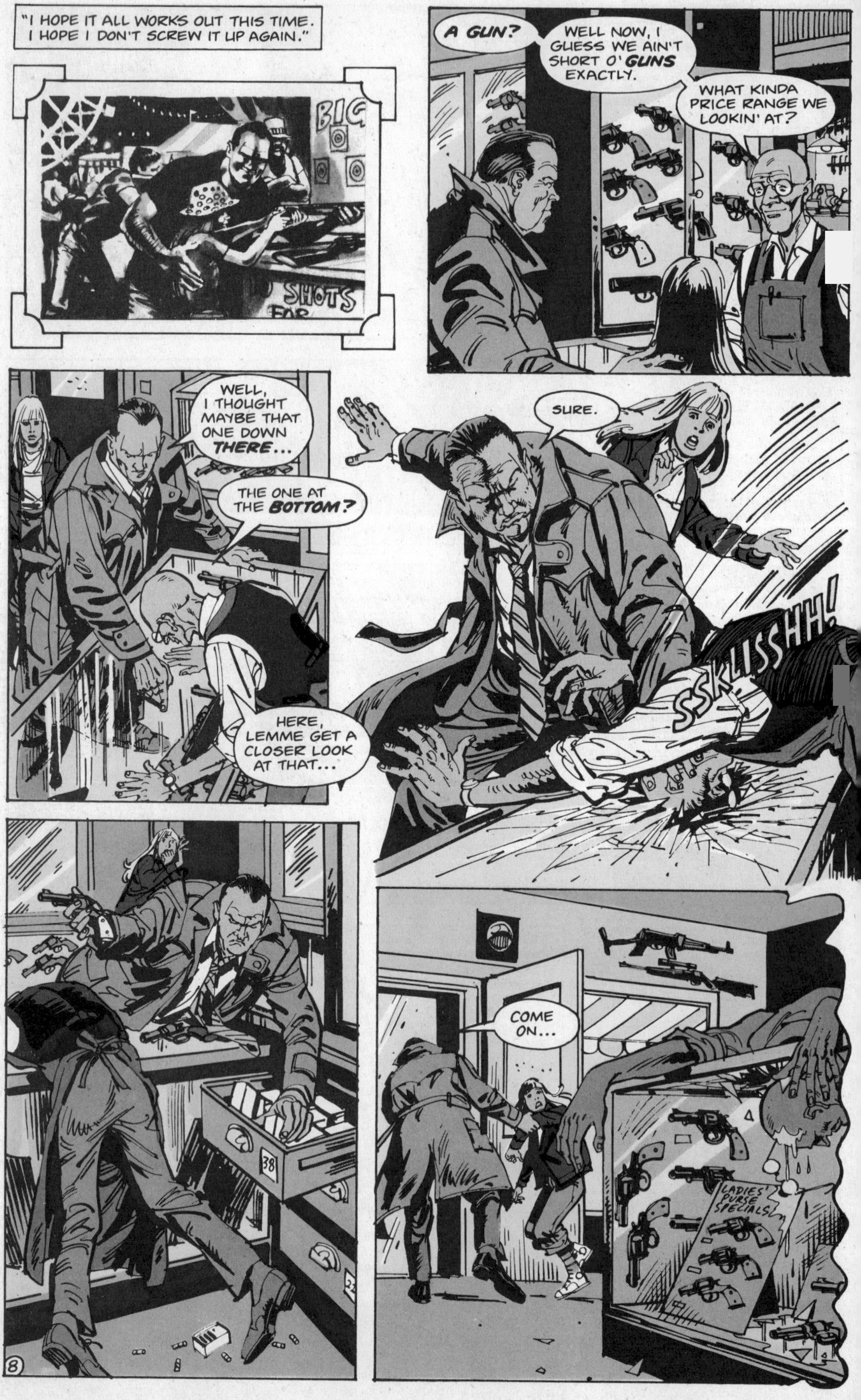
"I HOPE IT ALL WORKS OUT THIS TIME. I HOPE I DON'T SCREW IT UP AGAIN."
BIG
SHOTS
A GUN?
WELL NOW, I GUESS WE AIN'T SHORT O' GUNS EXACTLY.
WHAT KINDA PRICE RANGE WE LOOKIN' AT?
WELL, I THOUGHT MAYBE THAT ONE DOWN THERE...
THE ONE AT THE BOTTOM?
HERE, LEMME GET A CLOSER LOOK AT THAT...
SURE.
SSKLISSHH!
38
8
COME ON...
LADIES' PURSE SPECIALS

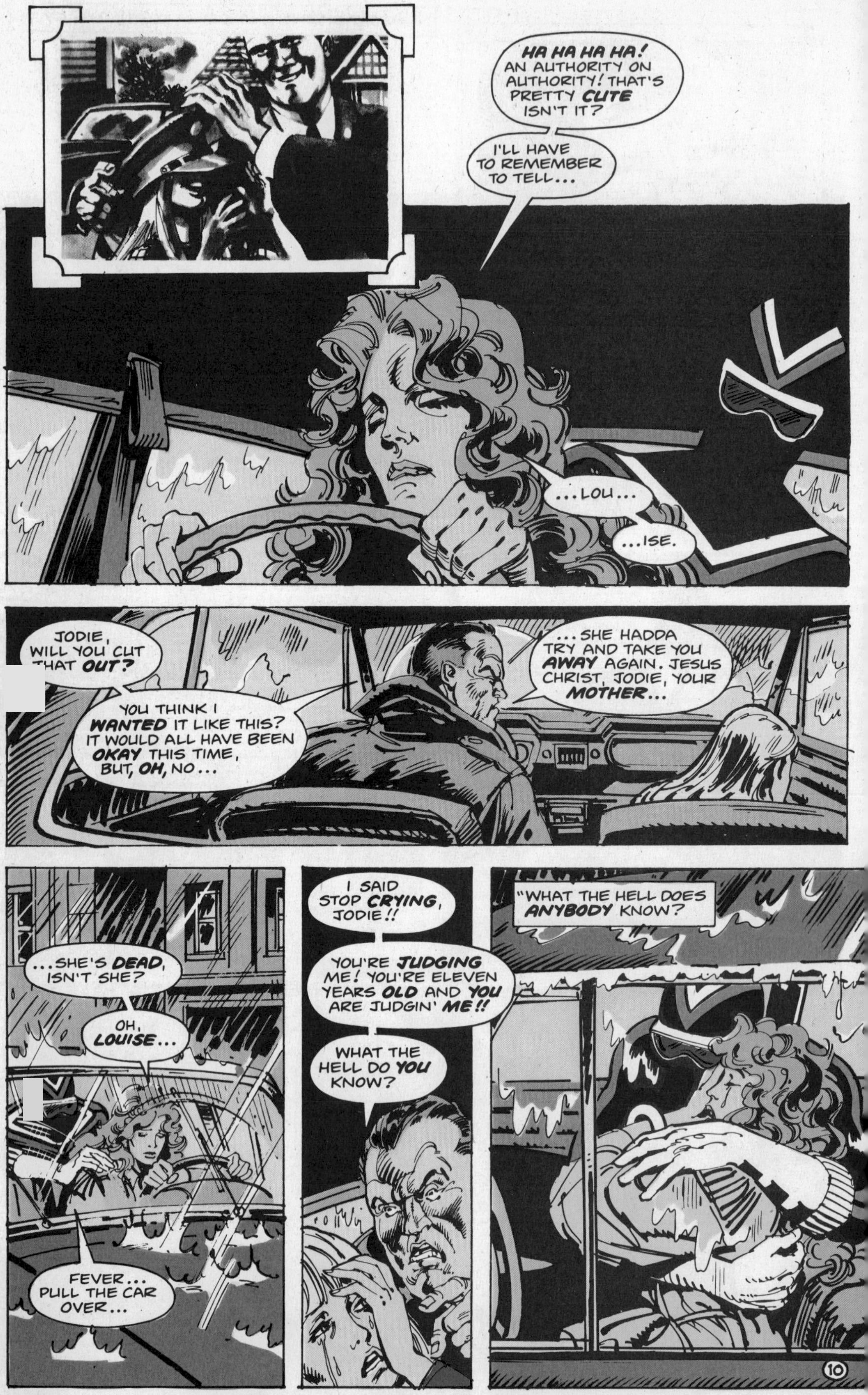
HA HA HA HA! AN AUTHORITY ON AUTHORITY! THAT'S PRETTY CUTE ISN'T IT?
I'LL HAVE TO REMEMBER TO TELL...
...LOU...
...ISE.
JODIE, WILL YOU CUT THAT OUT?
YOU THINK I WANTED IT LIKE THIS? IT WOULD ALL HAVE BEEN OKAY THIS TIME, BUT, OH, NO...
...SHE HADDA TRY AND TAKE YOU AWAY AGAIN. JESUS CHRIST, JODIE, YOUR MOTHER...
...SHE'S DEAD, ISN'T SHE?
OH, LOUISE...
FEVER... PULL THE CAR OVER...
I SAID STOP CRYING, JODIE!!
YOU'RE JUDGING ME! YOU'RE ELEVEN YEARS OLD AND YOU ARE JUDGIN' ME!!
WHAT THE HELL DO YOU KNOW?
"WHAT THE HELL DOES ANYBODY KNOW?

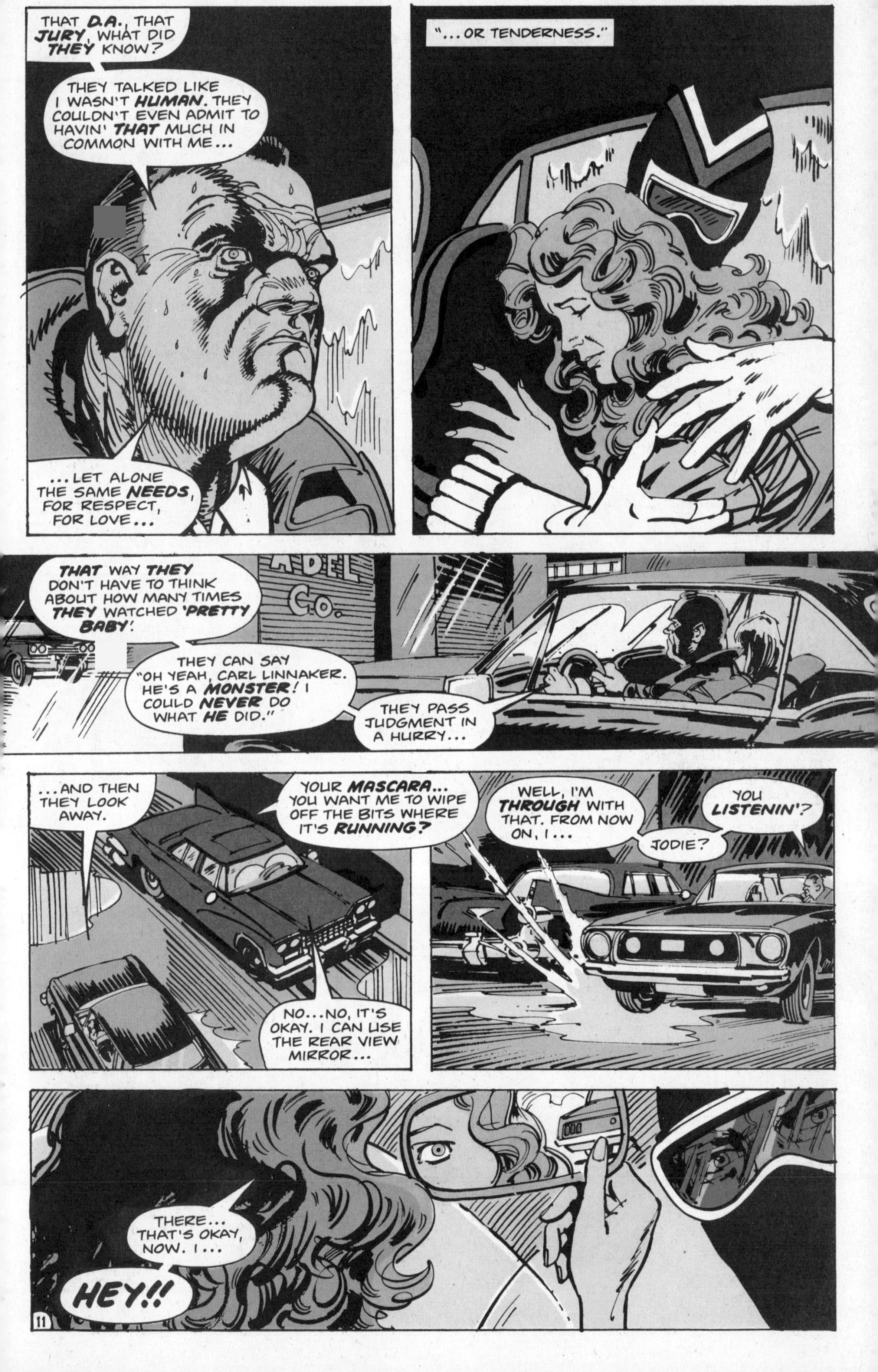

THAT D.A., THAT JURY, WHAT DID THEY KNOW?
THEY TALKED LIKE I WASN'T HUMAN. THEY COULDN'T EVEN ADMIT TO HAVIN' THAT MUCH IN COMMON WITH ME...
...LET ALONE THE SAME NEEDS, FOR RESPECT, FOR LOVE...
"...OR TENDERNESS."
THAT WAY THEY DON'T HAVE TO THINK ABOUT HOW MANY TIMES THEY WATCHED 'PRETTY BABY'.
THEY CAN SAY "OH YEAH, CARL LINNAKER. HE'S A MONSTER! I COULD NEVER DO WHAT HE DID."
THEY PASS JUDGMENT IN A HURRY...
...AND THEN THEY LOOK AWAY.
YOUR MASCARA... YOU WANT ME TO WIPE OFF THE BITS WHERE IT'S RUNNING?
NO...NO, IT'S OKAY. I CAN USE THE REAR VIEW MIRROR...
WELL, I'M THROUGH WITH THAT. FROM NOW ON, I...
JODIE?
YOU LISTENIN'?
THERE... THAT'S OKAY, NOW. I...
HEY!!
11

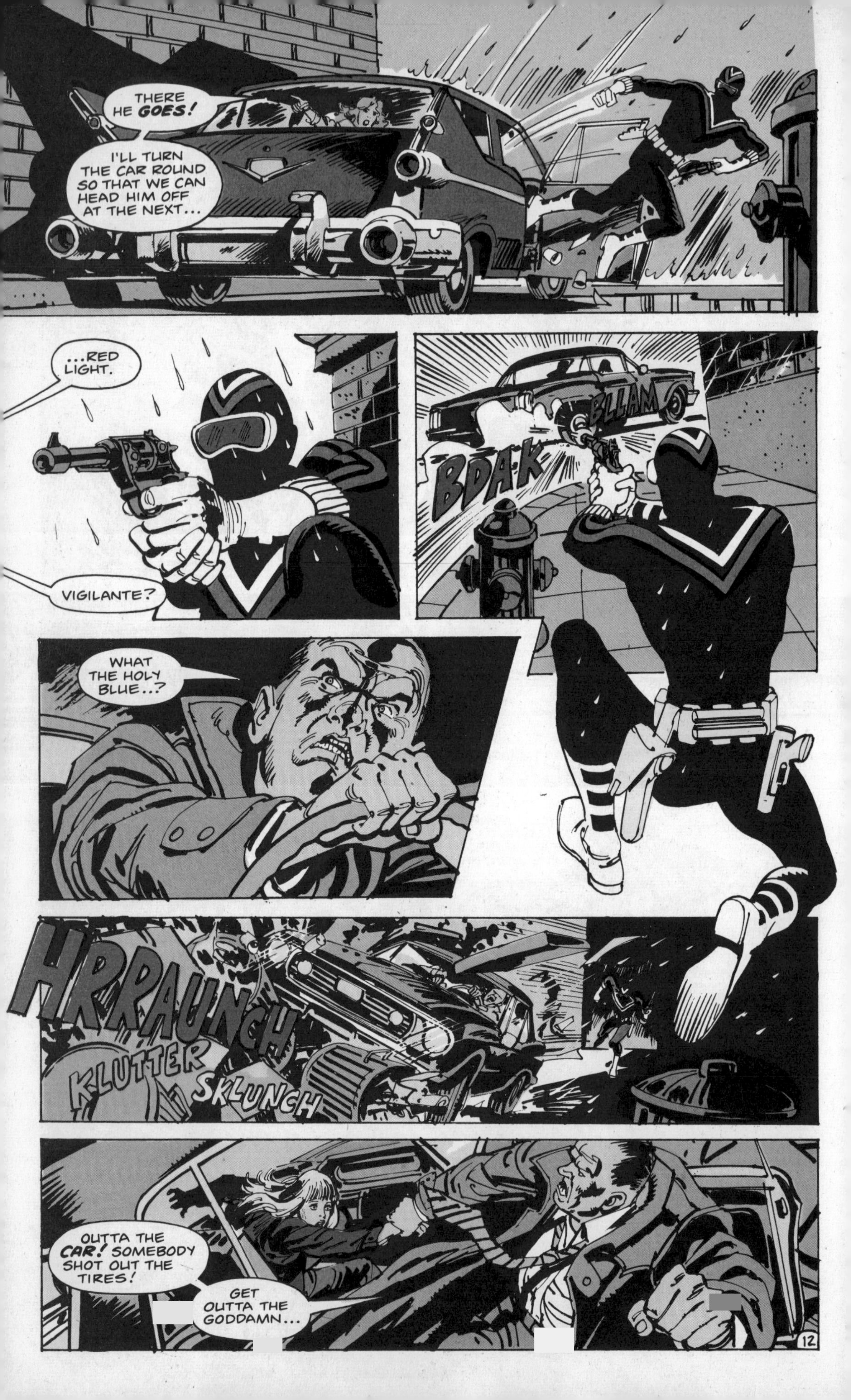
THERE HE GOES!
I'LL TURN THE CAR ROUND SO THAT WE CAN HEAD HIM OFF AT THE NEXT...
...RED LIGHT.
VIGILANTE?
BLLAM
BDAK
WHAT THE HOLY BLUE..?
HRRAUNCH
KLUTTER
SKLUNCH
OUTTA THE CAR! SOMEBODY SHOT OUT THE TIRES!
GET OUTTA THE GODDAMN...
12

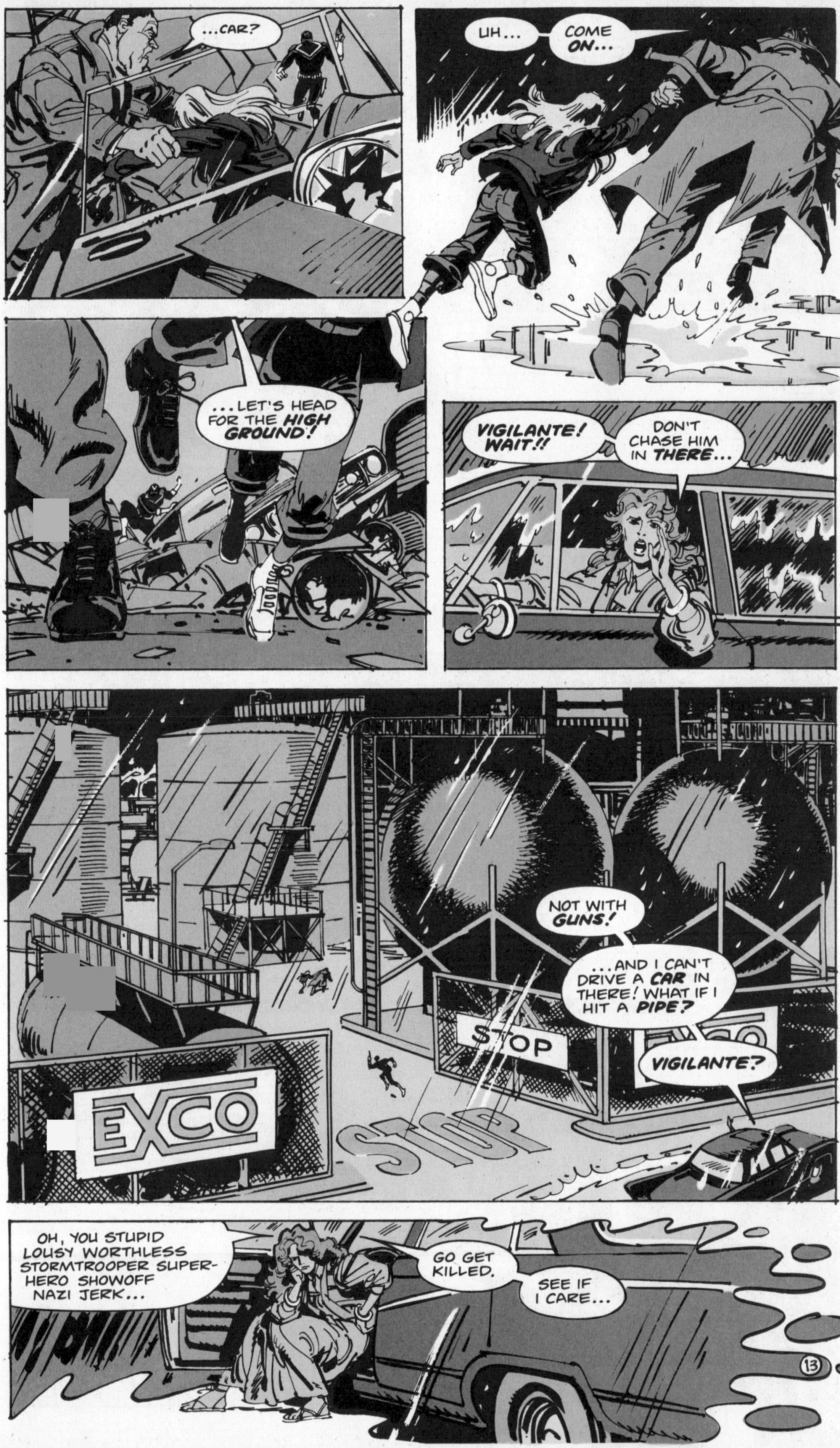
...CAR?
UH...
COME ON...
...LET'S HEAD FOR THE HIGH GROUND!
VIGILANTE! WAIT!!
DON'T CHASE HIM IN THERE...
NOT WITH GUNS!
...AND I CAN'T DRIVE A CAR IN THERE! WHAT IF I HIT A PIPE?
VIGILANTE?
EXCO
STOP
STOP
OH, YOU STUPID LOUSY WORTHLESS STORMTROOPER SUPER-HERO SHOWOFF NAZI JERK...
GO GET KILLED.
SEE IF I CARE...
13

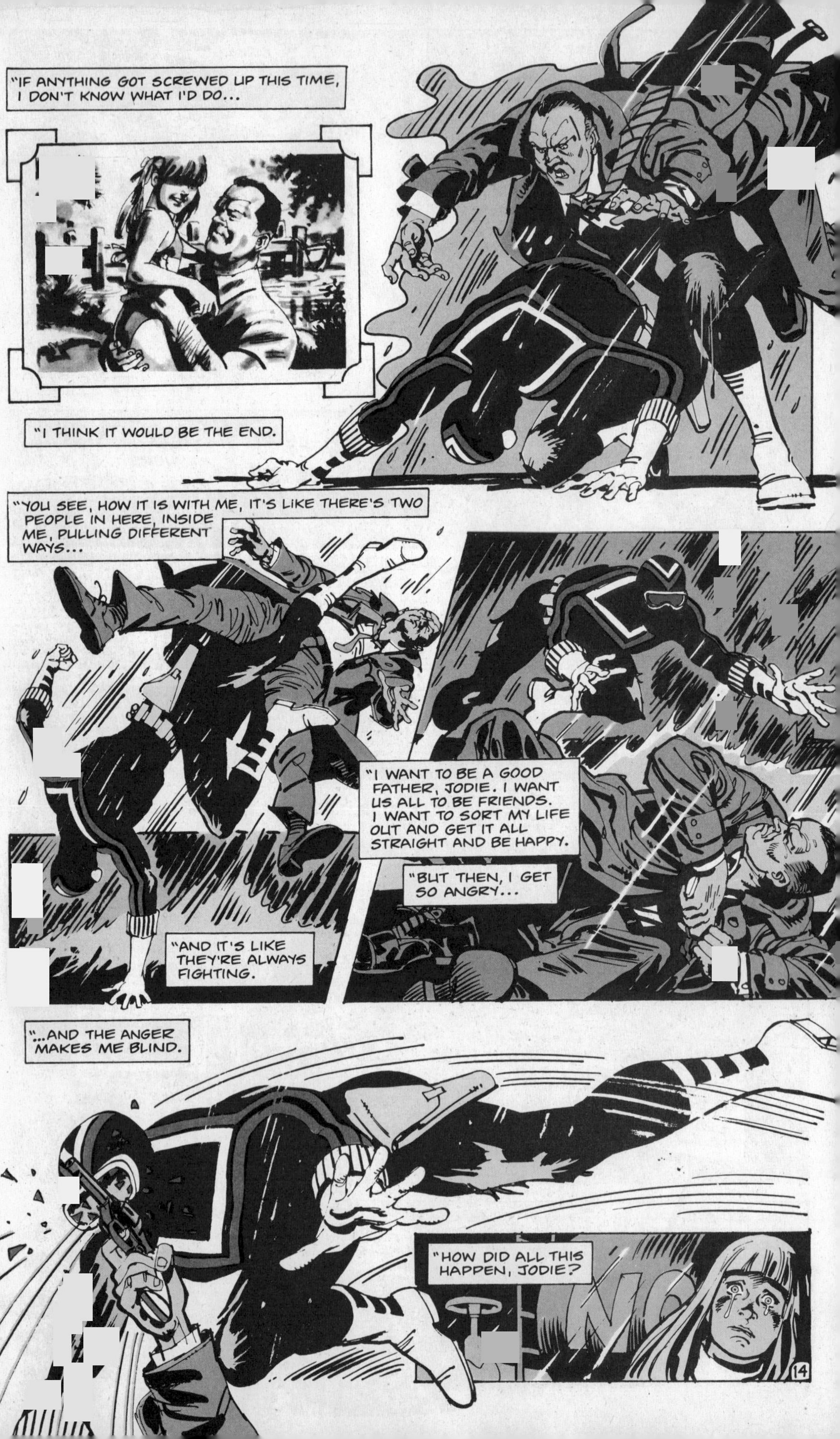

"IF ANYTHING GOT SCREWED UP THIS TIME, I DON'T KNOW WHAT I'D DO...
"I THINK IT WOULD BE THE END.
"YOU SEE, HOW IT IS WITH ME, IT'S LIKE THERE'S TWO PEOPLE IN HERE, INSIDE ME, PULLING DIFFERENT WAYS...
"AND IT'S LIKE THEY'RE ALWAYS FIGHTING.
"I WANT TO BE A GOOD FATHER, JODIE. I WANT US ALL TO BE FRIENDS. I WANT TO SORT MY LIFE OUT AND GET IT ALL STRAIGHT AND BE HAPPY.
"BUT THEN, I GET SO ANGRY...
"...AND THE ANGER MAKES ME BLIND.
"HOW DID ALL THIS HAPPEN, JODIE?

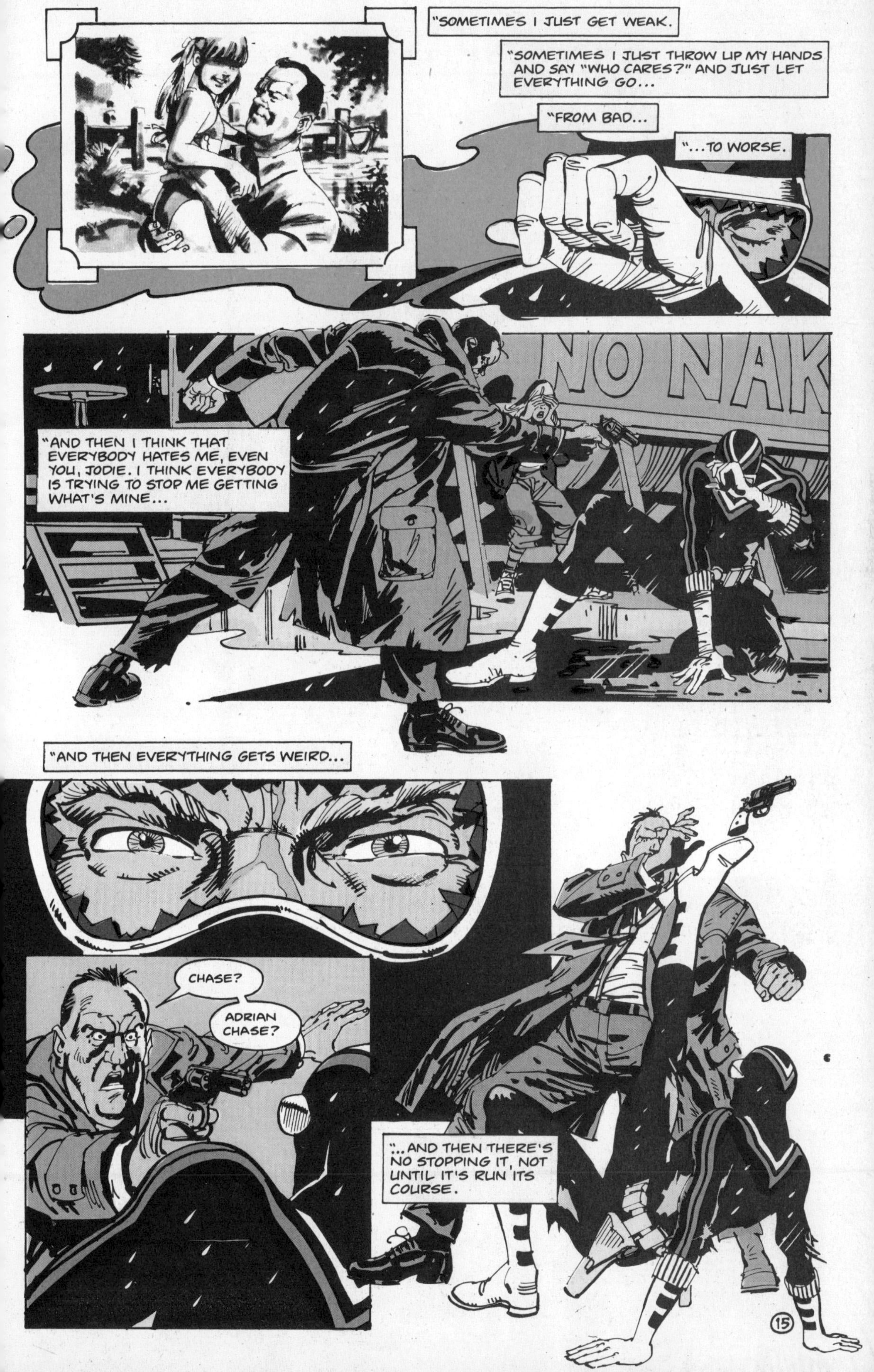
"SOMETIMES I JUST GET WEAK.
"SOMETIMES I JUST THROW UP MY HANDS AND SAY "WHO CARES?" AND JUST LET EVERYTHING GO...
"FROM BAD...
"...TO WORSE.
NO NAK
"AND THEN I THINK THAT EVERYBODY HATES ME, EVEN YOU, JODIE. I THINK EVERYBODY IS TRYING TO STOP ME GETTING WHAT'S MINE...
"AND THEN EVERYTHING GETS WEIRD...
CHASE?
ADRIAN CHASE?
"...AND THEN THERE'S NO STOPPING IT, NOT UNTIL IT'S RUN ITS COURSE.

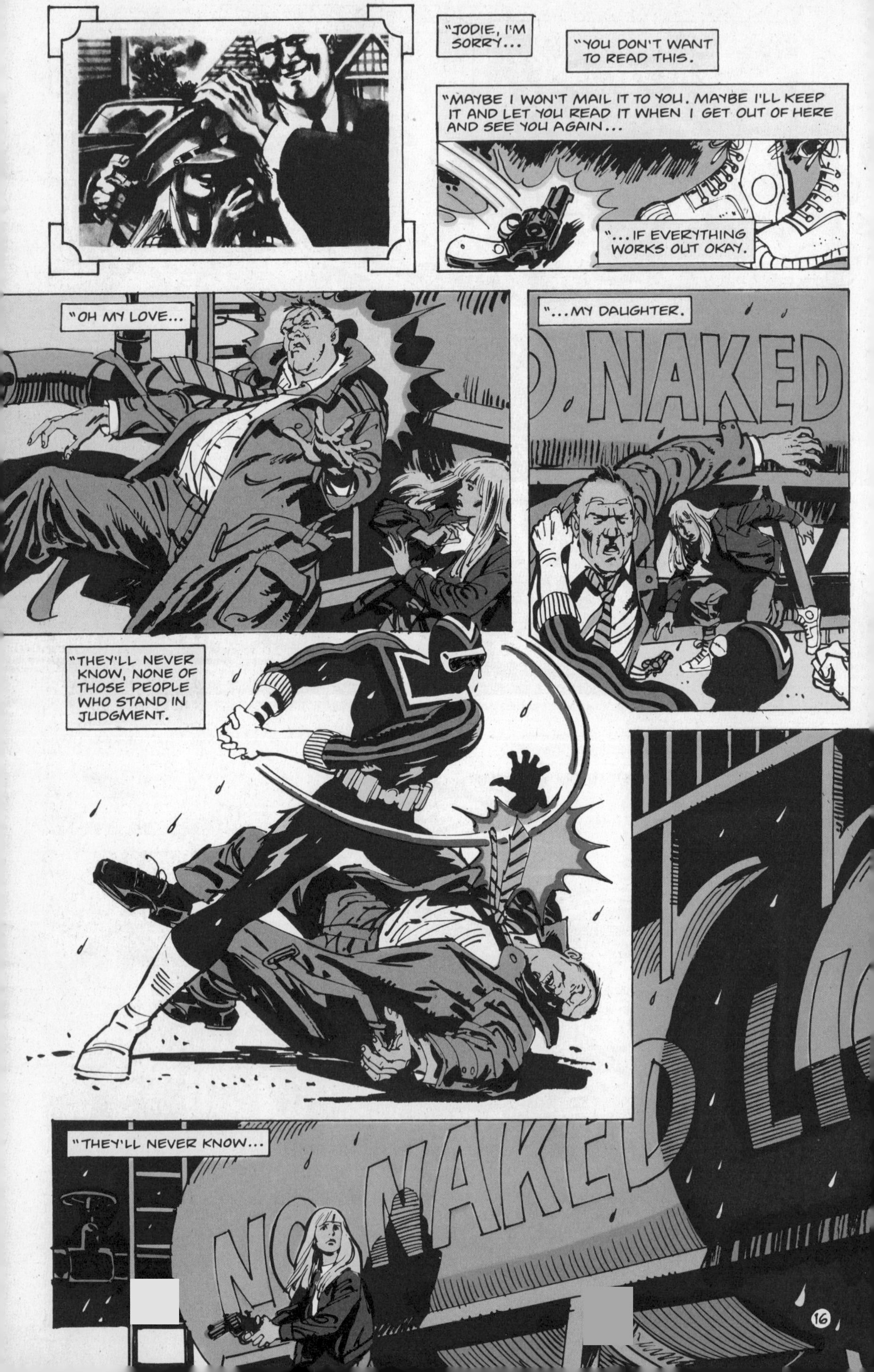
"JODIE, I'M SORRY...
"YOU DON'T WANT TO READ THIS.
"MAYBE I WON'T MAIL IT TO YOU. MAYBE I'LL KEEP IT AND LET YOU READ IT WHEN I GET OUT OF HERE AND SEE YOU AGAIN...
"...IF EVERYTHING WORKS OUT OKAY.
"OH MY LOVE...
"...MY DAUGHTER.
NAKED
"THEY'LL NEVER KNOW, NONE OF THOSE PEOPLE WHO STAND IN JUDGMENT.
"THEY'LL NEVER KNOW...
NO NAKED

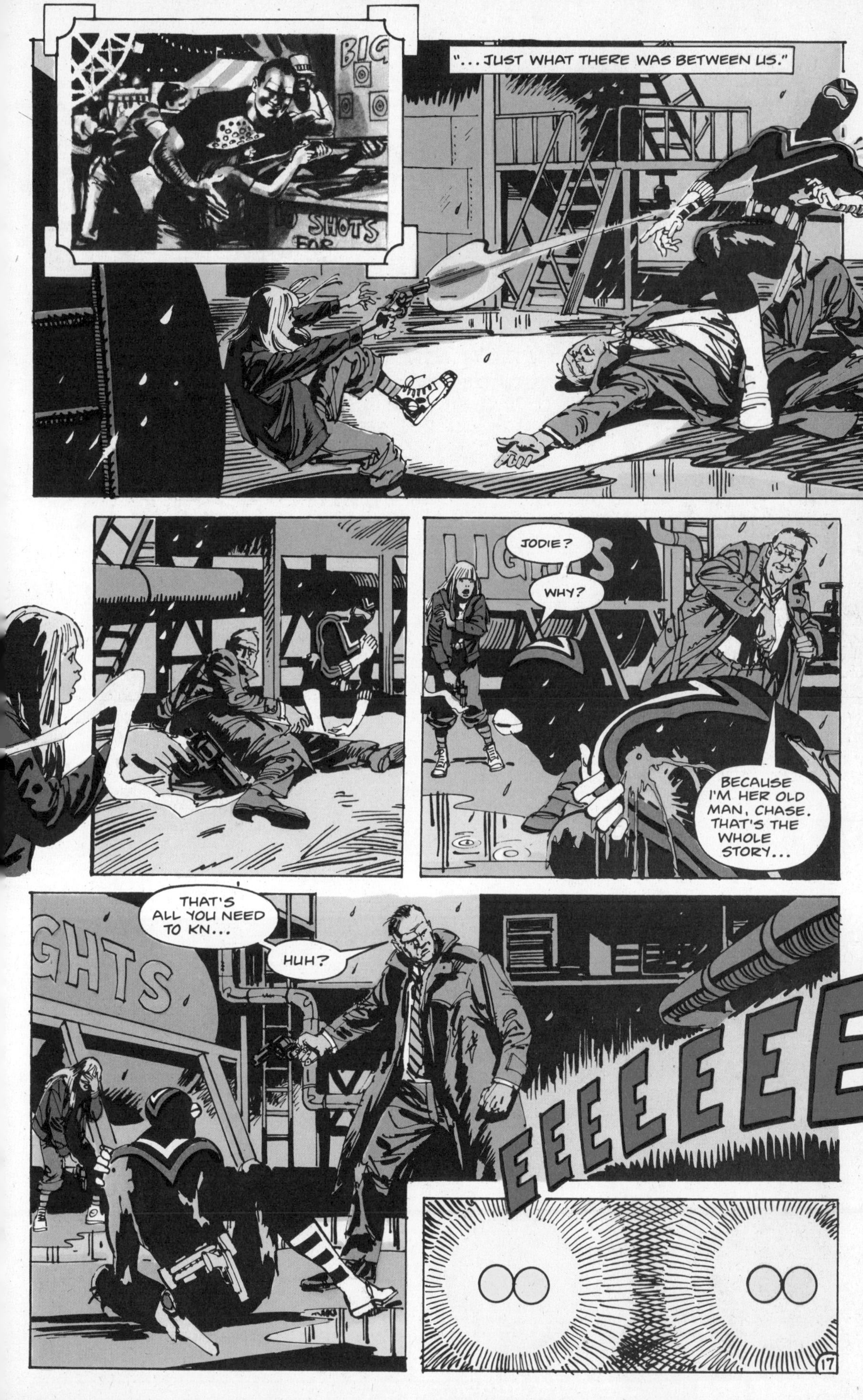

"... JUST WHAT THERE WAS BETWEEN US."
JODIE?
WHY?
BECAUSE I'M HER OLD MAN, CHASE. THAT'S THE WHOLE STORY...
THAT'S ALL YOU NEED TO KN...
HUH?
EEEEEEE

EEEEEEEEEEEEEEEEEEEEE

EEEEEEEEEE EE BWUMK

KLUTCH RRRRRRRR

OH...   OUUH...

FEVER!

FEVER, DON'T, DON'T MAKE ME...

18

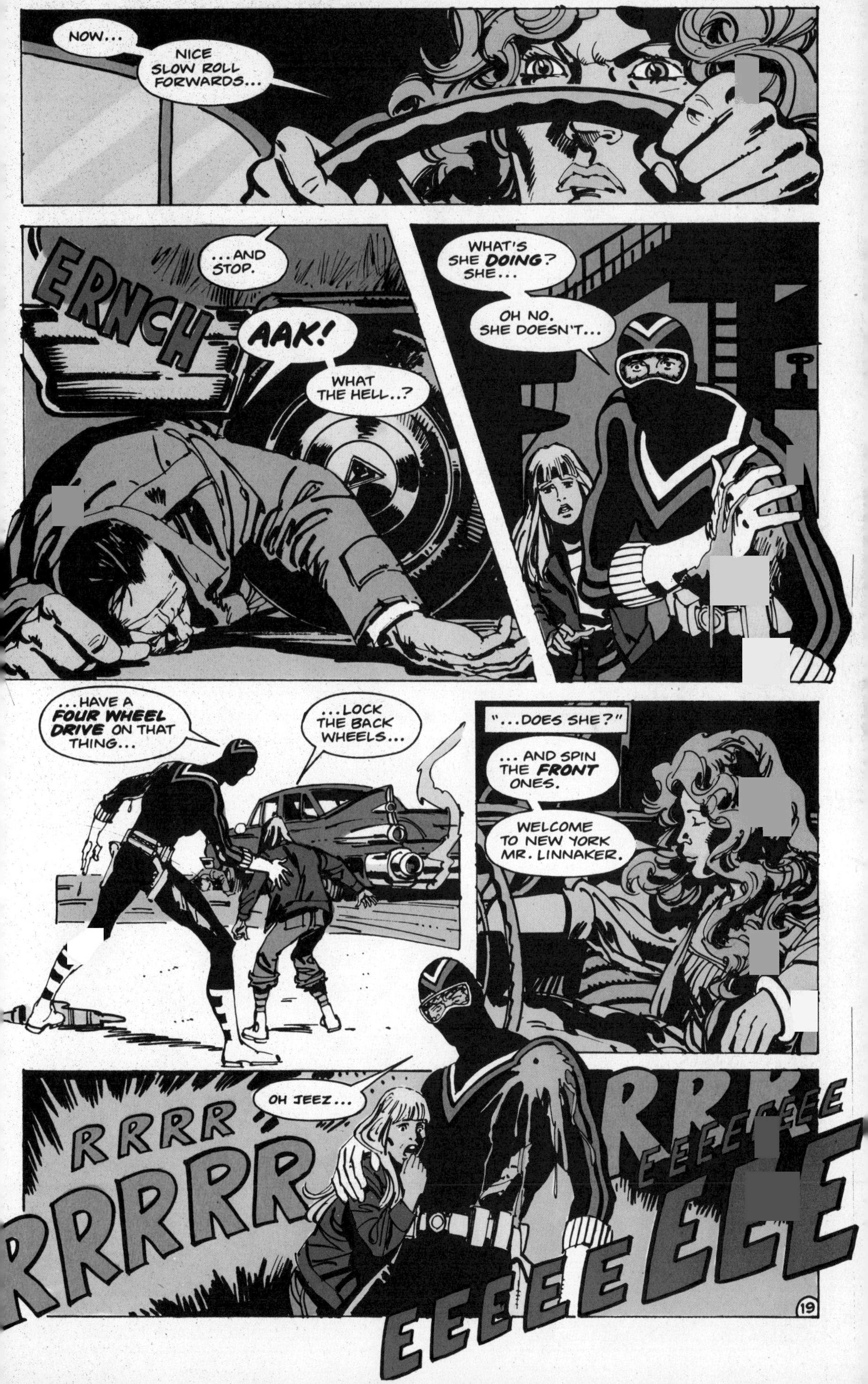
NOW...
NICE SLOW ROLL FORWARDS...
...AND STOP.
ERNCH
AAK!
WHAT THE HELL..?
WHAT'S SHE DOING? SHE...
OH NO. SHE DOESN'T...
...HAVE A FOUR WHEEL DRIVE ON THAT THING...
...LOCK THE BACK WHEELS...
"...DOES SHE?"
...AND SPIN THE FRONT ONES.
WELCOME TO NEW YORK MR. LINNAKER.
OH JEEZ...
RRRR
RRRRR
RRR
EEEEEEEEE
EEEEEEEEE

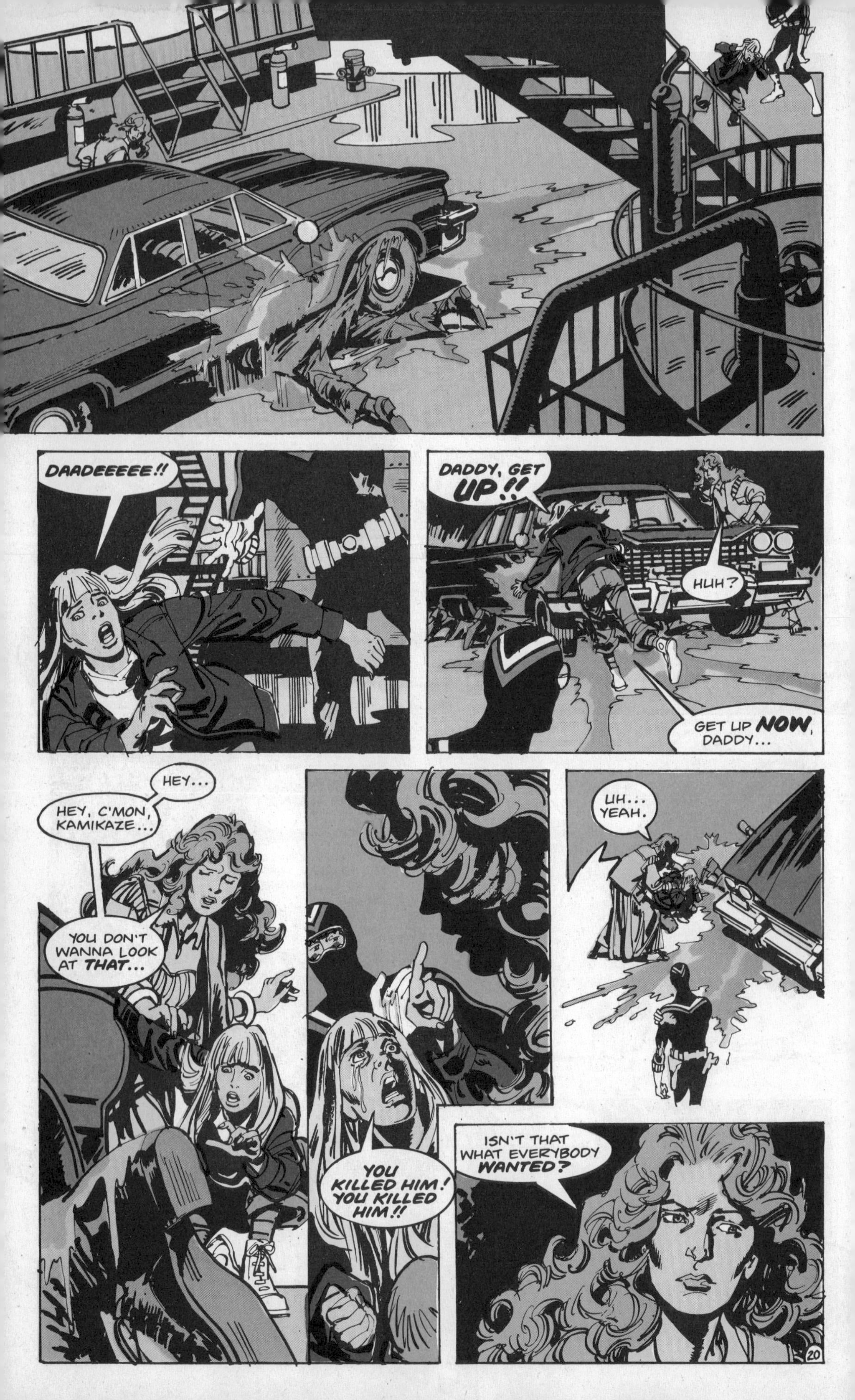

DAADEEEEE!!
DADDY, GET UP!!
HUH?
GET UP NOW, DADDY...
HEY...
HEY, C'MON, KAMIKAZE...
YOU DON'T WANNA LOOK AT THAT...
YOU KILLED HIM! YOU KILLED HIM!!
UH... YEAH.
ISN'T THAT WHAT EVERYBODY WANTED?

"THEY'LL NEVER MAKE SENSE OF IT, JODIE, BECAUSE NO MATTER HOW FAR INTO IT THEY DIG...

"...IT'S GOT NOTHING TO DO WITH THEM."

SHE'S OKAY.

I MEAN, SHE'S IN SHOCK AND SHE DOESN'T SEEM TO *REMEMBER* ANYTHING, BUT SHE'S NOT *HURT*.

YOU KNOW. *PHYSICALLY* SHE'S NOT HURT.

UH...

THAT THE EVENING EDITION YOU GOT THERE?

YUP.

ANYTHING INTERESTING IN IT?

PROSTITUTE MURDERED IN MARIJUANA MYSTERY

Neighbors found body and drugs in tenement horror. Details center pa

WOMAN SOUGHT

NOPE.

WHAT'S IN THAT ENVELOPE YOU GOT THERE?

LITT

21

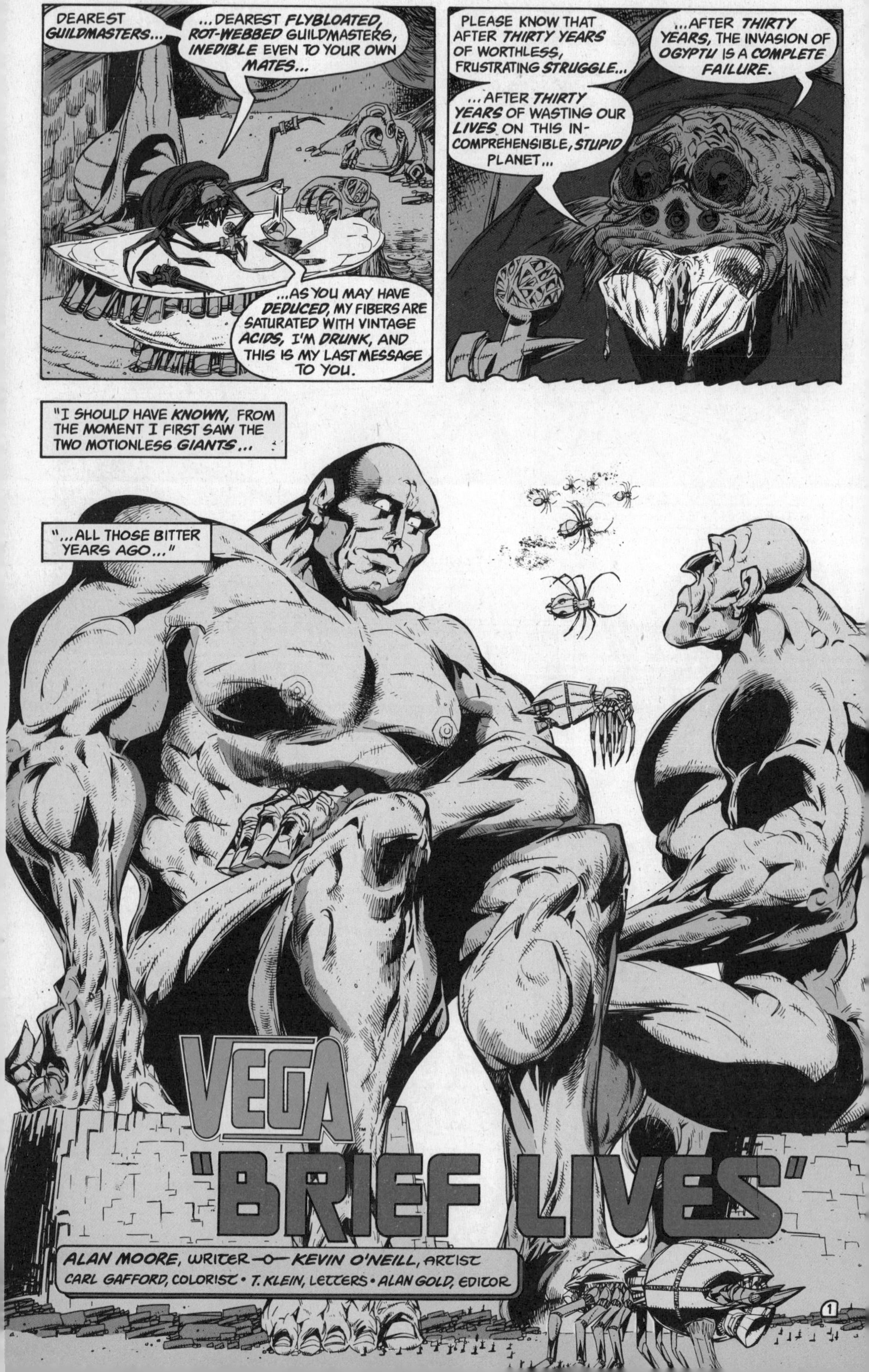
DEAREST GUILDMASTERS...
...DEAREST FLYBLOATED, ROT-WEBBED GUILDMASTERS, INEDIBLE EVEN TO YOUR OWN MATES...
...AS YOU MAY HAVE DEDUCED, MY FIBERS ARE SATURATED WITH VINTAGE ACIDS, I'M DRUNK, AND THIS IS MY LAST MESSAGE TO YOU.
PLEASE KNOW THAT AFTER THIRTY YEARS OF WORTHLESS, FRUSTRATING STRUGGLE...
...AFTER THIRTY YEARS OF WASTING OUR LIVES ON THIS IN-COMPREHENSIBLE, STUPID PLANET...
...AFTER THIRTY YEARS, THE INVASION OF OGYPTU IS A COMPLETE FAILURE.
"I SHOULD HAVE KNOWN, FROM THE MOMENT I FIRST SAW THE TWO MOTIONLESS GIANTS...
"...ALL THOSE BITTER YEARS AGO..."
VEGA
"BRIEF LIVES"
ALAN MOORE, WRITER KEVIN O'NEILL, ARTIST
CARL GAFFORD, COLORIST • T. KLEIN, LETTERS • ALAN GOLD, EDITOR
1

"IT TOOK TWENTY LUNAR RIPENINGS BEFORE WE REALIZED THAT WE WERE LOOKING AT AN ACTUAL *LIFE-FORM*..."

LAST SNOWCYCLE, THE STATUE ON THE *LEFT* HAD ITS EYES *FULLY OPEN*. NOW THEY'RE HALF *CLOSED*...

"...AND ANOTHER *TEN* BEFORE WE BEGAN TO *UNDERSTAND* THEM."

I BELIEVE THE GIANTS OPERATE IN A *DIFFERENT TIME FRAME*, FAR *SLOWER* THAN OUR OWN, WHERE THE BLINKING OF AN *EYE* LASTS TEN OF OUR *YEARS*...

"BUT I WAS MORE *HEADSTRONG* THEN, AND UNAWARE OF THE PROBLEM'S *MAGNITUDE*..."

I DON'T CARE *WHAT SPEED* THEY LIVE AT!

THEY HAVE BEEN INVADED BY THE *SPIDER GUILD* AND THEY SHALL LEARN TO *FEAR* US!

"THE DIFFICULTY WAS IN MAKING THE GIANTS *AWARE* THAT THEY HAD BEEN *CONQUERED*."

WE CAN'T *COMMUNICATE*... FOR *THEM*, WE'RE MOVING TOO FAST TO *SEE*.

WE'D HAVE TO STAND STILL FOR *DECADES* BEFORE THEY'D *NOTICE* US.

"BUT I DID NOT GIVE IN. AHH...HOW *FIERCE* I WAS IN MY YOUTH. HOW *RESOLUTE*..."

THEN THEY SHALL *FEEL* OUR PRESENCE. *PAIN* IS THE ONLY *UNIVERSAL LANGUAGE*!

GIVE ME THAT *GEMBURNER*...

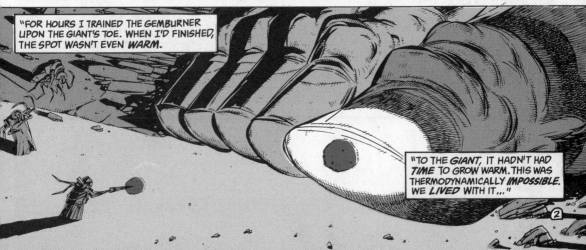

"FOR HOURS I TRAINED THE GEMBURNER UPON THE GIANT'S TOE. WHEN I'D FINISHED, THE SPOT WASN'T EVEN *WARM*.

"TO THE *GIANT*, IT HADN'T HAD *TIME* TO GROW WARM. THIS WAS THERMODYNAMICALLY *IMPOSSIBLE*. WE *LIVED* WITH IT..."

2

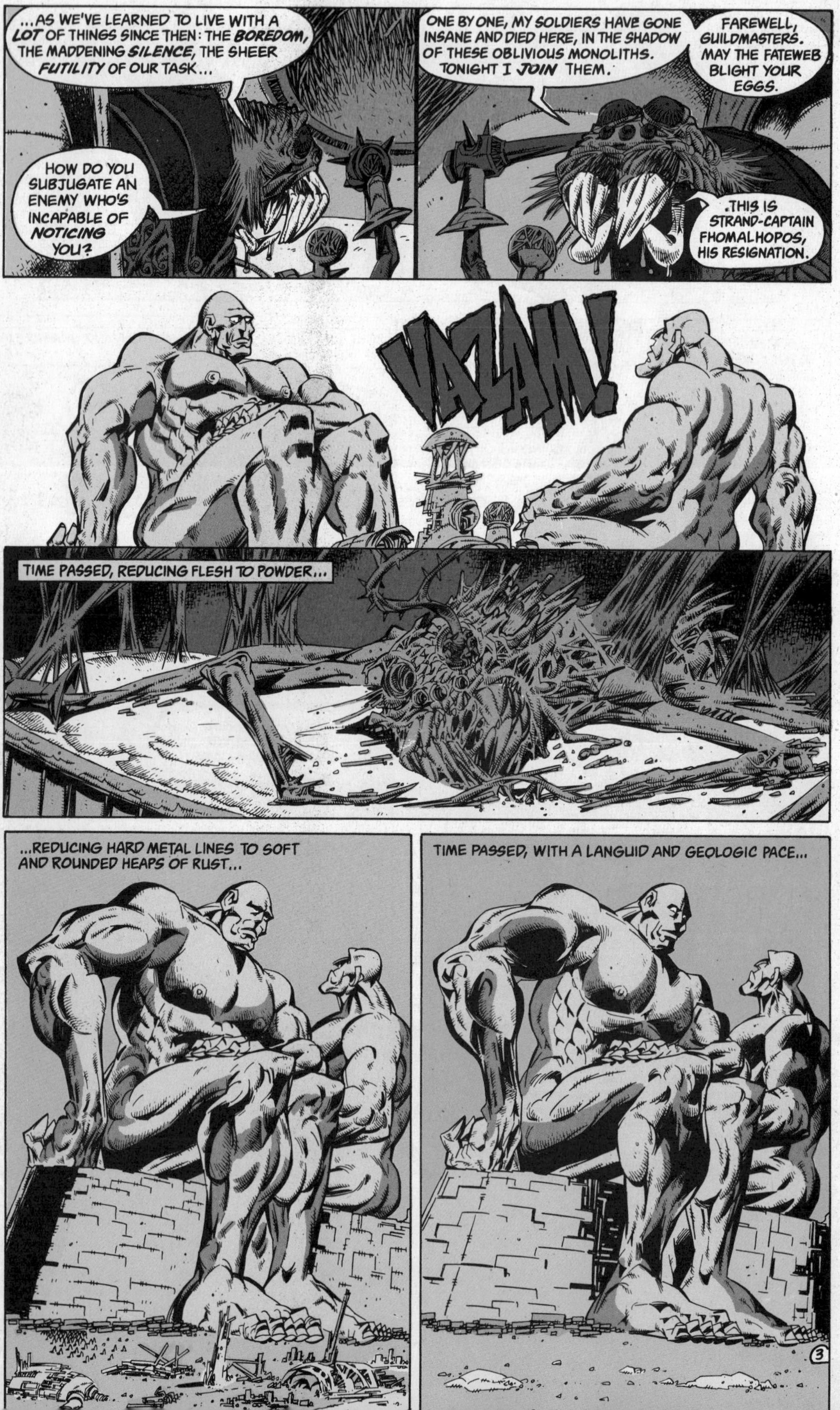
...AS WE'VE LEARNED TO LIVE WITH A LOT OF THINGS SINCE THEN: THE BOREDOM, THE MADDENING SILENCE, THE SHEER FUTILITY OF OUR TASK...
HOW DO YOU SUBJUGATE AN ENEMY WHO'S INCAPABLE OF NOTICING YOU?
ONE BY ONE, MY SOLDIERS HAVE GONE INSANE AND DIED HERE, IN THE SHADOW OF THESE OBLIVIOUS MONOLITHS. TONIGHT I JOIN THEM.
FAREWELL, GUILDMASTERS. MAY THE FATEWEB BLIGHT YOUR EGGS.
.THIS IS STRAND-CAPTAIN FHOMALHOPOS, HIS RESIGNATION.
VAZAM!
TIME PASSED, REDUCING FLESH TO POWDER...
...REDUCING HARD METAL LINES TO SOFT AND ROUNDED HEAPS OF RUST...
TIME PASSED, WITH A LANGUID AND GEOLOGIC PACE...
3

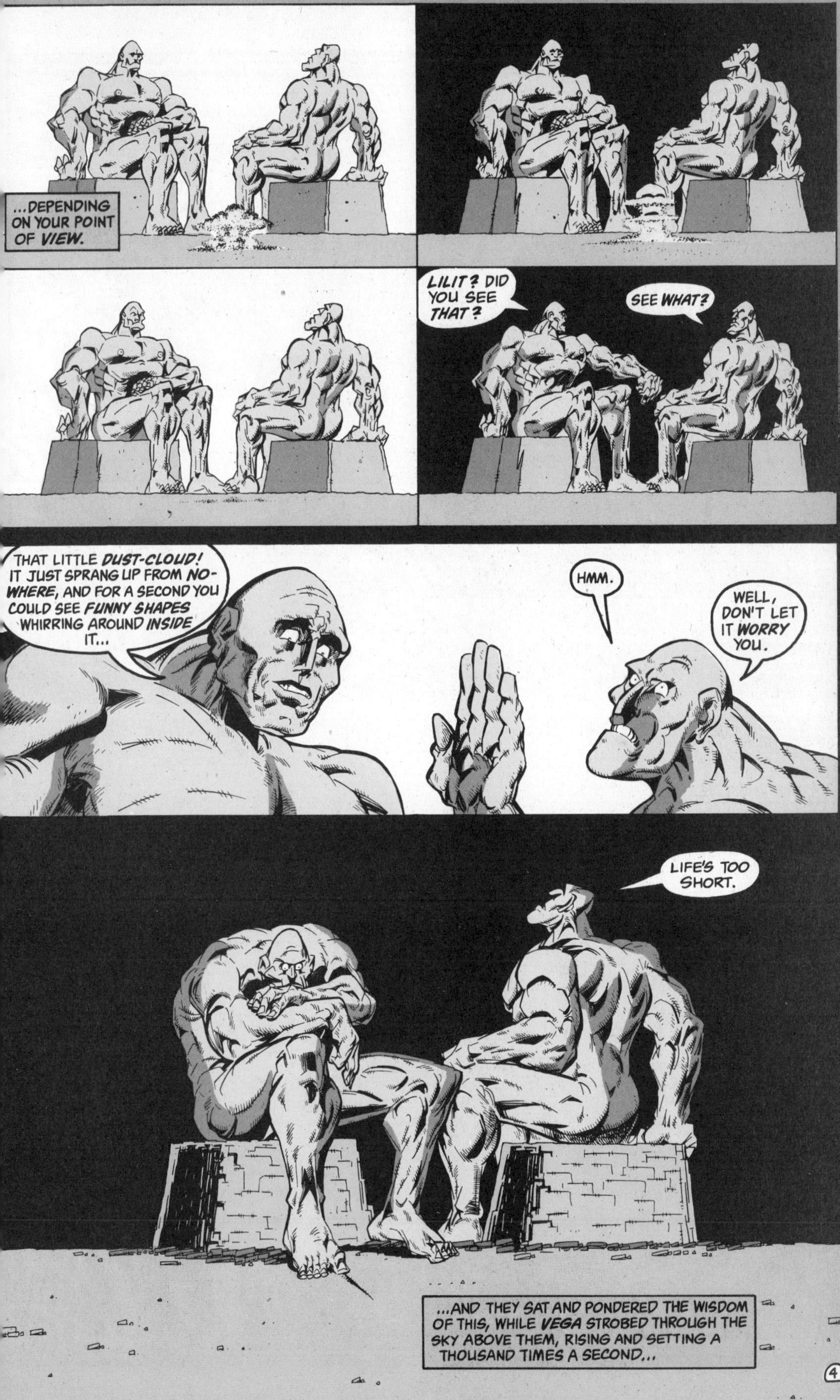
...DEPENDING ON YOUR POINT OF VIEW.
LILIT? DID YOU SEE THAT?
SEE WHAT?
THAT LITTLE DUST-CLOUD! IT JUST SPRANG UP FROM NO-WHERE, AND FOR A SECOND YOU COULD SEE FUNNY SHAPES WHIRRING AROUND INSIDE IT...
HMM.
WELL, DON'T LET IT WORRY YOU.
LIFE'S TOO SHORT.
...AND THEY SAT AND PONDERED THE WISDOM OF THIS, WHILE VEGA STROBED THROUGH THE SKY ABOVE THEM, RISING AND SETTING A THOUSAND TIMES A SECOND...
4

"THE MEN OF *CULACAO* BRAG AND JOSTLE AND SHAKE THEIR SPEARS, PINK-FACED WITH EXCITEMENT AND WITH DAWN.

"OUTSIDE THE VILLAGE THE GIANT MOLLUSKS GRAZE, ALIEN AND INDIFFERENT.

"I'VE TRIED TO GET MY *INTERPRETER* TO EXPLAIN THIS RITUAL TO ME, BUT THE CONCEPTS ARE TOO *ALIEN* TO GRASP.

"HIS NAME IS *MOPI.* HE HAS LONG, SOFT FINGERS AND SHORT, SOFT FUR.

"ONE OF THE CULACAONS DETACHES HIMSELF FROM THE MAIN HERD AND RUSHES SCREAMING AT THE NEAREST MOLLUSK.

"HE STABS THE EXPOSED VIOLET MEMBRANE OVER AND OVER WITH HIS SPEAR.

"EVERYONE CHEERS.

"SOON, HIS FELLOWS JOIN IN, EACH ASSAULTING THE SNAIL-THING OF THEIR CHOICE. THE ATMOSPHERE IS OVERWHELMINGLY *MASCULINE*...

"...BUT THEN IT *WOULD* BE.

"IMPOSSIBLE AS IT SEEMS, THERE ARE *NO FEMALE CULACAONS*.

"IT COULD ONLY HAPPEN IN...

VEGA™

A MAN'S WORLD

G-1874

ALAN MOORE, WRITER • *PARIS CULLINS,* PENCILS • *RICK MAGYAR,* INKS • *KLEIN,* LETTERS • *GAFF,* COLORS • *ALAN GOLD,* EDITOR

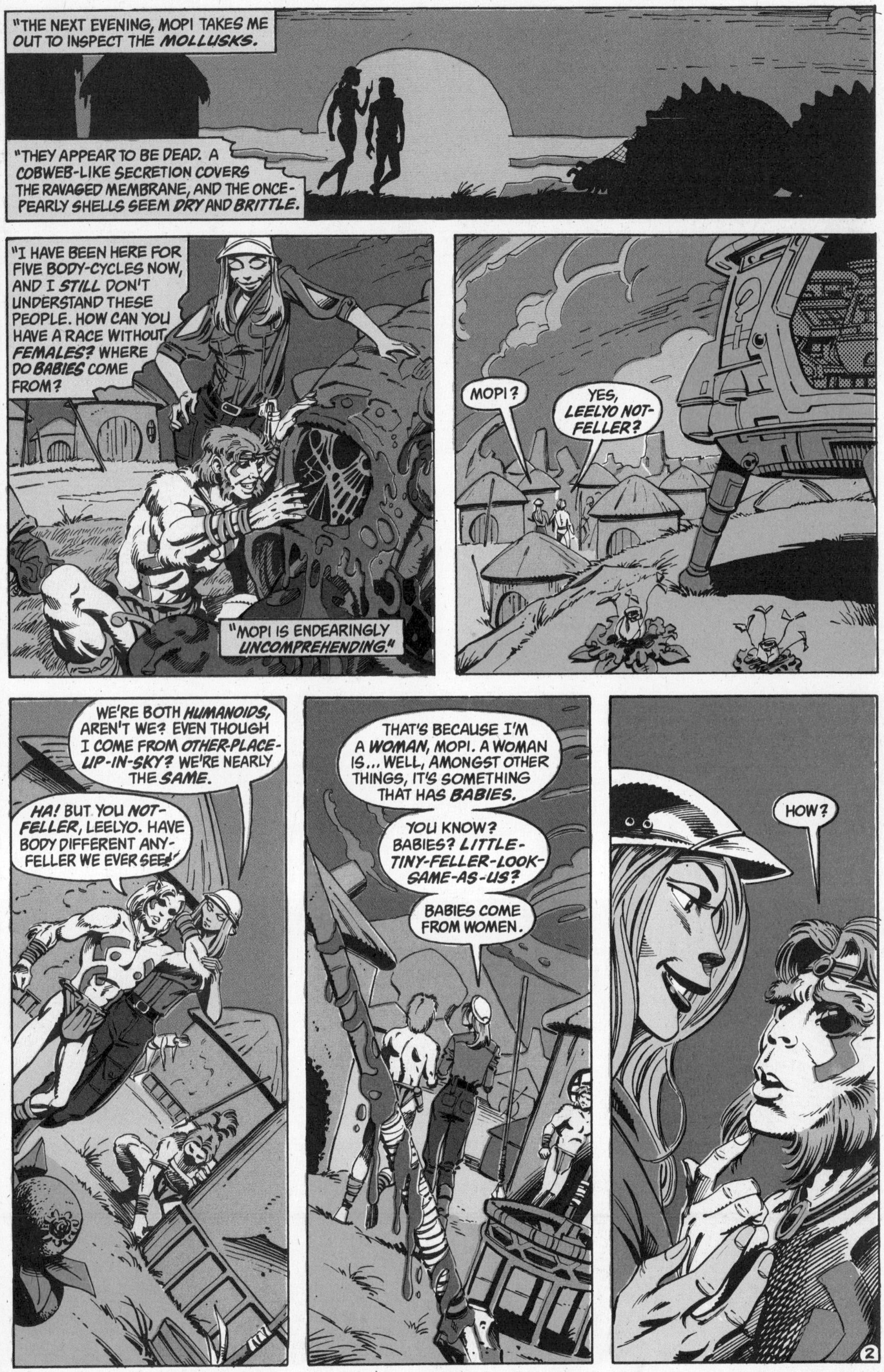

"THE NEXT EVENING, MOPI TAKES ME OUT TO INSPECT THE MOLLUSKS.
"THEY APPEAR TO BE DEAD. A COBWEB-LIKE SECRETION COVERS THE RAVAGED MEMBRANE, AND THE ONCE-PEARLY SHELLS SEEM DRY AND BRITTLE.
"I HAVE BEEN HERE FOR FIVE BODY-CYCLES NOW, AND I STILL DON'T UNDERSTAND THESE PEOPLE. HOW CAN YOU HAVE A RACE WITHOUT FEMALES? WHERE DO BABIES COME FROM?
"MOPI IS ENDEARINGLY UNCOMPREHENDING."
MOPI?
YES, LEELYO NOT-FELLER?
WE'RE BOTH HUMANOIDS, AREN'T WE? EVEN THOUGH I COME FROM OTHER-PLACE-UP-IN-SKY? WE'RE NEARLY THE SAME.
HA! BUT YOU NOT-FELLER, LEELYO. HAVE BODY DIFFERENT ANY-FELLER WE EVER SEE!
THAT'S BECAUSE I'M A WOMAN, MOPI. A WOMAN IS... WELL, AMONGST OTHER THINGS, IT'S SOMETHING THAT HAS BABIES.
YOU KNOW? BABIES? LITTLE-TINY-FELLER-LOOK-SAME-AS-US?
BABIES COME FROM WOMEN.
HOW?
2

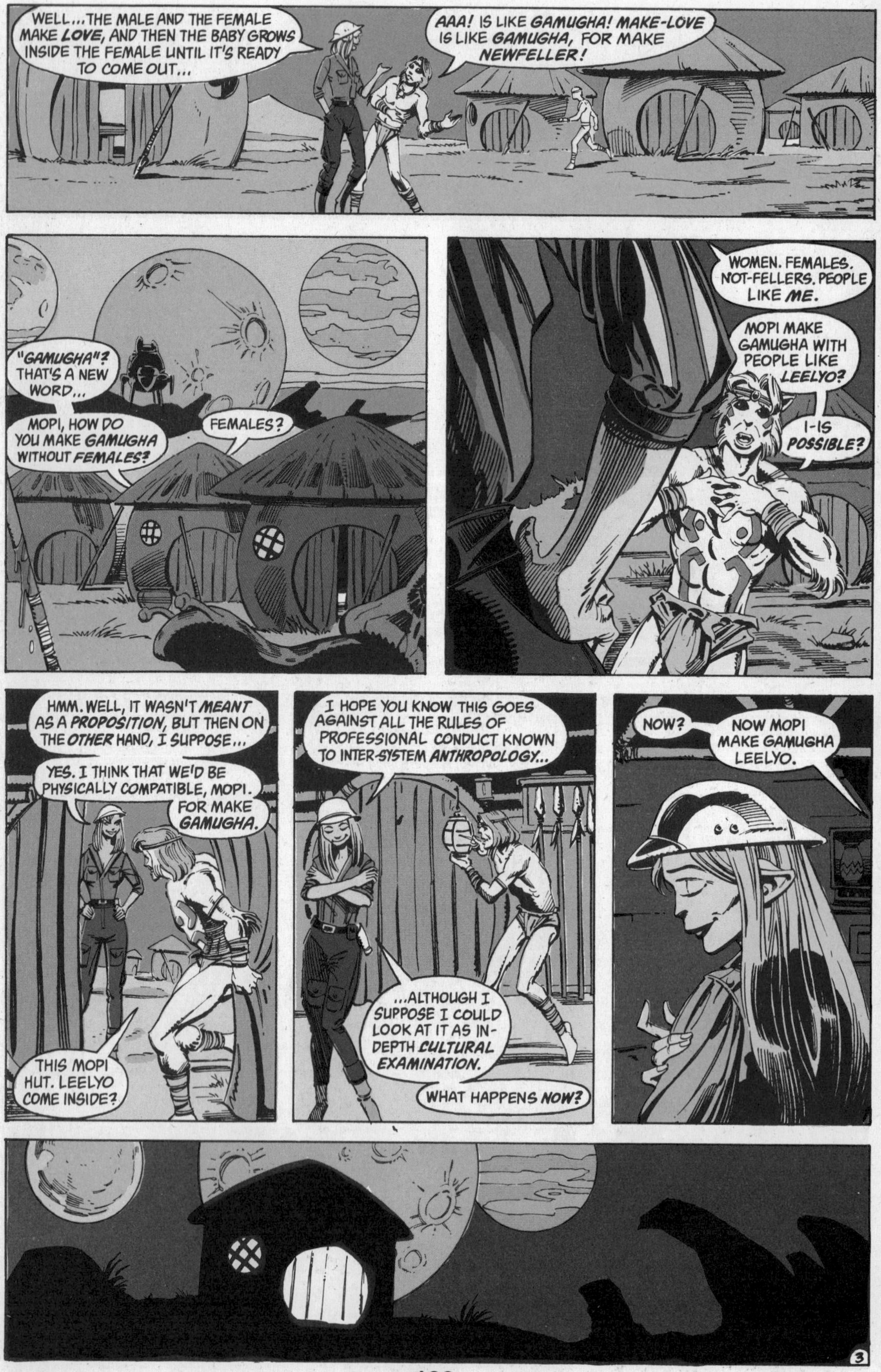
WELL... THE MALE AND THE FEMALE MAKE LOVE, AND THEN THE BABY GROWS INSIDE THE FEMALE UNTIL IT'S READY TO COME OUT...
AAA! IS LIKE GAMUGHA! MAKE-LOVE IS LIKE GAMUGHA, FOR MAKE NEWFELLER!
"GAMUGHA"? THAT'S A NEW WORD...
MOPI, HOW DO YOU MAKE GAMUGHA WITHOUT FEMALES?
FEMALES?
WOMEN. FEMALES. NOT-FELLERS. PEOPLE LIKE ME.
MOPI MAKE GAMUGHA WITH PEOPLE LIKE LEELYO?
I-IS POSSIBLE?
HMM. WELL, IT WASN'T MEANT AS A PROPOSITION, BUT THEN ON THE OTHER HAND, I SUPPOSE...
YES. I THINK THAT WE'D BE PHYSICALLY COMPATIBLE, MOPI.
FOR MAKE GAMUGHA.
THIS MOPI HUT. LEELYO COME INSIDE?
I HOPE YOU KNOW THIS GOES AGAINST ALL THE RULES OF PROFESSIONAL CONDUCT KNOWN TO INTER-SYSTEM ANTHROPOLOGY...
...ALTHOUGH I SUPPOSE I COULD LOOK AT IT AS IN-DEPTH CULTURAL EXAMINATION.
WHAT HAPPENS NOW?
NOW?
NOW MOPI MAKE GAMUGHA LEELYO.
3

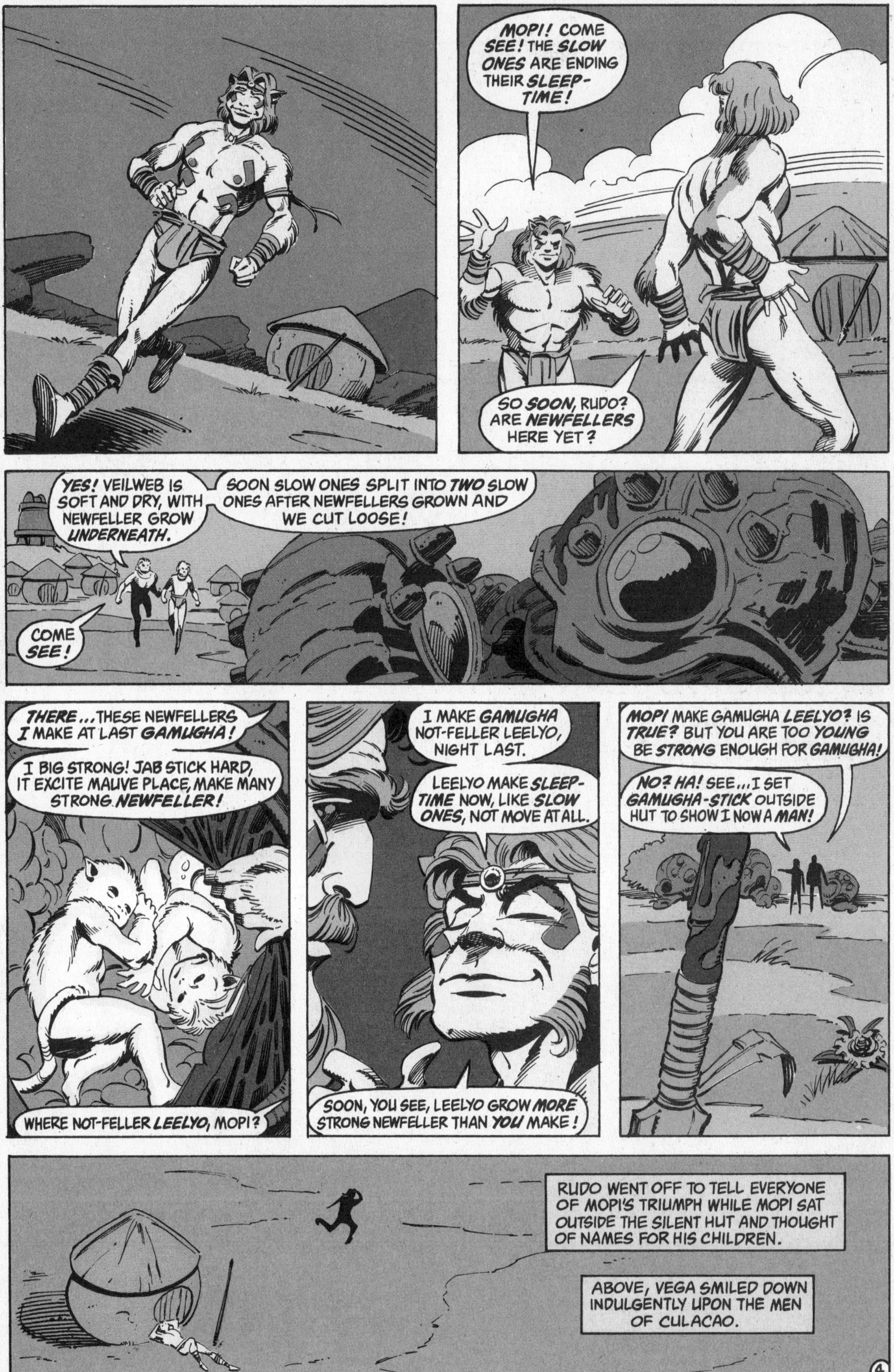

MOPI! COME SEE! THE SLOW ONES ARE ENDING THEIR SLEEP-TIME!
SO SOON, RUDO? ARE NEWFELLERS HERE YET?
YES! VEILWEB IS SOFT AND DRY, WITH NEWFELLER GROW UNDERNEATH.
SOON SLOW ONES SPLIT INTO TWO SLOW ONES AFTER NEWFELLERS GROWN AND WE CUT LOOSE!
COME SEE!
THERE... THESE NEWFELLERS I MAKE AT LAST GAMUGHA!
I BIG STRONG! JAB STICK HARD, IT EXCITE MAUVE PLACE, MAKE MANY STRONG NEWFELLER!
WHERE NOT-FELLER LEELYO, MOPI?
I MAKE GAMUGHA NOT-FELLER LEELYO, NIGHT LAST.
LEELYO MAKE SLEEP-TIME NOW, LIKE SLOW ONES, NOT MOVE AT ALL.
SOON, YOU SEE, LEELYO GROW MORE STRONG NEWFELLER THAN YOU MAKE!
MOPI MAKE GAMUGHA LEELYO? IS TRUE? BUT YOU ARE TOO YOUNG BE STRONG ENOUGH FOR GAMUGHA!
NO? HA! SEE... I SET GAMUGHA-STICK OUTSIDE HUT TO SHOW I NOW A MAN!
RUDO WENT OFF TO TELL EVERYONE OF MOPI'S TRIUMPH WHILE MOPI SAT OUTSIDE THE SILENT HUT AND THOUGHT OF NAMES FOR HIS CHILDREN.
ABOVE, VEGA SMILED DOWN INDULGENTLY UPON THE MEN OF CULACAO.
4

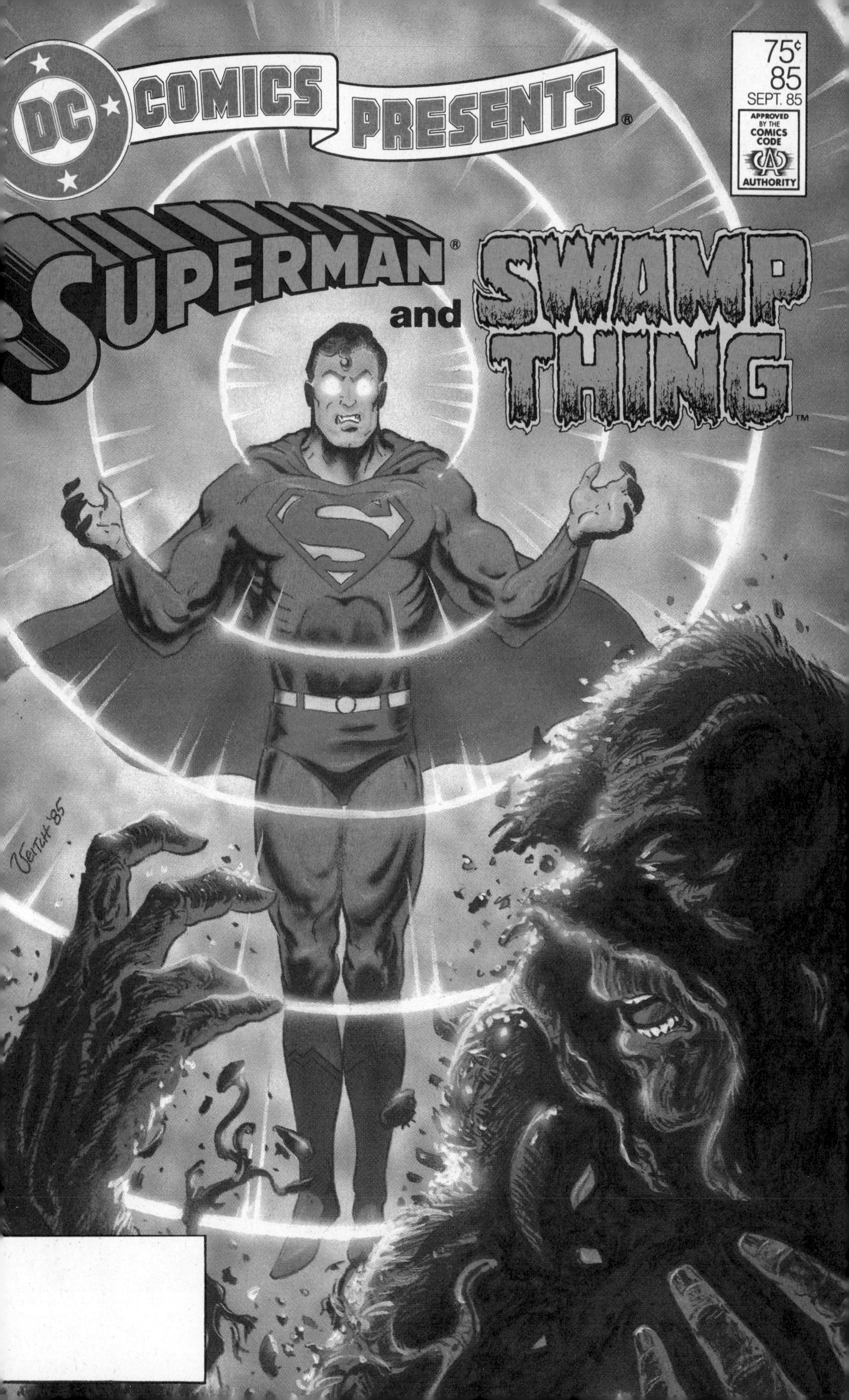
DC COMICS PRESENTS®
75¢
85
SEPT. 85
APPROVED BY THE COMICS CODE AUTHORITY
SUPERMAN®
and
SWAMP THING™
Veitch '85

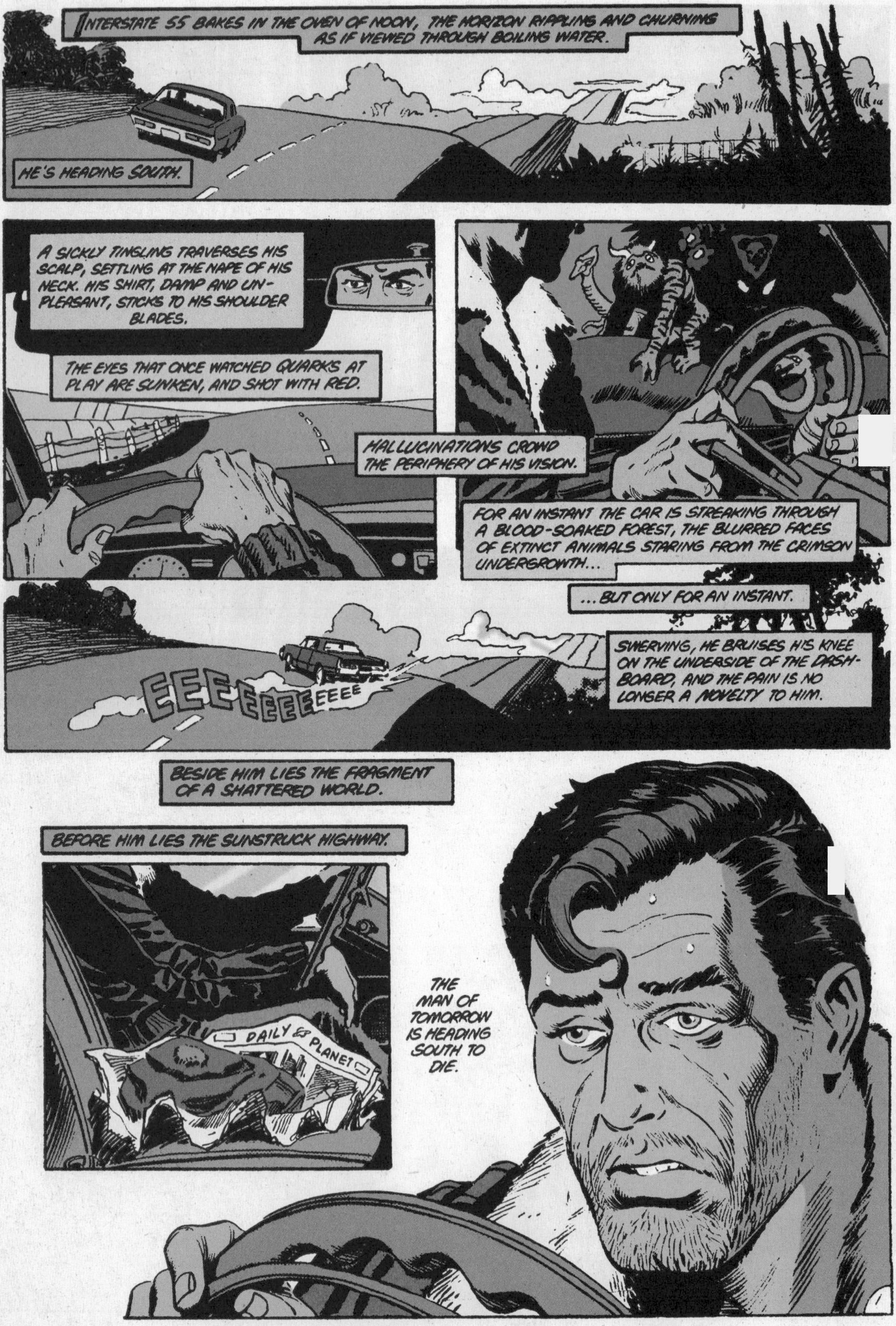
INTERSTATE 55 BAKES IN THE OVEN OF NOON, THE HORIZON RIPPLING AND CHURNING AS IF VIEWED THROUGH BOILING WATER.
HE'S HEADING SOUTH.
A SICKLY TINGLING TRAVERSES HIS SCALP, SETTLING AT THE NAPE OF HIS NECK. HIS SHIRT, DAMP AND UN-PLEASANT, STICKS TO HIS SHOULDER BLADES.
THE EYES THAT ONCE WATCHED QUARKS AT PLAY ARE SUNKEN, AND SHOT WITH RED.
HALLUCINATIONS CROWD THE PERIPHERY OF HIS VISION.
FOR AN INSTANT THE CAR IS STREAKING THROUGH A BLOOD-SOAKED FOREST, THE BLURRED FACES OF EXTINCT ANIMALS STARING FROM THE CRIMSON UNDERGROWTH...
...BUT ONLY FOR AN INSTANT.
EEEEEEEEEEE
SWERVING, HE BRUISES HIS KNEE ON THE UNDERSIDE OF THE DASH-BOARD, AND THE PAIN IS NO LONGER A NOVELTY TO HIM.
BESIDE HIM LIES THE FRAGMENT OF A SHATTERED WORLD.
BEFORE HIM LIES THE SUNSTRUCK HIGHWAY.
DAILY PLANET
THE MAN OF TOMORROW IS HEADING SOUTH TO DIE.

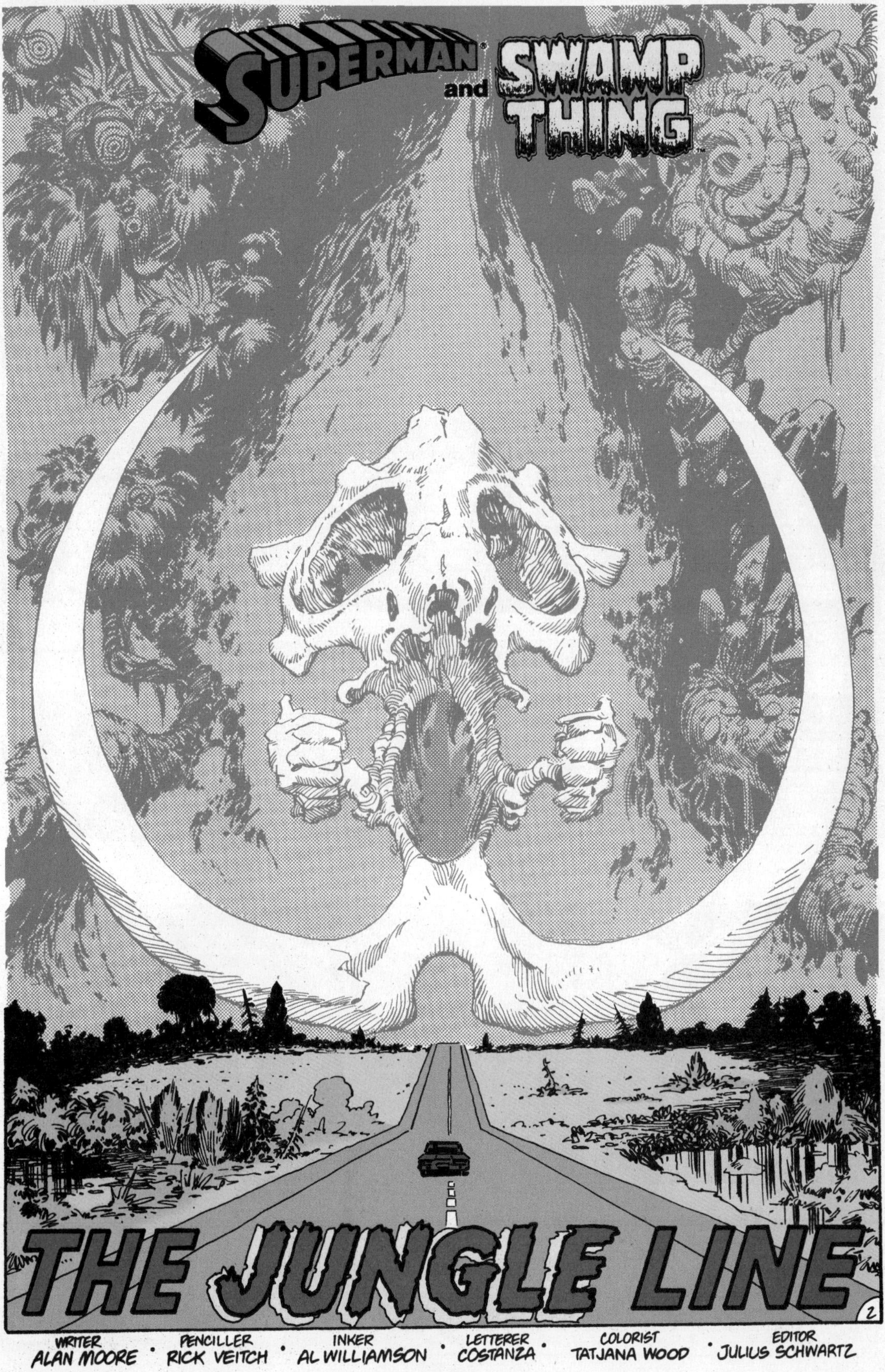
SUPERMAN and SWAMP THING
THE JUNGLE LINE
2

WRITER ALAN MOORE • PENCILLER RICK VEITCH • INKER AL WILLIAMSON • LETTERER COSTANZA • COLORIST TATJANA WOOD • EDITOR JULIUS SCHWARTZ

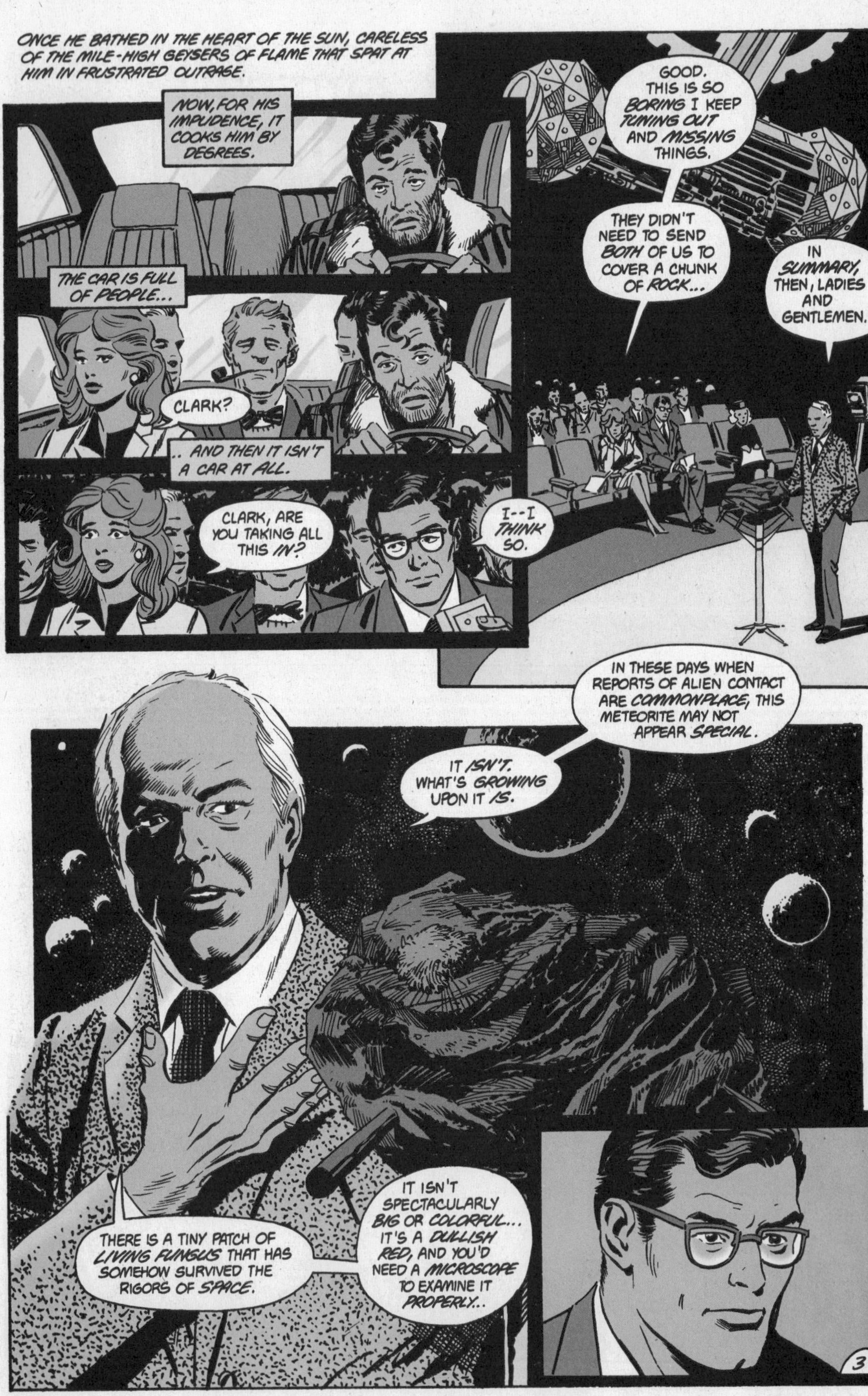
ONCE HE BATHED IN THE HEART OF THE SUN, CARELESS OF THE MILE-HIGH GEYSERS OF FLAME THAT SPAT AT HIM IN FRUSTRATED OUTRAGE.
NOW, FOR HIS IMPUDENCE, IT COOKS HIM BY DEGREES.
THE CAR IS FULL OF PEOPLE...
CLARK?
.. AND THEN IT ISN'T A CAR AT ALL.
CLARK, ARE YOU TAKING ALL THIS IN?
I--I THINK SO.
GOOD. THIS IS SO BORING I KEEP TUNING OUT AND MISSING THINGS.
THEY DIDN'T NEED TO SEND BOTH OF US TO COVER A CHUNK OF ROCK...
IN SUMMARY, THEN, LADIES AND GENTLEMEN...
IN THESE DAYS WHEN REPORTS OF ALIEN CONTACT ARE COMMONPLACE, THIS METEORITE MAY NOT APPEAR SPECIAL.
IT ISN'T. WHAT'S GROWING UPON IT IS.
THERE IS A TINY PATCH OF LIVING FUNGUS THAT HAS SOMEHOW SURVIVED THE RIGORS OF SPACE.
IT ISN'T SPECTACULARLY BIG OR COLORFUL... IT'S A DULLISH RED, AND YOU'D NEED A MICROSCOPE TO EXAMINE IT PROPERLY..
3

HOWEVER...THIS *LIFE FORM* HAS SURVIVED *DECADES*... POSSIBLY *CENTURIES*... IN AN *ABSOLUTE FRIGID VACUUM.*

TO *SCIENCE*, THIS IS AN *UN-PRECEDENTED* DISCOVERY.

DOES ANYONE HAVE ANY *QUESTIONS*?

YES? MS. *LANG*, I BELIEVE?

DR. *EVERETT*, IS THIS FIND *REALLY* THAT IMPORTANT?

AFTER ALL, FOR OVER *TWENTY YEARS* WE'VE HAD A LIVING ALIEN *JUST AS* INDESTRUCTIBLE UPON OUR PLANET.

AHH. YOU'RE TALKING ABOUT *SUPERMAN.*

WELL, THE *DIFFERENCE* IS THAT UNLIKE THIS *FUNGUS,* SUPERMAN COULD NOT BE EXPECTED TO LIE STILL THROUGH-OUT WHAT MAY BE *YEARS OF THOROUGH RESEARCH.*

ANY *OTHER* QUESTIONS?

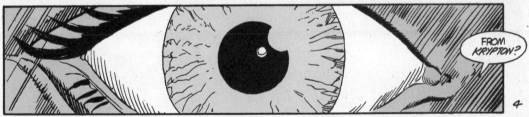

FROM *KRYPTON?*

4

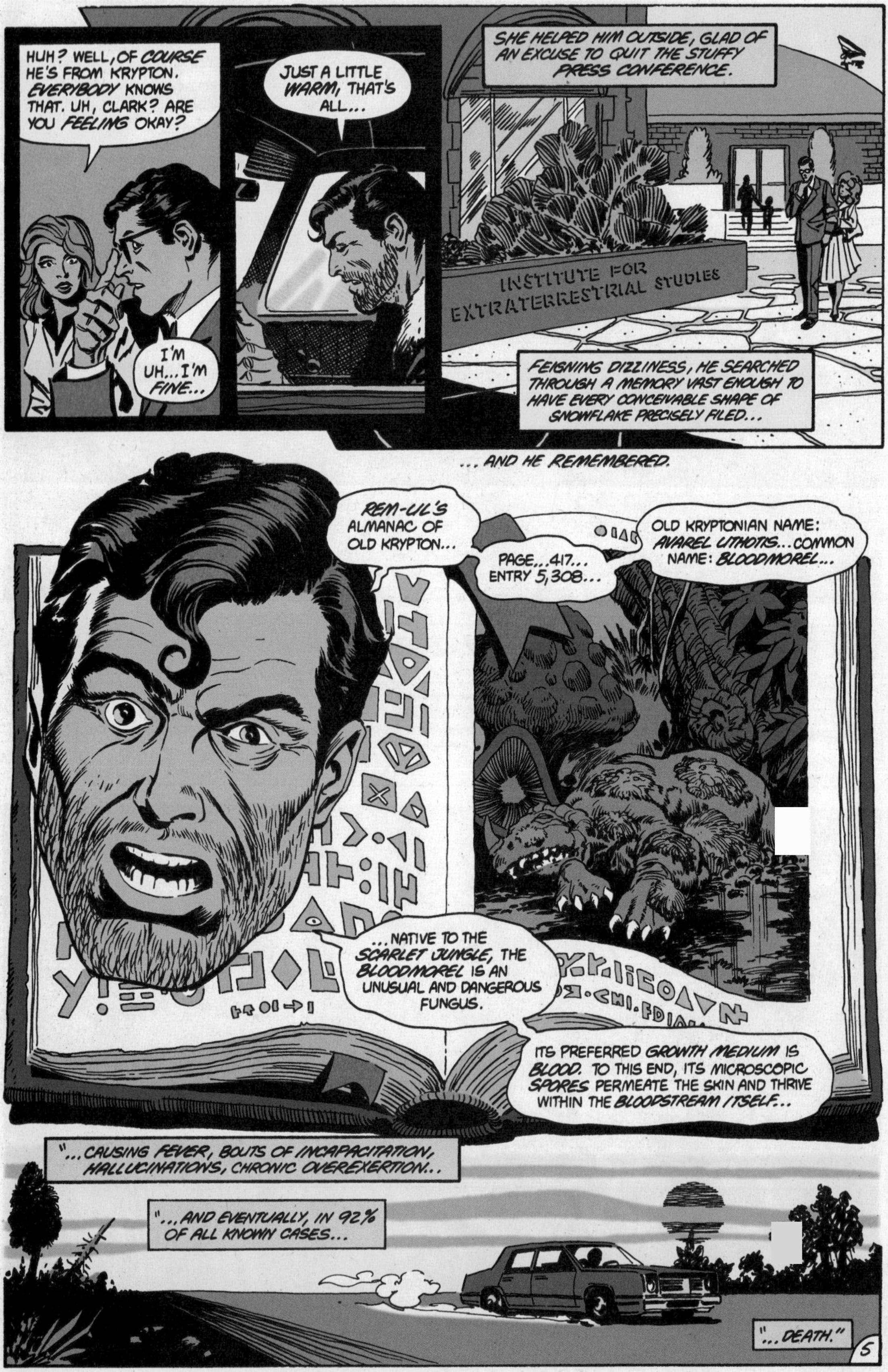
HUH? WELL, OF COURSE HE'S FROM KRYPTON. EVERYBODY KNOWS THAT. UH, CLARK? ARE YOU FEELING OKAY?
I'M UH...I'M FINE...
JUST A LITTLE WARM, THAT'S ALL...
SHE HELPED HIM OUTSIDE, GLAD OF AN EXCUSE TO QUIT THE STUFFY PRESS CONFERENCE.
INSTITUTE FOR EXTRATERRESTRIAL STUDIES
FEIGNING DIZZINESS, HE SEARCHED THROUGH A MEMORY VAST ENOUGH TO HAVE EVERY CONCEIVABLE SHAPE OF SNOWFLAKE PRECISELY FILED...
...AND HE REMEMBERED.
REM-UL'S ALMANAC OF OLD KRYPTON...
PAGE...417... ENTRY 5,308...
OLD KRYPTONIAN NAME: AVAREL UTHOTIS...COMMON NAME: BLOODMOREL...
...NATIVE TO THE SCARLET JUNGLE, THE BLOODMOREL IS AN UNUSUAL AND DANGEROUS FUNGUS.
ITS PREFERRED GROWTH MEDIUM IS BLOOD. TO THIS END, ITS MICROSCOPIC SPORES PERMEATE THE SKIN AND THRIVE WITHIN THE BLOODSTREAM ITSELF...
"...CAUSING FEVER, BOUTS OF INCAPACITATION, HALLUCINATIONS, CHRONIC OVEREXERTION...
"...AND EVENTUALLY, IN 92% OF ALL KNOWN CASES...
"...DEATH."
5

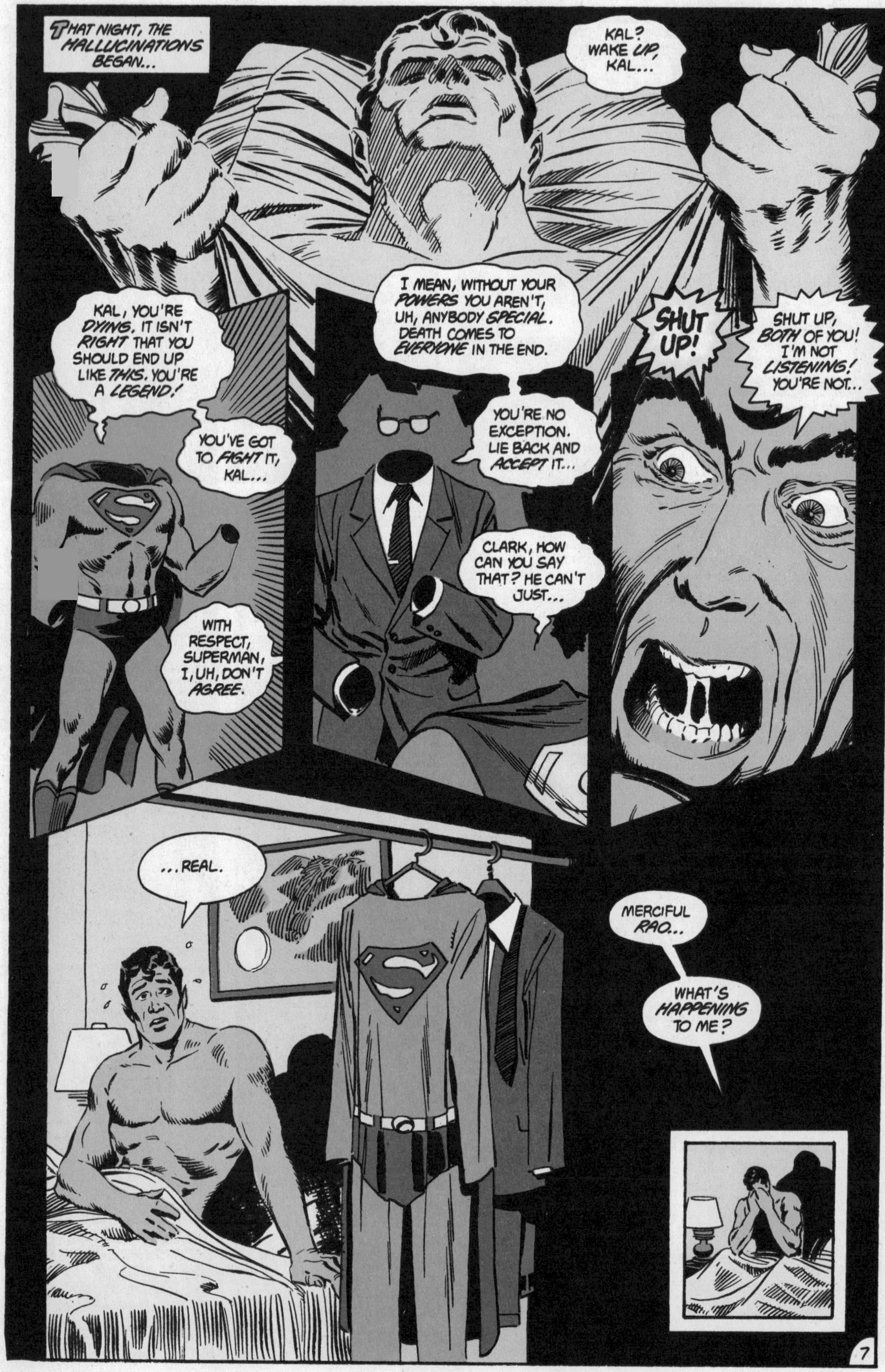
THAT NIGHT, THE HALLUCINATIONS BEGAN...
KAL? WAKE UP, KAL...
KAL, YOU'RE DYING. IT ISN'T RIGHT THAT YOU SHOULD END UP LIKE THIS. YOU'RE A LEGEND!
YOU'VE GOT TO FIGHT IT, KAL...
WITH RESPECT, SUPERMAN, I, UH, DON'T AGREE.
I MEAN, WITHOUT YOUR POWERS YOU AREN'T, UH, ANYBODY SPECIAL. DEATH COMES TO EVERYONE IN THE END.
YOU'RE NO EXCEPTION. LIE BACK AND ACCEPT IT...
CLARK, HOW CAN YOU SAY THAT? HE CAN'T JUST...
SHUT UP!
SHUT UP, BOTH OF YOU! I'M NOT LISTENING! YOU'RE NOT...
...REAL.
MERCIFUL RAO...
WHAT'S HAPPENING TO ME?
7

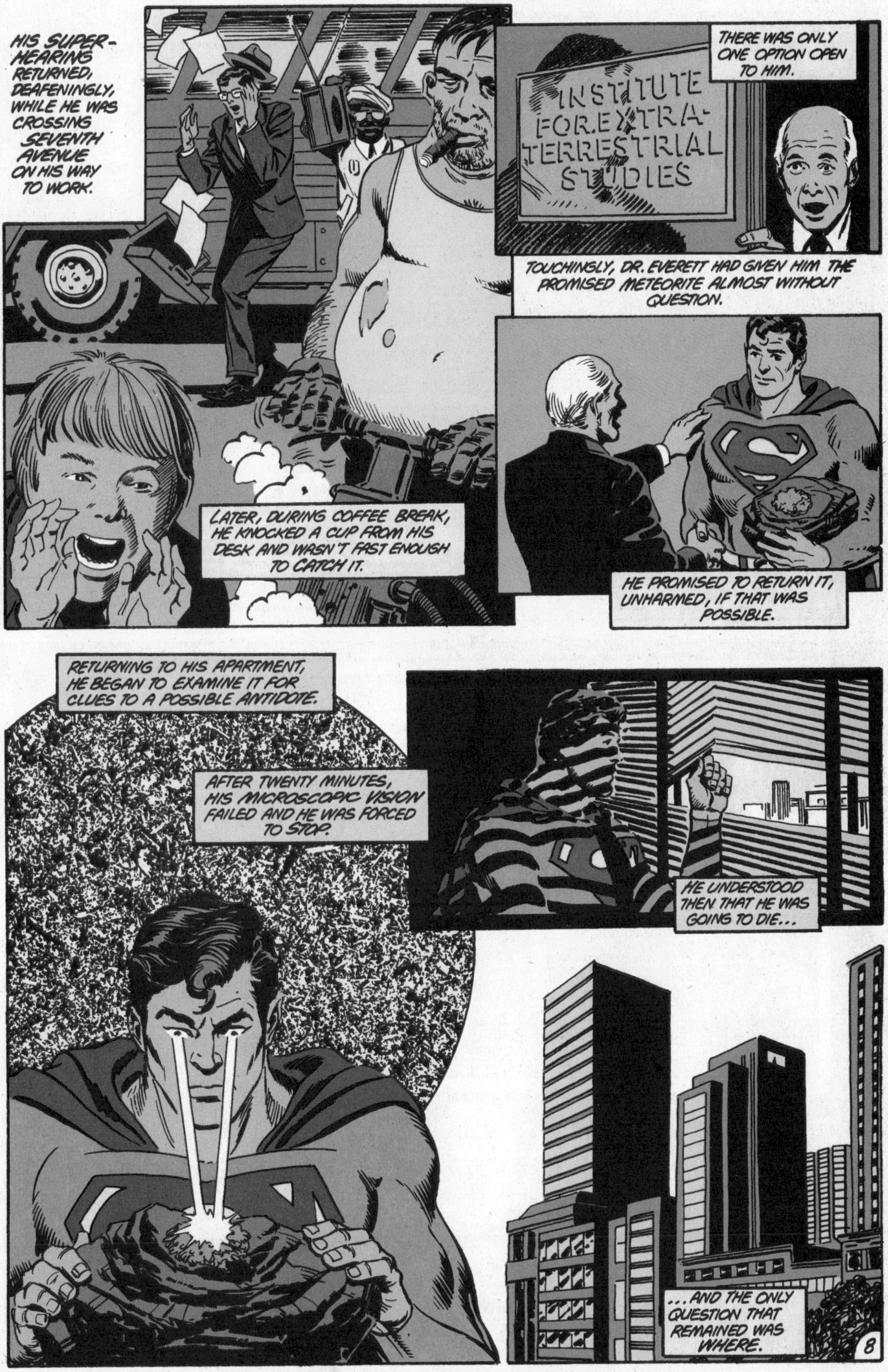

HIS SUPER-HEARING RETURNED, DEAFENINGLY, WHILE HE WAS CROSSING SEVENTH AVENUE ON HIS WAY TO WORK.
THERE WAS ONLY ONE OPTION OPEN TO HIM.
INSTITUTE FOR EXTRA-TERRESTRIAL STUDIES
TOUCHINGLY, DR. EVERETT HAD GIVEN HIM THE PROMISED METEORITE ALMOST WITHOUT QUESTION.
LATER, DURING COFFEE BREAK, HE KNOCKED A CUP FROM HIS DESK AND WASN'T FAST ENOUGH TO CATCH IT.
HE PROMISED TO RETURN IT, UNHARMED, IF THAT WAS POSSIBLE.
RETURNING TO HIS APARTMENT, HE BEGAN TO EXAMINE IT FOR CLUES TO A POSSIBLE ANTIDOTE.
AFTER TWENTY MINUTES, HIS MICROSCOPIC VISION FAILED AND HE WAS FORCED TO STOP.
HE UNDERSTOOD THEN THAT HE WAS GOING TO DIE...
...AND THE ONLY QUESTION THAT REMAINED WAS WHERE.
8

HE WANTED TO BE *ALONE* WHEN IT HAPPENED, BUT HIS *FORTRESS* WAS TOO *DISTANT,* AND FLYING WAS *UNTHINKABLE.*

COAST CITY

CENTRAL CITY

STAR CITY

HE ALSO ELIMINATED *GOTHAM, NEW YORK, WASHINGTON,* AND ALL OTHER CITIES FREQUENTED BY THE *SUPER-HERO COMMUNITY.*

*F*INALLY, HE BOUGHT A SECONDHAND CAR IN A *CASH* TRANSACTION UNDER THE NAME OF *CAL ELLIS.*

SUPER DEALS

AL'S USED CARS

TAKING THE *METEORITE,* JUST IN CASE, HE MADE FOR THE *ONE PLACE* IN AMERICA WITH *NO* INDIGENOUS *SUPERHUMANS...*

HE HEADED SOUTH.

BLAAAAAAAAA

HHROOM

140

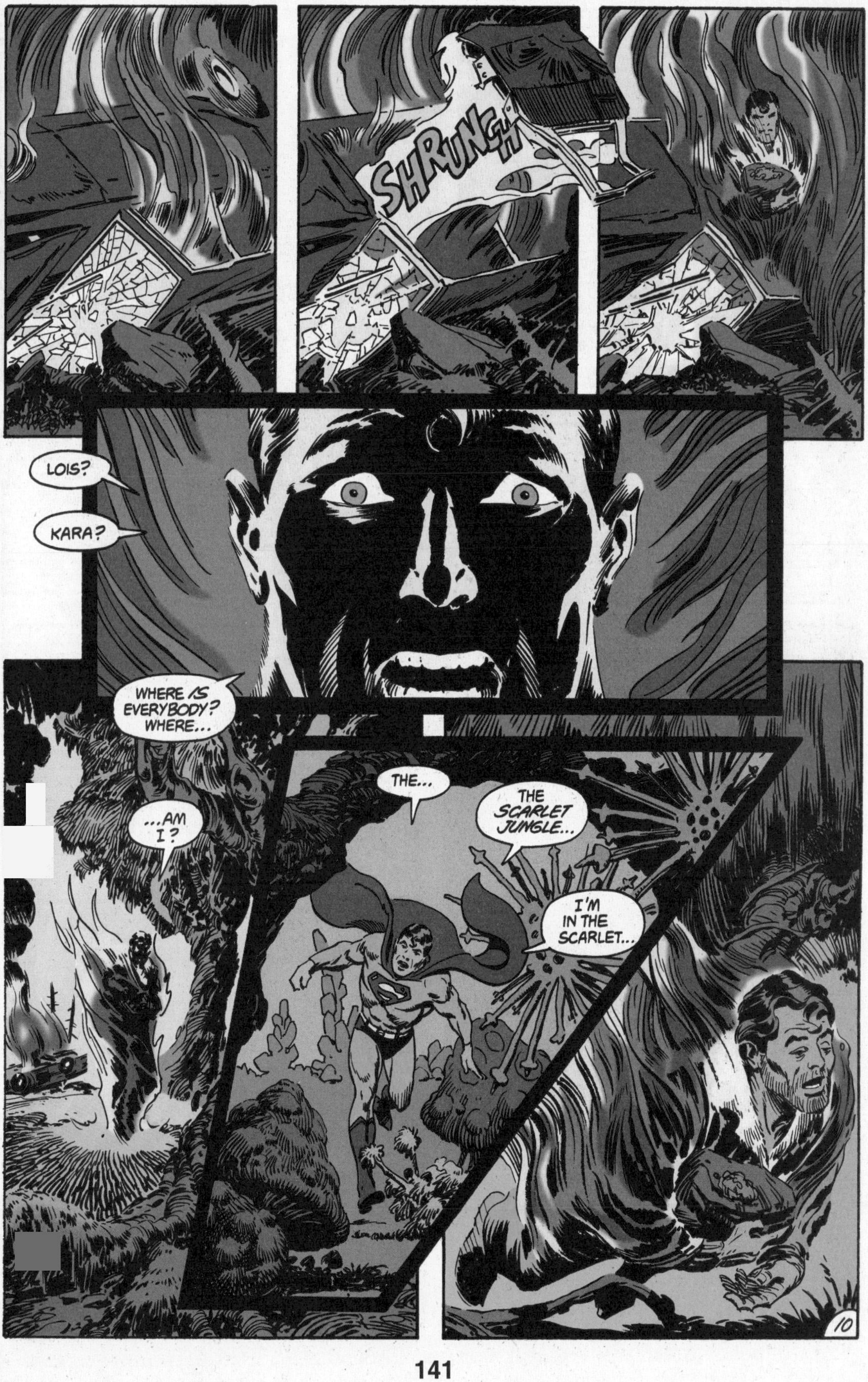
SHRUNCH
LOIS?
KARA?
WHERE IS EVERYBODY? WHERE...
...AM I?
THE...
THE SCARLET JUNGLE...
I'M IN THE SCARLET...
10

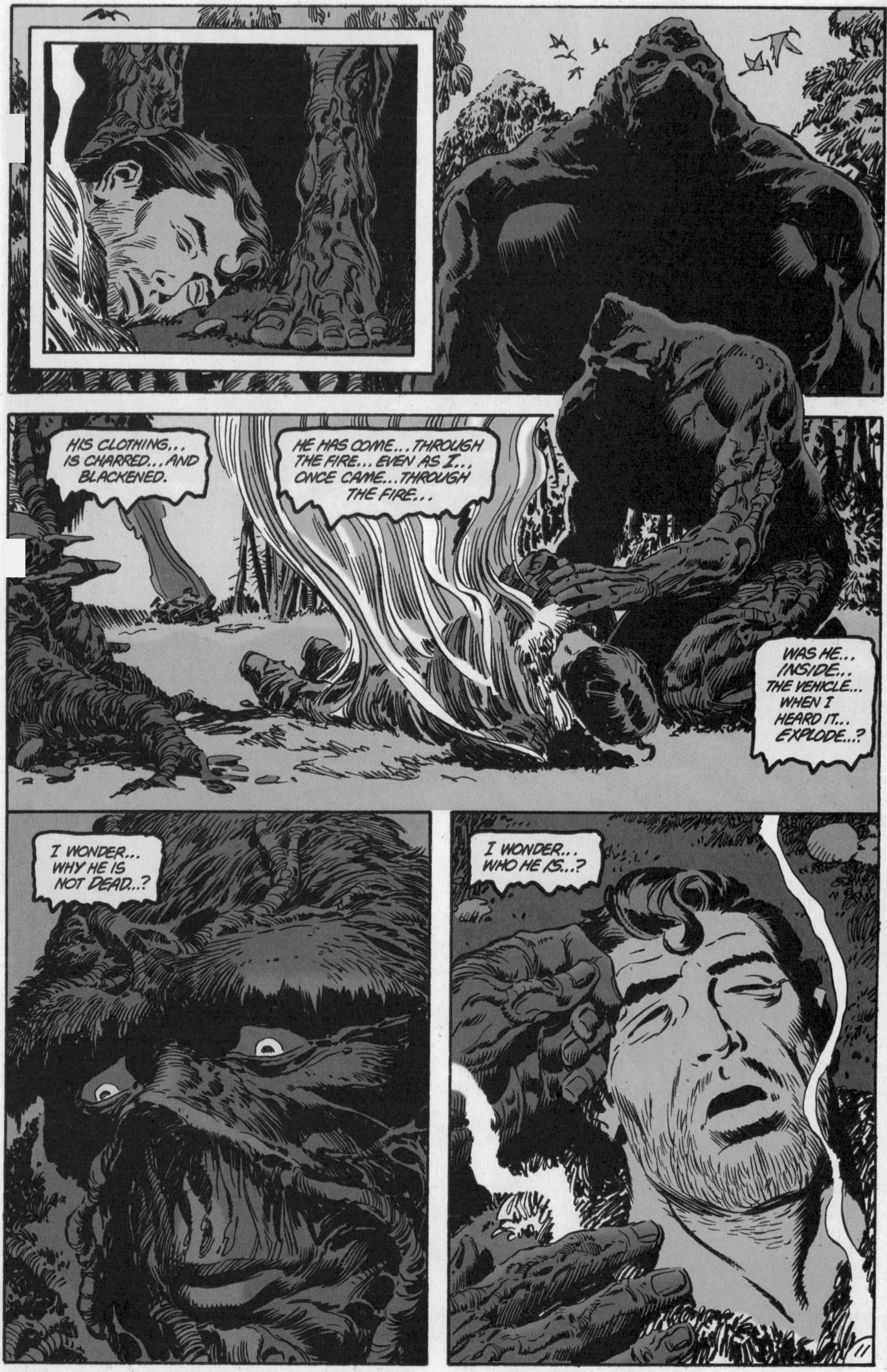
HIS CLOTHING... IS CHARRED... AND BLACKENED.
HE HAS COME... THROUGH THE FIRE... EVEN AS I... ONCE CAME... THROUGH THE FIRE...
WAS HE... INSIDE... THE VEHICLE... WHEN I HEARD IT... EXPLODE...?
I WONDER... WHY HE IS NOT DEAD...?
I WONDER... WHO HE IS...?

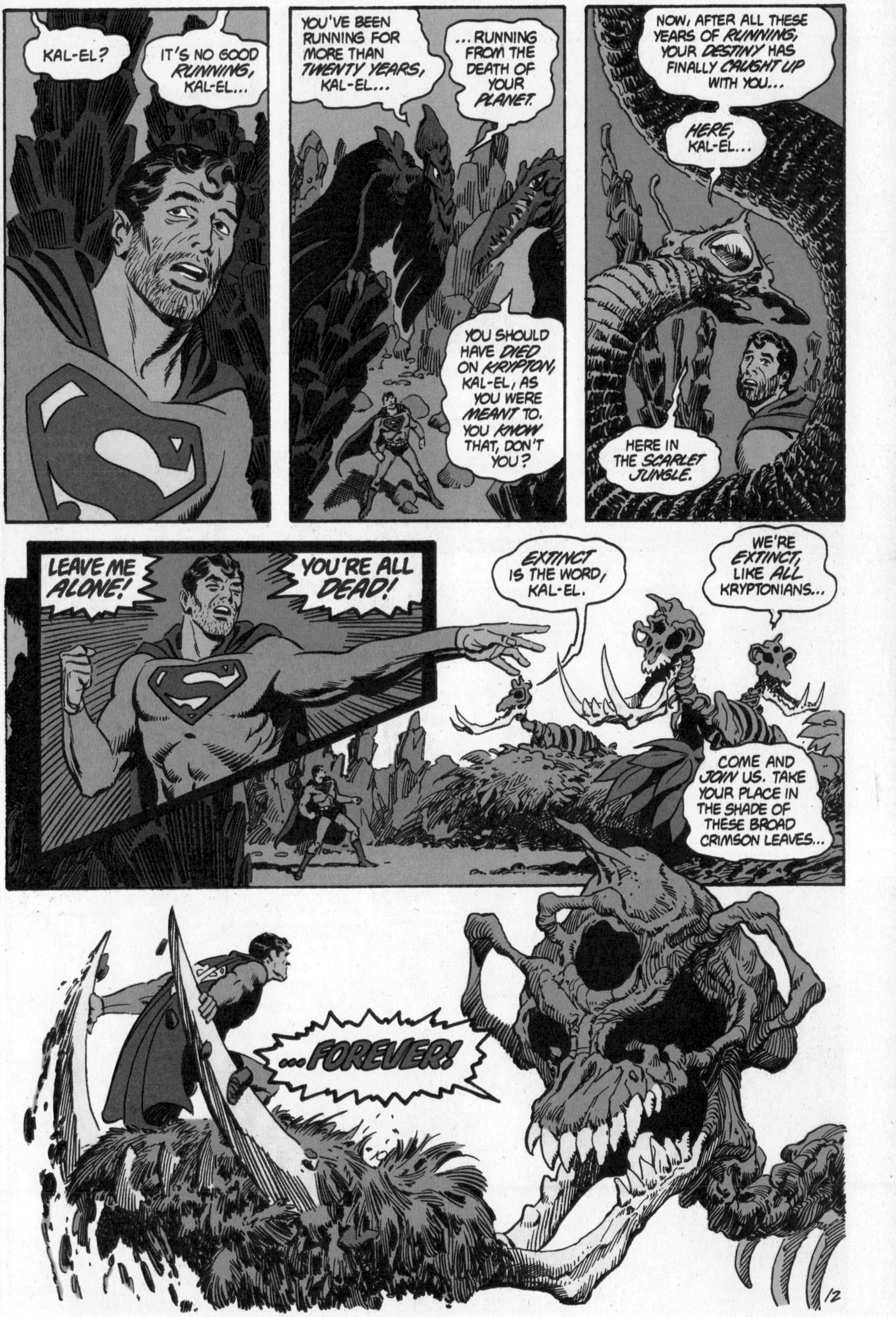

KAL-EL?
IT'S NO GOOD RUNNING, KAL-EL...
YOU'VE BEEN RUNNING FOR MORE THAN TWENTY YEARS, KAL-EL...
...RUNNING FROM THE DEATH OF YOUR PLANET.
YOU SHOULD HAVE DIED ON KRYPTON, KAL-EL, AS YOU WERE MEANT TO. YOU KNOW THAT, DON'T YOU?
NOW, AFTER ALL THESE YEARS OF RUNNING, YOUR DESTINY HAS FINALLY CAUGHT UP WITH YOU...
HERE, KAL-EL...
HERE IN THE SCARLET JUNGLE.
LEAVE ME ALONE!
YOU'RE ALL DEAD!
EXTINCT IS THE WORD, KAL-EL.
WE'RE EXTINCT, LIKE ALL KRYPTONIANS...
COME AND JOIN US. TAKE YOUR PLACE IN THE SHADE OF THESE BROAD CRIMSON LEAVES...
...FOREVER!
12

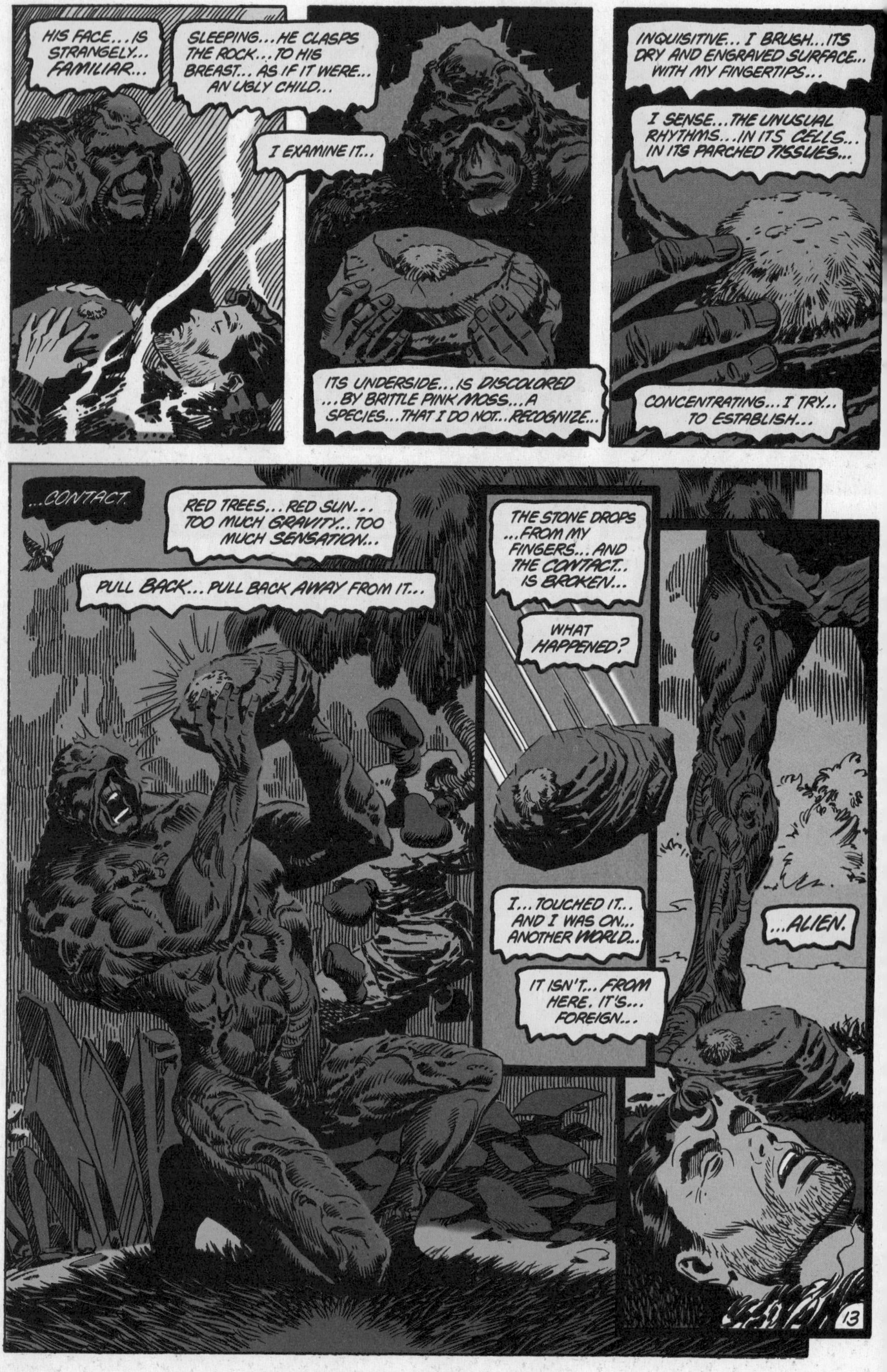
HIS FACE... IS STRANGELY... FAMILIAR...
SLEEPING... HE CLASPS THE ROCK... TO HIS BREAST... AS IF IT WERE... AN UGLY CHILD...
I EXAMINE IT...
ITS UNDERSIDE... IS DISCOLORED ...BY BRITTLE PINK MOSS... A SPECIES... THAT I DO NOT... RECOGNIZE...
INQUISITIVE... I BRUSH... ITS DRY AND ENGRAVED SURFACE... WITH MY FINGERTIPS...
I SENSE... THE UNUSUAL RHYTHMS... IN ITS CELLS... IN ITS PARCHED TISSUES...
CONCENTRATING... I TRY... TO ESTABLISH...
...CONTACT.
RED TREES... RED SUN... TOO MUCH GRAVITY... TOO MUCH SENSATION...
PULL BACK... PULL BACK AWAY FROM IT...
THE STONE DROPS ...FROM MY FINGERS... AND THE CONTACT... IS BROKEN...
WHAT HAPPENED?
I... TOUCHED IT... AND I WAS ON... ANOTHER WORLD...
IT ISN'T... FROM HERE. IT'S... FOREIGN...
...ALIEN.
13

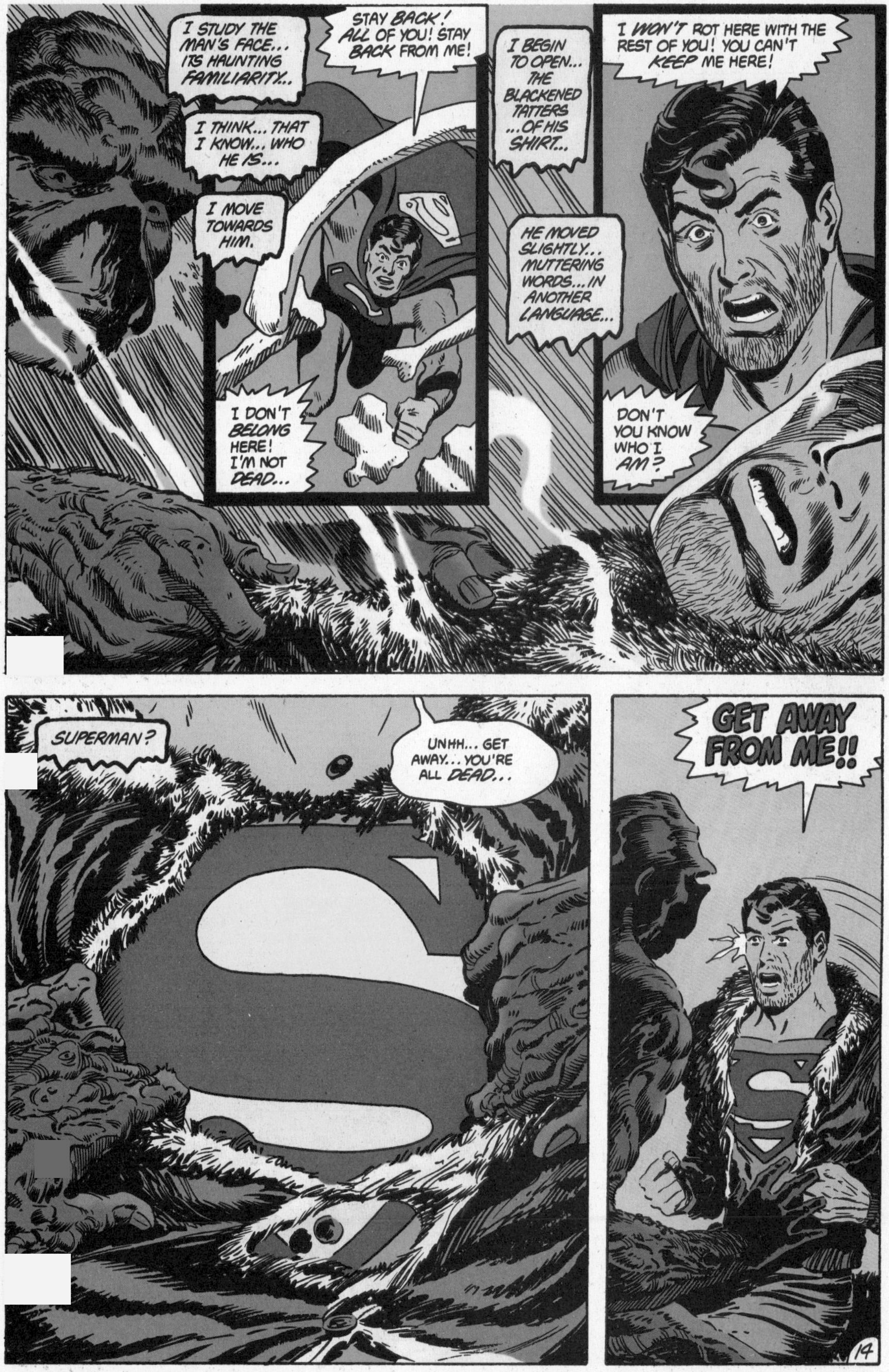
I STUDY THE MAN'S FACE... ITS HAUNTING FAMILIARITY...
I THINK... THAT I KNOW... WHO HE IS...
I MOVE TOWARDS HIM.
STAY BACK! ALL OF YOU! STAY BACK FROM ME!
I DON'T BELONG HERE! I'M NOT DEAD...
I BEGIN TO OPEN... THE BLACKENED TATTERS ...OF HIS SHIRT...
HE MOVED SLIGHTLY... MUTTERING WORDS... IN ANOTHER LANGUAGE...
I WON'T ROT HERE WITH THE REST OF YOU! YOU CAN'T KEEP ME HERE!
DON'T YOU KNOW WHO I AM?
SUPERMAN?
UNHH... GET AWAY... YOU'RE ALL DEAD...
GET AWAY FROM ME!!
14

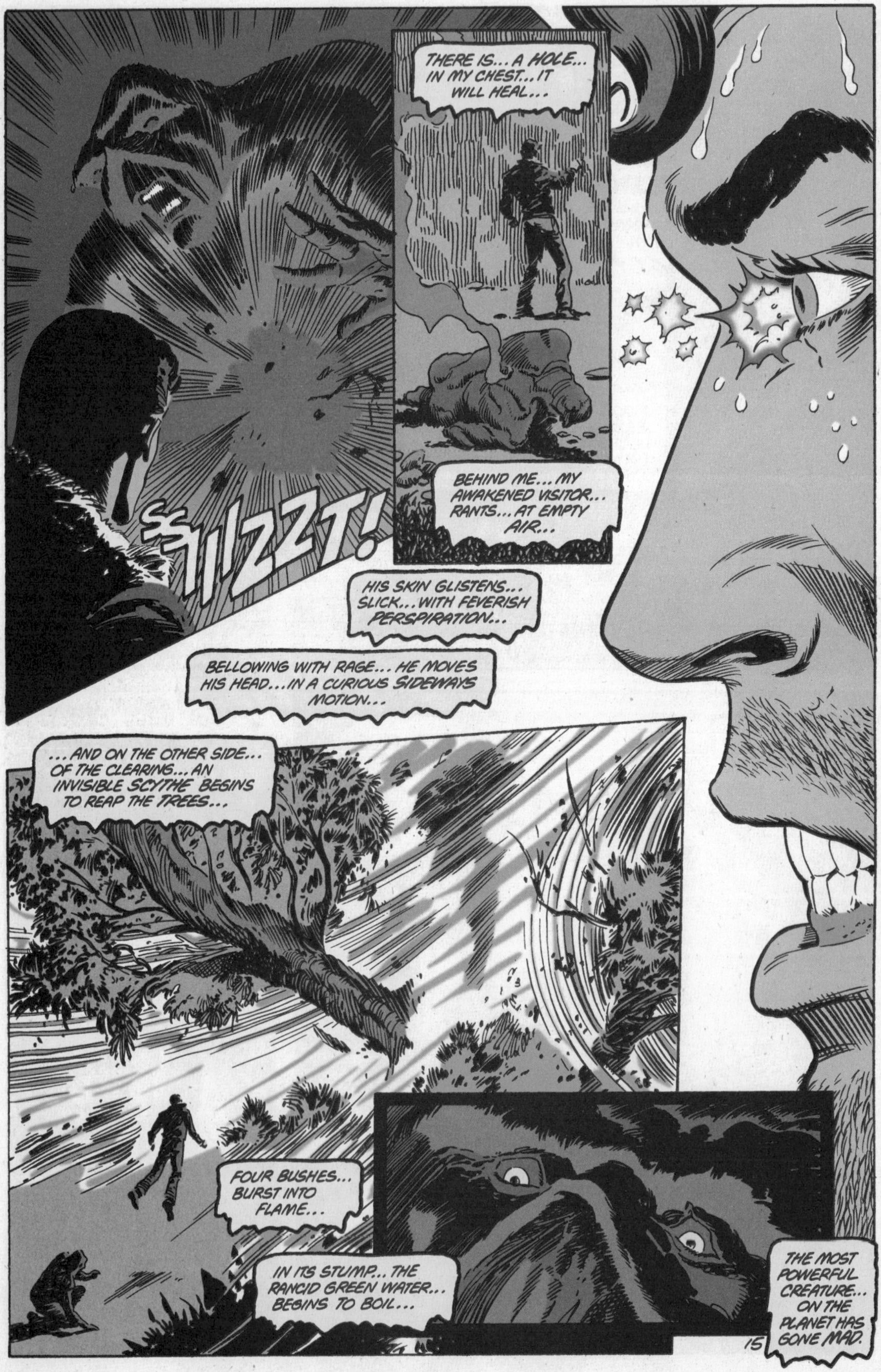
SSHHIZZZT!
THERE IS... A HOLE... IN MY CHEST... IT WILL HEAL...
BEHIND ME... MY AWAKENED VISITOR... RANTS... AT EMPTY AIR...
HIS SKIN GLISTENS... SLICK... WITH FEVERISH PERSPIRATION...
BELLOWING WITH RAGE... HE MOVES HIS HEAD... IN A CURIOUS SIDEWAYS MOTION...
...AND ON THE OTHER SIDE... OF THE CLEARING... AN INVISIBLE SCYTHE BEGINS TO REAP THE TREES...
FOUR BUSHES... BURST INTO FLAME...
IN ITS STUMP... THE RANCID GREEN WATER... BEGINS TO BOIL...
THE MOST POWERFUL CREATURE... ON THE PLANET HAS GONE MAD.
15

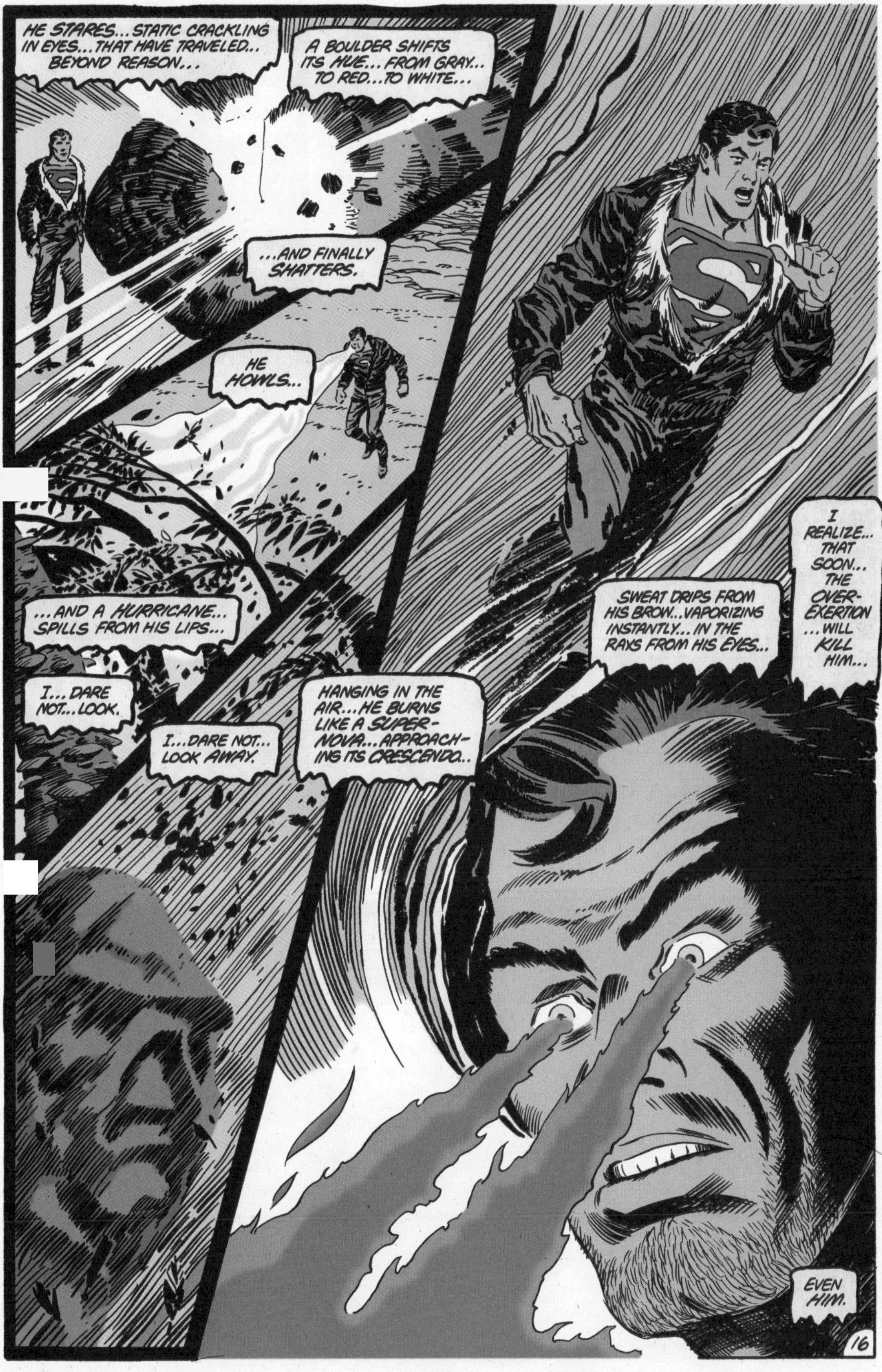
HE STARES... STATIC CRACKLING IN EYES... THAT HAVE TRAVELED... BEYOND REASON...
A BOULDER SHIFTS ITS HUE... FROM GRAY... TO RED... TO WHITE...
...AND FINALLY SHATTERS.
HE HOWLS...
...AND A HURRICANE... SPILLS FROM HIS LIPS...
I... DARE NOT... LOOK.
I... DARE NOT... LOOK AWAY.
HANGING IN THE AIR... HE BURNS LIKE A SUPER-NOVA... APPROACH-ING ITS CRESCENDO...
SWEAT DRIPS FROM HIS BROW... VAPORIZING INSTANTLY... IN THE RAYS FROM HIS EYES...
I REALIZE... THAT SOON... THE OVER-EXERTION ...WILL KILL HIM...
EVEN HIM.
16

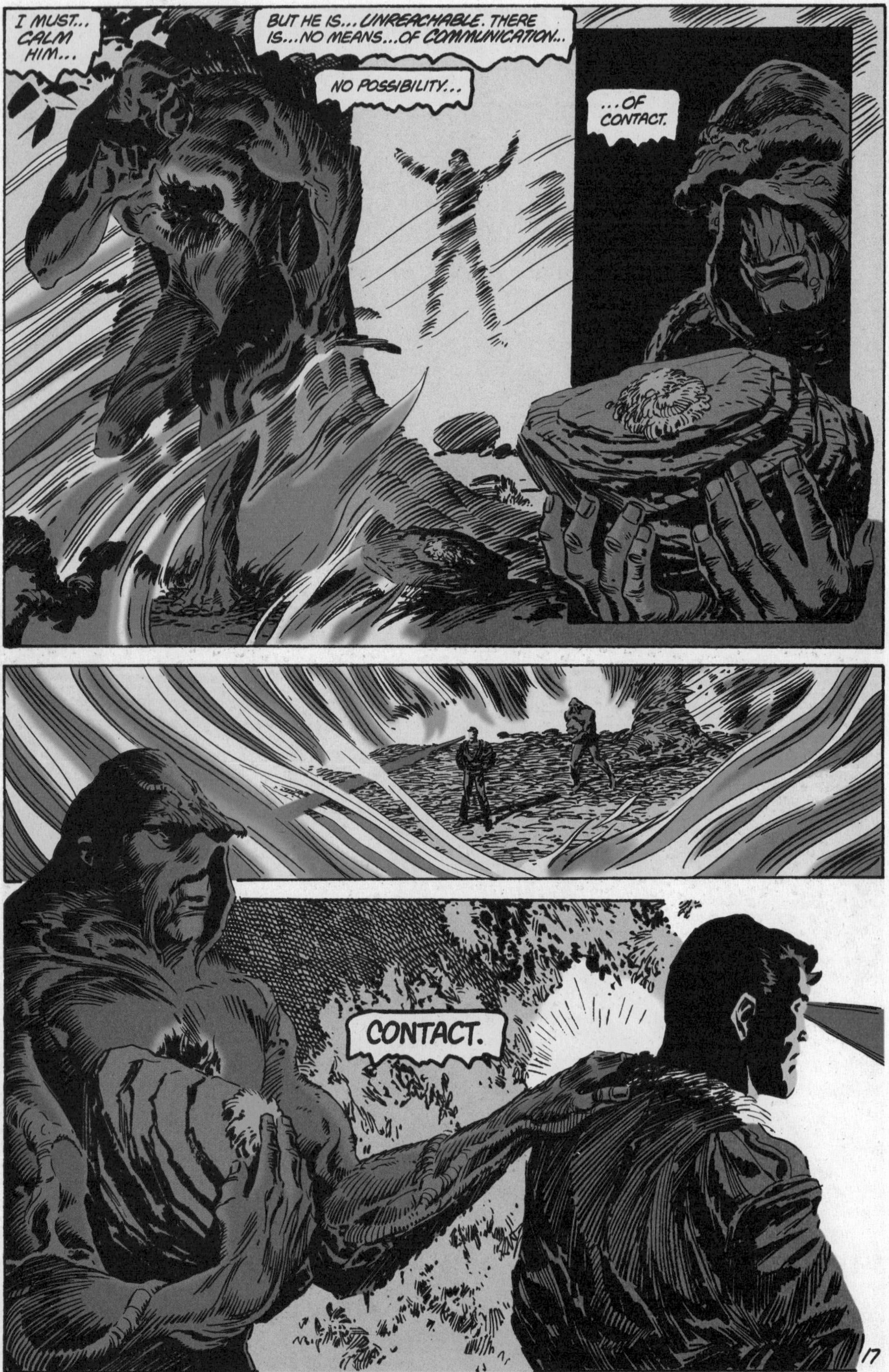
I MUST... CALM HIM...
BUT HE IS... UNREACHABLE. THERE IS... NO MEANS... OF COMMUNICATION...
NO POSSIBILITY...
...OF CONTACT.
CONTACT.
17

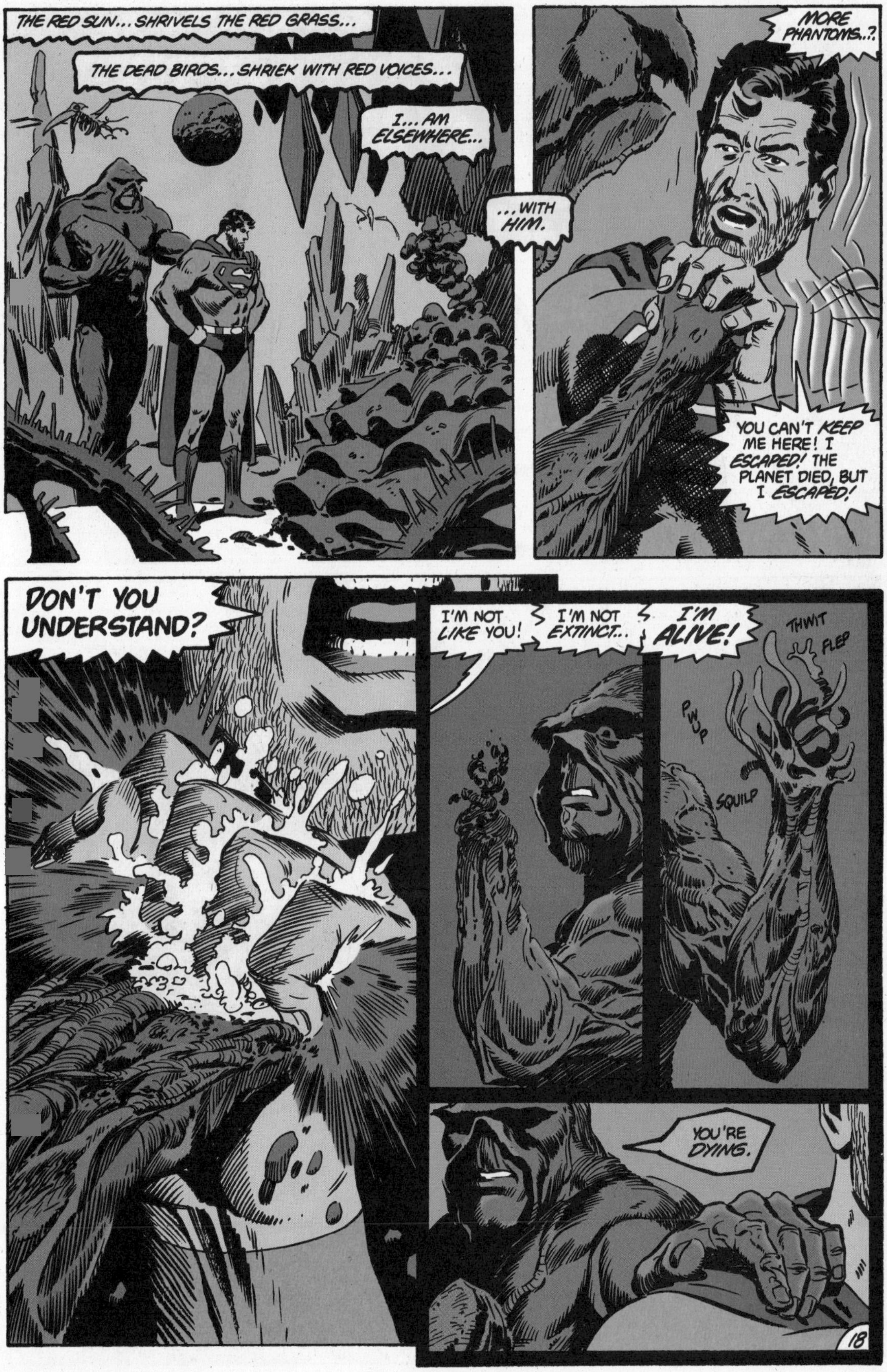

THE RED SUN... SHRIVELS THE RED GRASS...
THE DEAD BIRDS... SHRIEK WITH RED VOICES...
I... AM ELSEWHERE...
...WITH HIM.
MORE PHANTOMS..?
YOU CAN'T KEEP ME HERE! I ESCAPED! THE PLANET DIED, BUT I ESCAPED!
DON'T YOU UNDERSTAND?
I'M NOT LIKE YOU!
I'M NOT EXTINCT...
I'M ALIVE!
THWIT
FLEP
PWUP
SQUILP
YOU'RE DYING.
18

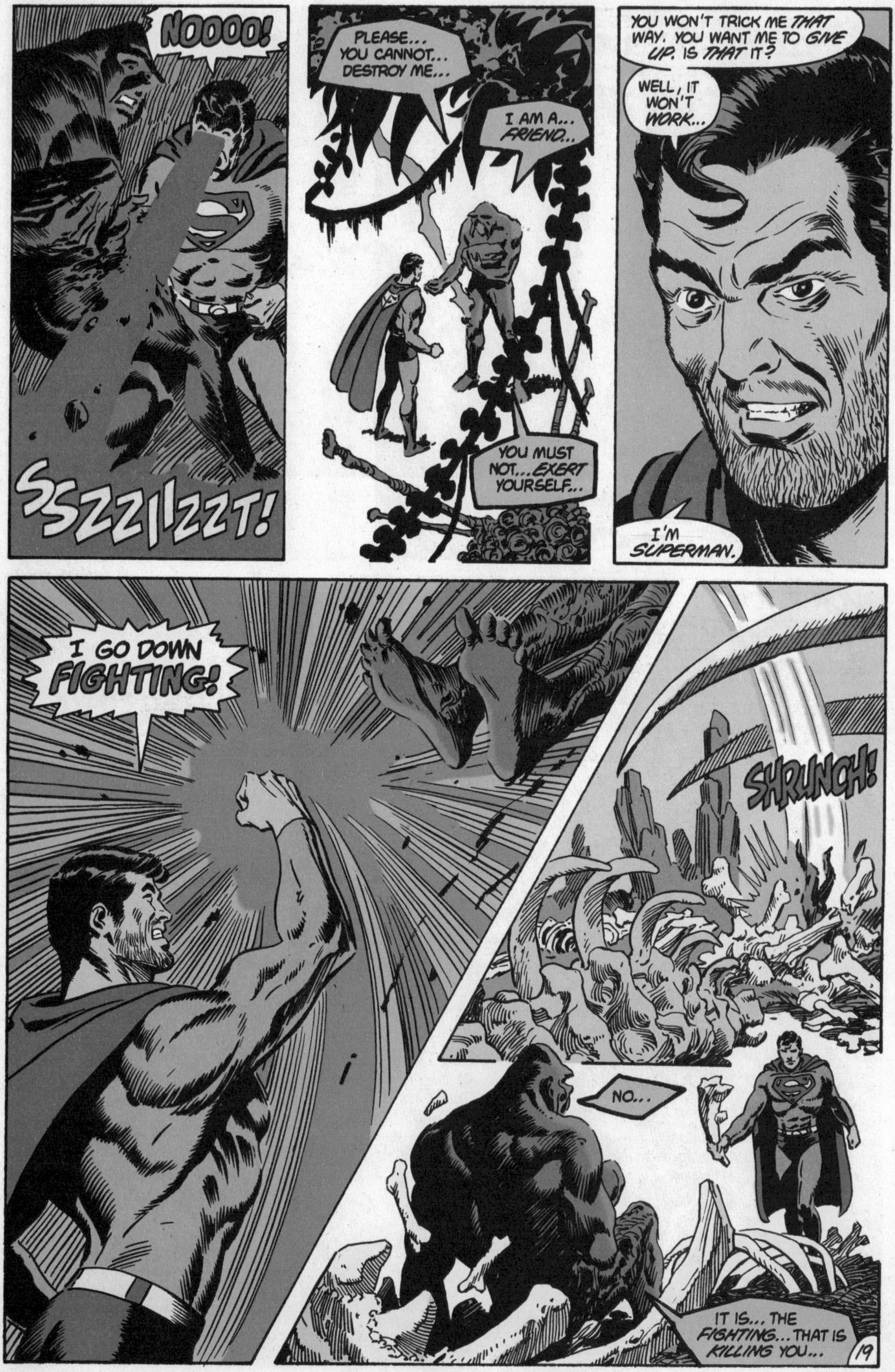
NOOOO!
SSZZII'ZZT!
PLEASE... YOU CANNOT... DESTROY ME...
I AM A... FRIEND...
YOU MUST NOT... EXERT YOURSELF...
YOU WON'T TRICK ME THAT WAY. YOU WANT ME TO GIVE UP. IS THAT IT?
WELL, IT WON'T WORK...
I'M SUPERMAN.
I GO DOWN FIGHTING!
SHRUNCH!
NO...
IT IS... THE FIGHTING... THAT IS KILLING YOU...
19

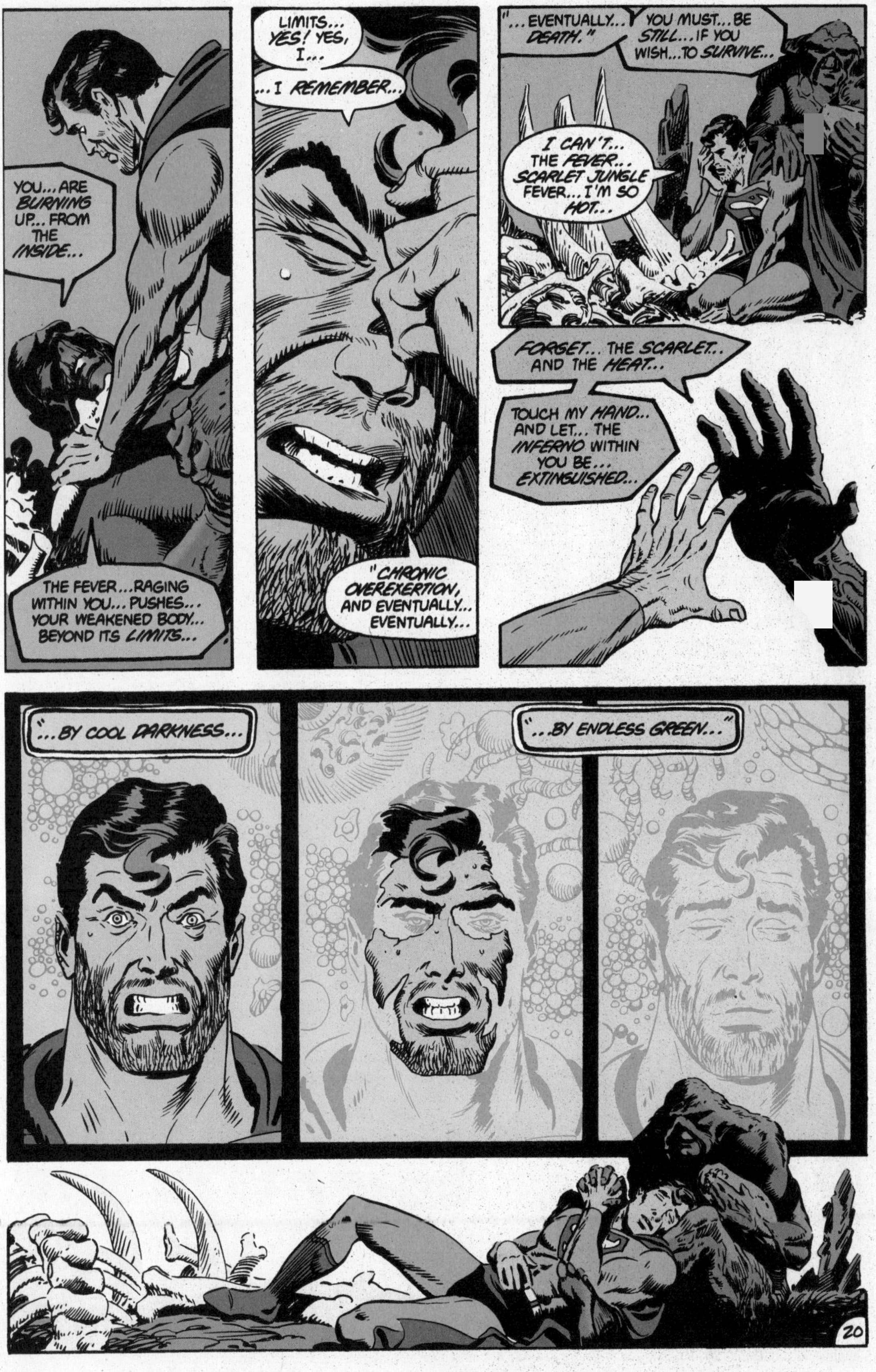

YOU... ARE BURNING UP... FROM THE INSIDE...
THE FEVER... RAGING WITHIN YOU... PUSHES... YOUR WEAKENED BODY... BEYOND ITS LIMITS...
LIMITS... YES! YES, I...
...I REMEMBER...
"CHRONIC OVEREXERTION, AND EVENTUALLY... EVENTUALLY...
"...EVENTUALLY... DEATH."
YOU MUST... BE STILL... IF YOU WISH... TO SURVIVE...
I CAN'T... THE FEVER... SCARLET JUNGLE FEVER... I'M SO HOT...
FORGET... THE SCARLET... AND THE HEAT...
TOUCH MY HAND... AND LET... THE INFERNO WITHIN YOU BE... EXTINGUISHED...
"...BY COOL DARKNESS...
"...BY ENDLESS GREEN..."
20

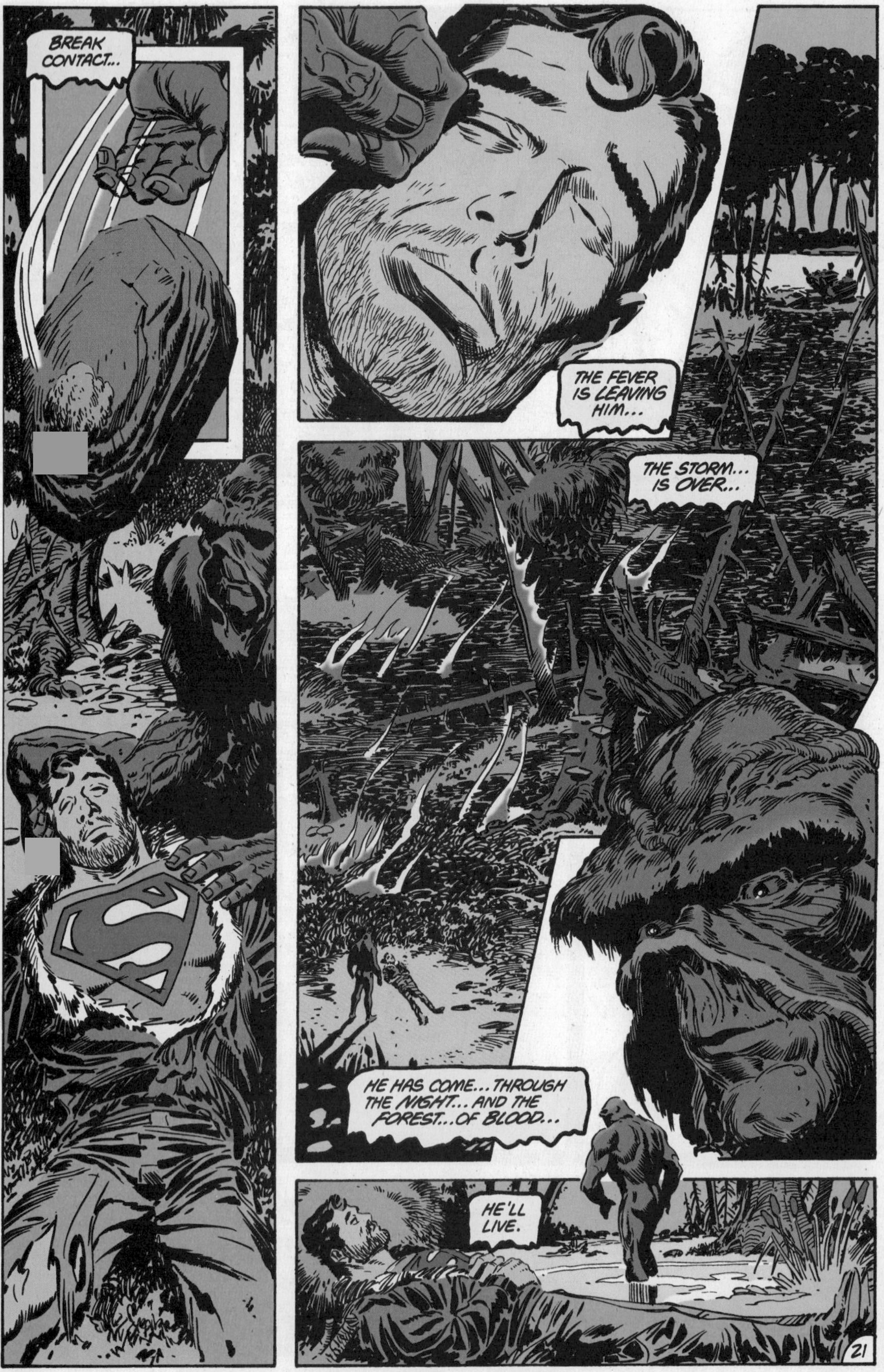
BREAK CONTACT...
THE FEVER IS LEAVING HIM...
THE STORM... IS OVER...
HE HAS COME...THROUGH THE NIGHT... AND THE FOREST...OF BLOOD...
HE'LL LIVE.
21

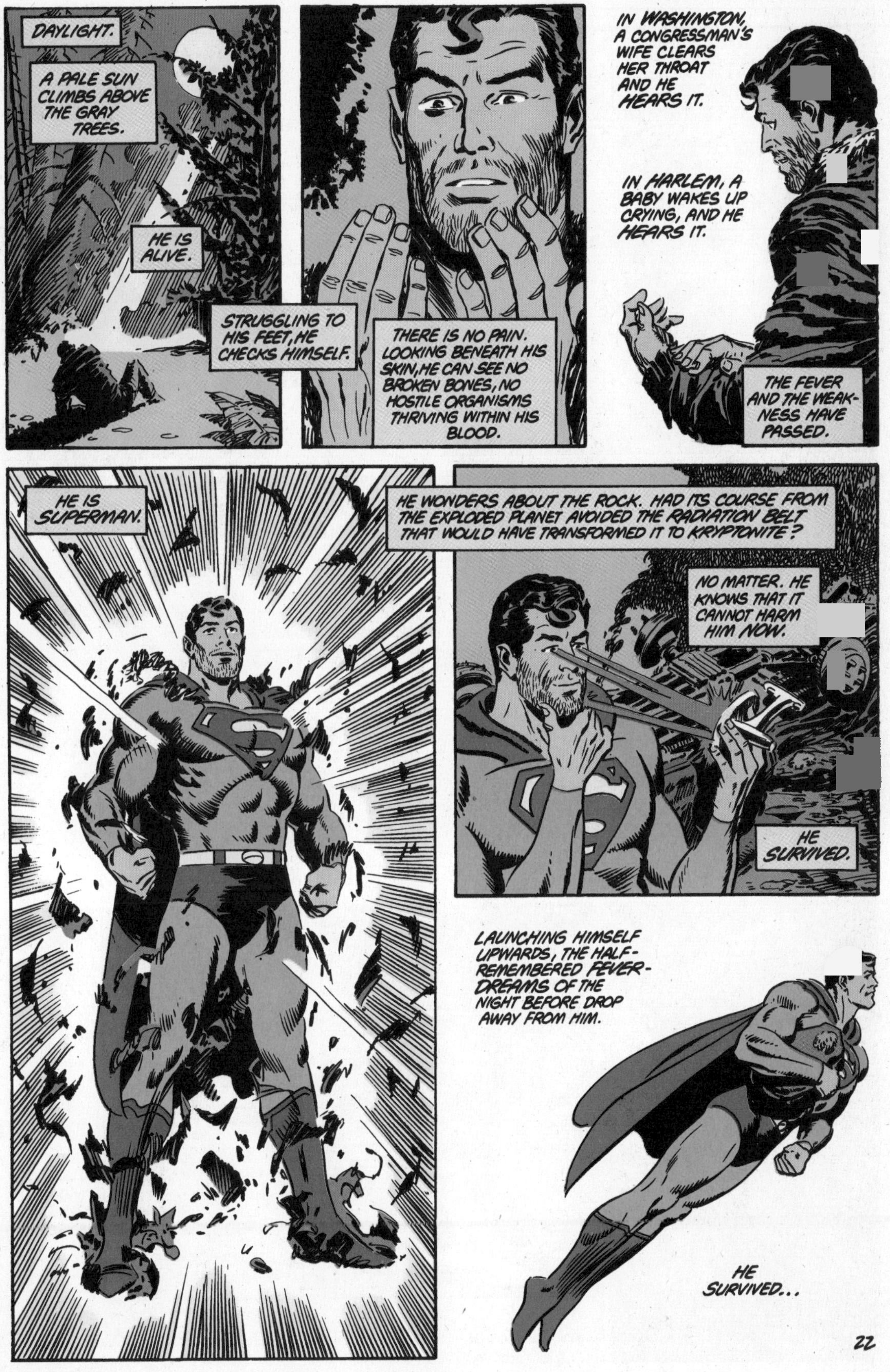
DAYLIGHT.
A PALE SUN CLIMBS ABOVE THE GRAY TREES.
HE IS ALIVE.
STRUGGLING TO HIS FEET, HE CHECKS HIMSELF.
THERE IS NO PAIN. LOOKING BENEATH HIS SKIN, HE CAN SEE NO BROKEN BONES, NO HOSTILE ORGANISMS THRIVING WITHIN HIS BLOOD.
IN WASHINGTON, A CONGRESSMAN'S WIFE CLEARS HER THROAT AND HE HEARS IT.
IN HARLEM, A BABY WAKES UP CRYING, AND HE HEARS IT.
THE FEVER AND THE WEAKNESS HAVE PASSED.
HE IS SUPERMAN.
HE WONDERS ABOUT THE ROCK. HAD ITS COURSE FROM THE EXPLODED PLANET AVOIDED THE RADIATION BELT THAT WOULD HAVE TRANSFORMED IT TO KRYPTONITE?
NO MATTER. HE KNOWS THAT IT CANNOT HARM HIM NOW.
HE SURVIVED.
LAUNCHING HIMSELF UPWARDS, THE HALF-REMEMBERED FEVER-DREAMS OF THE NIGHT BEFORE DROP AWAY FROM HIM.
HE SURVIVED...
22

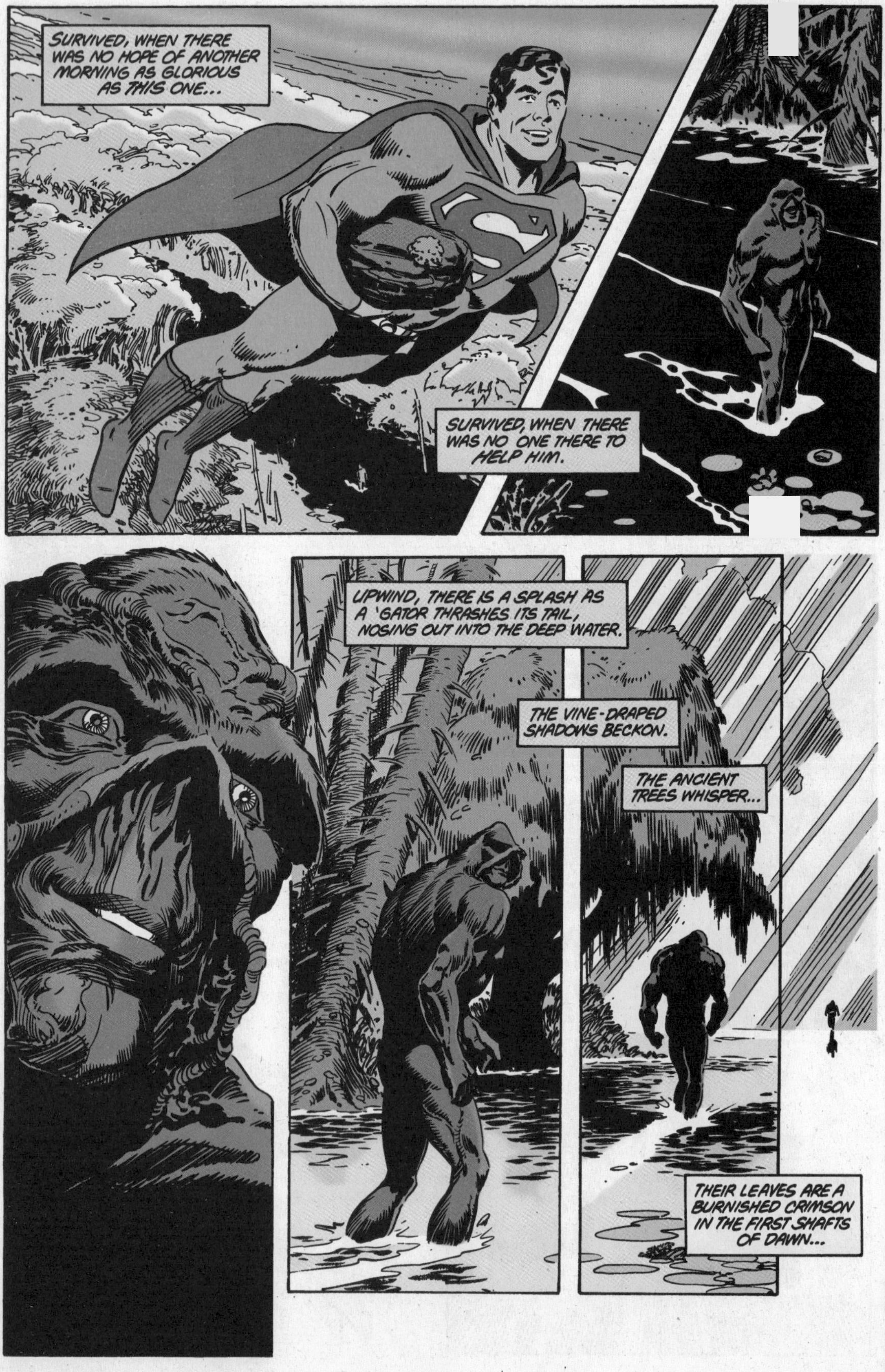
SURVIVED, WHEN THERE WAS NO HOPE OF ANOTHER MORNING AS GLORIOUS AS THIS ONE...
SURVIVED, WHEN THERE WAS NO ONE THERE TO HELP HIM.
UPWIND, THERE IS A SPLASH AS A 'GATOR THRASHES ITS TAIL, NOSING OUT INTO THE DEEP WATER.
THE VINE-DRAPED SHADOWS BECKON.
THE ANCIENT TREES WHISPER...
THEIR LEAVES ARE A BURNISHED CRIMSON IN THE FIRST SHAFTS OF DAWN...

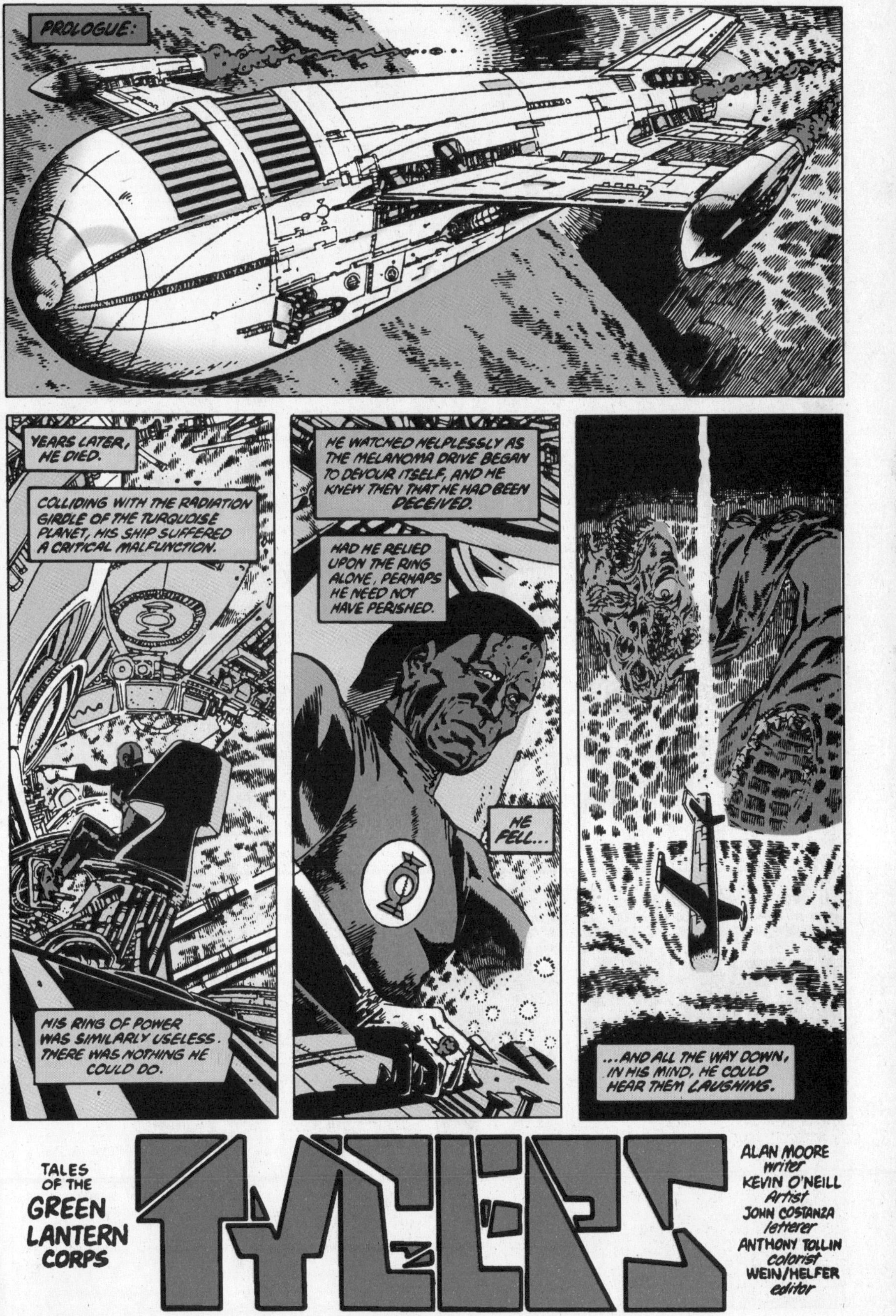
PROLOGUE:
YEARS LATER, HE DIED.
COLLIDING WITH THE RADIATION GIRDLE OF THE TURQUOISE PLANET, HIS SHIP SUFFERED A CRITICAL MALFUNCTION.
HIS RING OF POWER WAS SIMILARLY USELESS. THERE WAS NOTHING HE COULD DO.
HE WATCHED HELPLESSLY AS THE MELANOMA DRIVE BEGAN TO DEVOUR ITSELF, AND HE KNEW THEN THAT HE HAD BEEN DECEIVED.
HAD HE RELIED UPON THE RING ALONE, PERHAPS HE NEED NOT HAVE PERISHED.
HE FELL...
...AND ALL THE WAY DOWN, IN HIS MIND, HE COULD HEAR THEM LAUGHING.

TALES OF THE GREEN LANTERN CORPS

TYGERS

ALAN MOORE writer
KEVIN O'NEILL Artist
JOHN COSTANZA letterer
ANTHONY TOLLIN colorist
WEIN/HELFER editor

MANY YEARS EARLIER:

HMM.

TELL ME AGAIN WHAT YOU KNOW OF THE SPHERE BENEATH US.

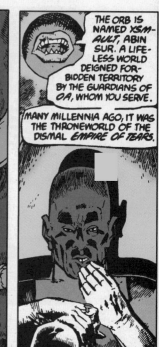

THE ORB IS NAMED XSM-AULT, ABIN SUR. A LIFE-LESS WORLD DEIGNED FOR-BIDDEN TERRITORY BY THE GUARDIANS OF OA, WHOM YOU SERVE.

MANY MILLENNIA AGO, IT WAS THE THRONEWORLD OF THE DISMAL *EMPIRE OF TEARS.*

"DURING THE NIGHT-EONS WHEN MAGIC HELD PROMINENCE, THE EMPIRE OF TEARS SPANNED THREE GALAXIES.

"ITS REGENTS, DEATHLESS AND MALIGN ESSENCES WHOSE CRUELTIES HAD GROWN TOO SOPHISTICATED FOR MORTAL FORM, REIGNED UNCHALLENGED..."

"...UNTIL THE ELDERS OF OA DECLARED THEMSELVES GUARDIANS OF THE UNIVERSE, COMMENCING WITH A PURGE OF DARK AND NECROMANTIC FACTIONS FROM THE STARWAYS.

"THE EMPIRE OF TEARS WAS NO MORE. THE DEMONS WERE CHAINED..."

...BUT NOT *DEAD.* THOUGH DISEMBODIED AND PHYSICALLY POWERLESS, THEIR SUBTLE AND DANGEROUS MINDS REMAIN ENTOMBED UPON YSMAULT.

IT IS A *CORPSE-WORLD,* HAUNTED BY ITS DEAD MASTERS, AND NONE MAY GO THERE SAVE BY THE GUARDIANS' LEAVE.

2

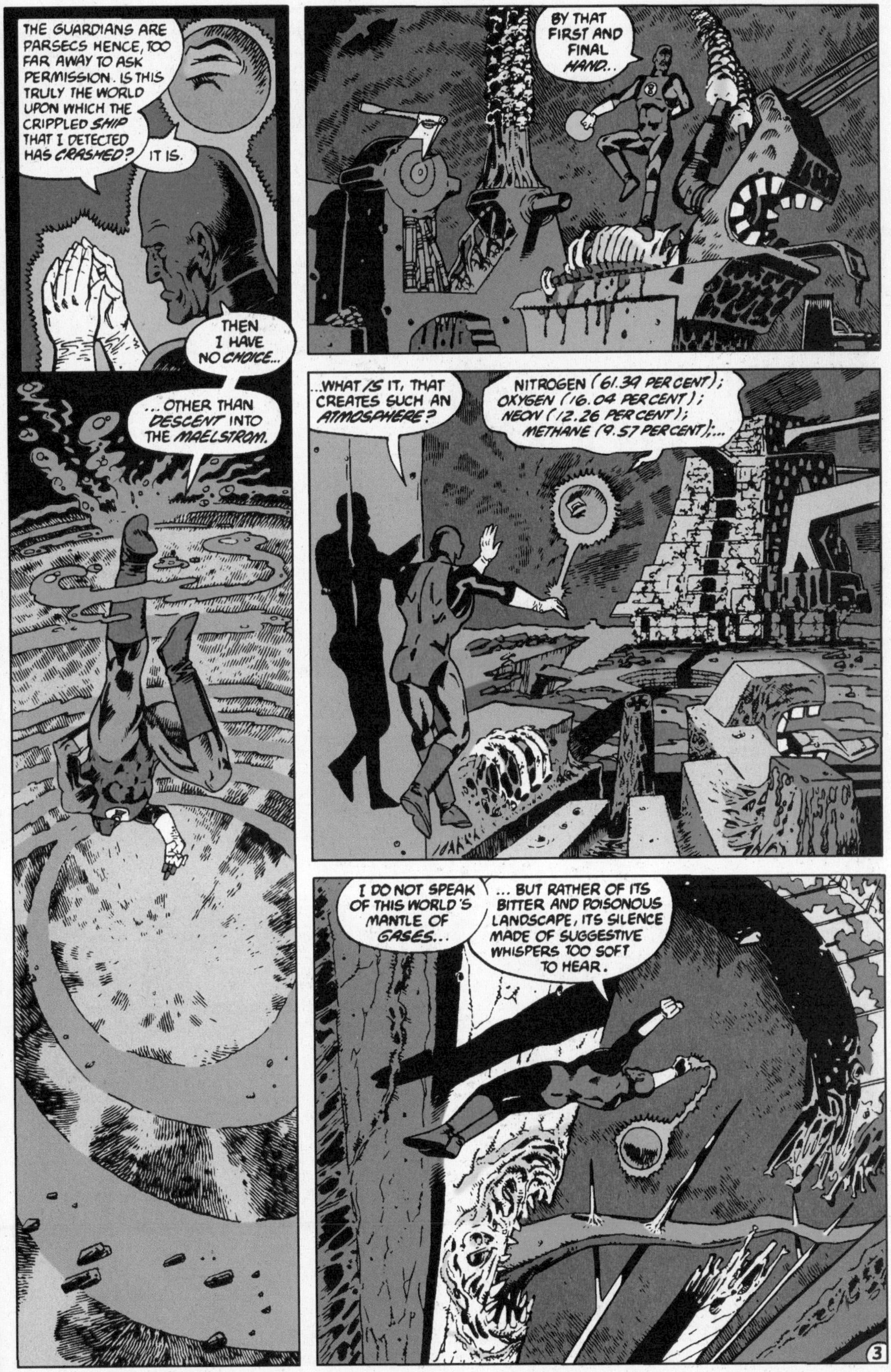
THE GUARDIANS ARE PARSECS HENCE, TOO FAR AWAY TO ASK PERMISSION. IS THIS TRULY THE WORLD UPON WHICH THE CRIPPLED SHIP THAT I DETECTED HAS CRASHED?
IT IS.
THEN I HAVE NO CHOICE...
BY THAT FIRST AND FINAL HAND...
...OTHER THAN DESCENT INTO THE MAELSTROM.
...WHAT IS IT, THAT CREATES SUCH AN ATMOSPHERE?
NITROGEN (61.39 PERCENT); OXYGEN (16.04 PERCENT); NEON (12.26 PERCENT); METHANE (9.57 PERCENT);...
I DO NOT SPEAK OF THIS WORLD'S MANTLE OF GASES...
... BUT RATHER OF ITS BITTER AND POISONOUS LANDSCAPE, ITS SILENCE MADE OF SUGGESTIVE WHISPERS TOO SOFT TO HEAR.
3

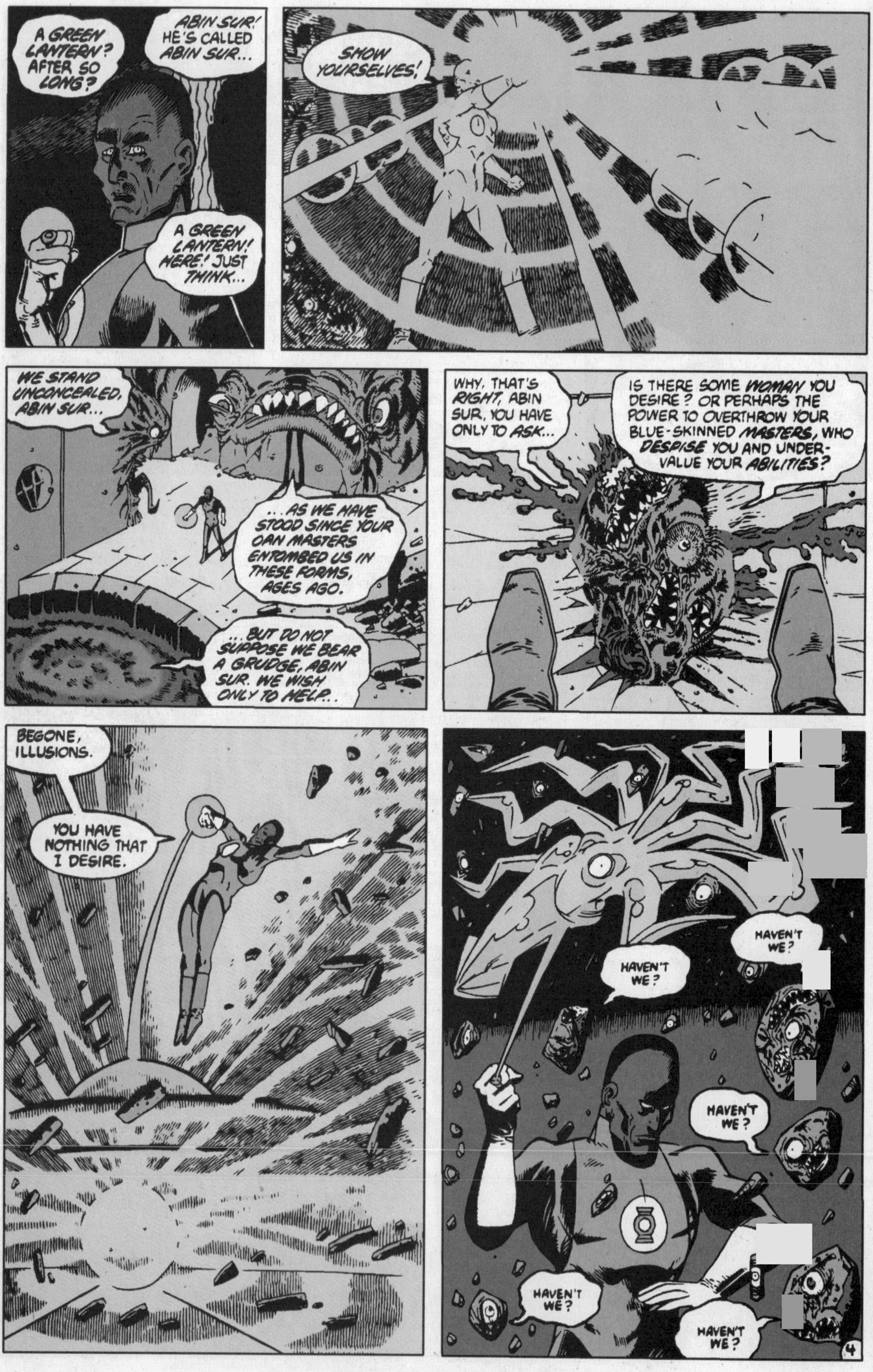
A GREEN LANTERN? AFTER SO LONG?
ABIN SUR! HE'S CALLED ABIN SUR...
A GREEN LANTERN! HERE! JUST THINK...
SHOW YOURSELVES!
WE STAND UNCONCEALED, ABIN SUR...
...AS WE HAVE STOOD SINCE YOUR OAN MASTERS ENTOMBED US IN THESE FORMS, AGES AGO.
...BUT DO NOT SUPPOSE WE BEAR A GRUDGE, ABIN SUR. WE WISH ONLY TO HELP...
WHY, THAT'S RIGHT, ABIN SUR. YOU HAVE ONLY TO ASK...
IS THERE SOME WOMAN YOU DESIRE? OR PERHAPS THE POWER TO OVERTHROW YOUR BLUE-SKINNED MASTERS, WHO DESPISE YOU AND UNDER-VALUE YOUR ABILITIES?
BEGONE, ILLUSIONS.
YOU HAVE NOTHING THAT I DESIRE.
HAVEN'T WE?
HAVEN'T WE?
HAVEN'T WE?
HAVEN'T WE?
HAVEN'T WE?

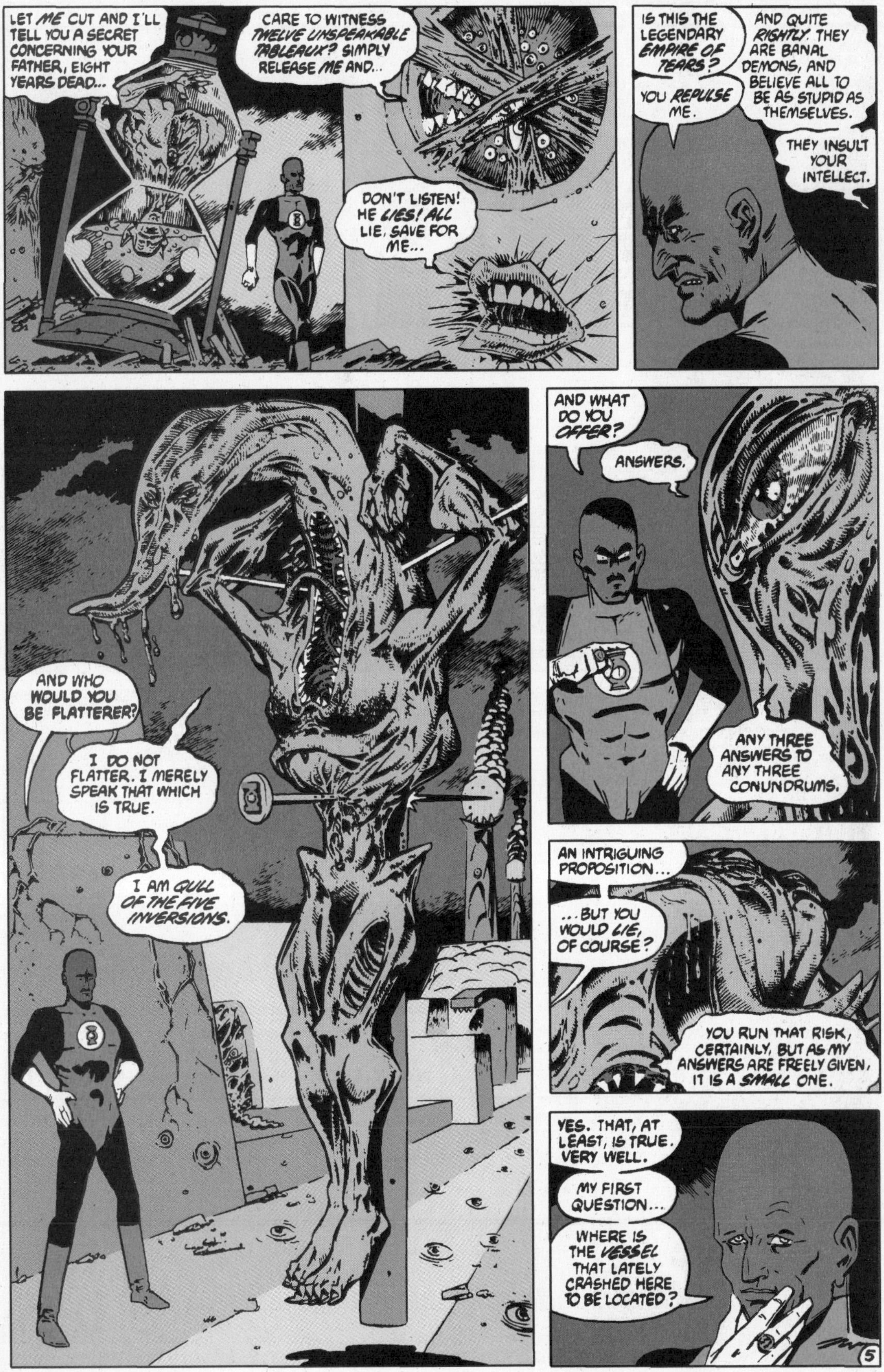
LET ME CUT AND I'LL TELL YOU A SECRET CONCERNING YOUR FATHER, EIGHT YEARS DEAD...
CARE TO WITNESS TWELVE UNSPEAKABLE TABLEAUX? SIMPLY RELEASE ME AND...
DON'T LISTEN! HE LIES! ALL LIE, SAVE FOR ME...
IS THIS THE LEGENDARY EMPIRE OF TEARS?
AND QUITE RIGHTLY. THEY ARE BANAL DEMONS, AND BELIEVE ALL TO BE AS STUPID AS THEMSELVES.
YOU REPULSE ME.
THEY INSULT YOUR INTELLECT.
AND WHO WOULD YOU BE FLATTERER?
I DO NOT FLATTER. I MERELY SPEAK THAT WHICH IS TRUE.
I AM QULL OF THE FIVE INVERSIONS.
AND WHAT DO YOU OFFER?
ANSWERS.
ANY THREE ANSWERS TO ANY THREE CONUNDRUMS.
AN INTRIGUING PROPOSITION...
...BUT YOU WOULD LIE, OF COURSE?
YOU RUN THAT RISK, CERTAINLY, BUT AS MY ANSWERS ARE FREELY GIVEN, IT IS A SMALL ONE.
YES. THAT, AT LEAST, IS TRUE. VERY WELL.
MY FIRST QUESTION...
WHERE IS THE VESSEL THAT LATELY CRASHED HERE TO BE LOCATED?
5

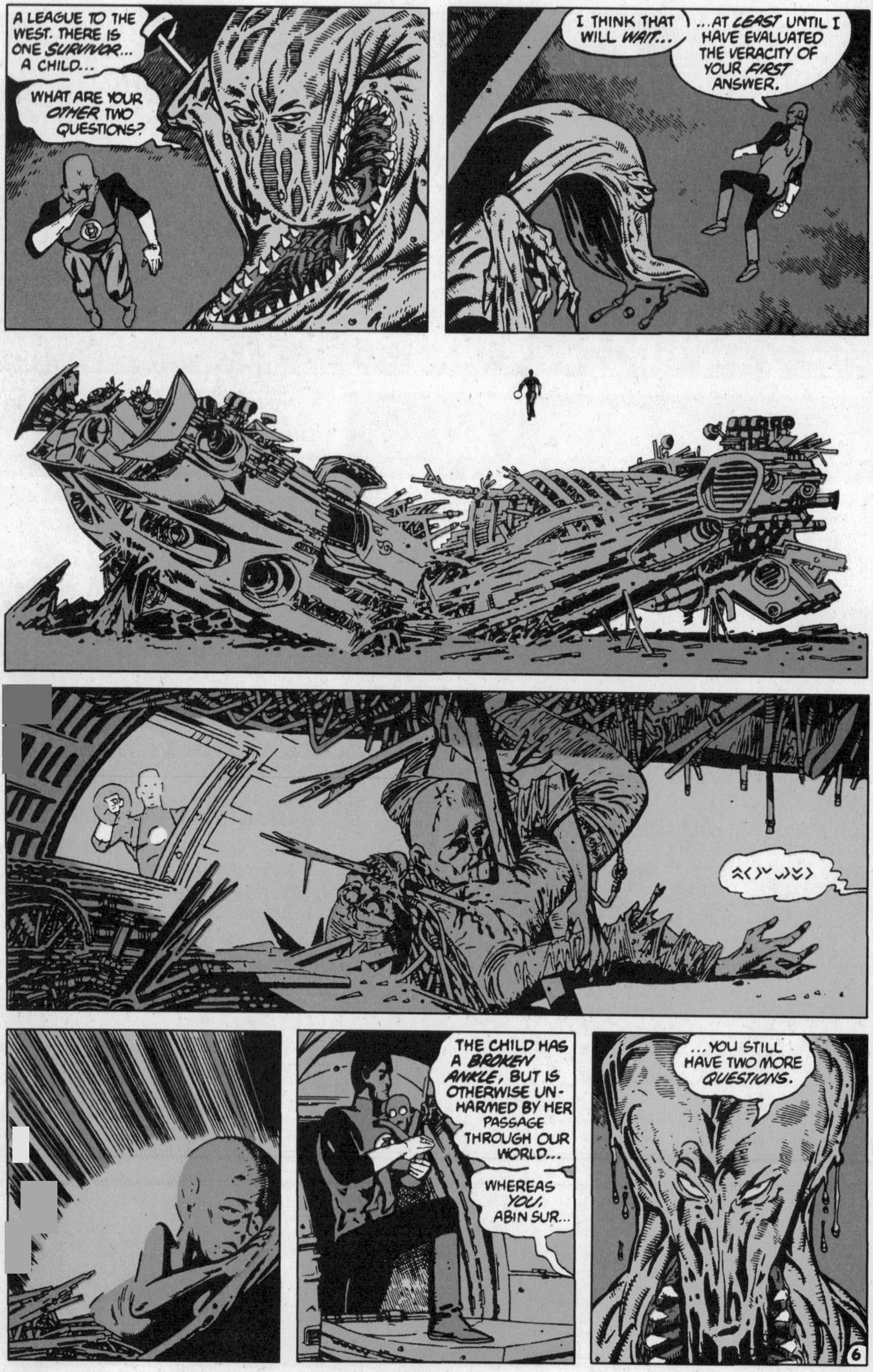
A LEAGUE TO THE WEST. THERE IS ONE SURVIVOR... A CHILD...
WHAT ARE YOUR OTHER TWO QUESTIONS?
I THINK THAT WILL WAIT...
...AT LEAST UNTIL I HAVE EVALUATED THE VERACITY OF YOUR FIRST ANSWER.
THE CHILD HAS A BROKEN ANKLE, BUT IS OTHERWISE UN-HARMED BY HER PASSAGE THROUGH OUR WORLD...
WHEREAS YOU, ABIN SUR...
...YOU STILL HAVE TWO MORE QUESTIONS.
6

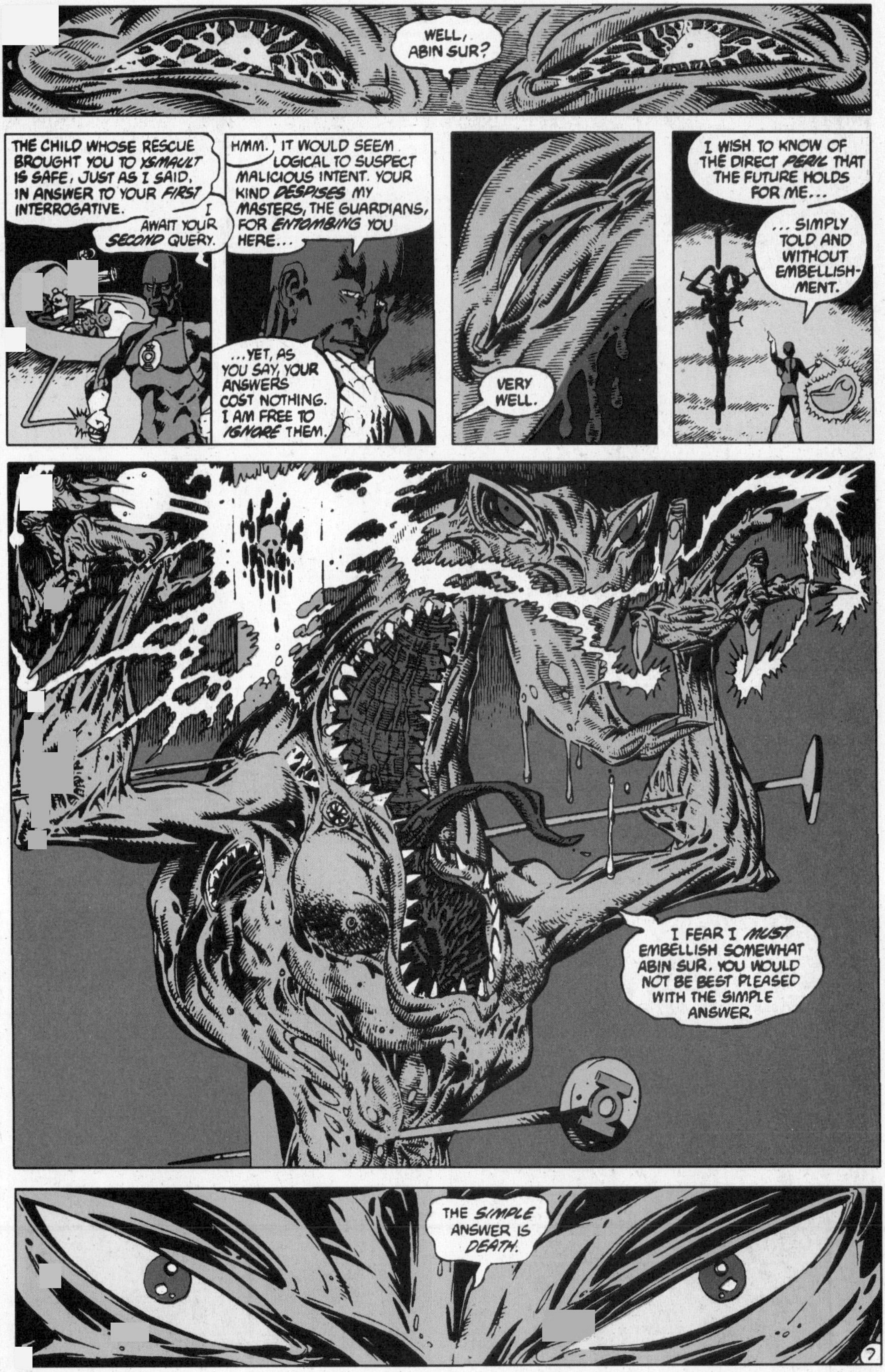
WELL, ABIN SUR?
THE CHILD WHOSE RESCUE BROUGHT YOU TO YSMAULT IS SAFE, JUST AS I SAID, IN ANSWER TO YOUR FIRST INTERROGATIVE.
I AWAIT YOUR SECOND QUERY.
HMM.
IT WOULD SEEM LOGICAL TO SUSPECT MALICIOUS INTENT. YOUR KIND DESPISES MY MASTERS, THE GUARDIANS, FOR ENTOMBING YOU HERE...
...YET, AS YOU SAY, YOUR ANSWERS COST NOTHING. I AM FREE TO IGNORE THEM.
VERY WELL.
I WISH TO KNOW OF THE DIRECT PERIL THAT THE FUTURE HOLDS FOR ME...
...SIMPLY TOLD AND WITHOUT EMBELLISHMENT.
I FEAR I MUST EMBELLISH SOMEWHAT ABIN SUR. YOU WOULD NOT BE BEST PLEASED WITH THE SIMPLE ANSWER.
THE SIMPLE ANSWER IS DEATH.
7

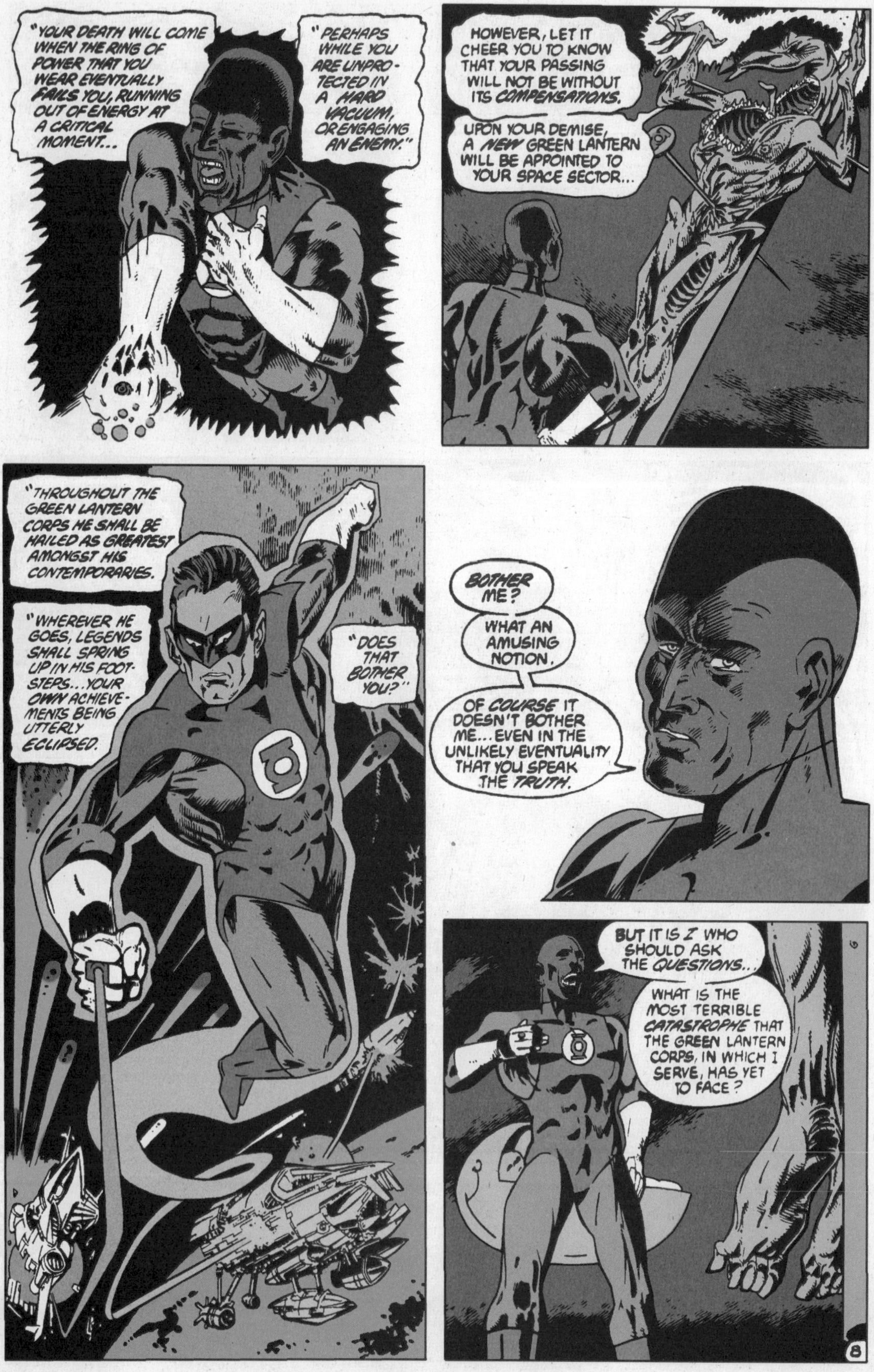
"YOUR DEATH WILL COME WHEN THE RING OF POWER THAT YOU WEAR EVENTUALLY FAILS YOU, RUNNING OUT OF ENERGY AT A CRITICAL MOMENT...
"PERHAPS WHILE YOU ARE UNPROTECTED IN A HARD VACUUM, OR ENGAGING AN ENEMY."
HOWEVER, LET IT CHEER YOU TO KNOW THAT YOUR PASSING WILL NOT BE WITHOUT ITS COMPENSATIONS.
UPON YOUR DEMISE, A NEW GREEN LANTERN WILL BE APPOINTED TO YOUR SPACE SECTOR...
"THROUGHOUT THE GREEN LANTERN CORPS HE SHALL BE HAILED AS GREATEST AMONGST HIS CONTEMPORARIES.
"WHEREVER HE GOES, LEGENDS SHALL SPRING UP IN HIS FOOTSTEPS... YOUR OWN ACHIEVEMENTS BEING UTTERLY ECLIPSED.
"DOES THAT BOTHER YOU?"
BOTHER ME?
WHAT AN AMUSING NOTION.
OF COURSE IT DOESN'T BOTHER ME... EVEN IN THE UNLIKELY EVENTUALITY THAT YOU SPEAK THE TRUTH.
BUT IT IS I WHO SHOULD ASK THE QUESTIONS...
WHAT IS THE MOST TERRIBLE CATASTROPHE THAT THE GREEN LANTERN CORPS, IN WHICH I SERVE, HAS YET TO FACE?
8

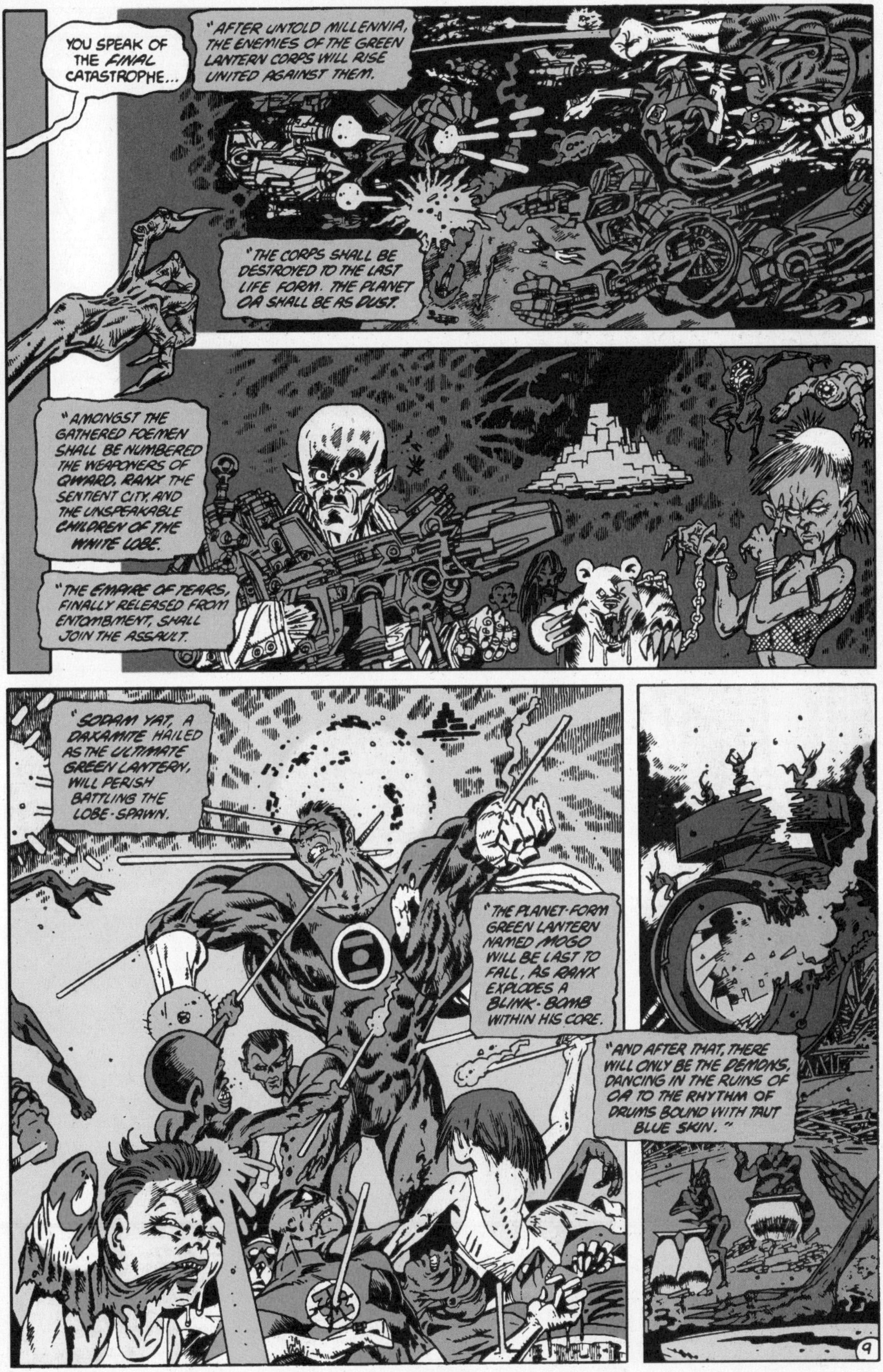
YOU SPEAK OF THE *FINAL* CATASTROPHE...
"AFTER UNTOLD MILLENNIA, THE ENEMIES OF THE GREEN LANTERN CORPS WILL RISE UNITED AGAINST THEM.
"THE CORPS SHALL BE DESTROYED TO THE LAST LIFE FORM. THE PLANET OA SHALL BE AS DUST.
"AMONGST THE GATHERED FOEMEN SHALL BE NUMBERED THE WEAPONERS OF QWARD, RANX THE SENTIENT CITY, AND THE UNSPEAKABLE CHILDREN OF THE WHITE LOBE.
"THE EMPIRE OF TEARS, FINALLY RELEASED FROM ENTOMBMENT, SHALL JOIN THE ASSAULT.
"SODAM YAT, A DAXAMITE HAILED AS THE ULTIMATE GREEN LANTERN, WILL PERISH BATTLING THE LOBE-SPAWN.
"THE PLANET-FORM GREEN LANTERN NAMED MOGO WILL BE LAST TO FALL, AS RANX EXPLODES A BLINK-BOMB WITHIN HIS CORE.
"AND AFTER THAT, THERE WILL ONLY BE THE DEMONS, DANCING IN THE RUINS OF OA TO THE RHYTHM OF DRUMS BOUND WITH TAUT BLUE SKIN."
9

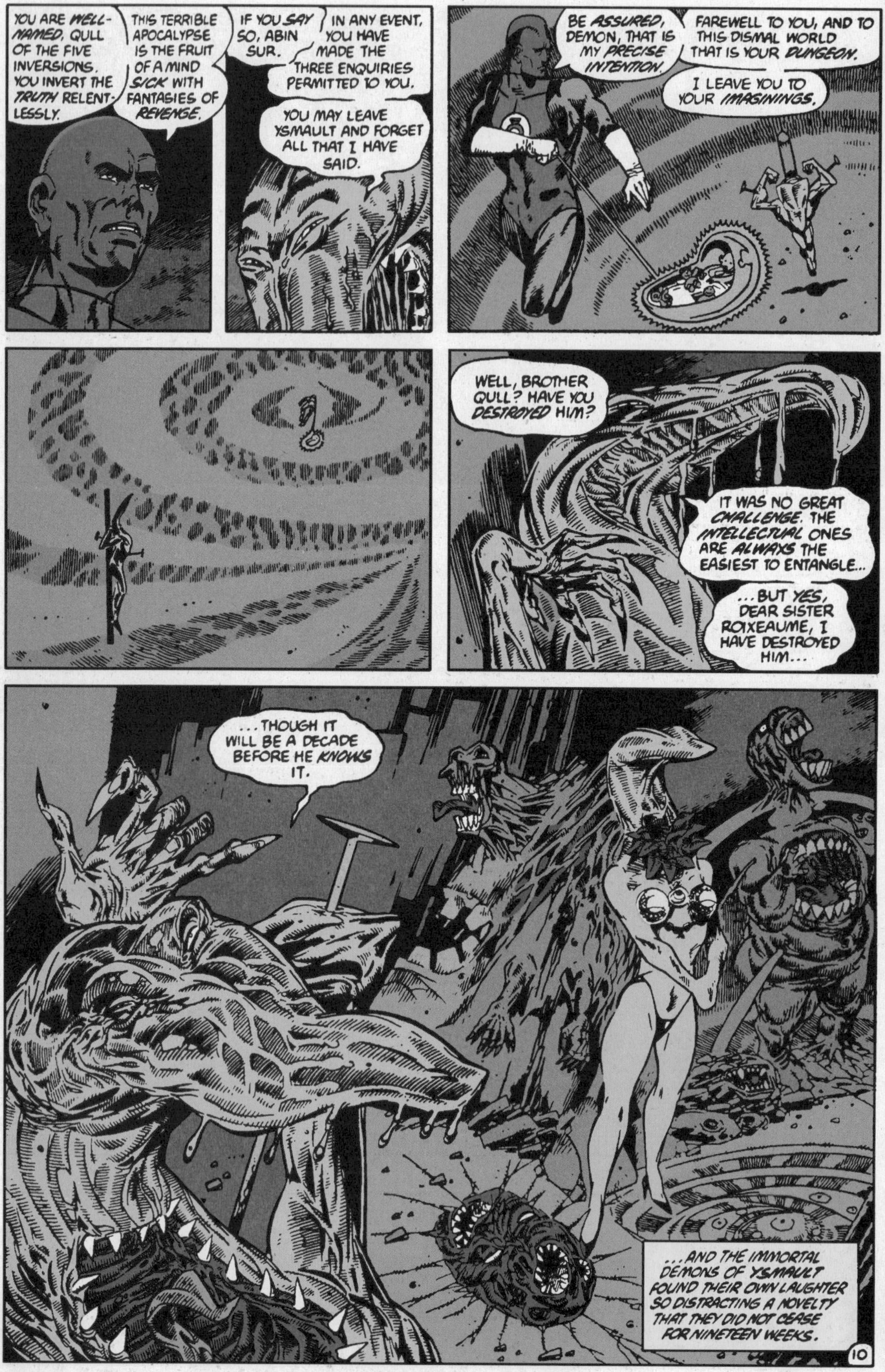
YOU ARE WELL-NAMED, QULL OF THE FIVE INVERSIONS. YOU INVERT THE TRUTH RELENTLESSLY.
THIS TERRIBLE APOCALYPSE IS THE FRUIT OF A MIND SICK WITH FANTASIES OF REVENGE.
IF YOU SAY SO, ABIN SUR.
IN ANY EVENT, YOU HAVE MADE THE THREE ENQUIRIES PERMITTED TO YOU.
YOU MAY LEAVE YSMAULT AND FORGET ALL THAT I HAVE SAID.
BE ASSURED, DEMON, THAT IS MY PRECISE INTENTION.
FAREWELL TO YOU, AND TO THIS DISMAL WORLD THAT IS YOUR DUNGEON.
I LEAVE YOU TO YOUR IMAGININGS.
WELL, BROTHER QULL? HAVE YOU DESTROYED HIM?
IT WAS NO GREAT CHALLENGE. THE INTELLECTUAL ONES ARE ALWAYS THE EASIEST TO ENTANGLE...
...BUT YES, DEAR SISTER ROIXEAUME, I HAVE DESTROYED HIM...
...THOUGH IT WILL BE A DECADE BEFORE HE KNOWS IT.
...AND THE IMMORTAL DEMONS OF YSMAULT FOUND THEIR OWN LAUGHTER SO DISTRACTING A NOVELTY THAT THEY DID NOT CEASE FOR NINETEEN WEEKS.
10

ABIN SUR'S RUMINATIONS UPON THE MATTER ENDURED FAR *LONGER*...

HMM.

SO *TELL* ME... IS THERE A CHANCE THAT YOU *MIGHT* RUN OUT OF ENERGIES AT SOME *VITAL* INSTANT, IRRE-SPECTIVE OF WHETHER QULL LIED?

A *REMOTE* CHANCE, BUT *YES*... IT *IS* POSSIBLE.

THEN I CAN SEE NO HARM IN OBSERVING *PRECAUTIONS*. PERHAPS ON *LONGER* MISSIONS I SHOULD TRAVEL BY *STARSHIP*, CONSERVING YOUR ENERGIES?

I HAVE NO OBJECTION TO THIS PROPOSAL.

GOOD.

THEN I MAY PUT THE EMPIRE OF TEARS AND THEIR MORBID *SPECULATIONS* ENTIRELY FROM MY *MIND*.

INCIDENTALLY, IS IT NOT TIME THAT I *RECHARGED* YOU? YOU MUST BE LOW ON *POWER*...

YOU RECHARGED ME BUT AN *HOUR* AGO, ABIN SUR.

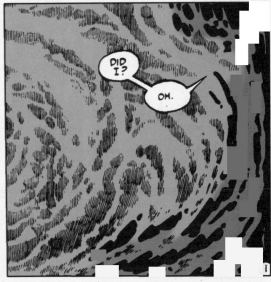

DID I?

OH.

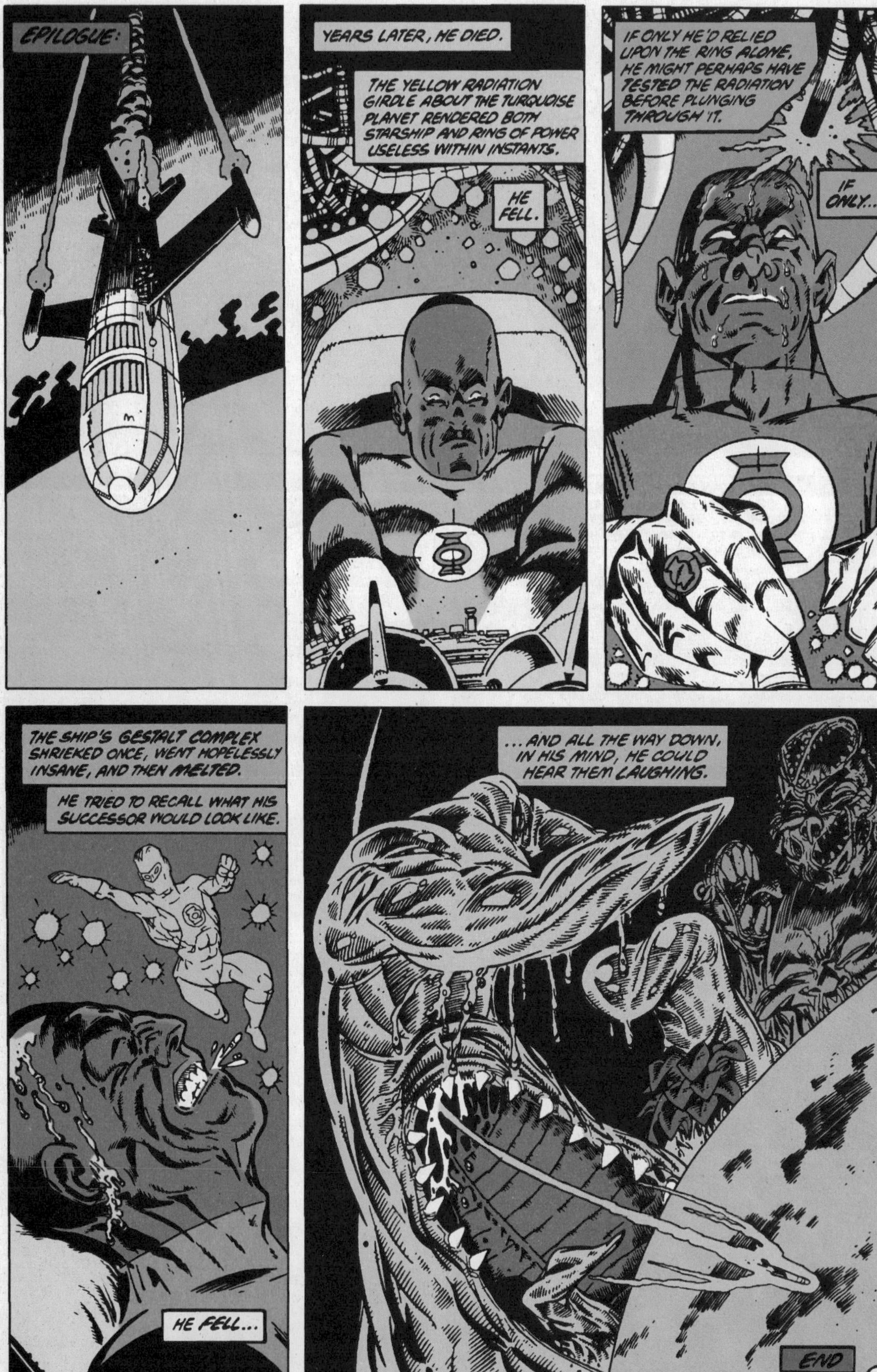
EPILOGUE:
YEARS LATER, HE DIED.
THE YELLOW RADIATION GIRDLE ABOUT THE TURQUOISE PLANET RENDERED BOTH STARSHIP AND RING OF POWER USELESS WITHIN INSTANTS.
HE FELL.
IF ONLY HE'D RELIED UPON THE RING ALONE, HE MIGHT PERHAPS HAVE TESTED THE RADIATION BEFORE PLUNGING THROUGH IT.
IF ONLY...
THE SHIP'S GESTALT COMPLEX SHRIEKED ONCE, WENT HOPELESSLY INSANE, AND THEN MELTED.
HE TRIED TO RECALL WHAT HIS SUCCESSOR WOULD LOOK LIKE.
HE FELL...
...AND ALL THE WAY DOWN, IN HIS MIND, HE COULD HEAR THEM LAUGHING.
END
12

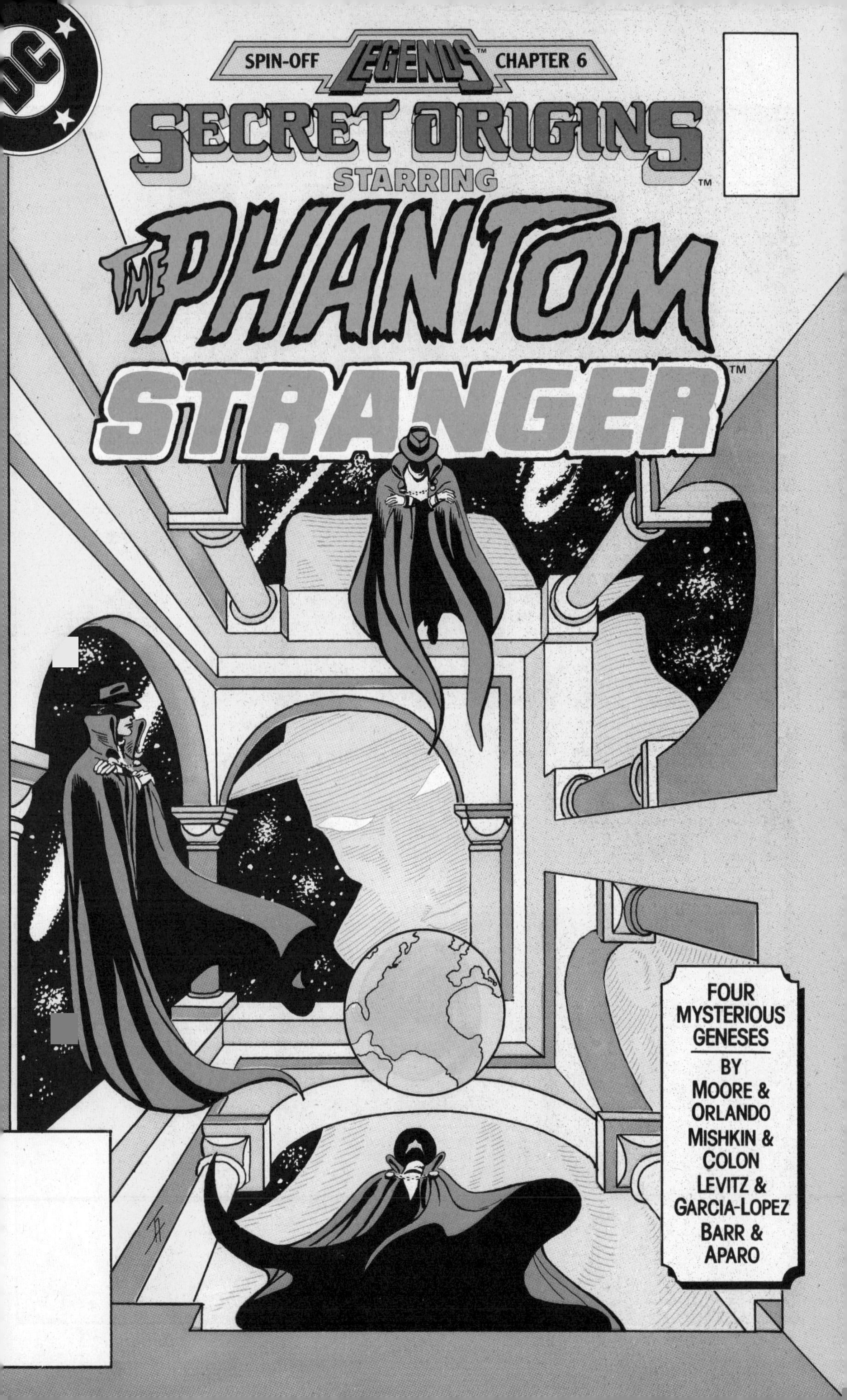

SPIN-OFF
LEGENDS™
CHAPTER 6
SECRET ORIGINS™
STARRING
THE PHANTOM STRANGER™
FOUR MYSTERIOUS GENESES
BY
MOORE & ORLANDO
MISHKIN & COLON
LEVITZ & GARCIA-LOPEZ
BARR & APARO

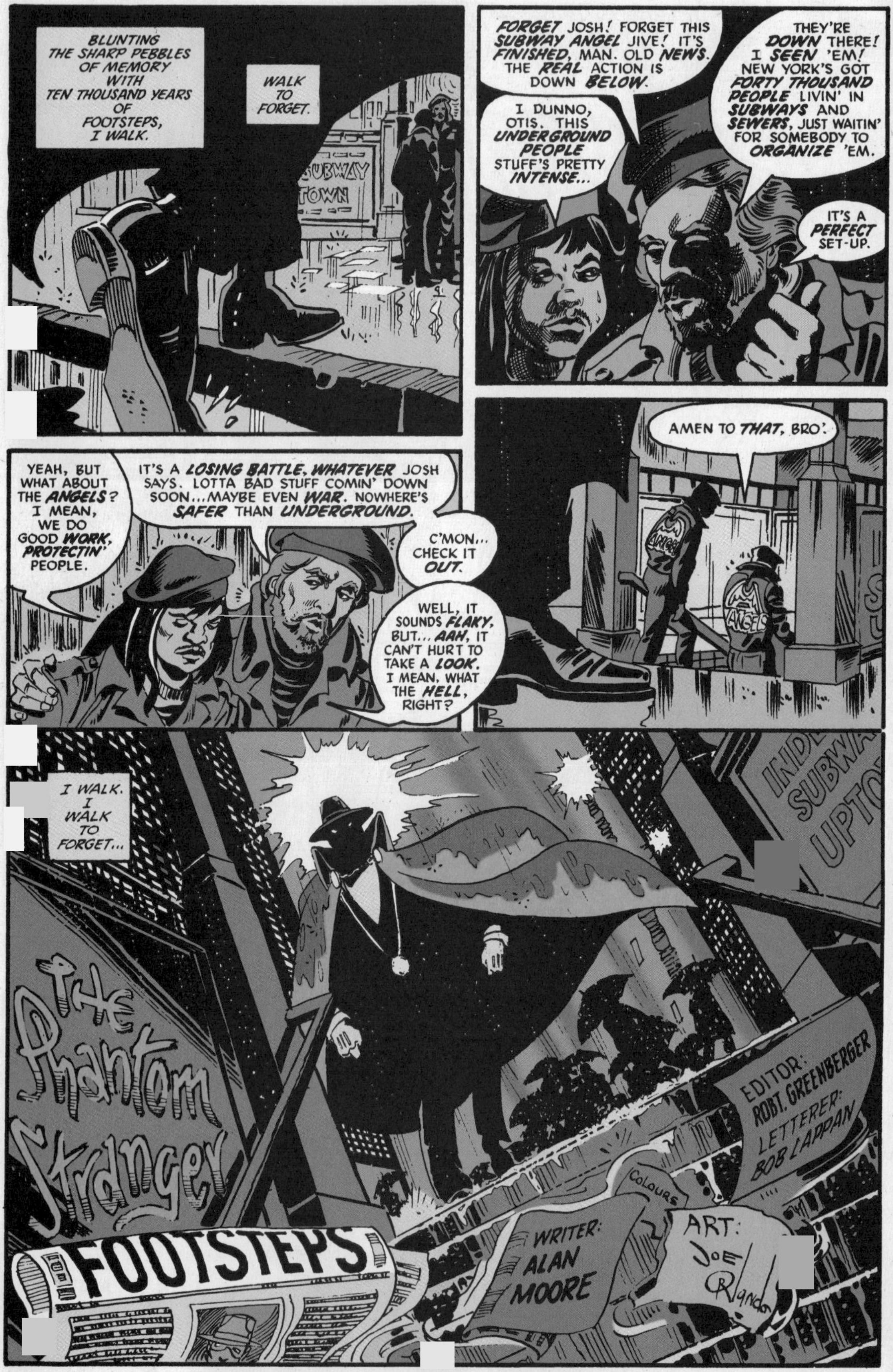

BLUNTING THE SHARP PEBBLES OF MEMORY WITH TEN THOUSAND YEARS OF FOOTSTEPS, I WALK.
WALK TO FORGET.
SUBWAY
TOWN
FORGET JOSH! FORGET THIS SUBWAY ANGEL JIVE! IT'S FINISHED, MAN. OLD NEWS. THE REAL ACTION IS DOWN BELOW.
I DUNNO, OTIS. THIS UNDERGROUND PEOPLE STUFF'S PRETTY INTENSE...
THEY'RE DOWN THERE! I SEEN 'EM! NEW YORK'S GOT FORTY THOUSAND PEOPLE LIVIN' IN SUBWAYS AND SEWERS, JUST WAITIN' FOR SOMEBODY TO ORGANIZE 'EM.
IT'S A PERFECT SET-UP.
YEAH, BUT WHAT ABOUT THE ANGELS? I MEAN, WE DO GOOD WORK, PROTECTIN' PEOPLE.
IT'S A LOSING BATTLE, WHATEVER JOSH SAYS. LOTTA BAD STUFF COMIN' DOWN SOON... MAYBE EVEN WAR. NOWHERE'S SAFER THAN UNDERGROUND.
C'MON... CHECK IT OUT.
WELL, IT SOUNDS FLAKY, BUT... AAH, IT CAN'T HURT TO TAKE A LOOK. I MEAN, WHAT THE HELL, RIGHT?
AMEN TO THAT, BRO'.
ANGELS
ANGELS
I WALK. I WALK TO FORGET...
SUBWA
UPTO
The Phantom Stranger
FOOTSTEPS
WRITER: ALAN MOORE
ART: JOE ORLANDO
COLOURS
EDITOR: ROBT. GREENBERGER
LETTERER: BOB LAPPAN

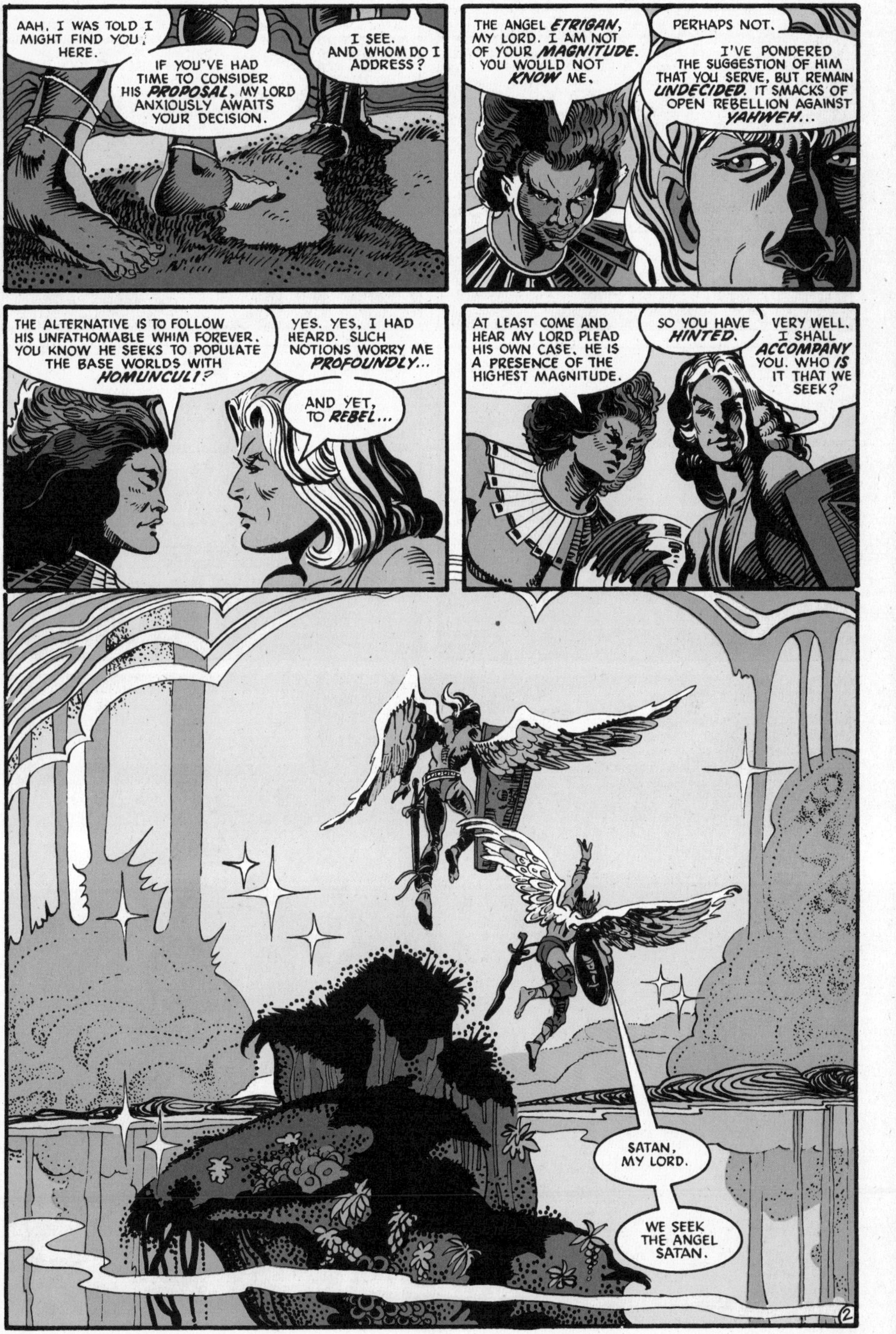
AAH, I WAS TOLD I MIGHT FIND YOU HERE.
IF YOU'VE HAD TIME TO CONSIDER HIS PROPOSAL, MY LORD ANXIOUSLY AWAITS YOUR DECISION.
I SEE. AND WHOM DO I ADDRESS?
THE ANGEL ETRIGAN, MY LORD. I AM NOT OF YOUR MAGNITUDE. YOU WOULD NOT KNOW ME.
PERHAPS NOT.
I'VE PONDERED THE SUGGESTION OF HIM THAT YOU SERVE, BUT REMAIN UNDECIDED. IT SMACKS OF OPEN REBELLION AGAINST YAHWEH...
THE ALTERNATIVE IS TO FOLLOW HIS UNFATHOMABLE WHIM FOREVER. YOU KNOW HE SEEKS TO POPULATE THE BASE WORLDS WITH HOMUNCULI?
YES. YES, I HAD HEARD. SUCH NOTIONS WORRY ME PROFOUNDLY...
AND YET, TO REBEL...
AT LEAST COME AND HEAR MY LORD PLEAD HIS OWN CASE. HE IS A PRESENCE OF THE HIGHEST MAGNITUDE.
SO YOU HAVE HINTED.
VERY WELL. I SHALL ACCOMPANY YOU. WHO IS IT THAT WE SEEK?
SATAN, MY LORD.
WE SEEK THE ANGEL SATAN.
2

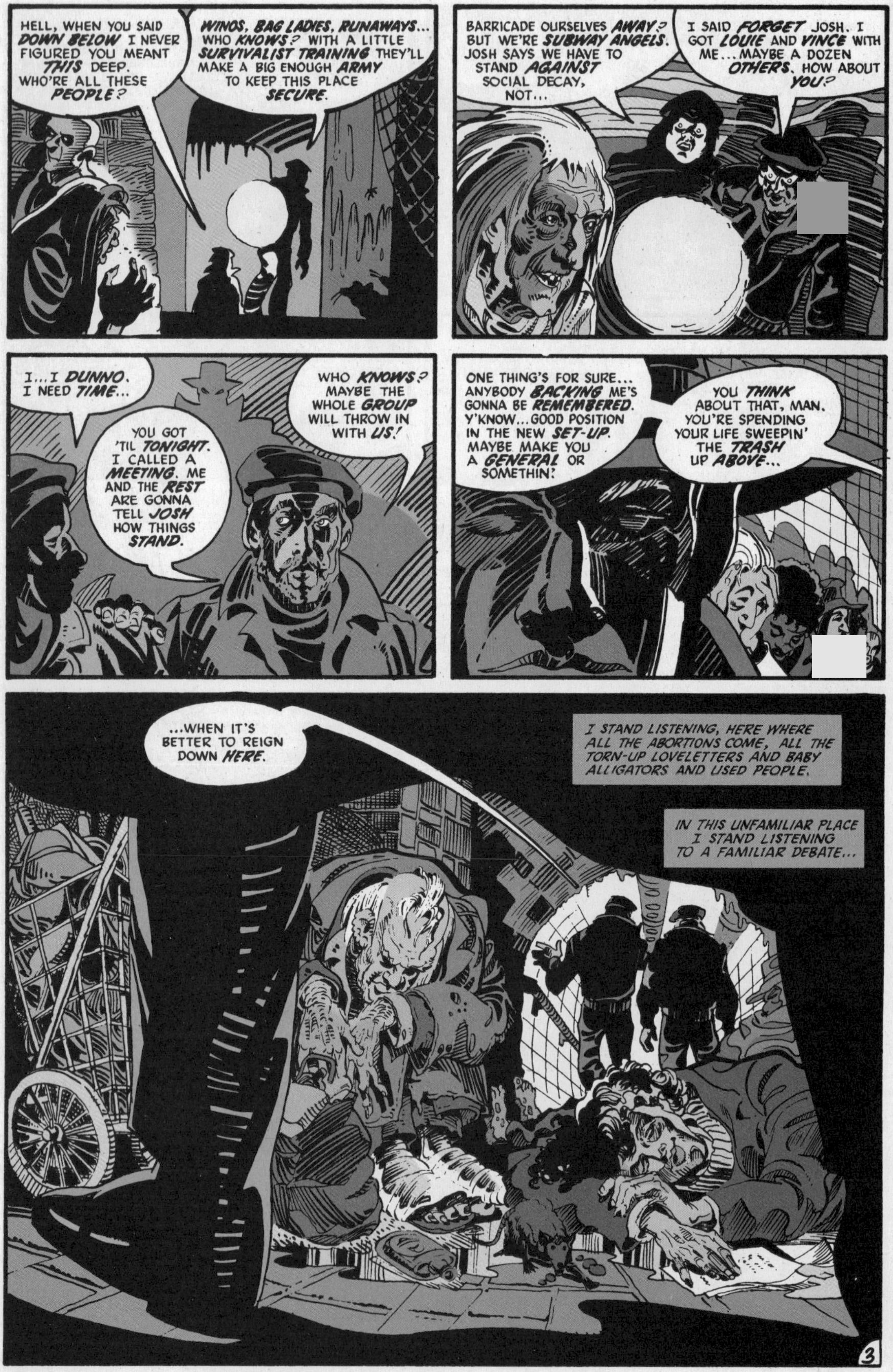
HELL, WHEN YOU SAID DOWN BELOW I NEVER FIGURED YOU MEANT THIS DEEP. WHO'RE ALL THESE PEOPLE?
WINOS, BAG LADIES, RUNAWAYS... WHO KNOWS? WITH A LITTLE SURVIVALIST TRAINING THEY'LL MAKE A BIG ENOUGH ARMY TO KEEP THIS PLACE SECURE.
BARRICADE OURSELVES AWAY? BUT WE'RE SUBWAY ANGELS. JOSH SAYS WE HAVE TO STAND AGAINST SOCIAL DECAY, NOT...
I SAID FORGET JOSH. I GOT LOUIE AND VINCE WITH ME... MAYBE A DOZEN OTHERS. HOW ABOUT YOU?
I...I DUNNO. I NEED TIME...
YOU GOT 'TIL TONIGHT. I CALLED A MEETING. ME AND THE REST ARE GONNA TELL JOSH HOW THINGS STAND.
WHO KNOWS? MAYBE THE WHOLE GROUP WILL THROW IN WITH US!
ONE THING'S FOR SURE... ANYBODY BACKING ME'S GONNA BE REMEMBERED. Y'KNOW...GOOD POSITION IN THE NEW SET-UP. MAYBE MAKE YOU A GENERAL OR SOMETHIN'.
YOU THINK ABOUT THAT, MAN. YOU'RE SPENDING YOUR LIFE SWEEPIN' THE TRASH UP ABOVE...
...WHEN IT'S BETTER TO REIGN DOWN HERE.
I STAND LISTENING, HERE WHERE ALL THE ABORTIONS COME, ALL THE TORN-UP LOVELETTERS AND BABY ALLIGATORS AND USED PEOPLE.
IN THIS UNFAMILIAR PLACE I STAND LISTENING TO A FAMILIAR DEBATE...
3

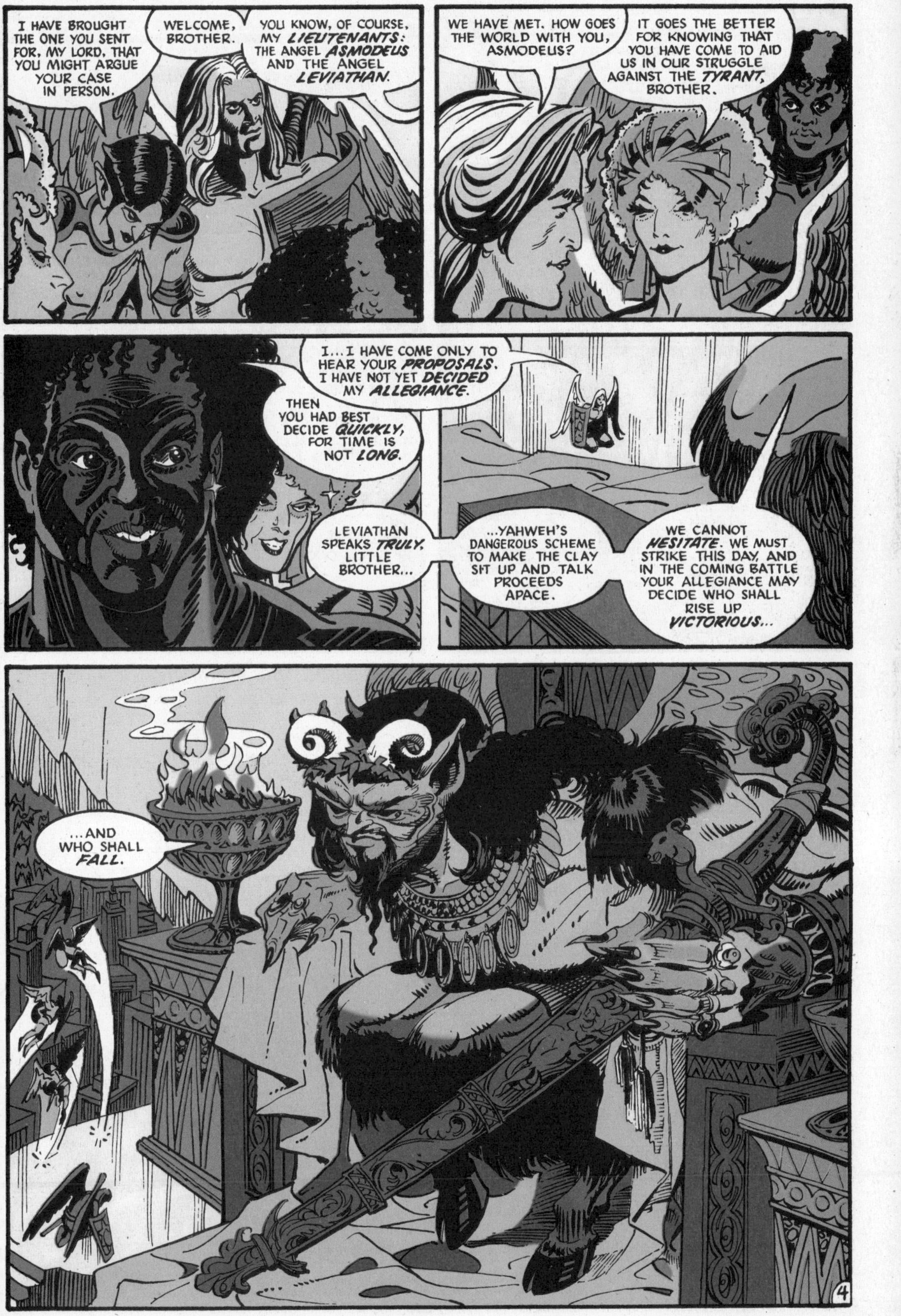
I HAVE BROUGHT THE ONE YOU SENT FOR, MY LORD, THAT YOU MIGHT ARGUE YOUR CASE IN PERSON.
WELCOME, BROTHER.
YOU KNOW, OF COURSE, MY LIEUTENANTS: THE ANGEL ASMODEUS AND THE ANGEL LEVIATHAN.
WE HAVE MET. HOW GOES THE WORLD WITH YOU, ASMODEUS?
IT GOES THE BETTER FOR KNOWING THAT YOU HAVE COME TO AID US IN OUR STRUGGLE AGAINST THE TYRANT, BROTHER.
I... I HAVE COME ONLY TO HEAR YOUR PROPOSALS. I HAVE NOT YET DECIDED MY ALLEGIANCE.
THEN YOU HAD BEST DECIDE QUICKLY, FOR TIME IS NOT LONG.
LEVIATHAN SPEAKS TRULY, LITTLE BROTHER...
...YAHWEH'S DANGEROUS SCHEME TO MAKE THE CLAY SIT UP AND TALK PROCEEDS APACE.
WE CANNOT HESITATE. WE MUST STRIKE THIS DAY, AND IN THE COMING BATTLE YOUR ALLEGIANCE MAY DECIDE WHO SHALL RISE UP VICTORIOUS...
...AND WHO SHALL FALL.
4

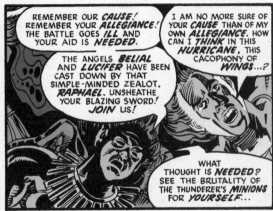

REMEMBER OUR *CAUSE!* REMEMBER YOUR *ALLEGIANCE!* THE BATTLE GOES *ILL* AND YOUR AID IS *NEEDED.*

THE ANGELS *BELIAL* AND *LUCIFER* HAVE BEEN CAST DOWN BY THAT SIMPLE-MINDED ZEALOT, *RAPHAEL.* UNSHEATHE YOUR BLAZING SWORD! *JOIN* US!

I AM NO MORE SURE OF YOUR *CAUSE* THAN OF MY OWN *ALLEGIANCE.* HOW CAN I *THINK* IN THIS *HURRICANE,* THIS CACOPHONY OF *WINGS...?*

WHAT THOUGHT IS *NEEDED?* SEE THE BRUTALITY OF THE THUNDERER'S *MINIONS* FOR *YOURSELF...*

HIS MAD-EYED SENTRIES HURL US DOWN TO THE BRINK OF THE *CHAOPLASM* ITSELF, WINGS BURNING WITH THE SPEED OF *DESCENT,* IMMORTAL BODIES FOREVER *BROKEN* AND *DEFORMED...*

WILL YOU NOT *HELP* US?

I--I *CANNOT.* YOU ARE *DAMNED...*

SO, DAMNED, IS IT?

BROTHER... LOOK *OUT!* YOU'RE *SLIPPING!*

NO MATTER. 'TIS BETTER TO BE ON THE SIDE OF THE *FALLEN* THAN ON NO SIDE AT *ALL...*

BETTER DAMNED BY FAAAAAA

173

OTIS? YOU *DOWN* HERE, MAN?

I CAUGHT UP WITH *JOSH* AND THE REST, BUT THEY WOULDN'T *TALK* TO ME HEY, WHO *NEEDS* IT, RIGHT?

I FIGURE I'M BETTER DOWN HERE WITH *YOU* GUYS.

OTIS? HEY, COME *ON,* MAN...

I *KNOW* I WASN'T MUCH HELP UP *ABOVE,* BUT I WAS KINDA *STRUNG OUT.* I FIGURE YOU COULD STILL USE ME HELPING YOU RUN THINGS DOWN *HERE,* THOUGH, RIGHT?

RIGHT, OTIS?

WRONG.

YOU DIDN'T DO *SNOT* TO HELP ME, MAN. ALL DEALS ARE *OFF.*

THAT *JACKET'LL* KEEP SOMEBODY *WARM.* GIVE IT *HERE.* YOU AIN'T NO *SUBWAY ANGEL.* AIN'T NO *SEWER SURVIVALIST* NEITHER.

YOU'RE *NOTHIN',* MAN. YOU'RE ON YOUR *OWN...*

...AND YOU SHOULDN'T HAVE *COME* HERE.

174

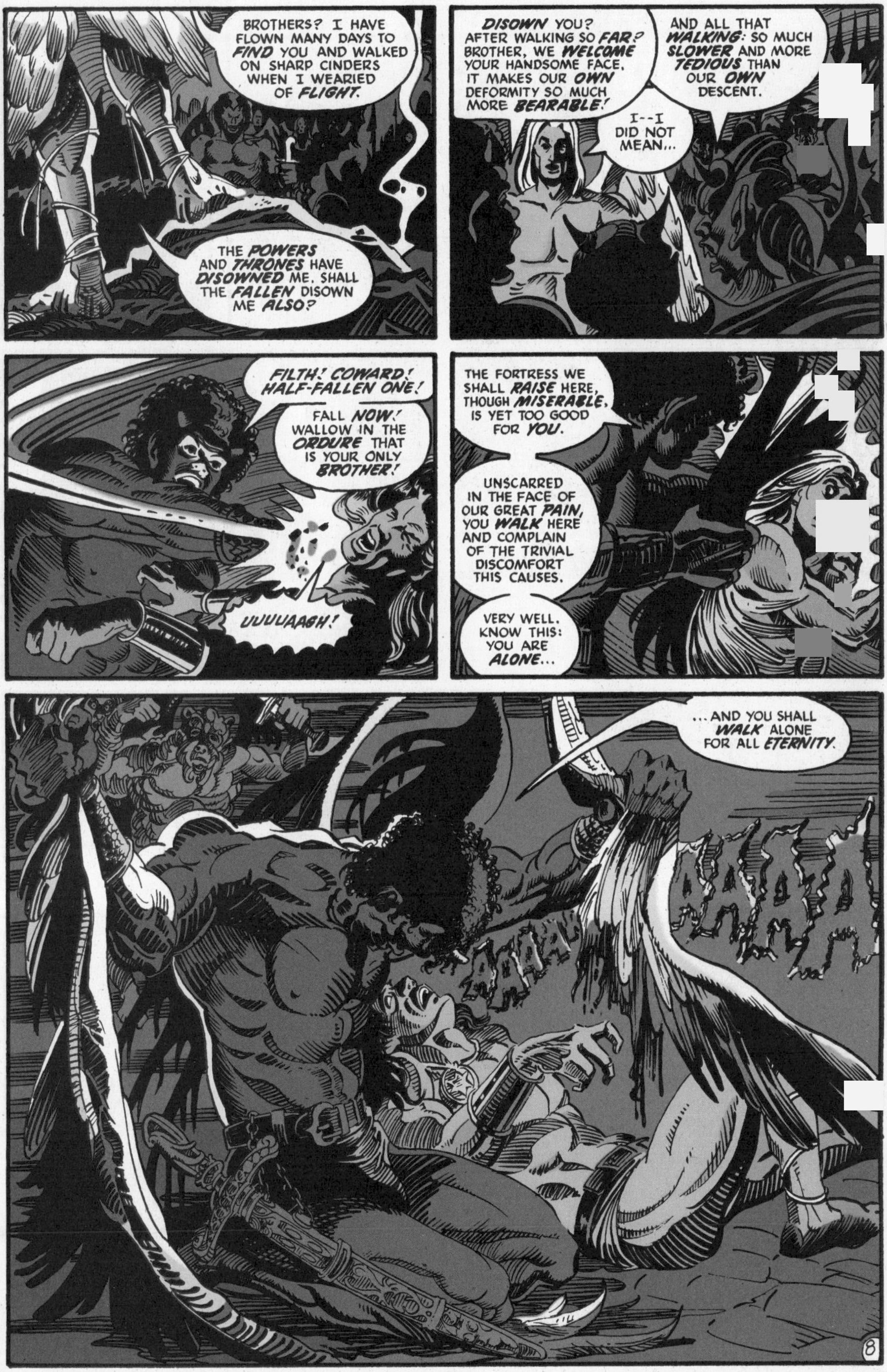
BROTHERS? I HAVE FLOWN MANY DAYS TO FIND YOU AND WALKED ON SHARP CINDERS WHEN I WEARIED OF FLIGHT.
THE POWERS AND THRONES HAVE DISOWNED ME. SHALL THE FALLEN DISOWN ME ALSO?
DISOWN YOU? AFTER WALKING SO FAR? BROTHER, WE WELCOME YOUR HANDSOME FACE. IT MAKES OUR OWN DEFORMITY SO MUCH MORE BEARABLE!
AND ALL THAT WALKING: SO MUCH SLOWER AND MORE TEDIOUS THAN OUR OWN DESCENT.
I--I DID NOT MEAN...
FILTH! COWARD! HALF-FALLEN ONE!
FALL NOW! WALLOW IN THE ORDURE THAT IS YOUR ONLY BROTHER!
UUUUAAGH!
THE FORTRESS WE SHALL RAISE HERE, THOUGH MISERABLE, IS YET TOO GOOD FOR YOU.
UNSCARRED IN THE FACE OF OUR GREAT PAIN, YOU WALK HERE AND COMPLAIN OF THE TRIVIAL DISCOMFORT THIS CAUSES.
VERY WELL. KNOW THIS: YOU ARE ALONE...
...AND YOU SHALL WALK ALONE FOR ALL ETERNITY.
8

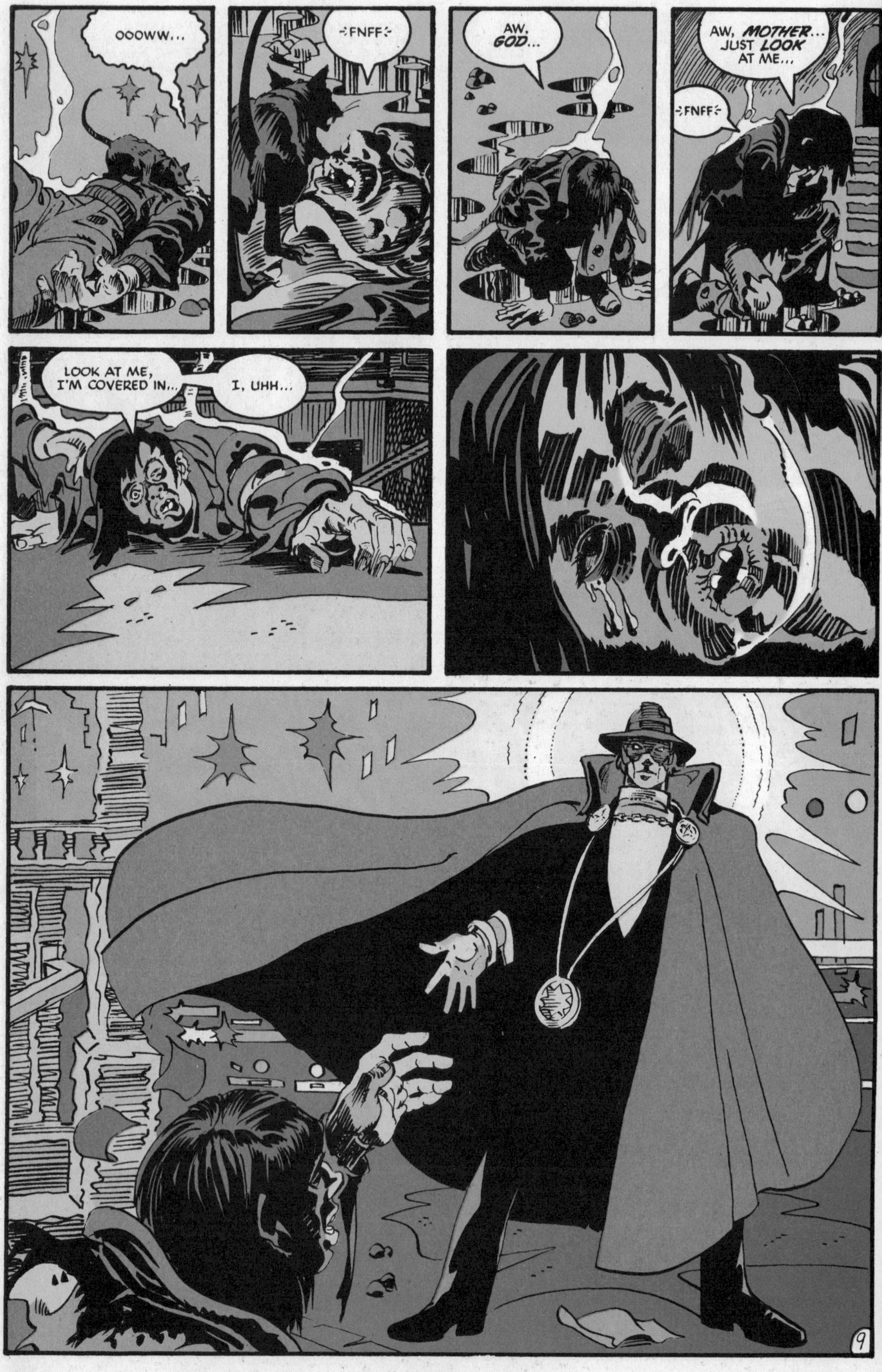
OOOWW...
-:FNFF:-
AW, GOD...
AW, MOTHER... JUST LOOK AT ME...
-:FNFF:-
LOOK AT ME, I'M COVERED IN...
I, UHH...
9

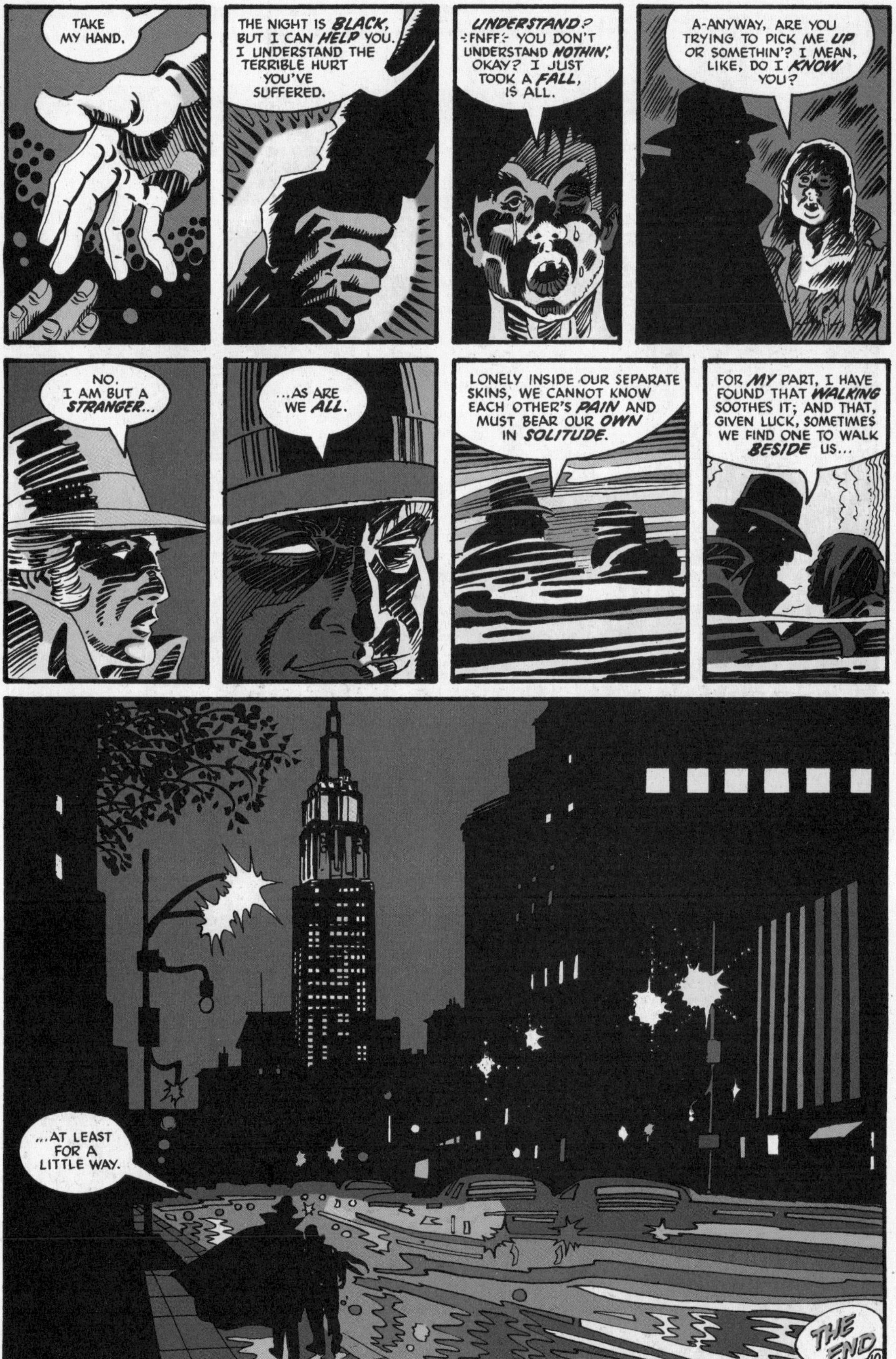
TAKE MY HAND.
THE NIGHT IS BLACK, BUT I CAN HELP YOU. I UNDERSTAND THE TERRIBLE HURT YOU'VE SUFFERED.
UNDERSTAND? -FNFF- YOU DON'T UNDERSTAND NOTHIN'! OKAY? I JUST TOOK A FALL, IS ALL.
A-ANYWAY, ARE YOU TRYING TO PICK ME UP OR SOMETHIN'? I MEAN, LIKE, DO I KNOW YOU?
NO. I AM BUT A STRANGER...
...AS ARE WE ALL.
LONELY INSIDE OUR SEPARATE SKINS, WE CANNOT KNOW EACH OTHER'S PAIN AND MUST BEAR OUR OWN IN SOLITUDE.
FOR MY PART, I HAVE FOUND THAT WALKING SOOTHES IT; AND THAT, GIVEN LUCK, SOMETIMES WE FIND ONE TO WALK BESIDE US...
...AT LEAST FOR A LITTLE WAY.
THE END
10

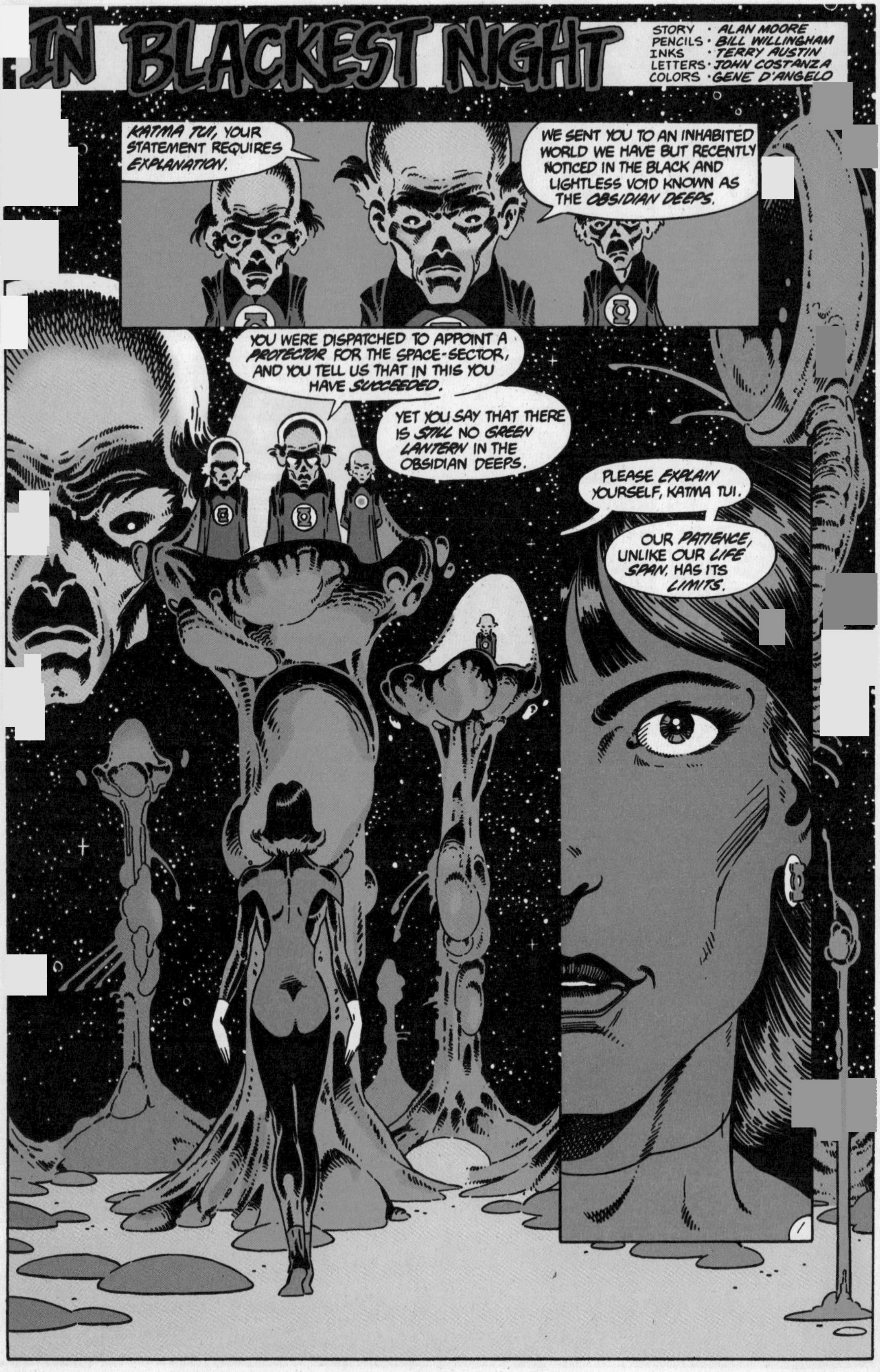
IN BLACKEST NIGHT
STORY · ALAN MOORE
PENCILS · BILL WILLINGHAM
INKS · TERRY AUSTIN
LETTERS · JOHN COSTANZA
COLORS · GENE D'ANGELO
KATMA TUI, YOUR STATEMENT REQUIRES EXPLANATION.
WE SENT YOU TO AN INHABITED WORLD WE HAVE BUT RECENTLY NOTICED IN THE BLACK AND LIGHTLESS VOID KNOWN AS THE OBSIDIAN DEEPS.
YOU WERE DISPATCHED TO APPOINT A PROTECTOR FOR THE SPACE-SECTOR, AND YOU TELL US THAT IN THIS YOU HAVE SUCCEEDED.
YET YOU SAY THAT THERE IS STILL NO GREEN LANTERN IN THE OBSIDIAN DEEPS.
PLEASE EXPLAIN YOURSELF, KATMA TUI.
OUR PATIENCE, UNLIKE OUR LIFE SPAN, HAS ITS LIMITS.
1

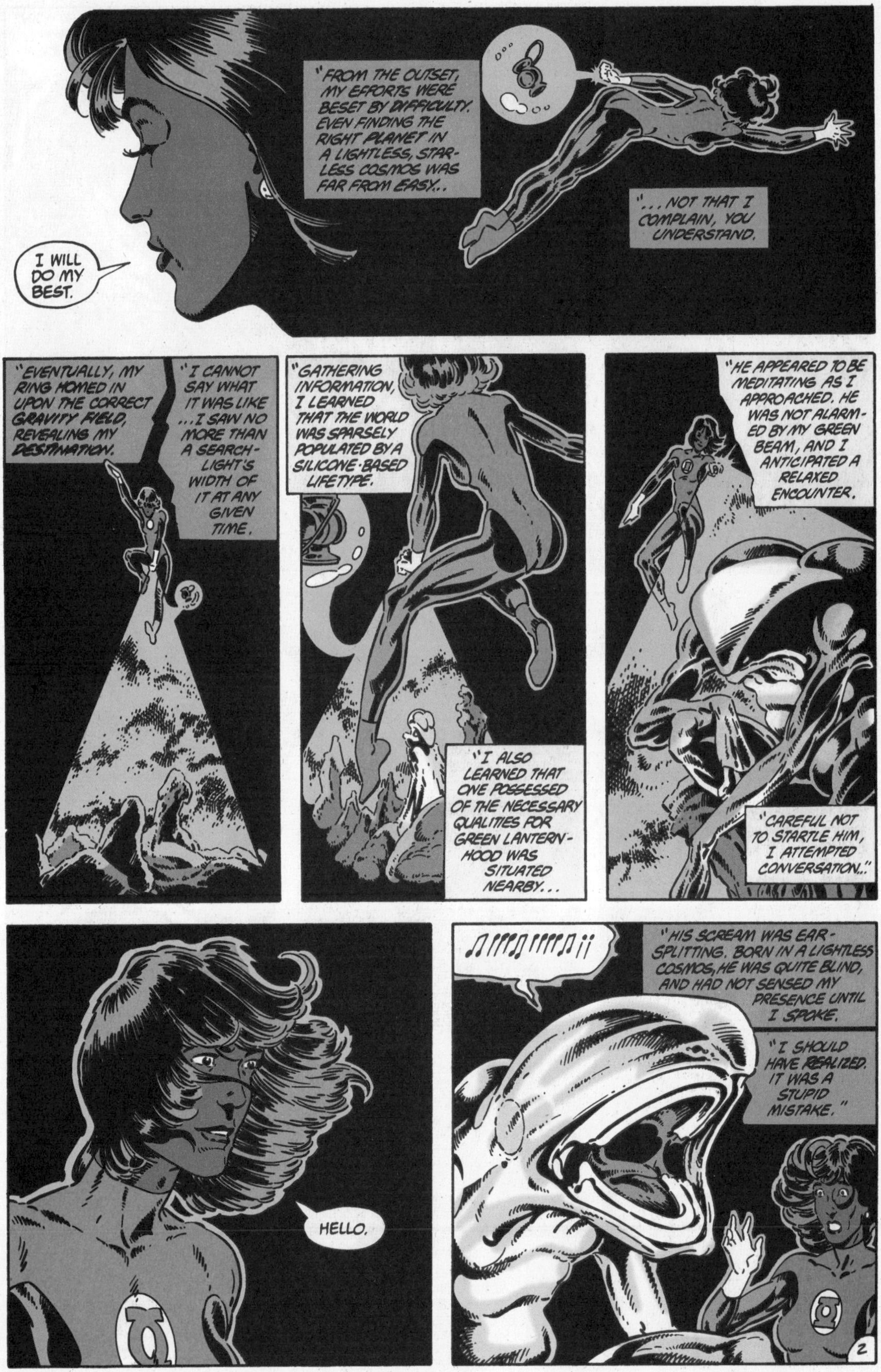
"FROM THE OUTSET, MY EFFORTS WERE BESET BY DIFFICULTY. EVEN FINDING THE RIGHT PLANET IN A LIGHTLESS, STARLESS COSMOS WAS FAR FROM EASY...
"...NOT THAT I COMPLAIN, YOU UNDERSTAND.
I WILL DO MY BEST.
"EVENTUALLY, MY RING HOMED IN UPON THE CORRECT GRAVITY FIELD, REVEALING MY DESTINATION.
"I CANNOT SAY WHAT IT WAS LIKE ...I SAW NO MORE THAN A SEARCH-LIGHT'S WIDTH OF IT AT ANY GIVEN TIME.
"GATHERING INFORMATION, I LEARNED THAT THE WORLD WAS SPARSELY POPULATED BY A SILICONE-BASED LIFETYPE.
"I ALSO LEARNED THAT ONE POSSESSED OF THE NECESSARY QUALITIES FOR GREEN LANTERN-HOOD WAS SITUATED NEARBY...
"HE APPEARED TO BE MEDITATING AS I APPROACHED. HE WAS NOT ALARMED BY MY GREEN BEAM, AND I ANTICIPATED A RELAXED ENCOUNTER.
"CAREFUL NOT TO STARTLE HIM, I ATTEMPTED CONVERSATION..."
HELLO.
"HIS SCREAM WAS EAR-SPLITTING. BORN IN A LIGHTLESS COSMOS, HE WAS QUITE BLIND, AND HAD NOT SENSED MY PRESENCE UNTIL I SPOKE.
"I SHOULD HAVE REALIZED. IT WAS A STUPID MISTAKE."
2

"USING MY RING TO TRANSLATE, I ATTEMPTED TO CALM HIM.

"HIS NAME WAS ROT LOP FAN.

"IT TOOK SOME LITTLE TIME, BUT AT LAST HE SEEMED TO UNDERSTAND THAT I MEANT NO HARM...

"...EVEN IF HE DID FIND ME IMPOSSIBLY GROTESQUE BY HIS STANDARDS."

SUCH A TERRIBLE PITY THAT YOU SHOULD BEAR THIS TACTILE DEFORMITY. YOUR VOICE SOUNDS SO KIND...

BUT THIS STORY OF YOURS...

YOU SAY THAT THERE ARE AREAS OF SOLID LAND FLOATING ABOVE THIS WORLD...

...AND THAT YOU COME FROM ONE SUCH PLACE TO INVITE ME INTO A LEAGUE OF PROTECTORS...?

YES. YOU WOULD MAKE A WORTHY MEMBER OF THE (UNTRANSLATABLE) CORPS.

THE WHAT? I DIDN'T CATCH THAT...

I'M SORRY, MY RING'S TRANSLATOR FUNCTION SEEMS TO BE SLIPPING, I SAID:

"THE (UNTRANSLATABLE) CORPS."

"I CHECKED THE RING. IT WORKED PERFECTLY.

"IT JUST COULDN'T TRANS- LATE THE WORDS 'GREEN' OR 'LANTERN' INTO A LANGUAGE WITH NO CONCEPT OF COLOR OR LIGHT."

AAH.

WE BEGIN TO PERCEIVE YOUR UNIQUE PROBLEM.

HOW DID YOU SOLVE IT?

3

"IT WAS DIFFICULT. WITHOUT THE BASIC IDEA OF LIGHT, THE WHOLE GREEN LANTERN CONCEPT IS INCOMPREHENSIBLE..."

THIS IS A *POWER RING*. IF YOU CONCENTRATE, IT EMITS A (*UNTRANSLATABLE*) OF (*UNTRANSLATABLE*) THAT YOU...

DARN.

"AND THEN THERE WAS THE OATH..."

IN (*UNTRANSLATABLE*), IN (*UNTRANSLATABLE*), NO EVIL SHALL ESCAPE MY (*UNTRANSLATABLE*). LET THOSE WHO WORSHIP EVIL'S MIGHT BEWARE MY POWER, (*UNTRANSLATABLE*).

MMM. PERHAPS IT *LOSES* SOMETHING...

"FINALLY, THOUGH IT SHAMES ME TO ADMIT IT, I GAVE UP."

STRANGER?

I AM SORRY THAT YOU CANNOT MAKE ME UNDERSTAND YOU. THOUGH WHAT YOU SAY IS ALIEN, IT HAS THE RING OF TRUTH...

SAY THAT AGAIN?

YOUR WORDS... I SAID THAT THEY HAD THE RING OF TRUTH, AND THAT...

"RING"! THAT'S IT! THE SOLUTION!

CERTAINLY IT'S *UNORTHODOX*, BUT I'M SURE THE GUARDIANS WILL TURN A (*UNTRANSLATABLE*) JUST THIS ONCE...

HERE, PUT THIS ON YOUR FINGER...

4

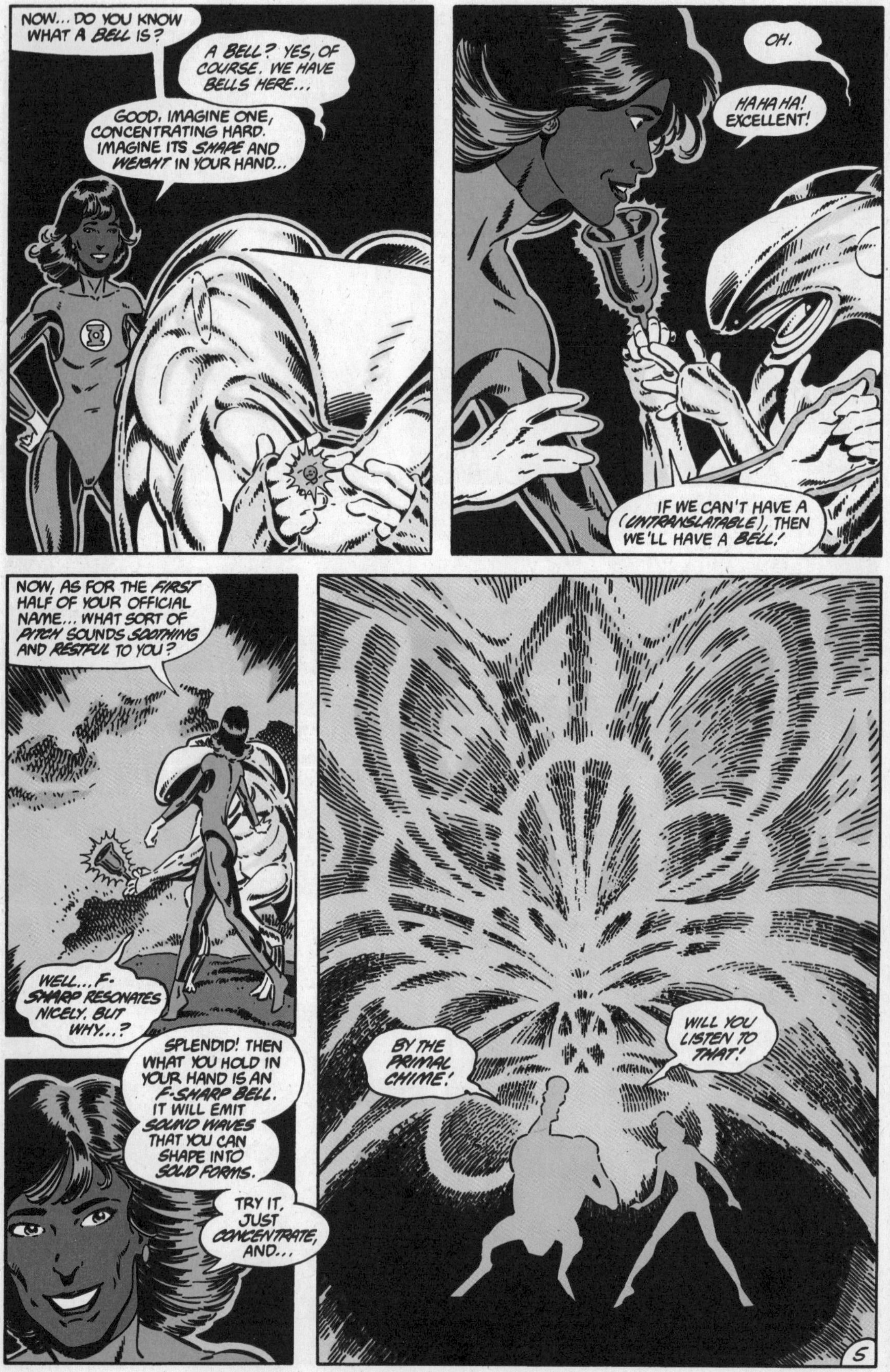
NOW... DO YOU KNOW WHAT A BELL IS?
A BELL? YES, OF COURSE. WE HAVE BELLS HERE...
GOOD. IMAGINE ONE, CONCENTRATING HARD. IMAGINE ITS SHAPE AND WEIGHT IN YOUR HAND...
OH.
HA HA HA! EXCELLENT!
IF WE CAN'T HAVE A (UNTRANSLATABLE), THEN WE'LL HAVE A BELL!
NOW, AS FOR THE FIRST HALF OF YOUR OFFICIAL NAME... WHAT SORT OF PITCH SOUNDS SOOTHING AND RESTFUL TO YOU?
WELL... F. SHARP RESONATES NICELY. BUT WHY...?
SPLENDID! THEN WHAT YOU HOLD IN YOUR HAND IS AN F-SHARP BELL. IT WILL EMIT SOUND WAVES THAT YOU CAN SHAPE INTO SOLID FORMS.
TRY IT, JUST CONCENTRATE, AND...
BY THE PRIMAL CHIME!
WILL YOU LISTEN TO THAT!
5

"I DECIDED TO TRY THE OATH AGAIN..."

PLACE YOUR HAND IN HERE, IT'S, UH, LIKE A SORT OF TUNING FORK. THEN YOU SAY...

HMM. NOW LET ME JUST THINK THIS THROUGH...

"EVENTUALLY, I HAD IT..."

IN LOUDEST DIN OR HUSH PROFOUND MY EARS CATCH EVIL'S SLIGHTEST SOUND LET THOSE WHO TOLL OUT EVIL'S KNELL BEWARE MY POWER: THE F-SHARP BELL!

"I CREATED A MODIFIED UNIFORM FOR HIM AND THEN LEFT.

"I DIDN'T MENTION THE RING'S WEAKNESS TO YELLOW OBJECTS. IN A COLORLESS COSMOS THERE SEEMED LITTLE POINT."

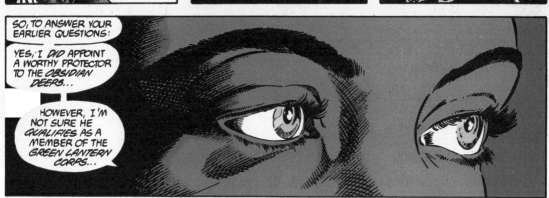

SO, TO ANSWER YOUR EARLIER QUESTIONS:

YES, I DID APPOINT A WORTHY PROTECTOR TO THE OBSIDIAN DEEPS...

HOWEVER, I'M NOT SURE HE QUALIFIES AS A MEMBER OF THE GREEN LANTERN CORPS...

...FOR IN TRUTH, HE'S NEVER EVEN HEARD OF US!

THAT SAID, HE'D APPRECIATE AN EARLY DECISION FROM YOU, CONCERNING HIS STATUS.

THANK YOU, KATMA TUI, WE'LL TRY NOT TO KEEP HIM IN THE DARK TOO LONG...

...AND FOUR CYCLES LATER, IN THE RECREATION COMPLEX, KATMA TUI REALIZED THAT FOR THE FIRST TIME IN MANY YEARS' SERVICE, SHE HAD HEARD A GUARDIAN MAKE A JOKE.

SHE FELT VAGUELY UNEASY FOR THE REST OF THAT DAY.

END

6

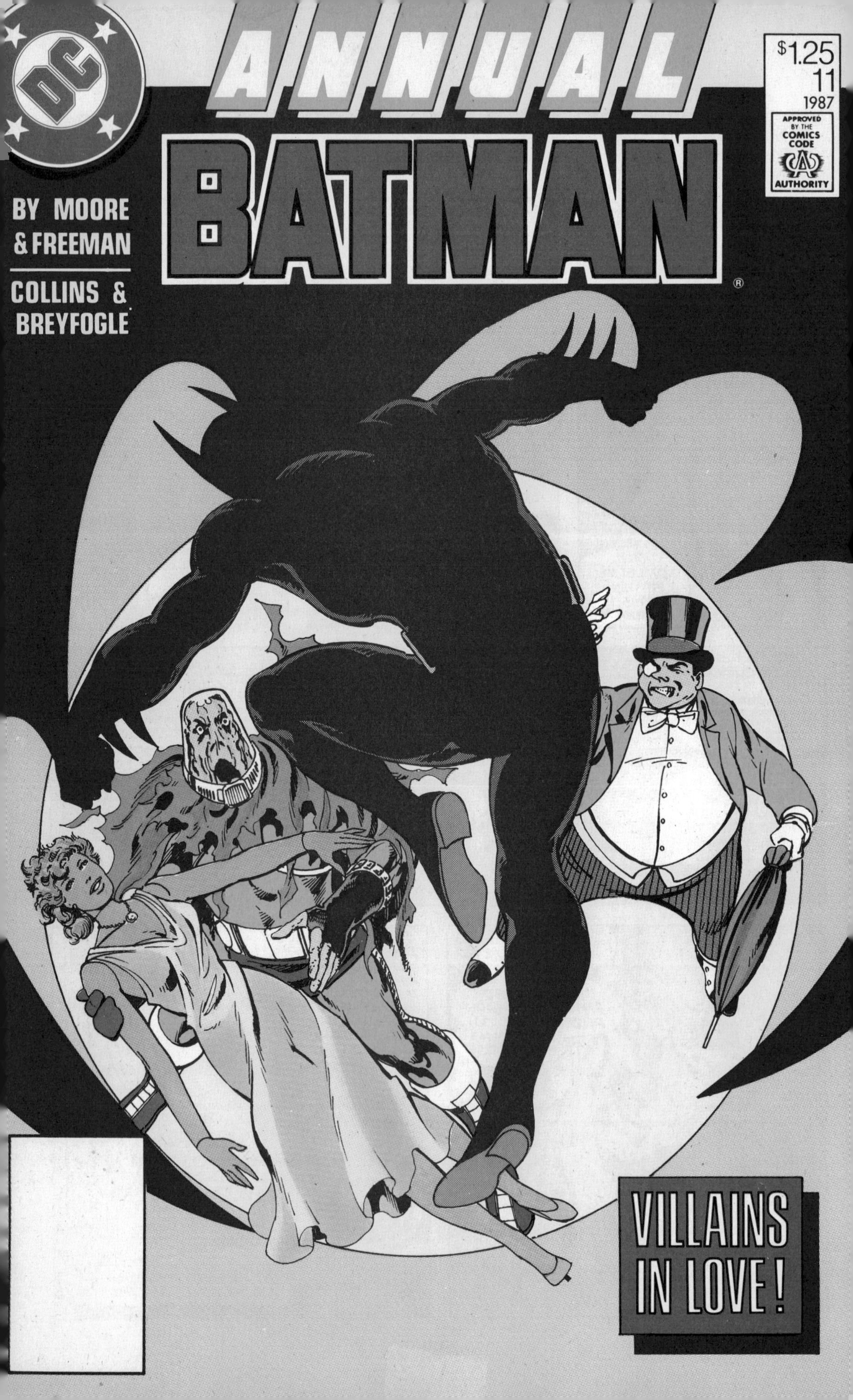

ANNUAL
BATMAN
$1.25
11
1987
APPROVED BY THE COMICS CODE AUTHORITY
BY MOORE & FREEMAN
COLLINS & BREYFOGLE
VILLAINS IN LOVE!

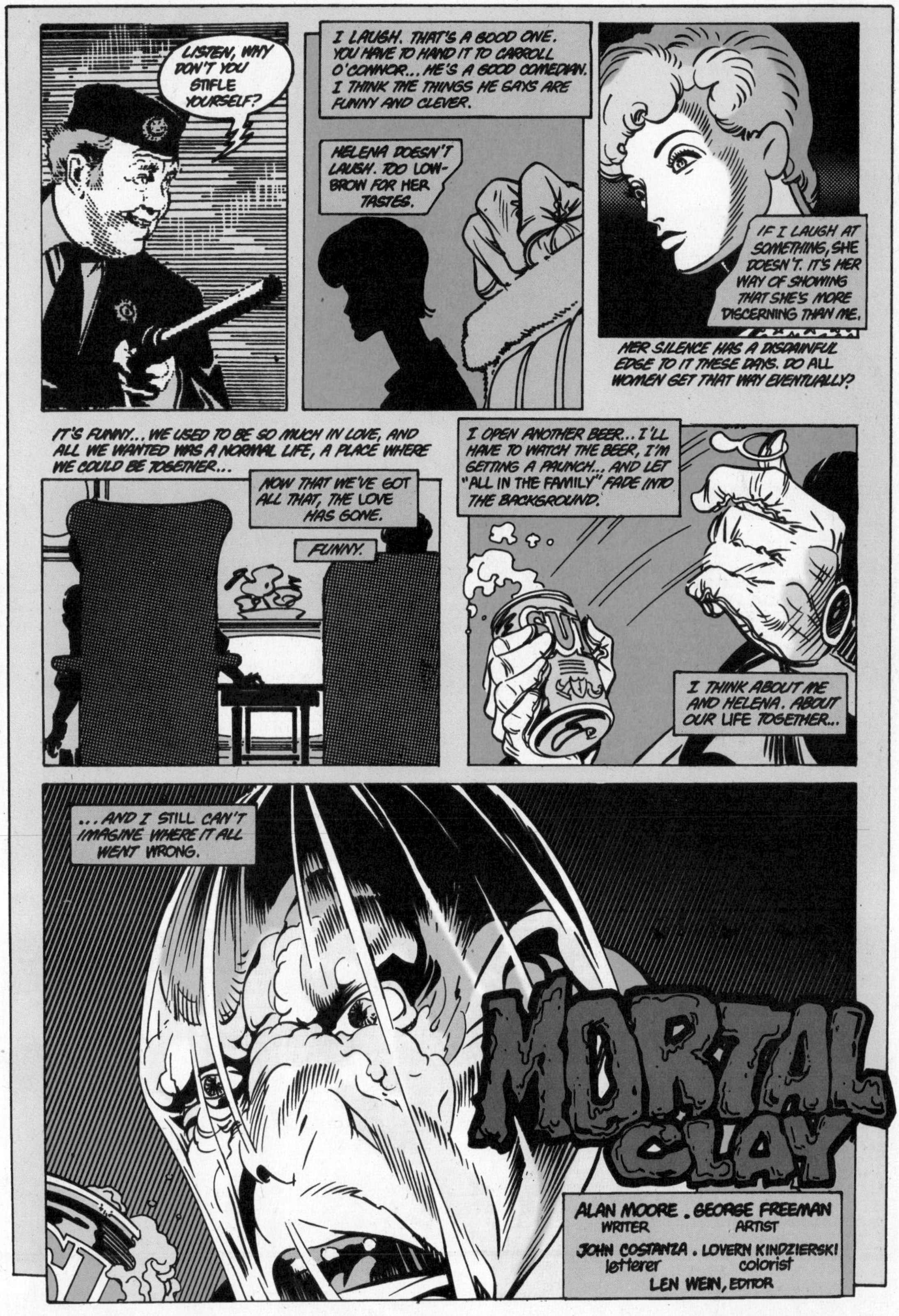

LISTEN, WHY DON'T YOU STIFLE YOURSELF?
I LAUGH. THAT'S A GOOD ONE. YOU HAVE TO HAND IT TO CARROLL O'CONNOR... HE'S A GOOD COMEDIAN. I THINK THE THINGS HE SAYS ARE FUNNY AND CLEVER.
HELENA DOESN'T LAUGH. TOO LOW-BROW FOR HER TASTES.
IF I LAUGH AT SOMETHING, SHE DOESN'T. IT'S HER WAY OF SHOWING THAT SHE'S MORE DISCERNING THAN ME.
HER SILENCE HAS A DISDAINFUL EDGE TO IT THESE DAYS. DO ALL WOMEN GET THAT WAY EVENTUALLY?
IT'S FUNNY... WE USED TO BE SO MUCH IN LOVE, AND ALL WE WANTED WAS A NORMAL LIFE, A PLACE WHERE WE COULD BE TOGETHER...
NOW THAT WE'VE GOT ALL THAT, THE LOVE HAS GONE.
FUNNY.
I OPEN ANOTHER BEER... I'LL HAVE TO WATCH THE BEER, I'M GETTING A PAUNCH... AND LET "ALL IN THE FAMILY" FADE INTO THE BACKGROUND.
I THINK ABOUT ME AND HELENA. ABOUT OUR LIFE TOGETHER...
...AND I STILL CAN'T IMAGINE WHERE IT ALL WENT WRONG.
MORTAL CLAY
ALAN MOORE . GEORGE FREEMAN
WRITER ARTIST
JOHN COSTANZA . LOVERN KINDZIERSKI
letterer colorist
LEN WEIN, EDITOR

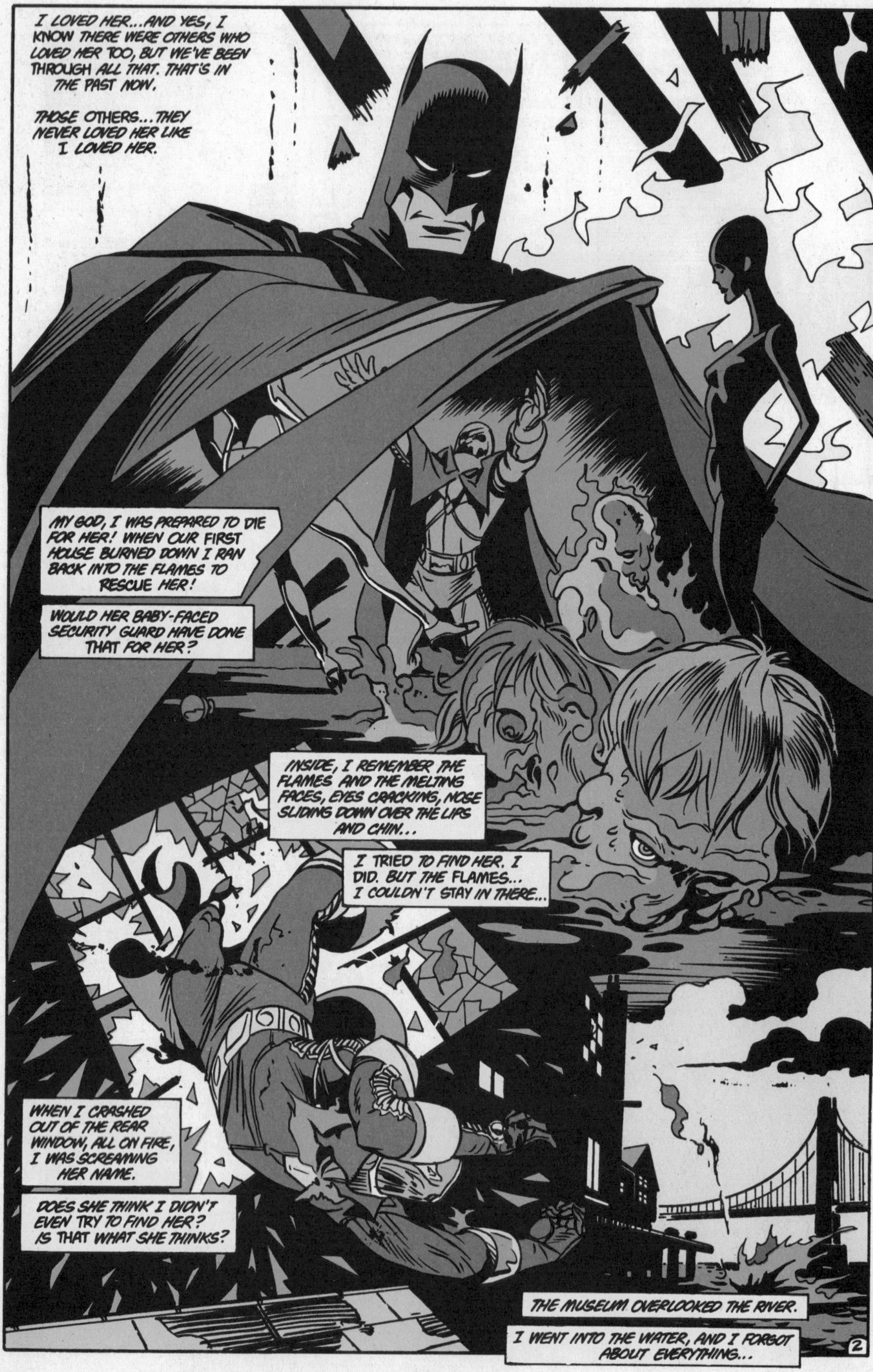
I LOVED HER...AND YES, I KNOW THERE WERE OTHERS WHO LOVED HER TOO, BUT WE'VE BEEN THROUGH ALL THAT. THAT'S IN THE PAST NOW.
THOSE OTHERS...THEY NEVER LOVED HER LIKE I LOVED HER.
MY GOD, I WAS PREPARED TO DIE FOR HER! WHEN OUR FIRST HOUSE BURNED DOWN I RAN BACK INTO THE FLAMES TO RESCUE HER!
WOULD HER BABY-FACED SECURITY GUARD HAVE DONE THAT FOR HER?
INSIDE, I REMEMBER THE FLAMES AND THE MELTING FACES, EYES CRACKING, NOSE SLIDING DOWN OVER THE LIPS AND CHIN...
I TRIED TO FIND HER. I DID. BUT THE FLAMES... I COULDN'T STAY IN THERE...
WHEN I CRASHED OUT OF THE REAR WINDOW, ALL ON FIRE, I WAS SCREAMING HER NAME.
DOES SHE THINK I DIDN'T EVEN TRY TO FIND HER? IS THAT WHAT SHE THINKS?
THE MUSEUM OVERLOOKED THE RIVER.
I WENT INTO THE WATER, AND I FORGOT ABOUT EVERYTHING...
2

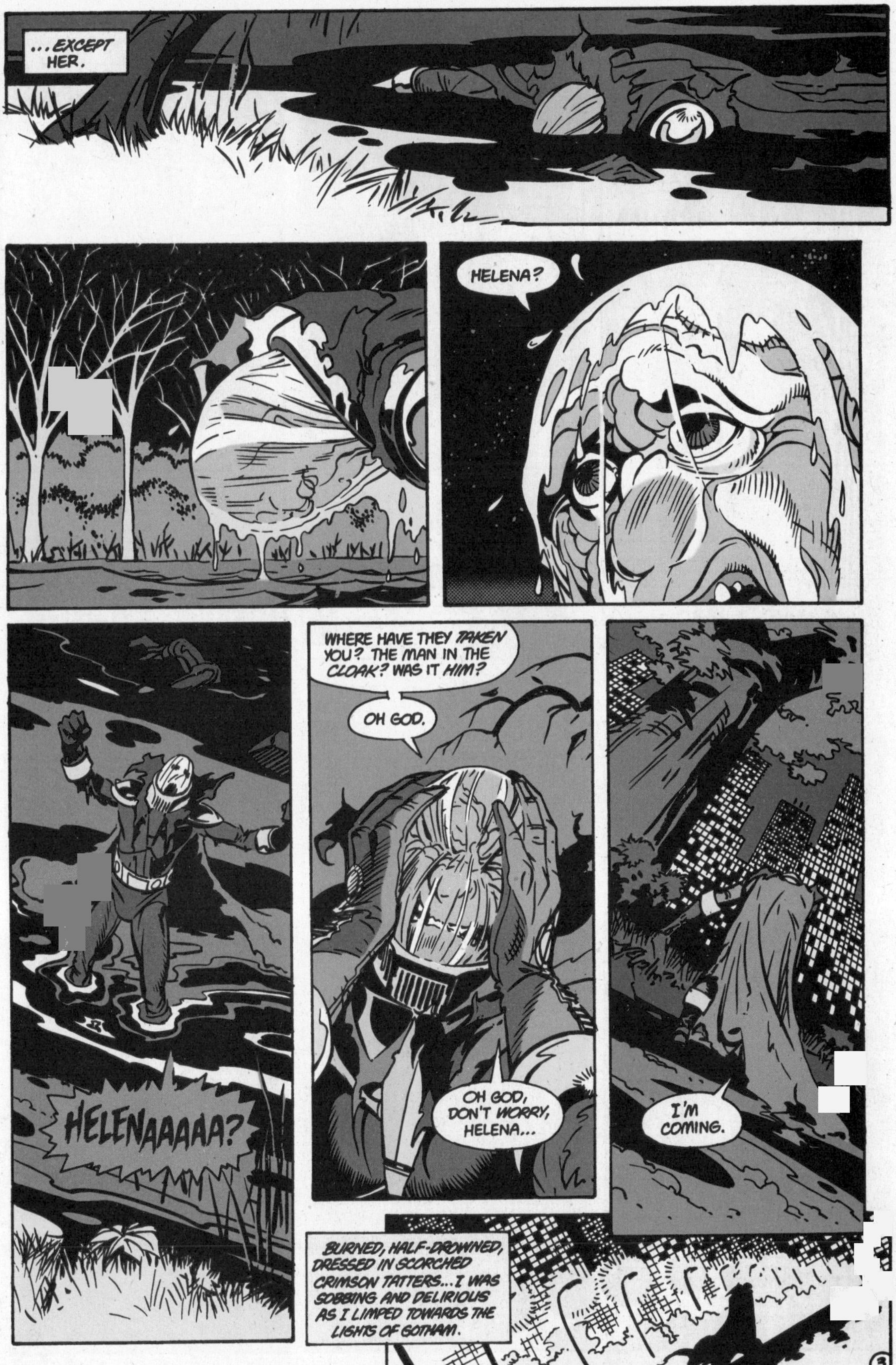
...EXCEPT HER.
HELENA?
HELENAAAAA?
WHERE HAVE THEY TAKEN YOU? THE MAN IN THE CLOAK? WAS IT HIM?
OH GOD.
OH GOD, DON'T WORRY, HELENA...
I'M COMING.
BURNED, HALF-DROWNED, DRESSED IN SCORCHED CRIMSON TATTERS... I WAS SOBBING AND DELIRIOUS AS I LIMPED TOWARDS THE LIGHTS OF GOTHAM.
3

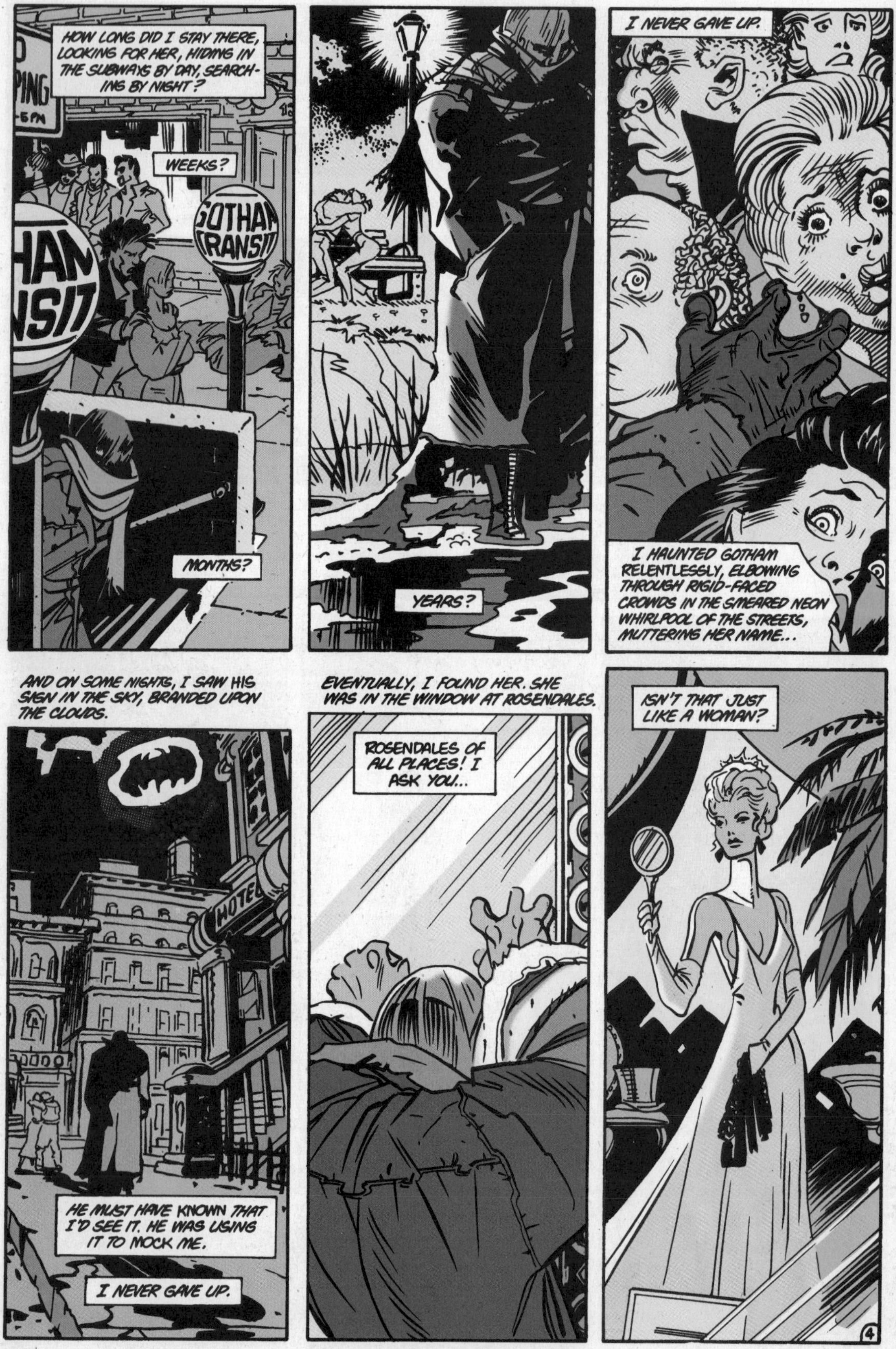
HOW LONG DID I STAY THERE, LOOKING FOR HER, HIDING IN THE SUBWAYS BY DAY, SEARCHING BY NIGHT?
WEEKS?
MONTHS?
YEARS?
I NEVER GAVE UP.
I HAUNTED GOTHAM RELENTLESSLY, ELBOWING THROUGH RIGID-FACED CROWDS IN THE SMEARED NEON WHIRLPOOL OF THE STREETS, MUTTERING HER NAME...
AND ON SOME NIGHTS, I SAW HIS SIGN IN THE SKY, BRANDED UPON THE CLOUDS.
HE MUST HAVE KNOWN THAT I'D SEE IT. HE WAS USING IT TO MOCK ME.
I NEVER GAVE UP.
EVENTUALLY, I FOUND HER. SHE WAS IN THE WINDOW AT ROSENDALES.
ROSENDALES OF ALL PLACES! I ASK YOU...
ISN'T THAT JUST LIKE A WOMAN?
4

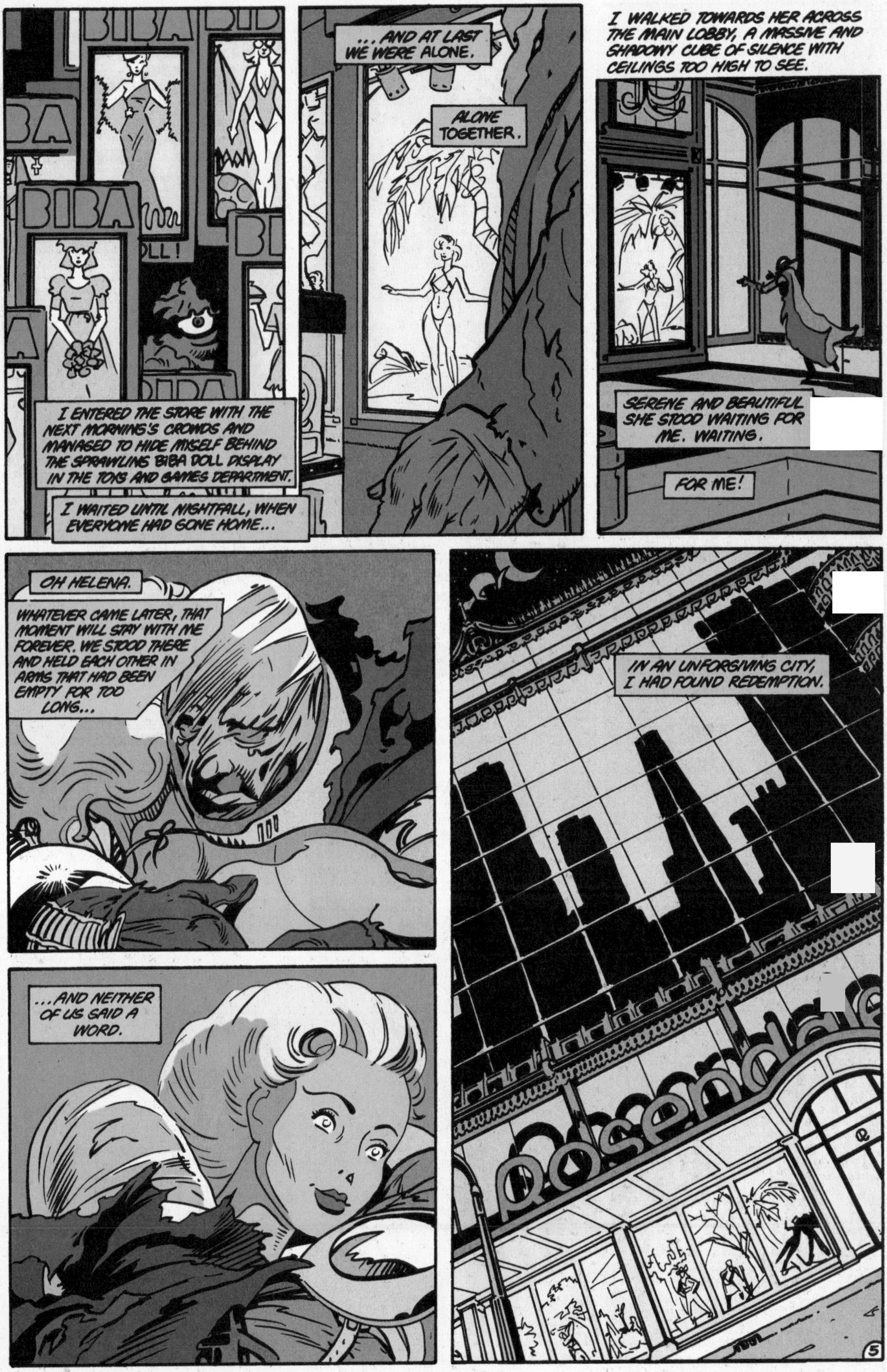

BIBA
BIBA
DOLL!
I ENTERED THE STORE WITH THE NEXT MORNING'S CROWDS AND MANAGED TO HIDE MYSELF BEHIND THE SPRAWLING BIBA DOLL DISPLAY IN THE TOYS AND GAMES DEPARTMENT.
I WAITED UNTIL NIGHTFALL, WHEN EVERYONE HAD GONE HOME...
...AND AT LAST WE WERE ALONE.
ALONE TOGETHER.
I WALKED TOWARDS HER ACROSS THE MAIN LOBBY, A MASSIVE AND SHADOWY CUBE OF SILENCE WITH CEILINGS TOO HIGH TO SEE.
SERENE AND BEAUTIFUL SHE STOOD WAITING FOR ME. WAITING.
FOR ME!
OH HELENA.
WHATEVER CAME LATER, THAT MOMENT WILL STAY WITH ME FOREVER. WE STOOD THERE AND HELD EACH OTHER IN ARMS THAT HAD BEEN EMPTY FOR TOO LONG...
...AND NEITHER OF US SAID A WORD.
IN AN UNFORGIVING CITY, I HAD FOUND REDEMPTION.
Rosendale
5

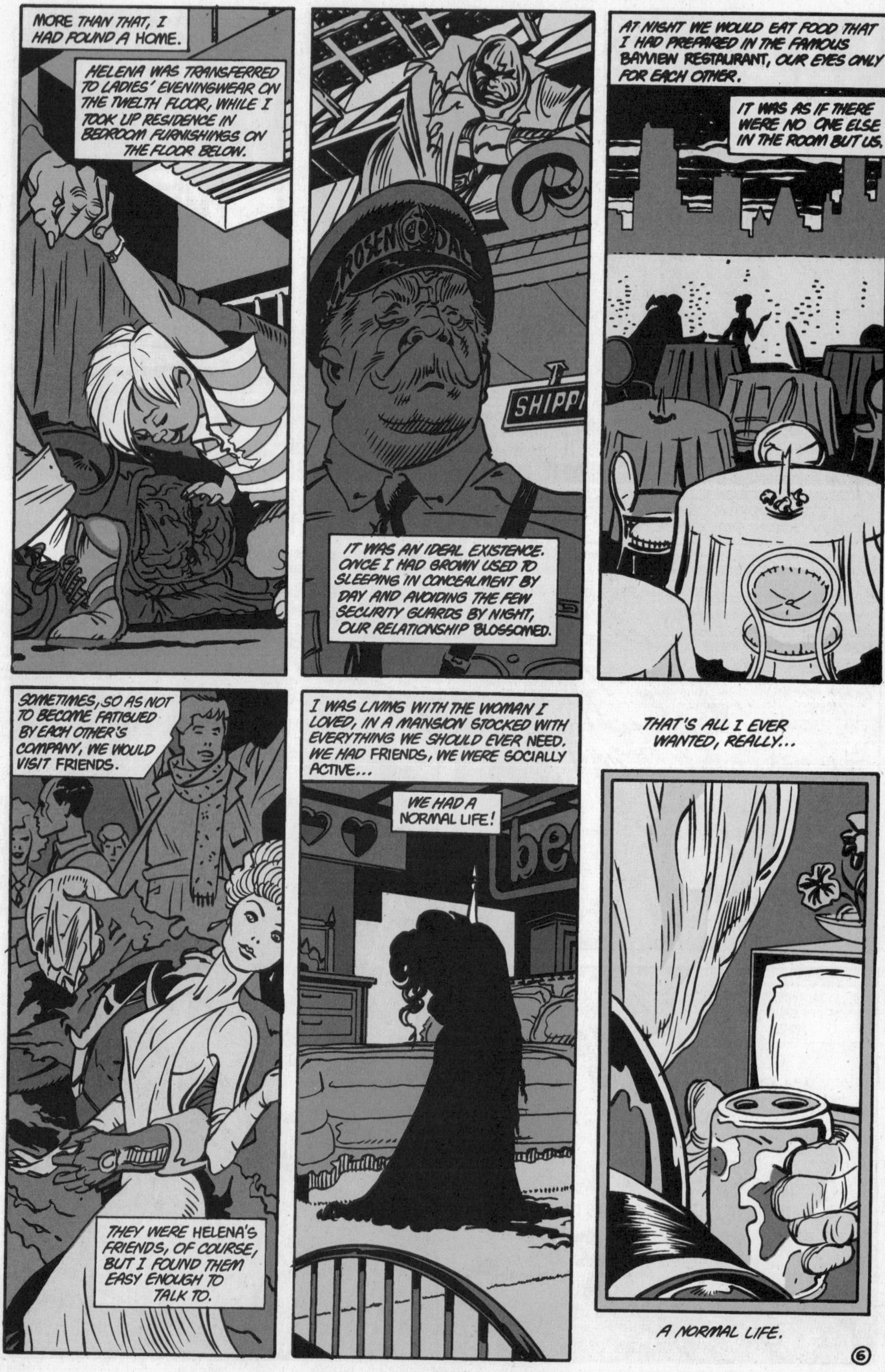
MORE THAN THAT, I HAD FOUND A HOME.
HELENA WAS TRANSFERRED TO LADIES' EVENINGWEAR ON THE TWELTH FLOOR, WHILE I TOOK UP RESIDENCE IN BEDROOM FURNISHINGS ON THE FLOOR BELOW.
ROSEN DAL
SHIPP
IT WAS AN IDEAL EXISTENCE. ONCE I HAD GROWN USED TO SLEEPING IN CONCEALMENT BY DAY AND AVOIDING THE FEW SECURITY GUARDS BY NIGHT, OUR RELATIONSHIP BLOSSOMED.
AT NIGHT WE WOULD EAT FOOD THAT I HAD PREPARED IN THE FAMOUS BAYVIEW RESTAURANT, OUR EYES ONLY FOR EACH OTHER.
IT WAS AS IF THERE WERE NO ONE ELSE IN THE ROOM BUT US.
SOMETIMES, SO AS NOT TO BECOME FATIGUED BY EACH OTHER'S COMPANY, WE WOULD VISIT FRIENDS.
THEY WERE HELENA'S FRIENDS, OF COURSE, BUT I FOUND THEM EASY ENOUGH TO TALK TO.
I WAS LIVING WITH THE WOMAN I LOVED, IN A MANSION STOCKED WITH EVERYTHING WE SHOULD EVER NEED. WE HAD FRIENDS, WE WERE SOCIALLY ACTIVE...
WE HAD A NORMAL LIFE!
be
THAT'S ALL I EVER WANTED, REALLY...
A NORMAL LIFE.
6

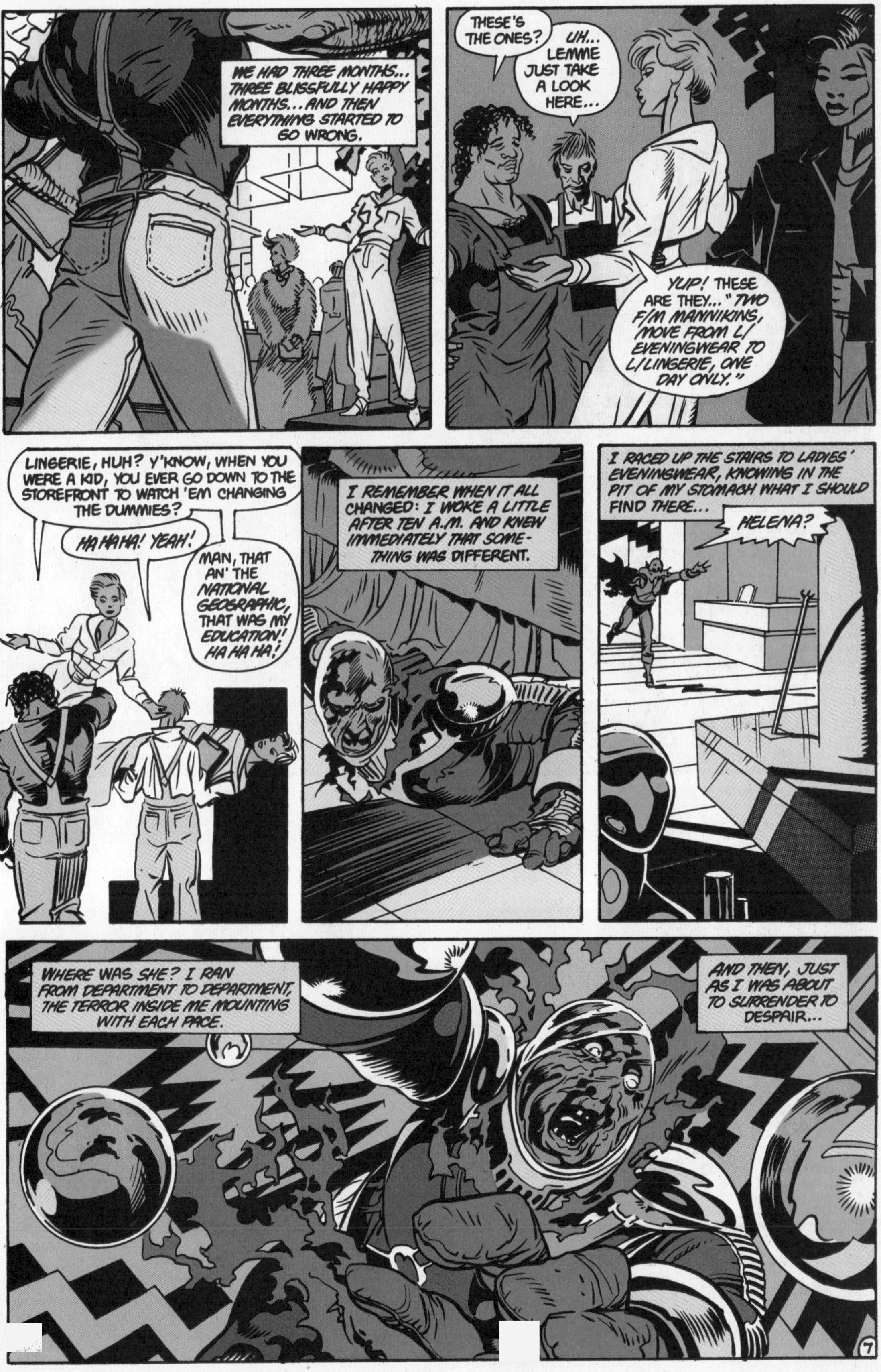
WE HAD THREE MONTHS... THREE BLISSFULLY HAPPY MONTHS... AND THEN EVERYTHING STARTED TO GO WRONG.
THESE'S THE ONES?
UH... LEMME JUST TAKE A LOOK HERE...
YUP! THESE ARE THEY... "TWO F/M MANNIKINS, MOVE FROM L/ EVENINGWEAR TO L/LINGERIE, ONE DAY ONLY."
LINGERIE, HUH? Y'KNOW, WHEN YOU WERE A KID, YOU EVER GO DOWN TO THE STOREFRONT TO WATCH 'EM CHANGING THE DUMMIES?
HA HA HA! YEAH!
MAN, THAT AN' THE NATIONAL GEOGRAPHIC, THAT WAS MY EDUCATION! HA HA HA!
I REMEMBER WHEN IT ALL CHANGED: I WOKE A LITTLE AFTER TEN A.M. AND KNEW IMMEDIATELY THAT SOME-THING WAS DIFFERENT.
I RACED UP THE STAIRS TO LADIES' EVENINGWEAR, KNOWING IN THE PIT OF MY STOMACH WHAT I SHOULD FIND THERE...
HELENA?
WHERE WAS SHE? I RAN FROM DEPARTMENT TO DEPARTMENT, THE TERROR INSIDE ME MOUNTING WITH EACH PACE.
AND THEN, JUST AS I WAS ABOUT TO SURRENDER TO DESPAIR...
7

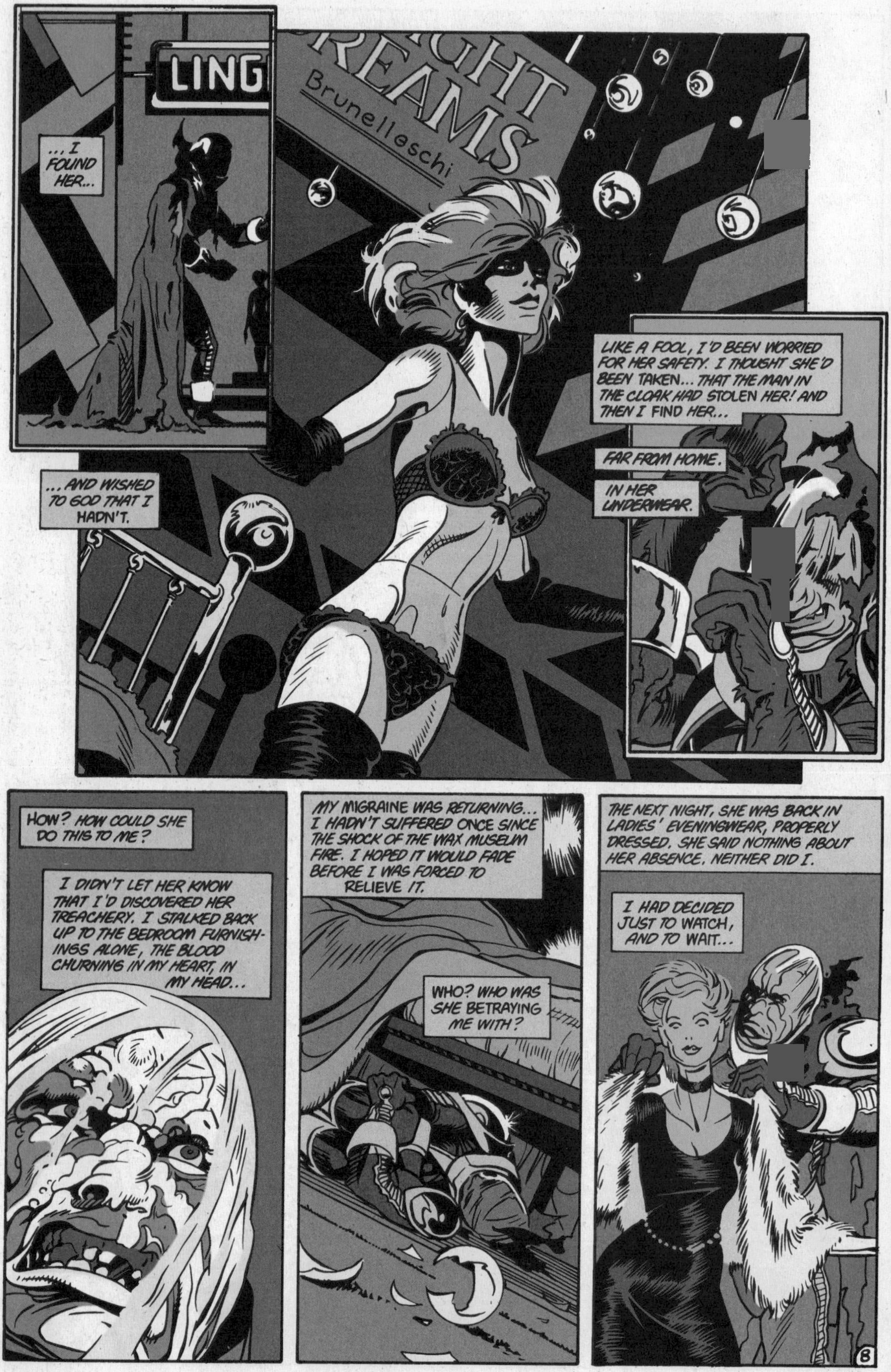
LING
..., I FOUND HER...
REAMS
Brunelleschi
...AND WISHED TO GOD THAT I HADN'T.
LIKE A FOOL, I'D BEEN WORRIED FOR HER SAFETY. I THOUGHT SHE'D BEEN TAKEN... THAT THE MAN IN THE CLOAK HAD STOLEN HER! AND THEN I FIND HER...
FAR FROM HOME.
IN HER UNDERWEAR.
HOW? HOW COULD SHE DO THIS TO ME?
I DIDN'T LET HER KNOW THAT I'D DISCOVERED HER TREACHERY. I STALKED BACK UP TO THE BEDROOM FURNISH-INGS ALONE, THE BLOOD CHURNING IN MY HEART, IN MY HEAD...
MY MIGRAINE WAS RETURNING... I HADN'T SUFFERED ONCE SINCE THE SHOCK OF THE WAX MUSEUM FIRE. I HOPED IT WOULD FADE BEFORE I WAS FORCED TO RELIEVE IT.
WHO? WHO WAS SHE BETRAYING ME WITH?
THE NEXT NIGHT, SHE WAS BACK IN LADIES' EVENINGWEAR, PROPERLY DRESSED. SHE SAID NOTHING ABOUT HER ABSENCE. NEITHER DID I.
I HAD DECIDED JUST TO WATCH, AND TO WAIT...
8

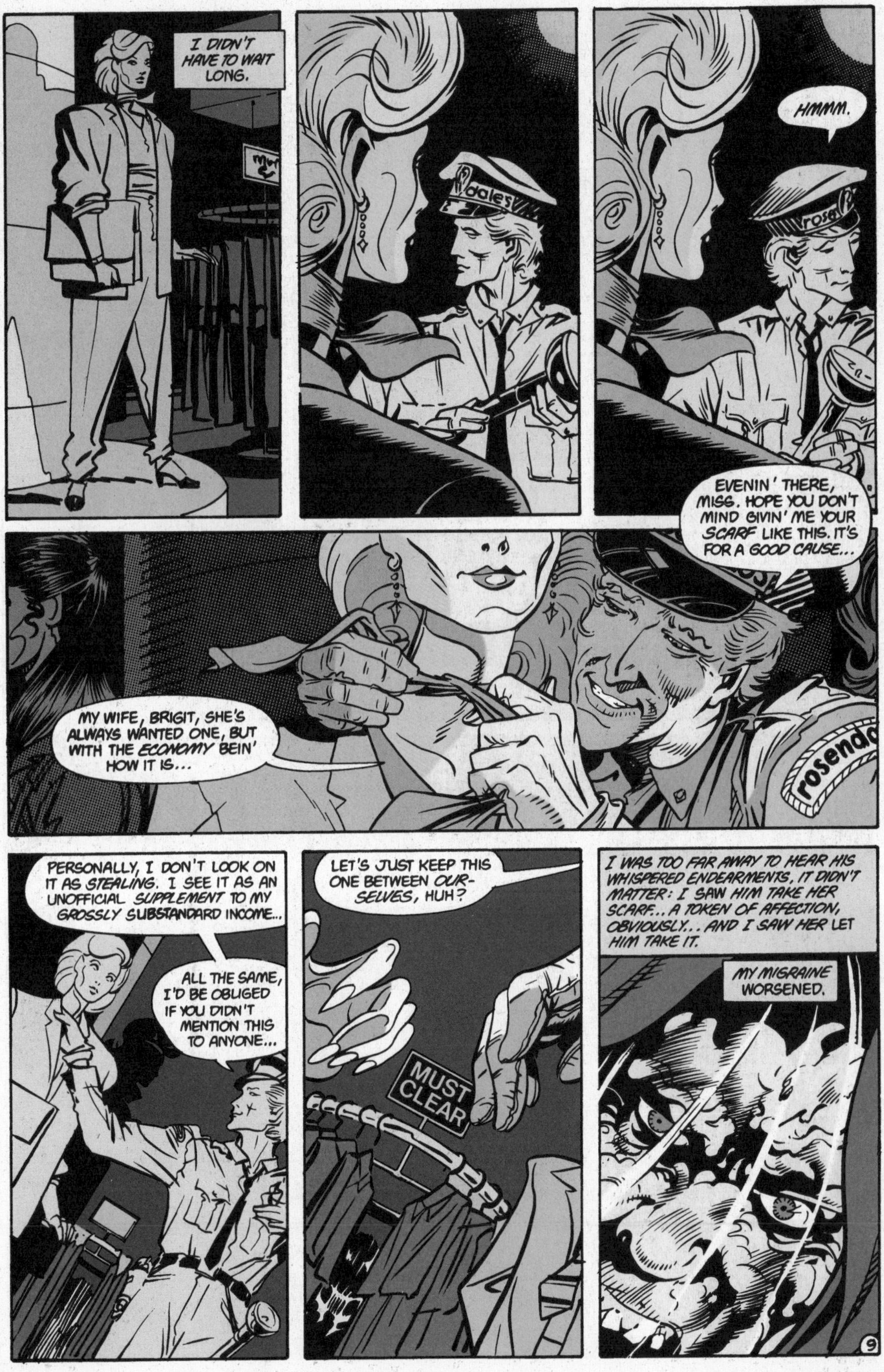
I DIDN'T HAVE TO WAIT LONG.
HMMM.
EVENIN' THERE, MISS. HOPE YOU DON'T MIND GIVIN' ME YOUR SCARF LIKE THIS. IT'S FOR A GOOD CAUSE...
MY WIFE, BRIGIT, SHE'S ALWAYS WANTED ONE, BUT WITH THE ECONOMY BEIN' HOW IT IS...
rosendo
PERSONALLY, I DON'T LOOK ON IT AS STEALING. I SEE IT AS AN UNOFFICIAL SUPPLEMENT TO MY GROSSLY SUBSTANDARD INCOME...
ALL THE SAME, I'D BE OBLIGED IF YOU DIDN'T MENTION THIS TO ANYONE...
LET'S JUST KEEP THIS ONE BETWEEN OURSELVES, HUH?
MUST CLEAR
I WAS TOO FAR AWAY TO HEAR HIS WHISPERED ENDEARMENTS. IT DIDN'T MATTER: I SAW HIM TAKE HER SCARF... A TOKEN OF AFFECTION, OBVIOUSLY... AND I SAW HER LET HIM TAKE IT.
MY MIGRAINE WORSENED.
9

I WAITED FOR HIM TO LEAVE, AND THEN I SLIPPED OUT UNOBSERVED. I DIDN'T WANT TO MAKE A SCENE IN FRONT OF HELENA.

ISN'T THAT RIDICULOUS? I STILL LOVED HER...

...AFTER ALL SHE'D DONE TO ME.

SHDUNF

rosendale

HEY... IS THERE SOMEBODY BACK THERE? RAY? IS THAT YOU BACK THERE, FOOLIN' AROUND?

HELLO?

ALL RIGHT... WHOEVER IT IS, YOU BETTER COME OUT NICE AN' EASY...

AND I WANTA BE ABLE TO SEE YOUR...

...HANDS.

AAAAAAAAAA!

ARIAAHHHH!

DDRANN!

DRANN!

10

194

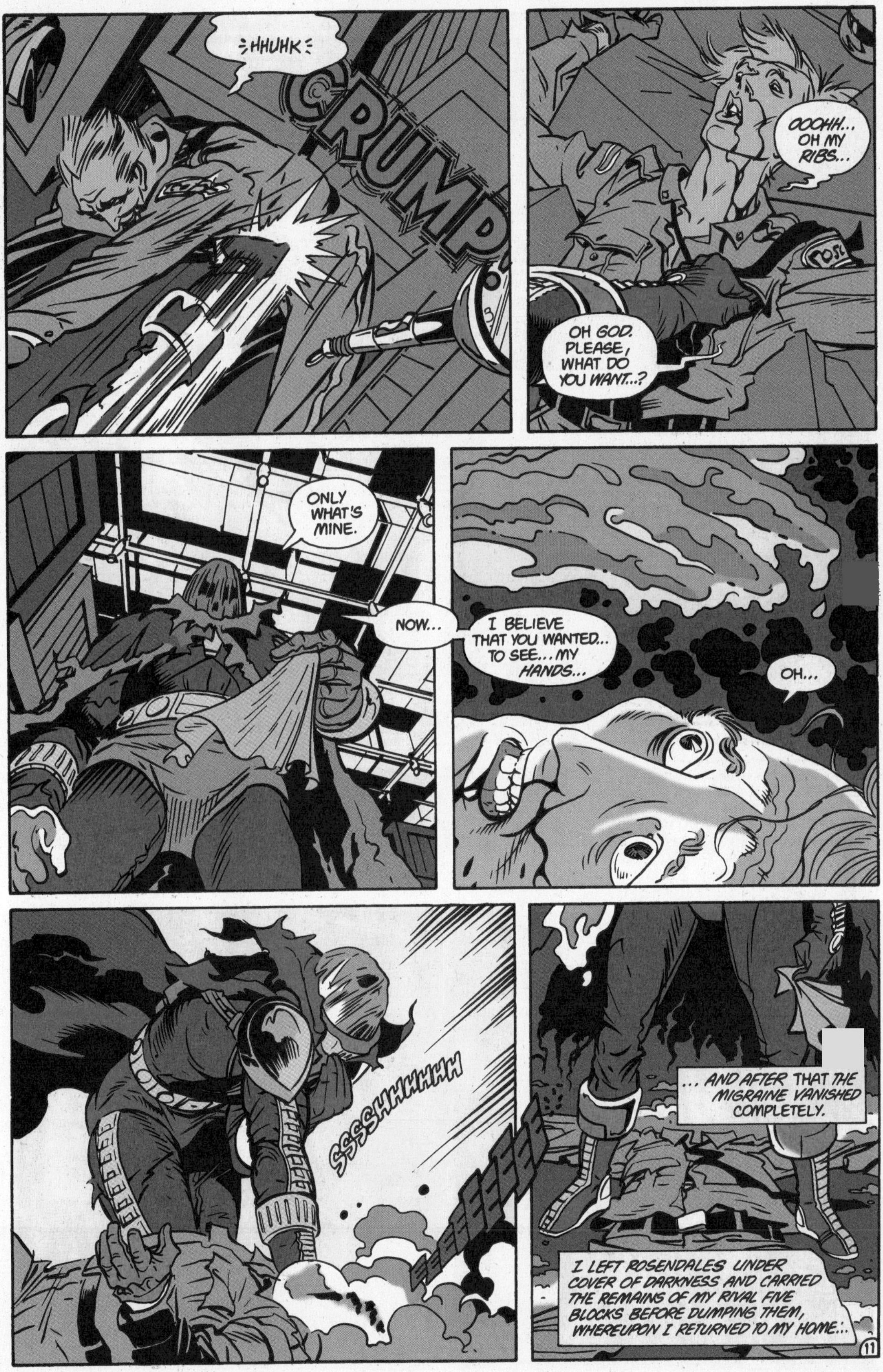

HHUHK
CRUMP
OOOHH... OH MY RIBS...
OH GOD. PLEASE, WHAT DO YOU WANT...?
ONLY WHAT'S MINE.
NOW...
I BELIEVE THAT YOU WANTED... TO SEE... MY HANDS...
OH...
SSSSHHHHHHH
... AND AFTER THAT THE MIGRAINE VANISHED COMPLETELY.
I LEFT ROSENDALES UNDER COVER OF DARKNESS AND CARRIED THE REMAINS OF MY RIVAL FIVE BLOCKS BEFORE DUMPING THEM, WHEREUPON I RETURNED TO MY HOME...
11

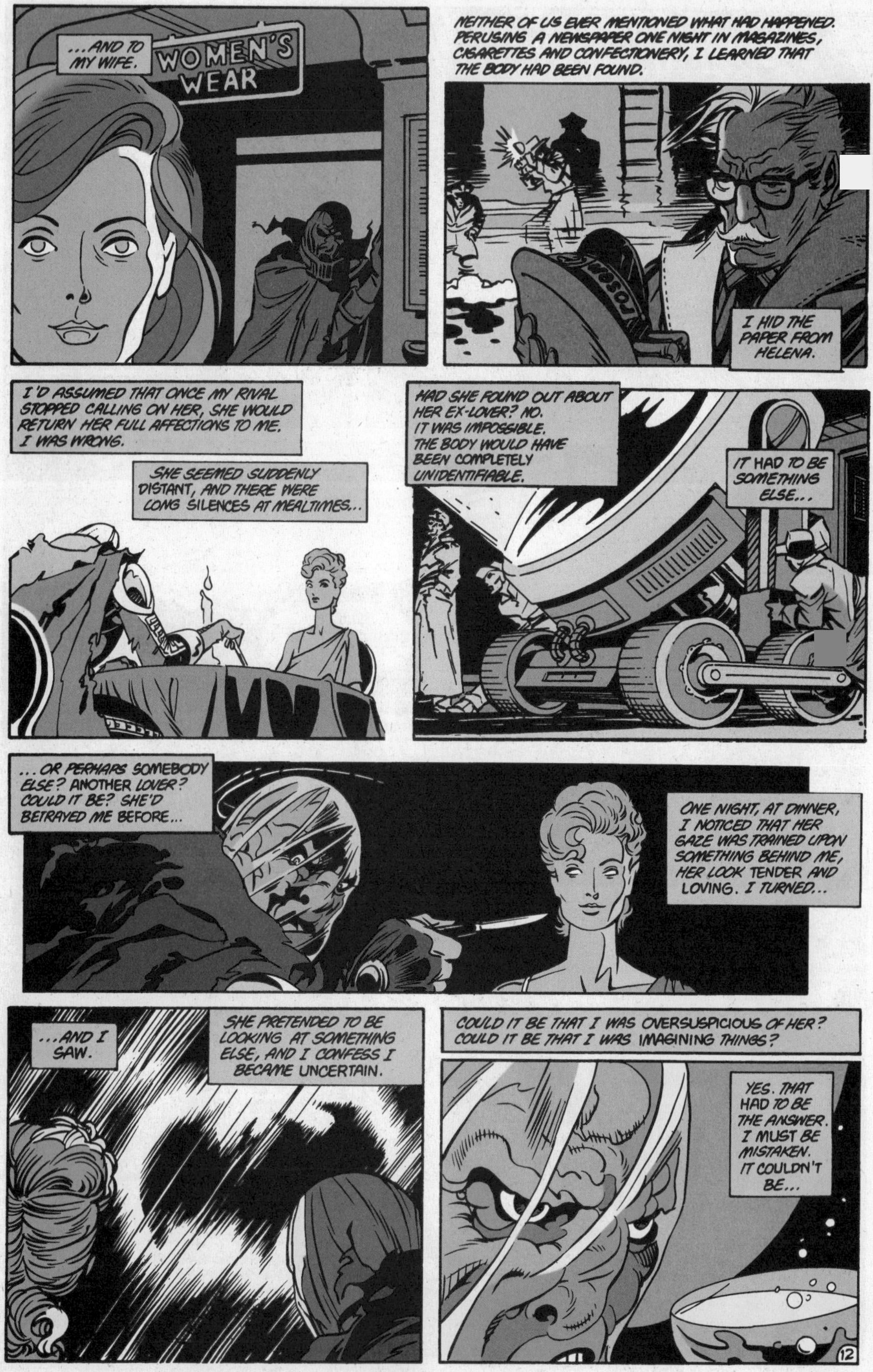
...AND TO MY WIFE.
WOMEN'S WEAR
NEITHER OF US EVER MENTIONED WHAT HAD HAPPENED. PERUSING A NEWSPAPER ONE NIGHT IN MAGAZINES, CIGARETTES AND CONFECTIONERY, I LEARNED THAT THE BODY HAD BEEN FOUND.
I HID THE PAPER FROM HELENA.
I'D ASSUMED THAT ONCE MY RIVAL STOPPED CALLING ON HER, SHE WOULD RETURN HER FULL AFFECTIONS TO ME. I WAS WRONG.
SHE SEEMED SUDDENLY DISTANT, AND THERE WERE LONG SILENCES AT MEALTIMES...
HAD SHE FOUND OUT ABOUT HER EX-LOVER? NO. IT WAS IMPOSSIBLE. THE BODY WOULD HAVE BEEN COMPLETELY UNIDENTIFIABLE.
IT HAD TO BE SOMETHING ELSE...
...OR PERHAPS SOMEBODY ELSE? ANOTHER LOVER? COULD IT BE? SHE'D BETRAYED ME BEFORE...
ONE NIGHT, AT DINNER, I NOTICED THAT HER GAZE WAS TRAINED UPON SOMETHING BEHIND ME, HER LOOK TENDER AND LOVING. I TURNED...
...AND I SAW.
SHE PRETENDED TO BE LOOKING AT SOMETHING ELSE, AND I CONFESS I BECAME UNCERTAIN.
COULD IT BE THAT I WAS OVERSUSPICIOUS OF HER? COULD IT BE THAT I WAS IMAGINING THINGS?
YES. THAT HAD TO BE THE ANSWER. I MUST BE MISTAKEN. IT COULDN'T BE...
12

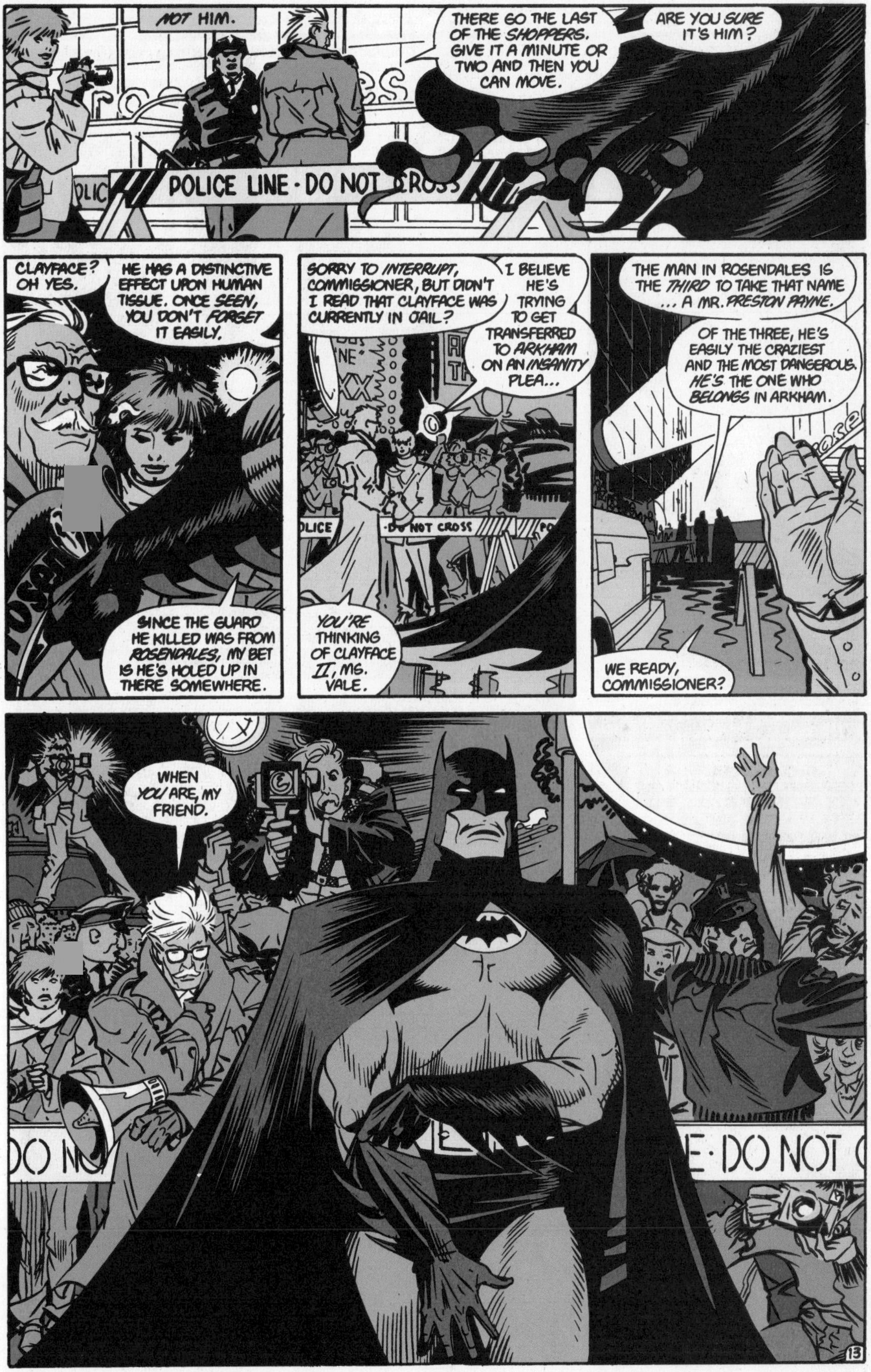
NOT HIM.
THERE GO THE LAST OF THE SHOPPERS. GIVE IT A MINUTE OR TWO AND THEN YOU CAN MOVE.
ARE YOU SURE IT'S HIM?
POLICE LINE - DO NOT CROSS
CLAYFACE? OH YES.
HE HAS A DISTINCTIVE EFFECT UPON HUMAN TISSUE. ONCE SEEN, YOU DON'T FORGET IT EASILY.
SINCE THE GUARD HE KILLED WAS FROM ROSENDALES, MY BET IS HE'S HOLED UP IN THERE SOMEWHERE.
SORRY TO INTERRUPT, COMMISSIONER, BUT DIDN'T I READ THAT CLAYFACE WAS CURRENTLY IN JAIL?
I BELIEVE HE'S TRYING TO GET TRANSFERRED TO ARKHAM ON AN INSANITY PLEA...
YOU'RE THINKING OF CLAYFACE II, MS. VALE.
THE MAN IN ROSENDALES IS THE THIRD TO TAKE THAT NAME ... A MR. PRESTON PAYNE.
OF THE THREE, HE'S EASILY THE CRAZIEST AND THE MOST DANGEROUS. HE'S THE ONE WHO BELONGS IN ARKHAM.
WE READY, COMMISSIONER?
WHEN YOU ARE, MY FRIEND.
DO NO
E - DO NOT
13

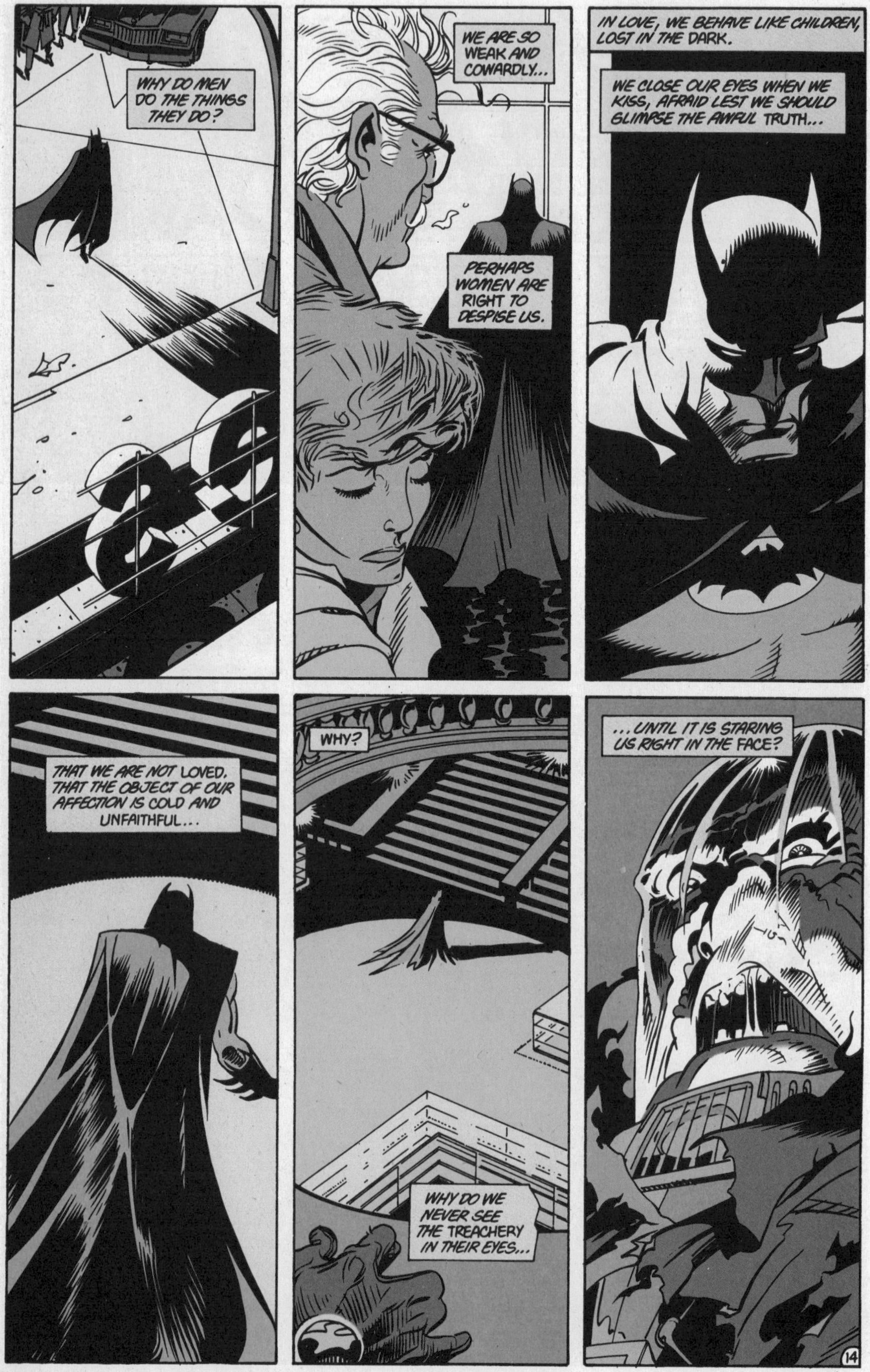
WHY DO MEN DO THE THINGS THEY DO?
WE ARE SO WEAK AND COWARDLY...
PERHAPS WOMEN ARE RIGHT TO DESPISE US.
IN LOVE, WE BEHAVE LIKE CHILDREN, LOST IN THE DARK.
WE CLOSE OUR EYES WHEN WE KISS, AFRAID LEST WE SHOULD GLIMPSE THE AWFUL TRUTH...
THAT WE ARE NOT LOVED. THAT THE OBJECT OF OUR AFFECTION IS COLD AND UNFAITHFUL...
WHY?
WHY DO WE NEVER SEE THE TREACHERY IN THEIR EYES...
...UNTIL IT IS STARING US RIGHT IN THE FACE?
14

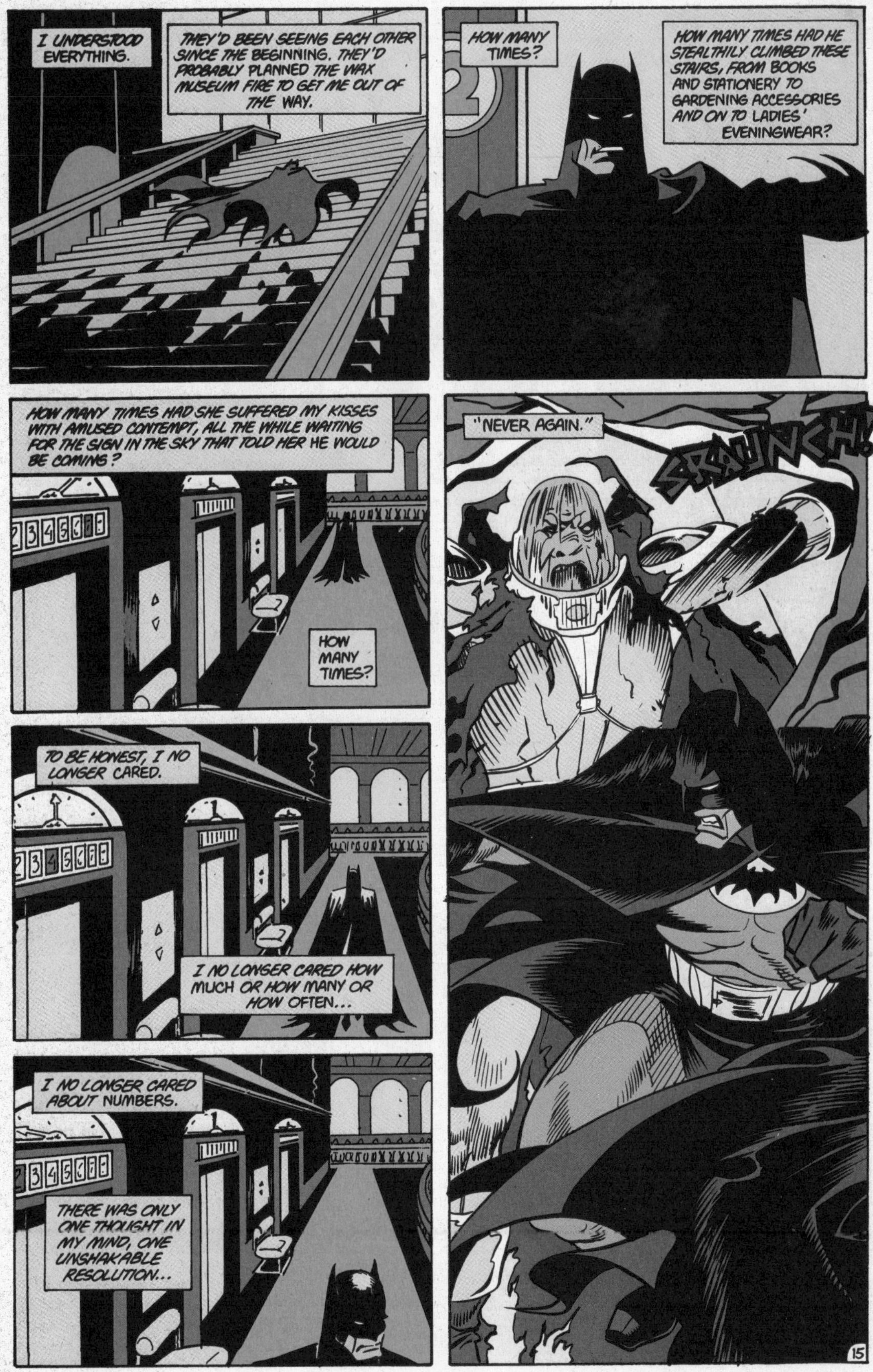
I UNDERSTOOD EVERYTHING.
THEY'D BEEN SEEING EACH OTHER SINCE THE BEGINNING. THEY'D PROBABLY PLANNED THE WAX MUSEUM FIRE TO GET ME OUT OF THE WAY.
HOW MANY TIMES?
HOW MANY TIMES HAD HE STEALTHILY CLIMBED THESE STAIRS, FROM BOOKS AND STATIONERY TO GARDENING ACCESSORIES AND ON TO LADIES' EVENINGWEAR?
HOW MANY TIMES HAD SHE SUFFERED MY KISSES WITH AMUSED CONTEMPT, ALL THE WHILE WAITING FOR THE SIGN IN THE SKY THAT TOLD HER HE WOULD BE COMING?
HOW MANY TIMES?
TO BE HONEST, I NO LONGER CARED.
I NO LONGER CARED HOW MUCH OR HOW MANY OR HOW OFTEN...
I NO LONGER CARED ABOUT NUMBERS.
THERE WAS ONLY ONE THOUGHT IN MY MIND, ONE UNSHAKABLE RESOLUTION...
"NEVER AGAIN."
SKRAUNCH!
15

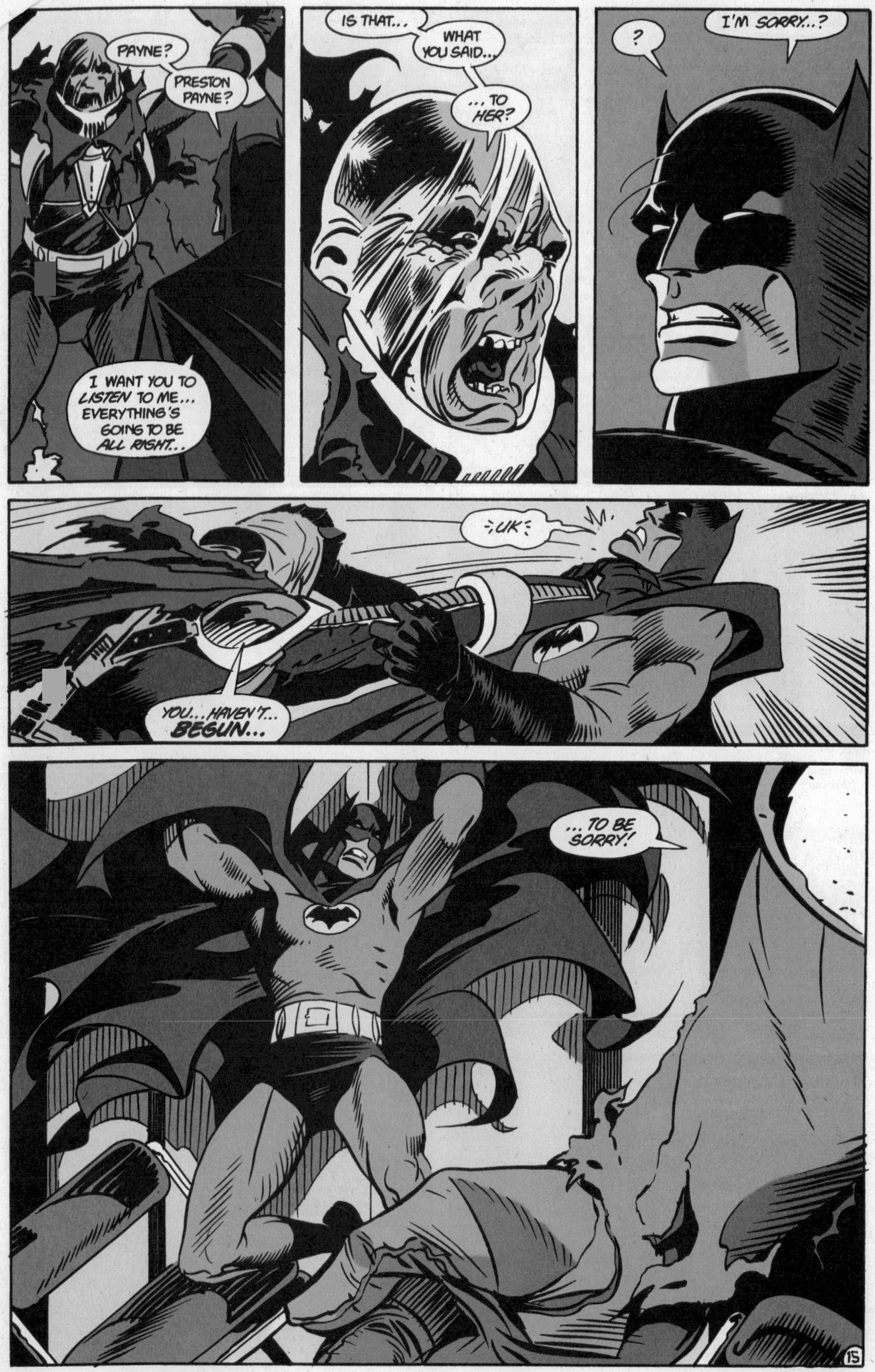
PAYNE?
PRESTON PAYNE?
I WANT YOU TO LISTEN TO ME... EVERYTHING'S GOING TO BE ALL RIGHT...
IS THAT...
WHAT YOU SAID...
...TO HER?
?
I'M SORRY...?
UK
YOU... HAVEN'T... BEGUN...
...TO BE SORRY!
15

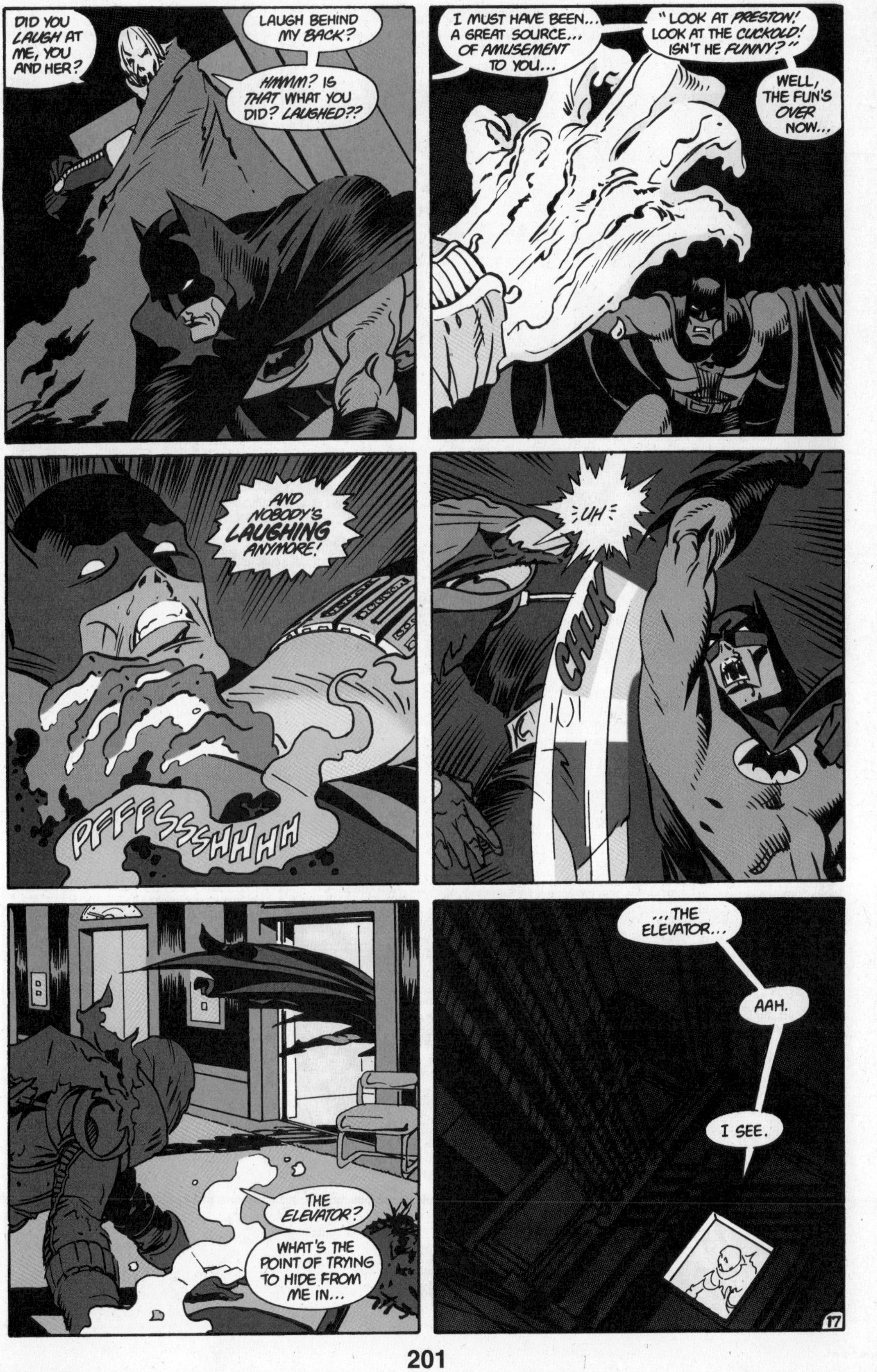
DID YOU LAUGH AT ME, YOU AND HER?
LAUGH BEHIND MY BACK?
HMMM? IS THAT WHAT YOU DID? LAUGHED??
I MUST HAVE BEEN... A GREAT SOURCE... OF AMUSEMENT TO YOU...
"LOOK AT PRESTON! LOOK AT THE CUCKOLD! ISN'T HE FUNNY?"
WELL, THE FUN'S OVER NOW...
AND NOBODY'S LAUGHING ANYMORE!
PFFFSSSHHHHH
UH
CHUK
THE ELEVATOR?
WHAT'S THE POINT OF TRYING TO HIDE FROM ME IN...
...THE ELEVATOR...
AAH.
I SEE.
17

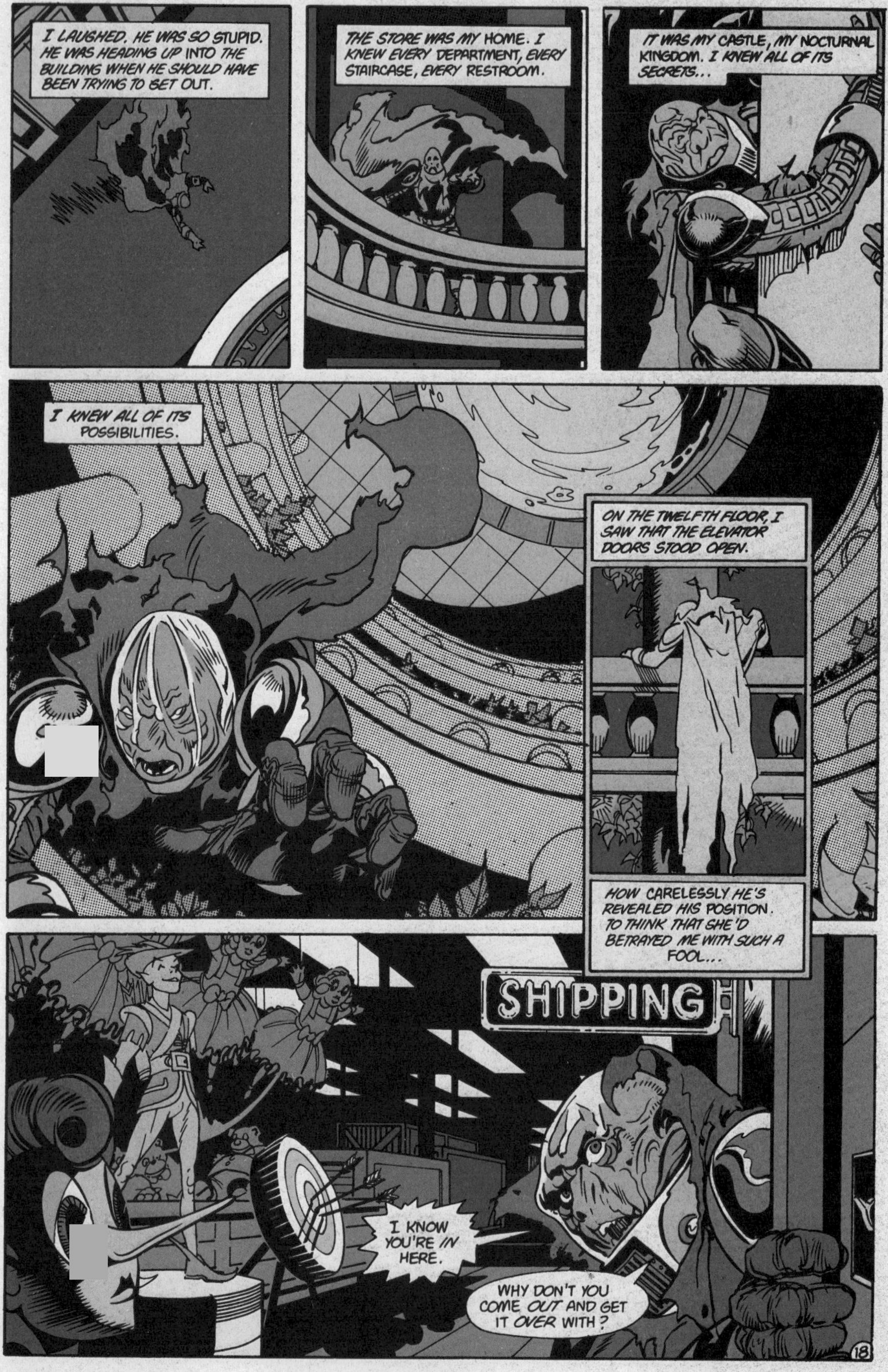
I LAUGHED. HE WAS SO STUPID. HE WAS HEADING UP INTO THE BUILDING WHEN HE SHOULD HAVE BEEN TRYING TO GET OUT.
THE STORE WAS MY HOME. I KNEW EVERY DEPARTMENT, EVERY STAIRCASE, EVERY RESTROOM.
IT WAS MY CASTLE, MY NOCTURNAL KINGDOM. I KNEW ALL OF ITS SECRETS...
I KNEW ALL OF ITS POSSIBILITIES.
ON THE TWELFTH FLOOR, I SAW THAT THE ELEVATOR DOORS STOOD OPEN.
HOW CARELESSLY HE'S REVEALED HIS POSITION. TO THINK THAT SHE'D BETRAYED ME WITH SUCH A FOOL...
SHIPPING
I KNOW YOU'RE IN HERE.
WHY DON'T YOU COME OUT AND GET IT OVER WITH?
18

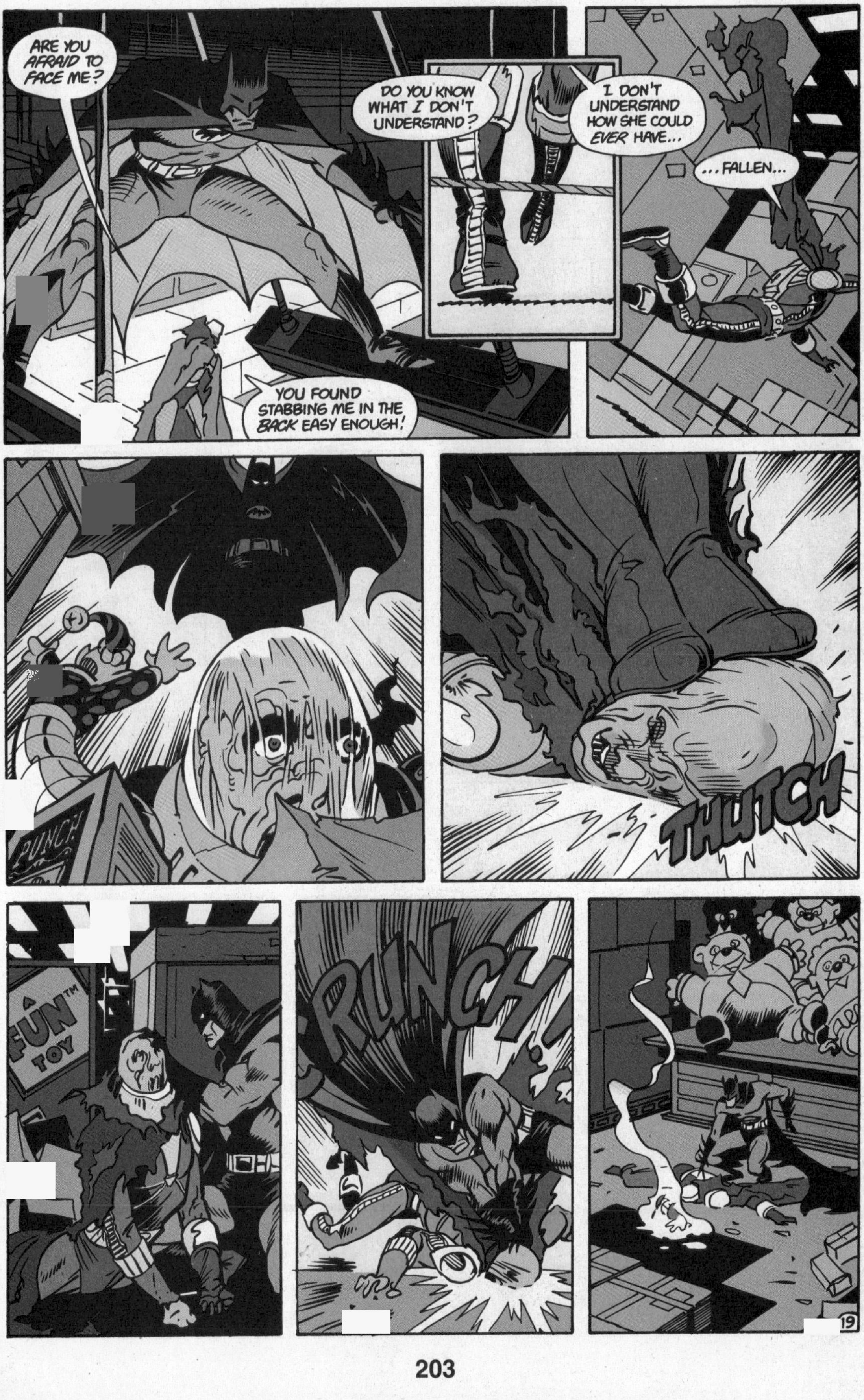

ARE YOU AFRAID TO FACE ME?
YOU FOUND STABBING ME IN THE BACK EASY ENOUGH!
DO YOU KNOW WHAT I DON'T UNDERSTAND?
I DON'T UNDERSTAND HOW SHE COULD EVER HAVE...
...FALLEN...
PUNCH
THWTCH
A FUN™ TOY
CRUNCH!
19

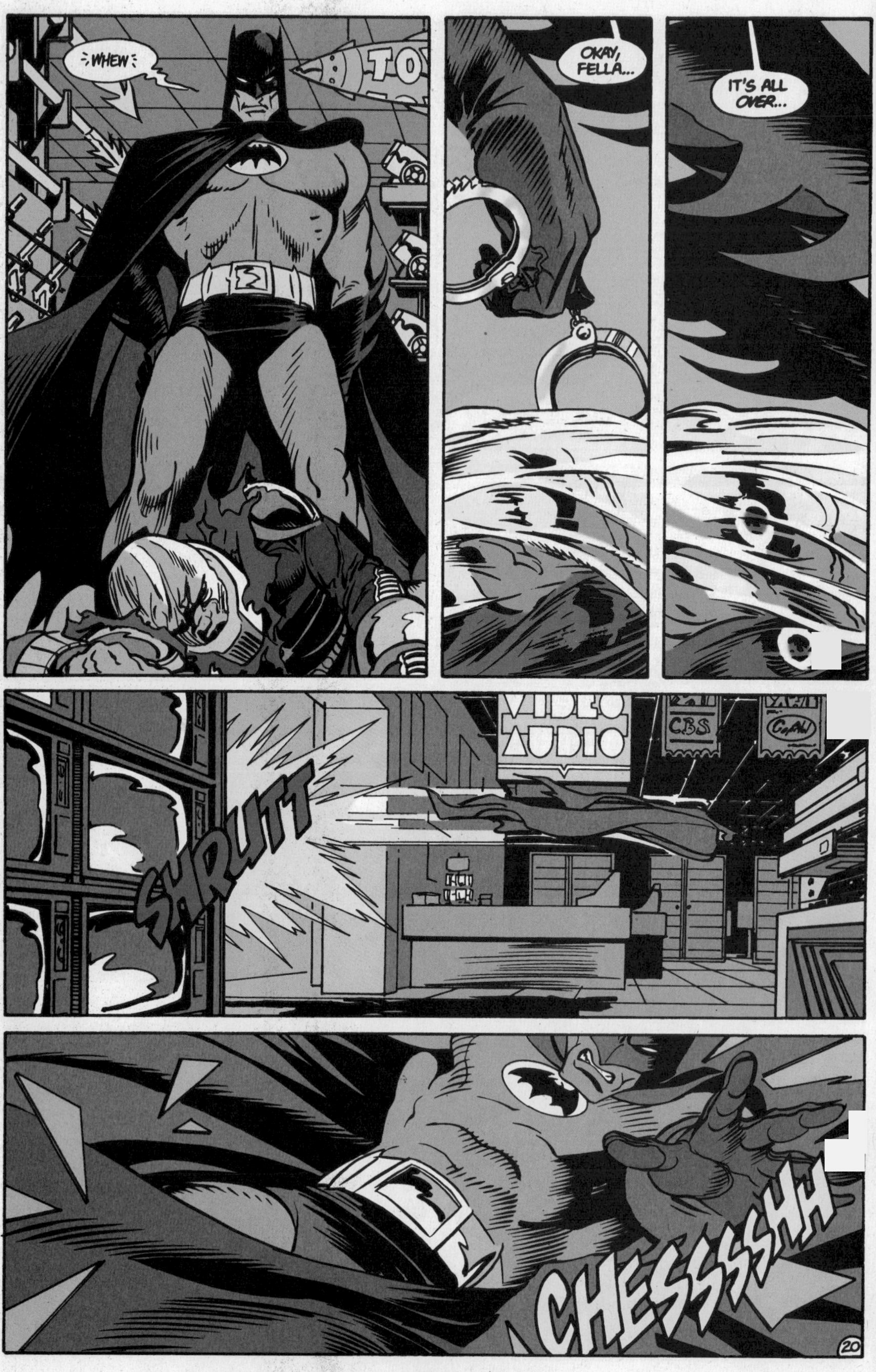
WHEW
OKAY, FELLA...
IT'S ALL OVER...
VIDEO AUDIO
CBS
SHRUTT
CHESSSSHH
20

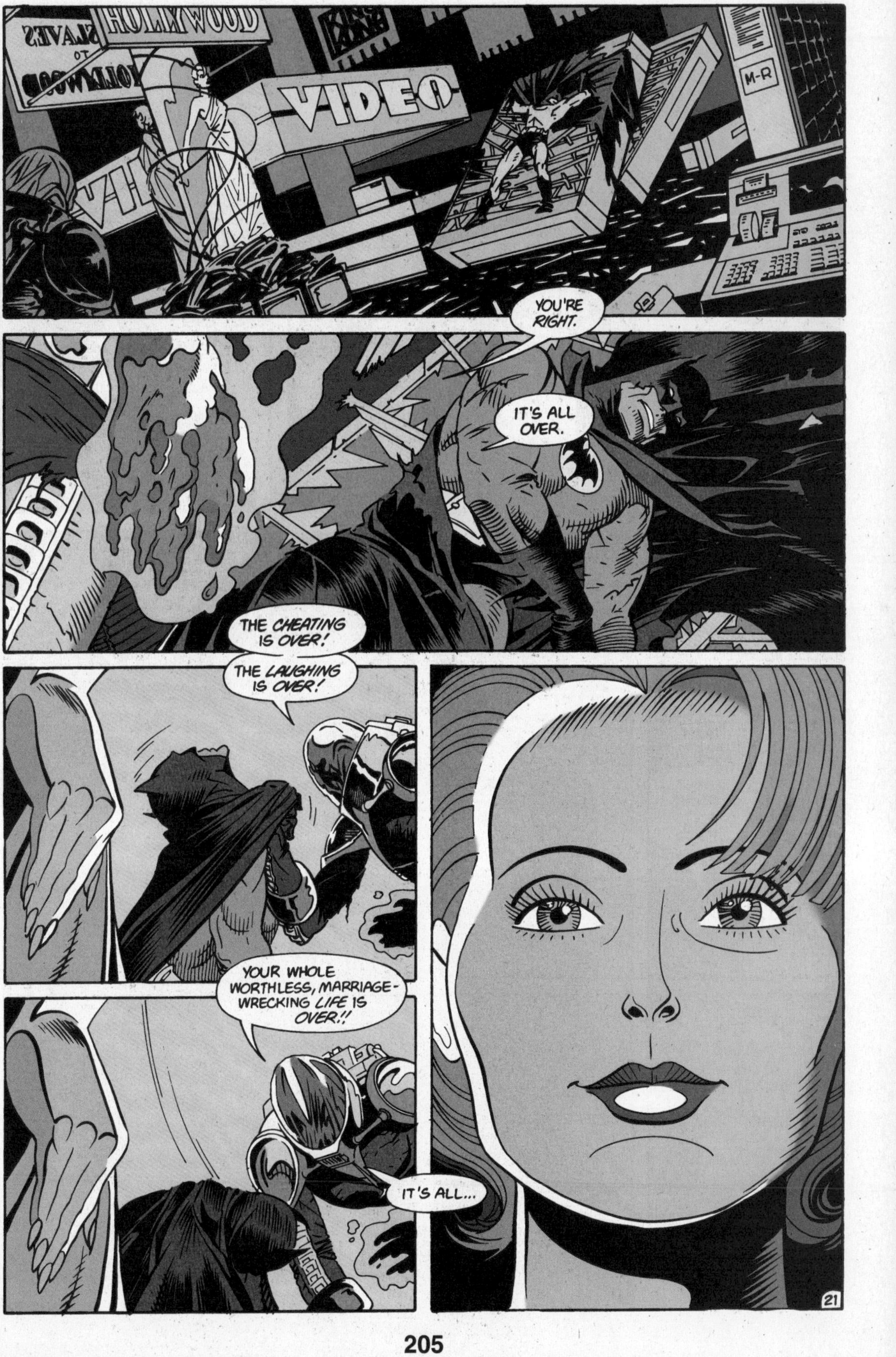
HOLLYWOOD
SLAVES TO HOLLYWOOD
VIDEO
M-R
YOU'RE RIGHT.
IT'S ALL OVER.
THE CHEATING IS OVER!
THE LAUGHING IS OVER!
YOUR WHOLE WORTHLESS, MARRIAGE-WRECKING LIFE IS OVER!!
IT'S ALL...
21

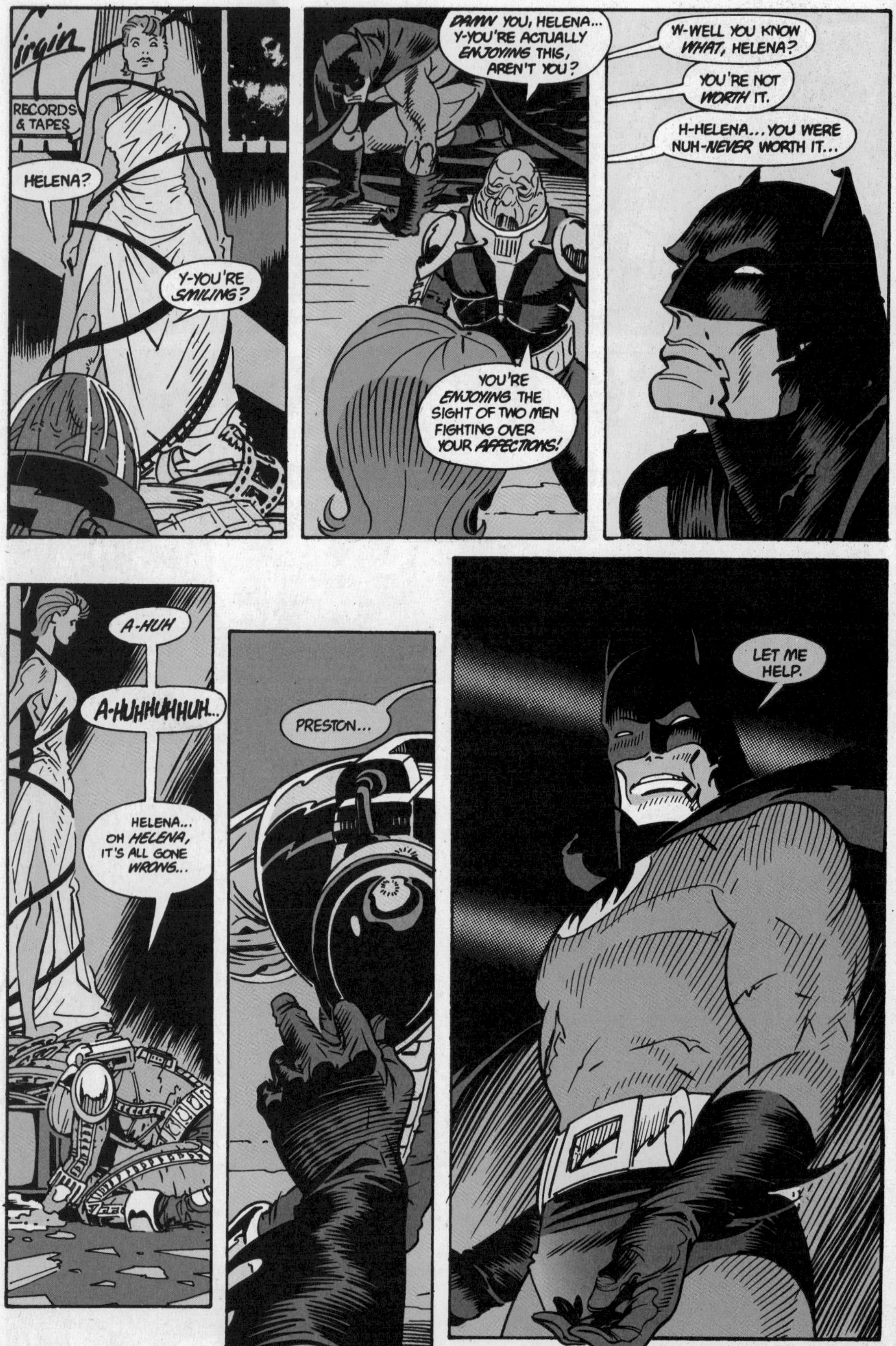
Virgin
RECORDS & TAPES
HELENA?
Y-YOU'RE SMILING?
DAMN YOU, HELENA... Y-YOU'RE ACTUALLY ENJOYING THIS, AREN'T YOU?
YOU'RE ENJOYING THE SIGHT OF TWO MEN FIGHTING OVER YOUR AFFECTIONS!
W-WELL YOU KNOW WHAT, HELENA?
YOU'RE NOT WORTH IT.
H-HELENA... YOU WERE NUH-NEVER WORTH IT...
A-HUH
A-HUHHUHHUH...
HELENA... OH HELENA, IT'S ALL GONE WRONG...
PRESTON...
LET ME HELP.
22

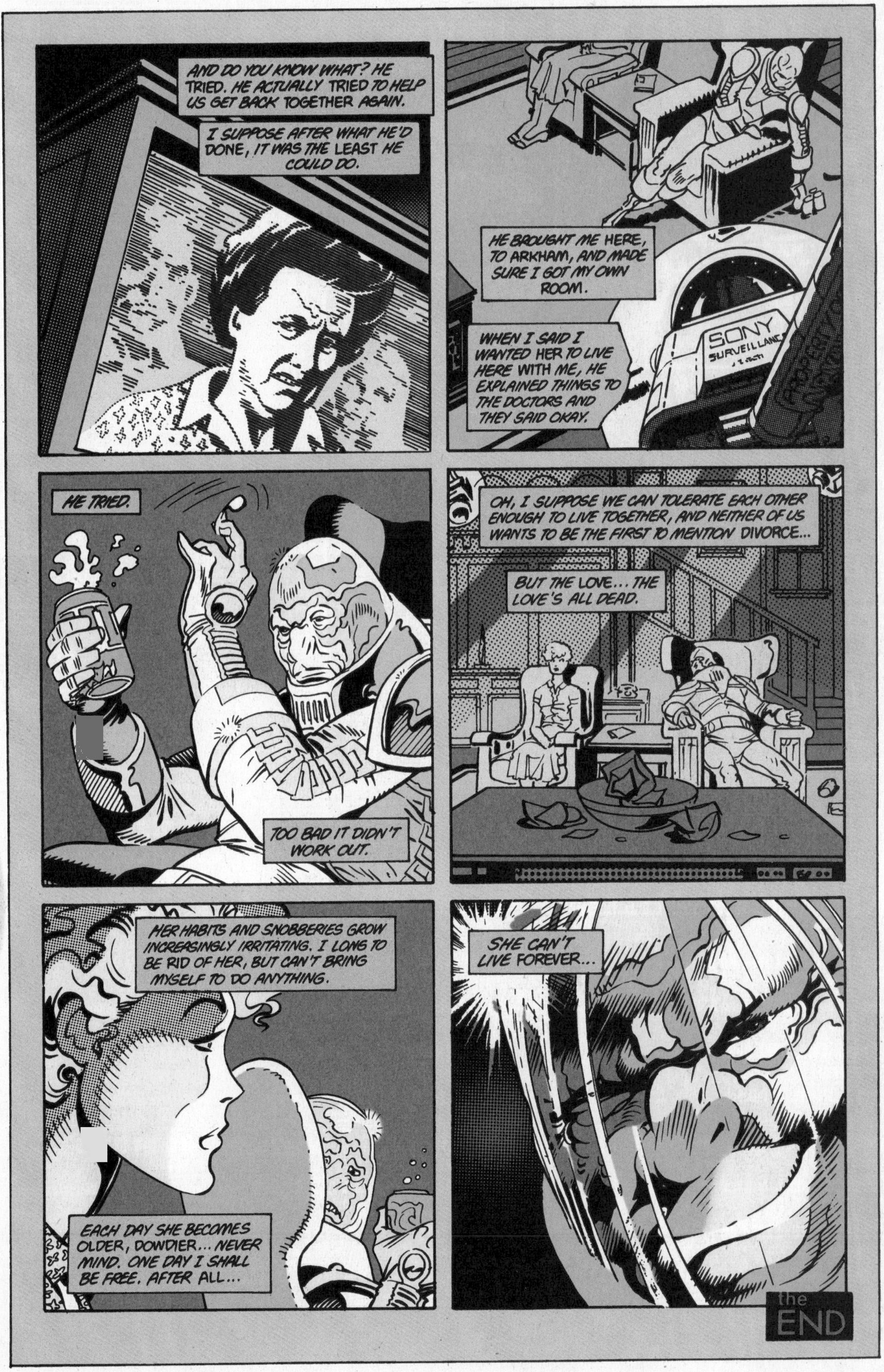
AND DO YOU KNOW WHAT? HE TRIED. HE ACTUALLY TRIED TO HELP US GET BACK TOGETHER AGAIN.
I SUPPOSE AFTER WHAT HE'D DONE, IT WAS THE LEAST HE COULD DO.
HE BROUGHT ME HERE, TO ARKHAM, AND MADE SURE I GOT MY OWN ROOM.
WHEN I SAID I WANTED HER TO LIVE HERE WITH ME, HE EXPLAINED THINGS TO THE DOCTORS AND THEY SAID OKAY.
SONY
SURVEILLANCE
HE TRIED.
TOO BAD IT DIDN'T WORK OUT.
OH, I SUPPOSE WE CAN TOLERATE EACH OTHER ENOUGH TO LIVE TOGETHER, AND NEITHER OF US WANTS TO BE THE FIRST TO MENTION DIVORCE...
BUT THE LOVE... THE LOVE'S ALL DEAD.
HER HABITS AND SNOBBERIES GROW INCREASINGLY IRRITATING. I LONG TO BE RID OF HER, BUT CAN'T BRING MYSELF TO DO ANYTHING.
EACH DAY SHE BECOMES OLDER, DOWDIER... NEVER MIND. ONE DAY I SHALL BE FREE. AFTER ALL...
SHE CAN'T LIVE FOREVER...
the END

OTHER BOOKS BY ALAN MOORE

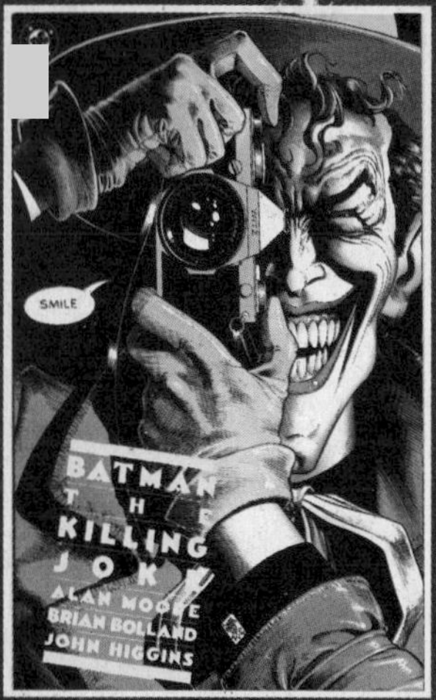
SMILE
BATMAN THE KILLING JOKE
ALAN MOORE
BRIAN BOLLAND
JOHN HIGGINS

BATMAN: THE KILLING JOKE
WITH BRIAN BOLLAND

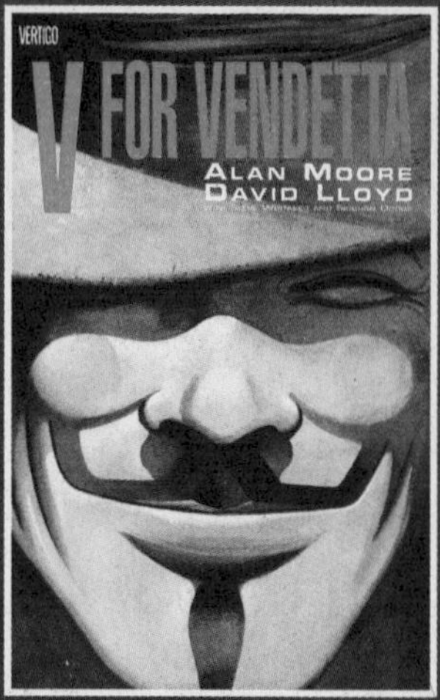
VERTIGO
V FOR VENDETTA
ALAN MOORE
DAVID LLOYD

V FOR VENDETTA
WITH DAVID LLOYD

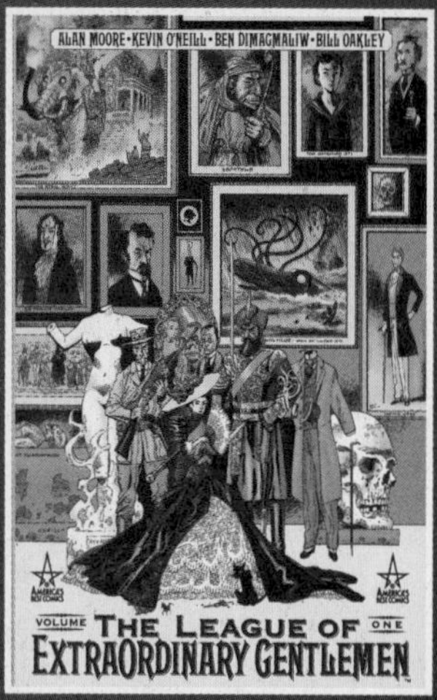
ALAN MOORE • KEVIN O'NEILL • BEN DIMAGMALIW • BILL OAKLEY
VOLUME ONE
THE LEAGUE OF EXTRAORDINARY GENTLEMEN

THE LEAGUE OF EXTRAORDINARY GENTLEMEN WITH KEVIN O'NEILL

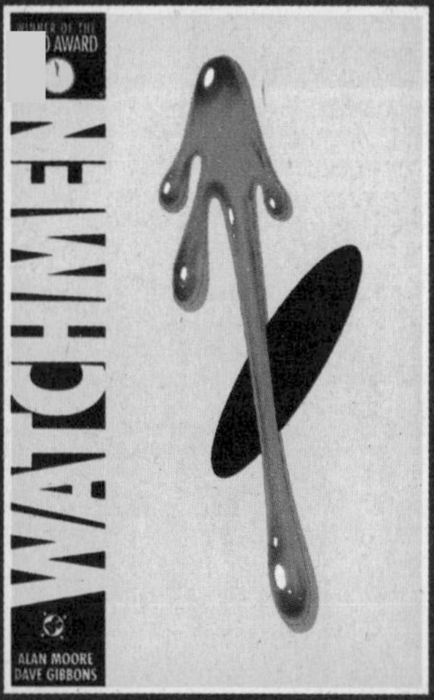
WATCHMEN
ALAN MOORE
DAVE GIBBONS

WATCHMEN
WITH DAVE GIBBONS

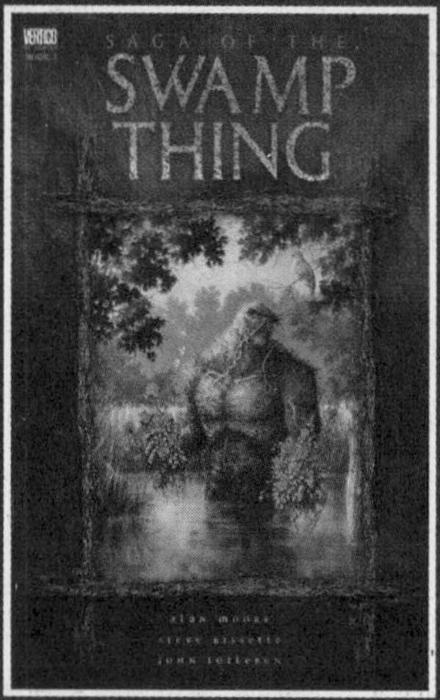
VERTIGO
SAGA OF THE
SWAMP THING

SAGA OF THE SWAMP THING
WITH STEVE BISSETTE, JOHN TOTLEBEN AND VARIOUS

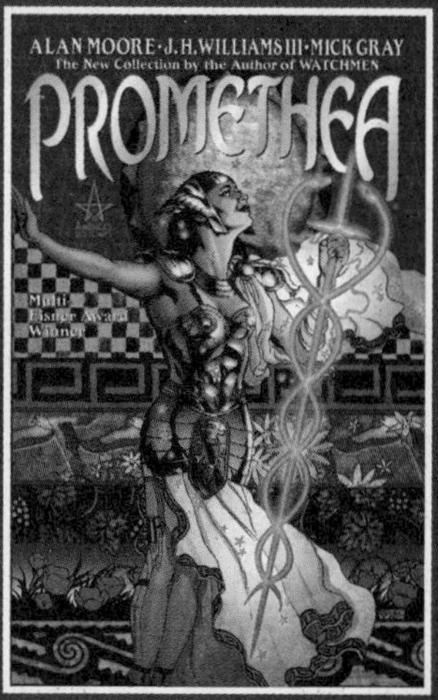
ALAN MOORE • J.H.WILLIAMS III • MICK GRAY
The New Collection by the Author of WATCHMEN
PROMETHEA

PROMETHEA BOOK ONE
WITH J.H. WILLIAMS III AND MICK GRAY

ALSO FROM VERTIGO

SWAMP THING: LOVE AND DEATH
BOOK TWO
with S. Bissette/J. Totleben/S. McManus

SWAMP THING: THE CURSE
BOOK THREE
with S. Bissette/J. Totleben

SWAMP THING: A MURDER OF CROWS
BOOK FOUR
with S. Bissette/J. Totleben/various

SWAMP THING: EARTH TO EARTH
BOOK FIVE
with S. Bissette/J. Totleben/various

SWAMP THING: REUNION
BOOK SIX
with S. Bissette/J. Totleben/various

ALSO FROM AMERICA'S BEST COMICS

TOM STRONG
BOOK ONE
with Chris Sprouse/Alan Gordon/various

TOM STRONG
BOOK TWO
with Chris Sprouse/Alan Gordon/various

PROMETHEA
BOOK TWO
with J.H. Williams III/Mick Gray

PROMETHEA
BOOK THREE
with J.H. Williams III/Mick Gray

TOP 10
BOOK ONE
with Gene Ha/Zander Cannon

TOP 10
BOOK TWO
with Gene Ha/Zander Cannon

TOMORROW STORIES
BOOK ONE
with K. Nowlan/R. Veitch/various